STOP

This is the back of the book!

This manga collection is translated into English but oriented in right-to-left reading format at the creator's request, maintaining the artwork's visual orientation as originally published in Japan. If you've never read manga in this way before, take a look at the diagram below to give yourself an idea of how to go about it. Basically, you'll be starting in the upper right corner and will read each balloon and panel moving right to left. It may take some getting used to, but you should get the hang of it very quickly. Have fun!

1
GET YOUR HANDS OFF SIR INTEGRA!!
2
YOU FREAK OF NATURE!!
3
HEH, HEHE HEH
AH HAH HEH.
HEH HAH HEH
HEH HEH
4
THERE'S NO WAY FOR YOU TO WIN, ANDERSON.
5
WALKING AWAY QUIETLY WOULD BE IN YOUR BEST INTEREST.
6
JUST EFTER AH FINISH YE AFF, FOOL WENCH...
7
THEN YOU'D BEST HURRY. IF YOU DALLY...
8
...THE ONE WHOSE HEAD YOU CUT OFF WILL COME BACK TO LIFE.

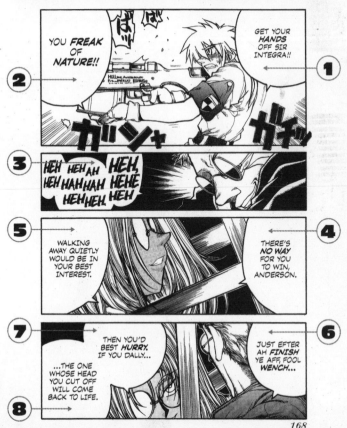

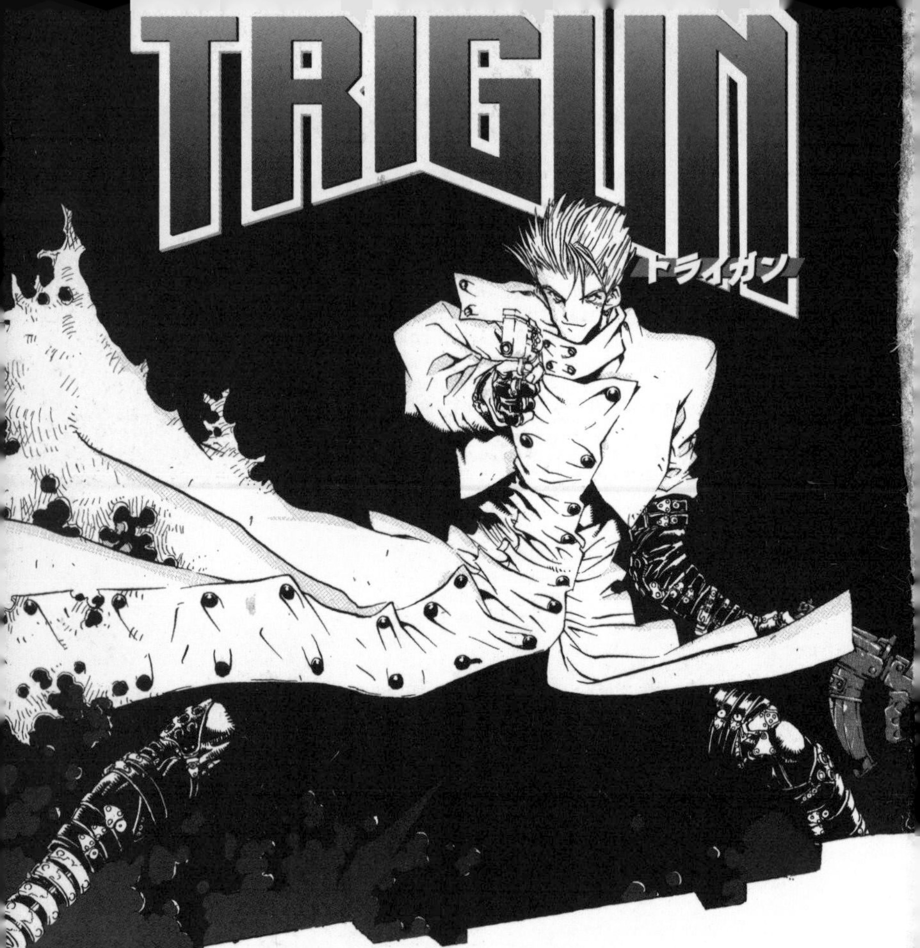
TRIGUN
トライガン

BERSERK

Created by Kentaro Miura, *Berserk* is manga mayhem to the extreme—violent, horrifying, and mercilessly funny—and the wellspring for the internationally popular anime series. Not for the squeamish or the easily offended, *Berserk* asks for no quarter—and offers none!

VOLUME 1:
ISBN-10: 1-59307-020-9
ISBN-13: 978-1-59307-020-5

VOLUME 2:
ISBN-10: 1-59307-021-7
ISBN-13: 978-1-59307-021-2

VOLUME 3:
ISBN-10: 1-59307-022-5
ISBN-13: 978-1-59307-022-9

VOLUME 4:
ISBN-10: 1-59307-203-1
ISBN-13: 978-1-59307-203-2

VOLUME 5:
ISBN-10: 1-59307-251-1
ISBN-13: 978-1-59307-251-3

VOLUME 6:
ISBN-10: 1-59307-252-X
ISBN-13: 978-1-59307-252-0

VOLUME 7:
ISBN-10: 1-59307-328-3
ISBN-13: 978-1-59307-328-2

VOLUME 8:
ISBN-10: 1-59307-329-1
ISBN-13: 978-1-59307-329-9

VOLUME 9:
ISBN-10: 1-59307-330-5
ISBN-13: 978-1-59307-330-5

VOLUME 10:
ISBN-10: 1-59307-331-3
ISBN-13: 978-1-59307-331-2

VOLUME 11:
ISBN-10: 1-59307-470-0
ISBN-13: 978-1-59307-470-8

VOLUME 12:
ISBN-10: 1-59307-484-0
ISBN-13: 978-1-59307-484-5

VOLUME 13:
ISBN-10: 1-59307-500-6
ISBN-13: 978-1-59307-500-2

VOLUME 14:
ISBN-10: 1-59307-501-4
ISBN-13: 978-1-59307-501-9

VOLUME 15:
ISBN-10: 1-59307-577-4
ISBN-13: 978-1-59307-577-4

Presented uncensored in the original Japanese format!

$13.95 Each!

DMP
Digital Manga Publishing
™

DARK HORSE MANGA

dmpbooks.com   darkhorse.com

AVAILABLE AT YOUR LOCAL COMICS SHOP OR BOOKSTORE
To find a comics shop near your area, call 1-888-266-4226. For more information or to order direct: •On the web: darkhorse.com •E-mail: mailorder@darkhorse.com •Phone: 1-800-862-0052 Mon.-Fri. 9 A.M. to 5 P.M. Pacific Time.

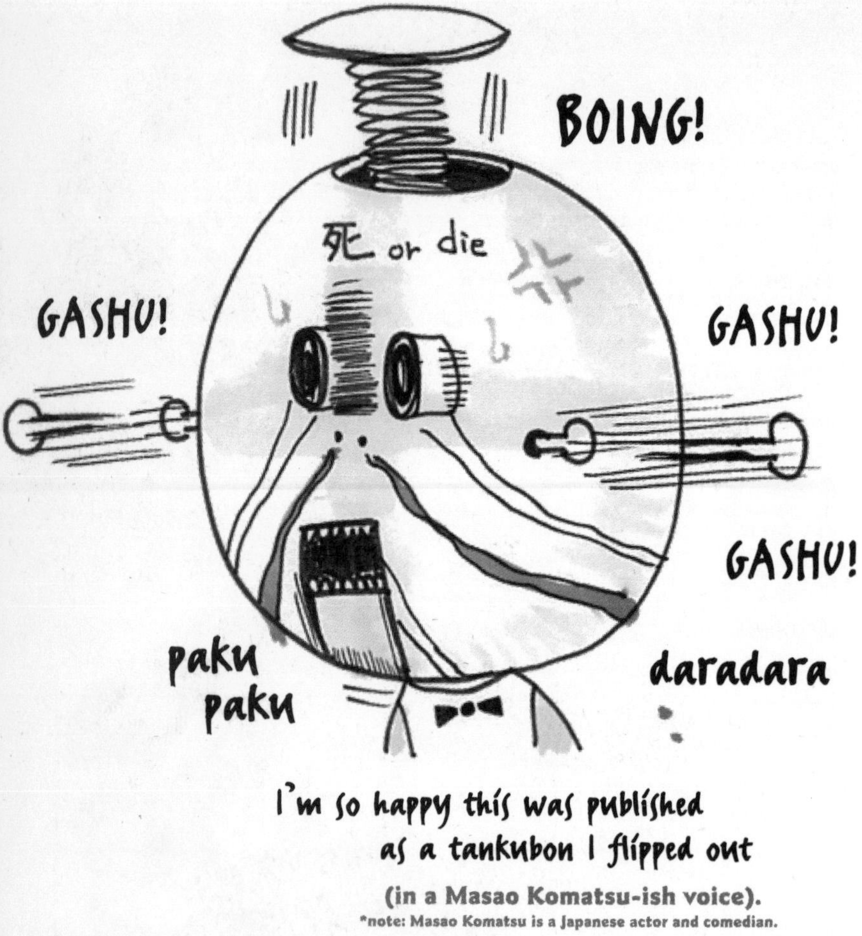
BOING!
死 or die
GASHU!
GASHU!
GASHU!
paku
paku
daradara

I'm so happy this was published
as a tankubon I flipped out
(in a Masao Komatsu-ish voice).

*note: Masao Komatsu is a Japanese actor and comedian.

Hailing from Adachi Ward, Tokyo

KOHTA HIRANO

Hobby = Being obnoxious.
Favorite Words/Practices = "Only thing better than food? More food!" Absurd Fear.
Favorite Country = Germany (because of the Nazi's*).
Favorite Voice Actor = Nachi Nozawa (because of the Nachi).

*note: forgive the joke, the nazi theme comes later, then you'll get it.

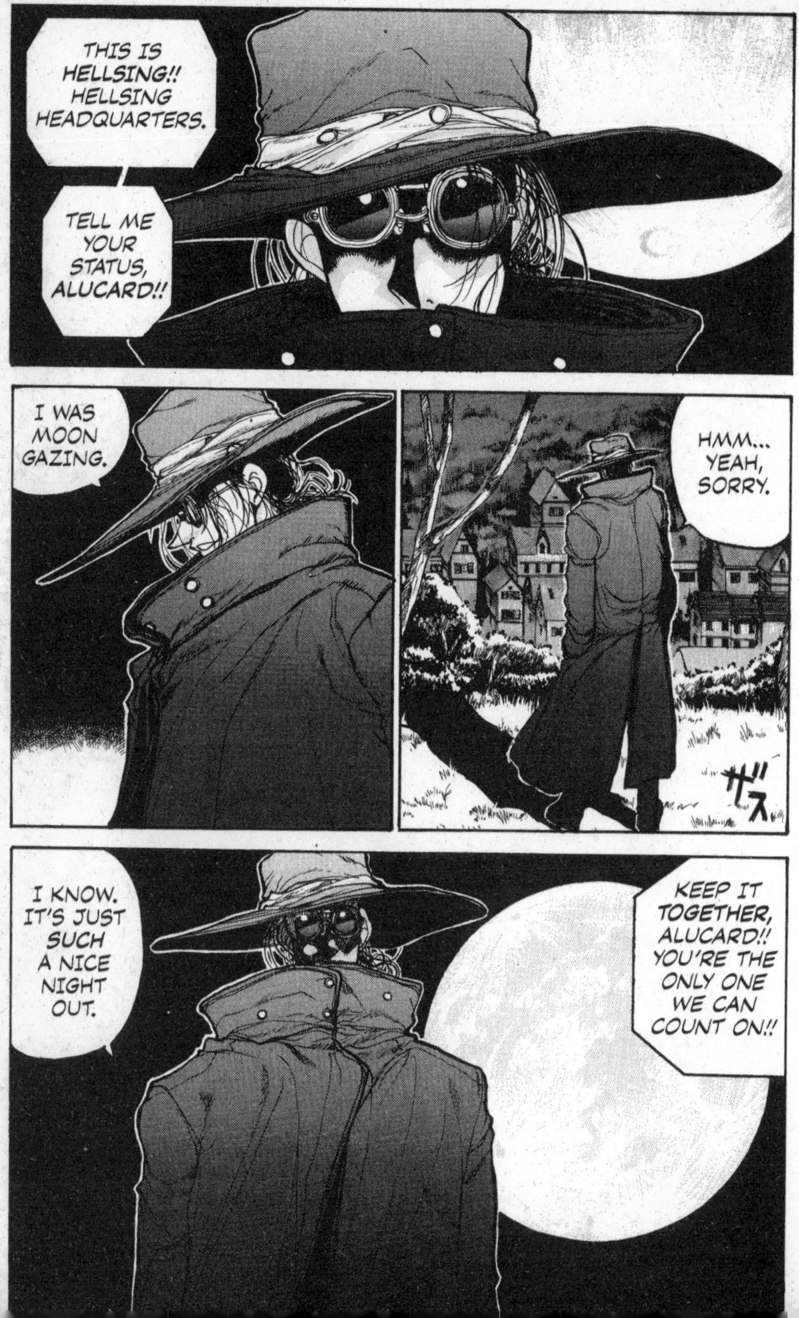
THIS IS HELLSING!! HELLSING HEADQUARTERS.
TELL ME YOUR STATUS, ALUCARD!!
HMM... YEAH, SORRY.
ザス
I WAS MOON GAZING.
KEEP IT TOGETHER, ALUCARD!! YOU'RE THE ONLY ONE WE CAN COUNT ON!!
I KNOW. IT'S JUST SUCH A NICE NIGHT OUT.

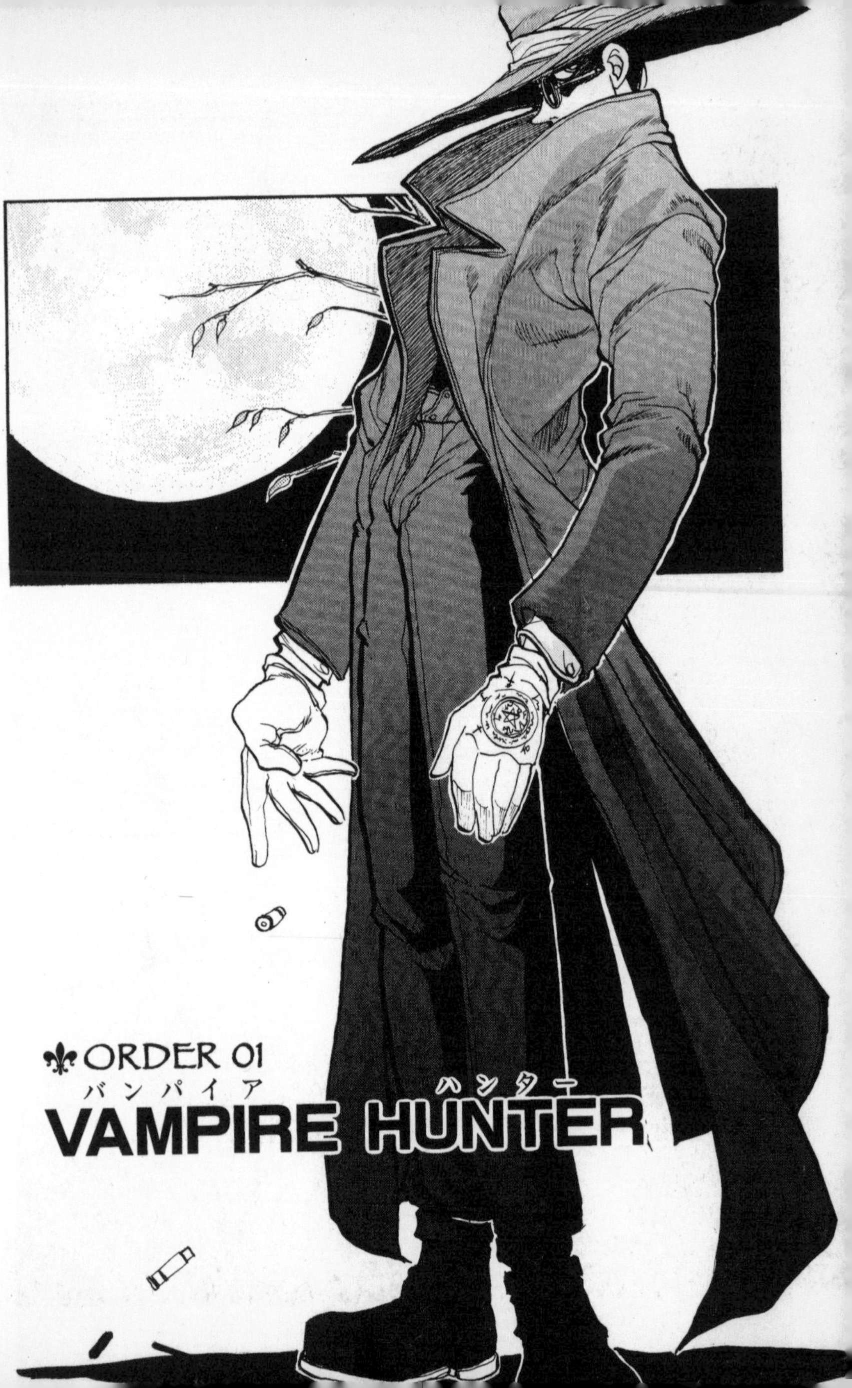
ORDER 01
バンパイア ハンター
VAMPIRE HUNTER

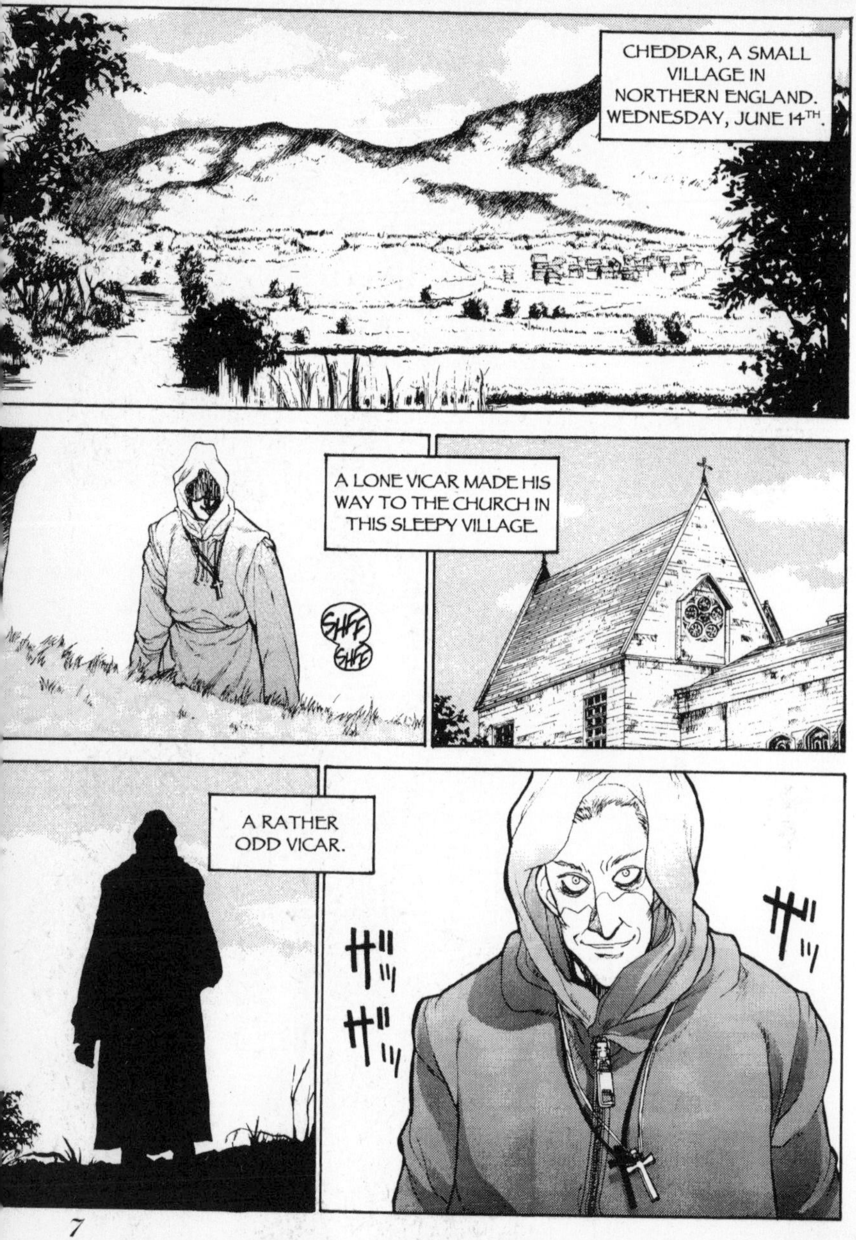
CHEDDAR, A SMALL VILLAGE IN NORTHERN ENGLAND. WEDNESDAY, JUNE 14TH.
A LONE VICAR MADE HIS WAY TO THE CHURCH IN THIS SLEEPY VILLAGE.
SHFF
SHFF
ザッ
ザッ
ザッ
A RATHER ODD VICAR.

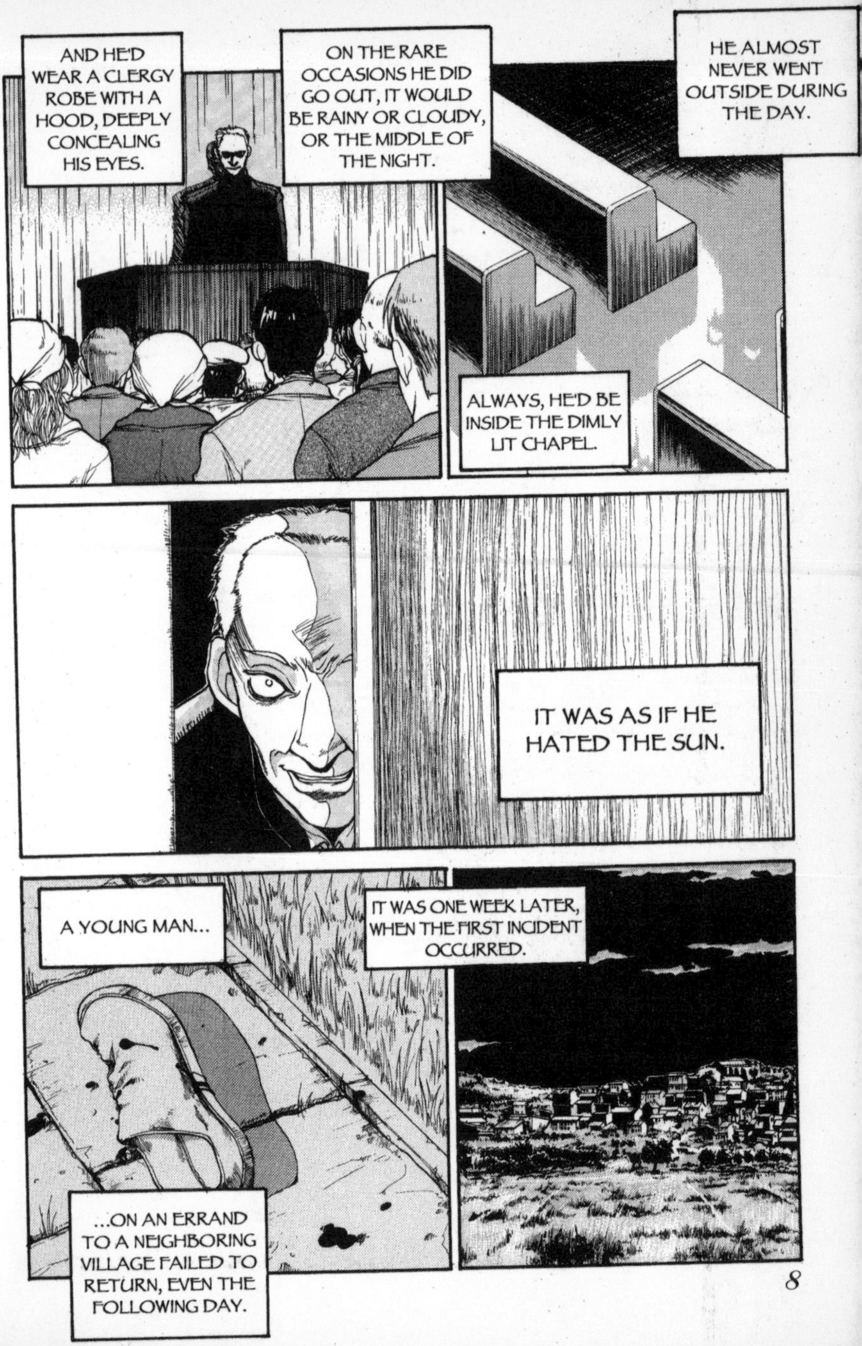
HE ALMOST NEVER WENT OUTSIDE DURING THE DAY.
ALWAYS, HE'D BE INSIDE THE DIMLY LIT CHAPEL.
ON THE RARE OCCASIONS HE DID GO OUT, IT WOULD BE RAINY OR CLOUDY, OR THE MIDDLE OF THE NIGHT.
AND HE'D WEAR A CLERGY ROBE WITH A HOOD, DEEPLY CONCEALING HIS EYES.
IT WAS AS IF HE HATED THE SUN.
IT WAS ONE WEEK LATER, WHEN THE FIRST INCIDENT OCCURRED.
A YOUNG MAN...
...ON AN ERRAND TO A NEIGHBORING VILLAGE FAILED TO RETURN, EVEN THE FOLLOWING DAY.

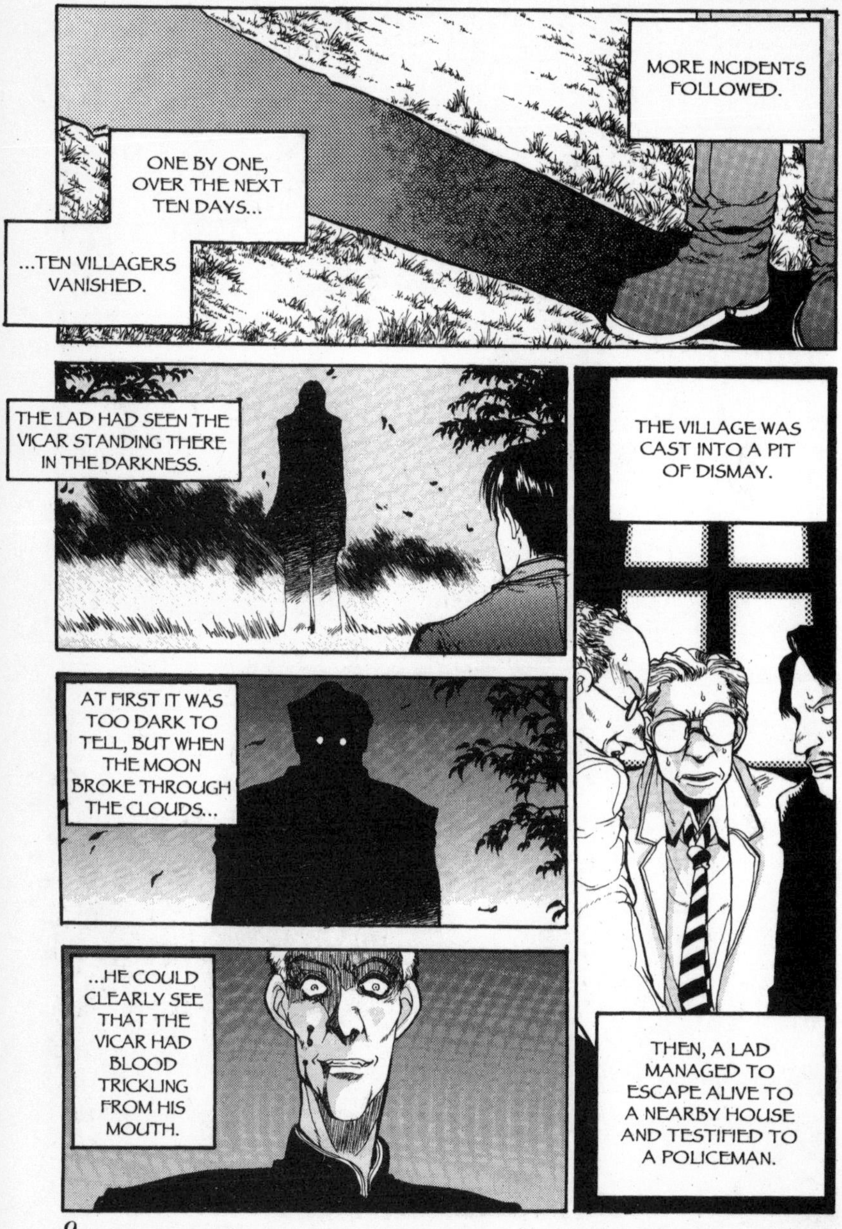
MORE INCIDENTS FOLLOWED.
ONE BY ONE, OVER THE NEXT TEN DAYS...
...TEN VILLAGERS VANISHED.
THE VILLAGE WAS CAST INTO A PIT OF DISMAY.
THEN, A LAD MANAGED TO ESCAPE ALIVE TO A NEARBY HOUSE AND TESTIFIED TO A POLICEMAN.
THE LAD HAD SEEN THE VICAR STANDING THERE IN THE DARKNESS.
AT FIRST IT WAS TOO DARK TO TELL, BUT WHEN THE MOON BROKE THROUGH THE CLOUDS...
...HE COULD CLEARLY SEE THAT THE VICAR HAD BLOOD TRICKLING FROM HIS MOUTH.

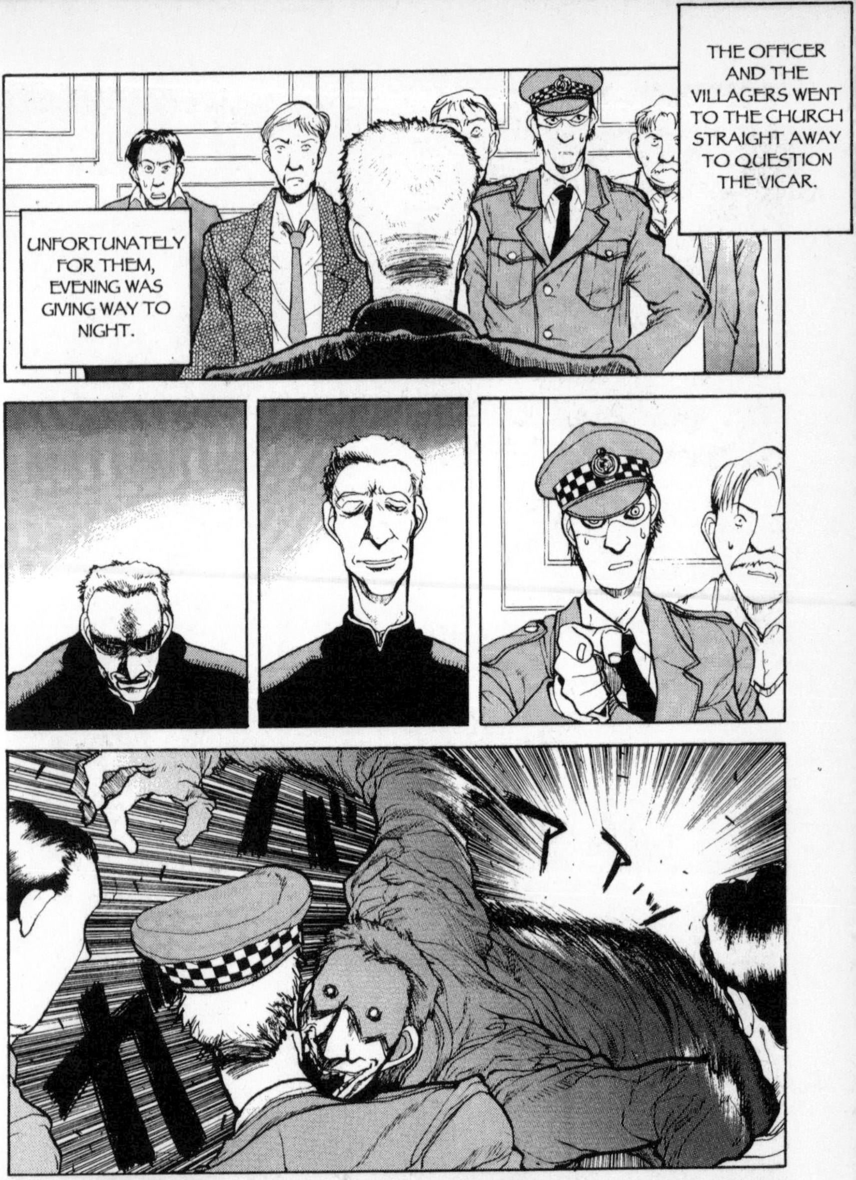
THE OFFICER AND THE VILLAGERS WENT TO THE CHURCH STRAIGHT AWAY TO QUESTION THE VICAR.
UNFORTUNATELY FOR THEM, EVENING WAS GIVING WAY TO NIGHT.

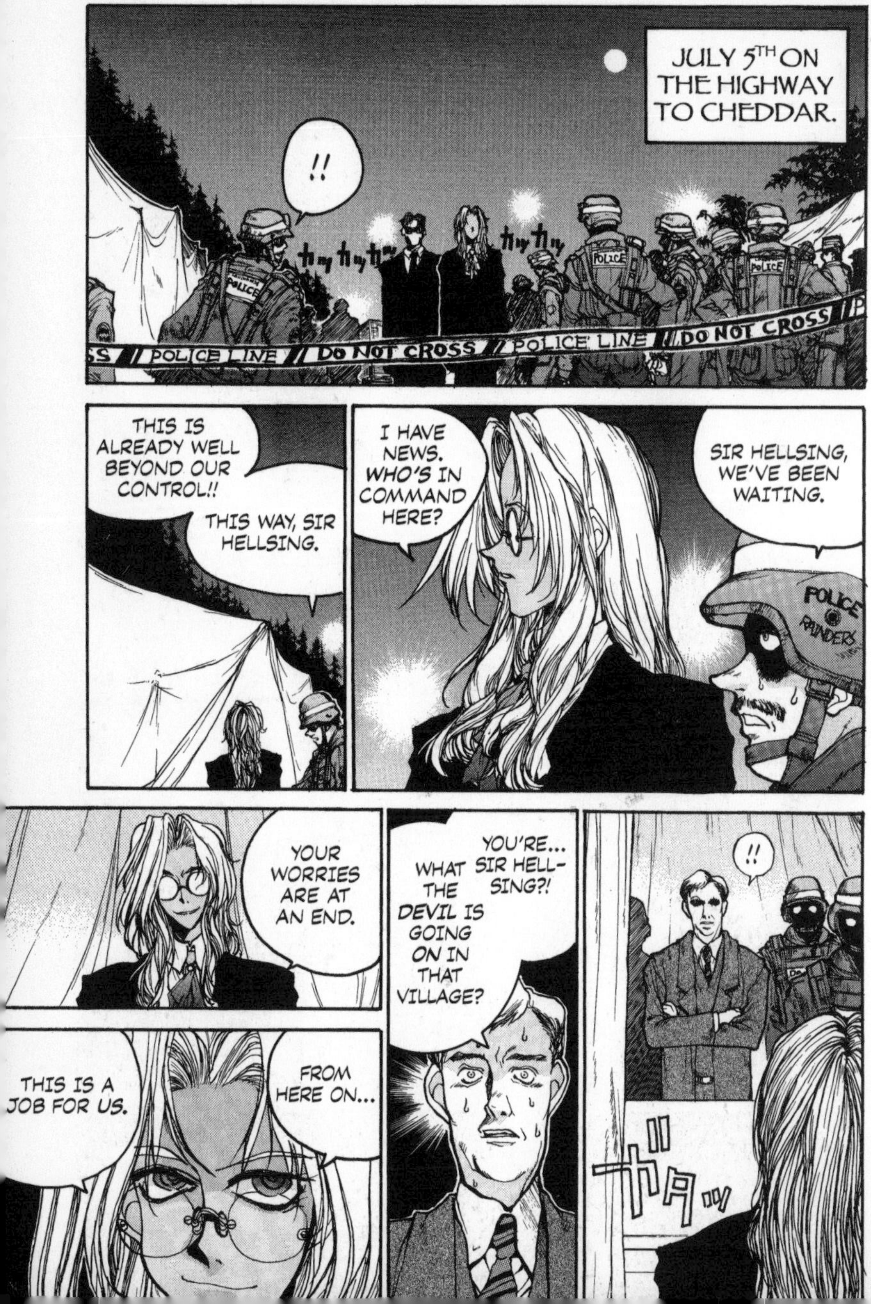

JULY 5TH ON THE HIGHWAY TO CHEDDAR.
!!
POLICE LINE
DO NOT CROSS
SIR HELLSING, WE'VE BEEN WAITING.
I HAVE NEWS. WHO'S IN COMMAND HERE?
THIS IS ALREADY WELL BEYOND OUR CONTROL!!
THIS WAY, SIR HELLSING.
!!
YOU'RE... SIR HELL-SING?!
WHAT THE DEVIL IS GOING ON IN THAT VILLAGE?
YOUR WORRIES ARE AT AN END.
FROM HERE ON...
THIS IS A JOB FOR US.

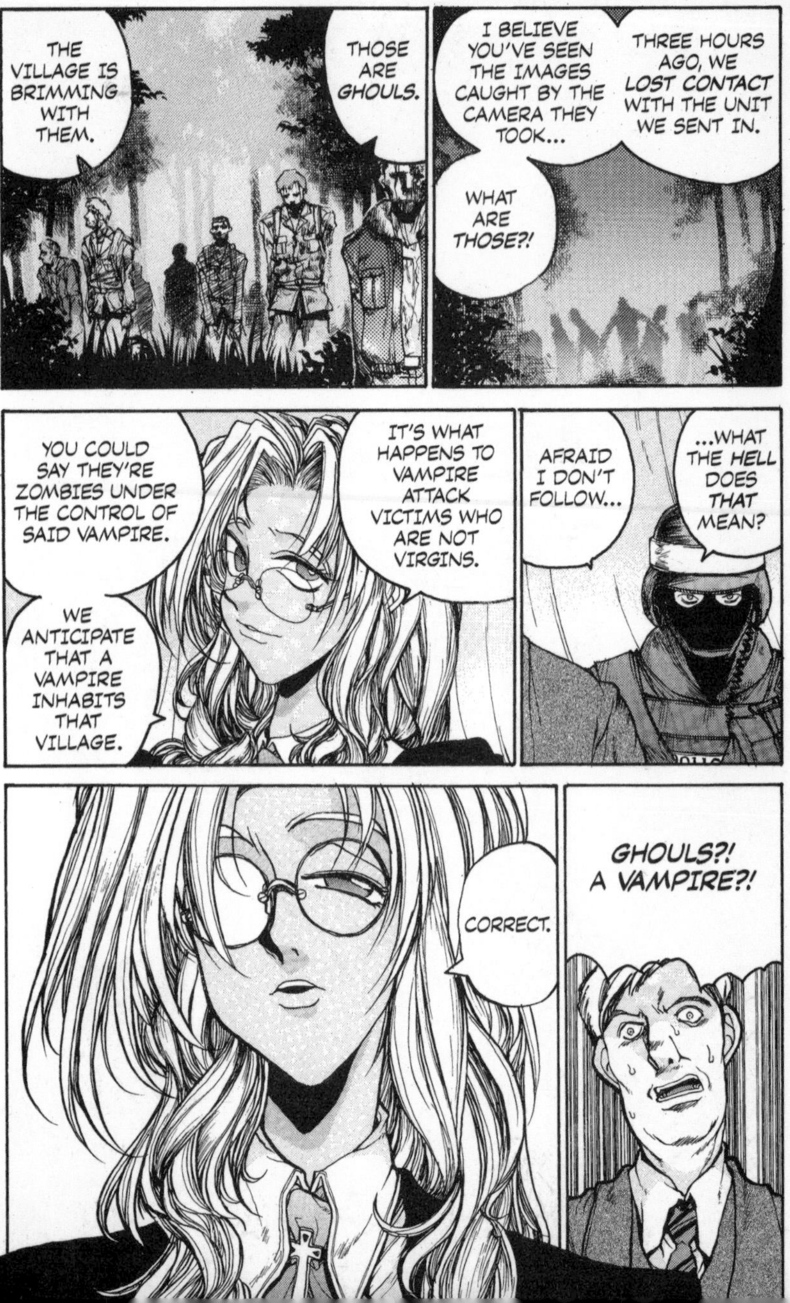
THREE HOURS AGO, WE LOST CONTACT WITH THE UNIT WE SENT IN.
I BELIEVE YOU'VE SEEN THE IMAGES CAUGHT BY THE CAMERA THEY TOOK...
WHAT ARE THOSE?!
THOSE ARE GHOULS.
THE VILLAGE IS BRIMMING WITH THEM.
...WHAT THE HELL DOES THAT MEAN?
AFRAID I DON'T FOLLOW...
IT'S WHAT HAPPENS TO VAMPIRE ATTACK VICTIMS WHO ARE NOT VIRGINS.
YOU COULD SAY THEY'RE ZOMBIES UNDER THE CONTROL OF SAID VAMPIRE.
WE ANTICIPATE THAT A VAMPIRE INHABITS THAT VILLAGE.
GHOULS?! A VAMPIRE?!
CORRECT.

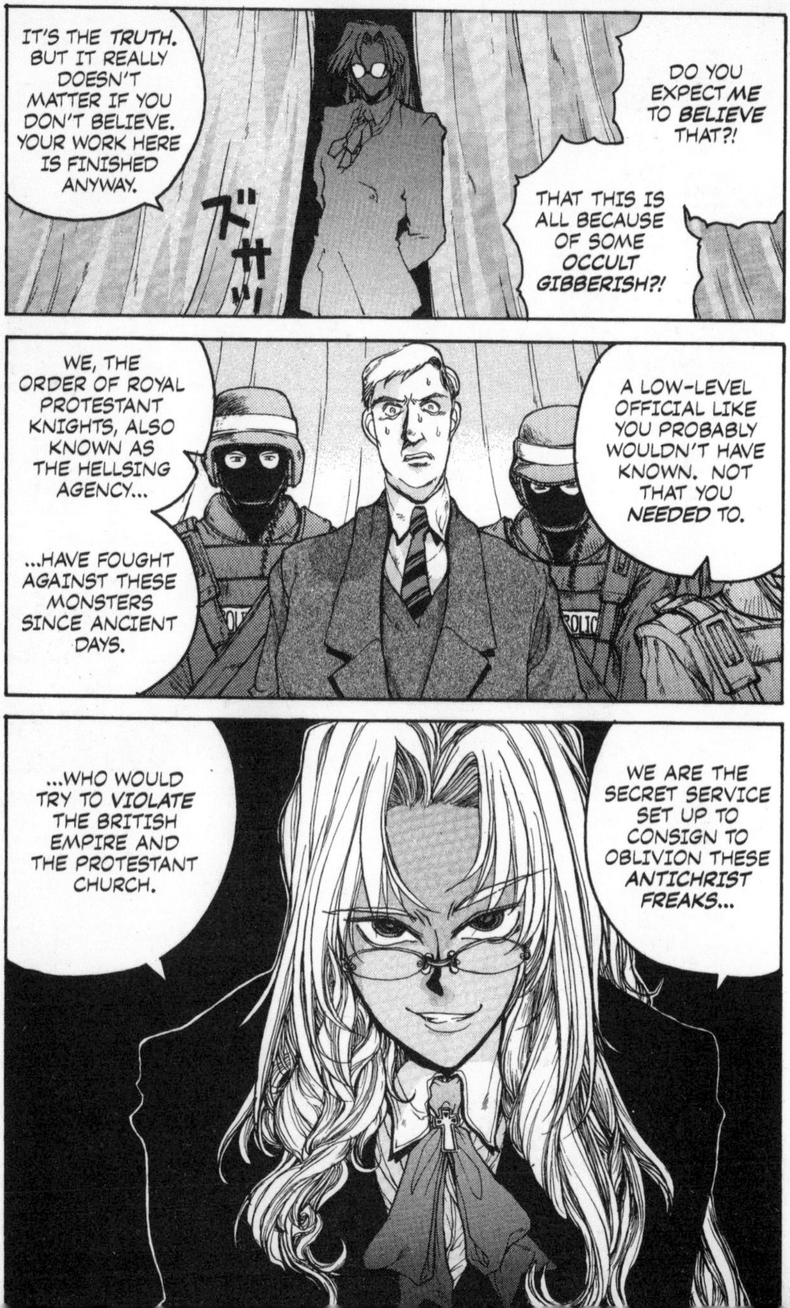
DO YOU EXPECT *ME* TO *BELIEVE* THAT?!
THAT THIS IS ALL BECAUSE OF SOME *OCCULT GIBBERISH?!*
IT'S THE *TRUTH.* BUT IT REALLY DOESN'T MATTER IF YOU DON'T BELIEVE. YOUR WORK HERE IS FINISHED ANYWAY.
ズサッ
A LOW-LEVEL OFFICIAL LIKE YOU PROBABLY WOULDN'T HAVE KNOWN. NOT THAT YOU *NEEDED* TO.
WE, THE ORDER OF ROYAL PROTESTANT KNIGHTS, ALSO KNOWN AS THE HELLSING AGENCY...
...HAVE FOUGHT AGAINST THESE MONSTERS SINCE ANCIENT DAYS.
WE ARE THE SECRET SERVICE SET UP TO CONSIGN TO OBLIVION THESE *ANTICHRIST FREAKS...*
...WHO WOULD TRY TO *VIOLATE* THE BRITISH EMPIRE AND THE PROTESTANT CHURCH.

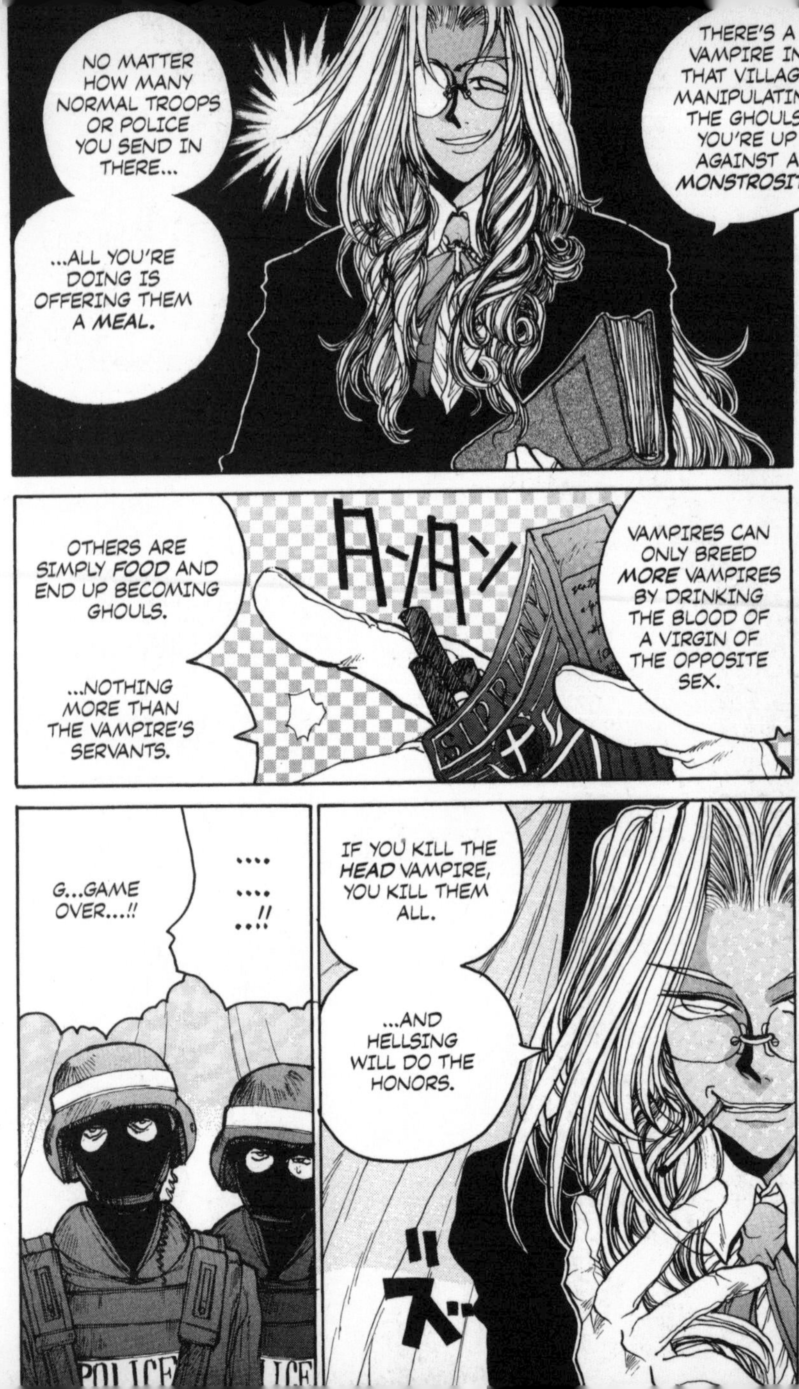
THERE'S A VAMPIRE IN THAT VILLAGE MANIPULATING THE GHOULS. YOU'RE UP AGAINST A *MONSTROSITY.*
NO MATTER HOW MANY NORMAL TROOPS OR POLICE YOU SEND IN THERE...
...ALL YOU'RE DOING IS OFFERING THEM A *MEAL.*
VAMPIRES CAN ONLY BREED *MORE* VAMPIRES BY DRINKING THE BLOOD OF A VIRGIN OF THE OPPOSITE SEX.
OTHERS ARE SIMPLY *FOOD* AND END UP BECOMING GHOULS.
...NOTHING MORE THAN THE VAMPIRE'S SERVANTS.
IF YOU KILL THE *HEAD* VAMPIRE, YOU KILL THEM ALL.
...AND HELLSING WILL DO THE HONORS.
....!!
G...GAME OVER...!!
POLICE
POLICE

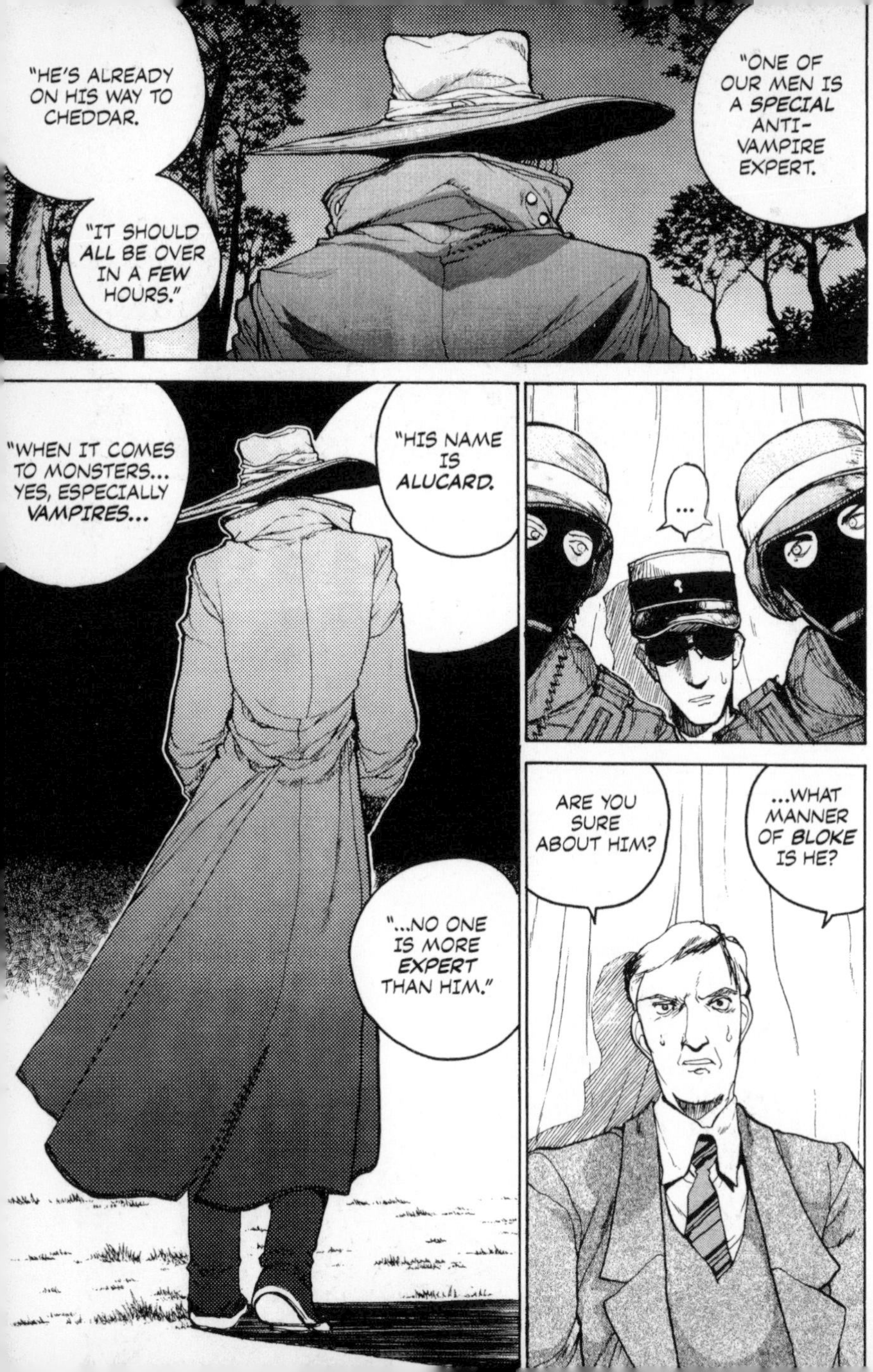
"ONE OF OUR MEN IS A SPECIAL ANTI-VAMPIRE EXPERT.
"HE'S ALREADY ON HIS WAY TO CHEDDAR.
"IT SHOULD ALL BE OVER IN A FEW HOURS."
...
...WHAT MANNER OF BLOKE IS HE?
ARE YOU SURE ABOUT HIM?
"HIS NAME IS ALUCARD.
"WHEN IT COMES TO MONSTERS... YES, ESPECIALLY VAMPIRES...
"...NO ONE IS MORE EXPERT THAN HIM."

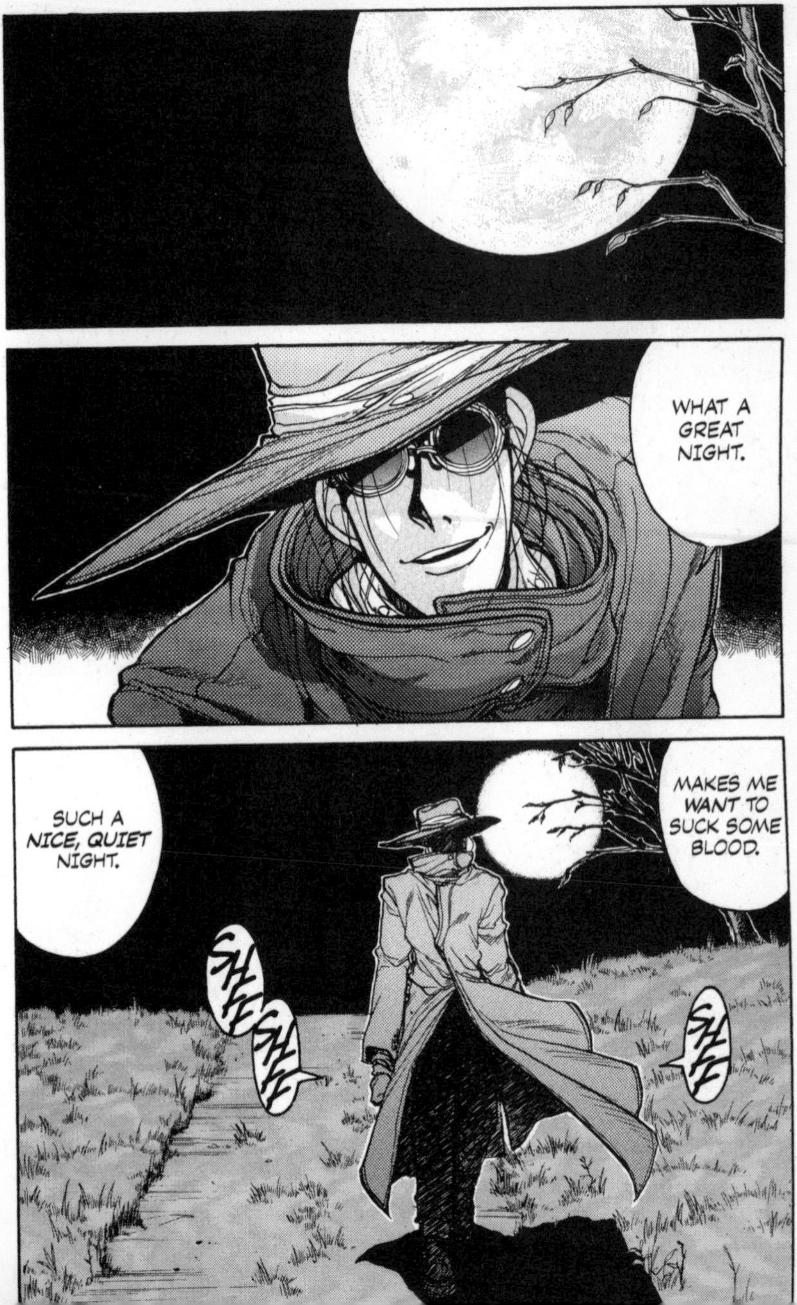
WHAT A GREAT NIGHT.
MAKES ME WANT TO SUCK SOME BLOOD.
SUCH A NICE, QUIET NIGHT.

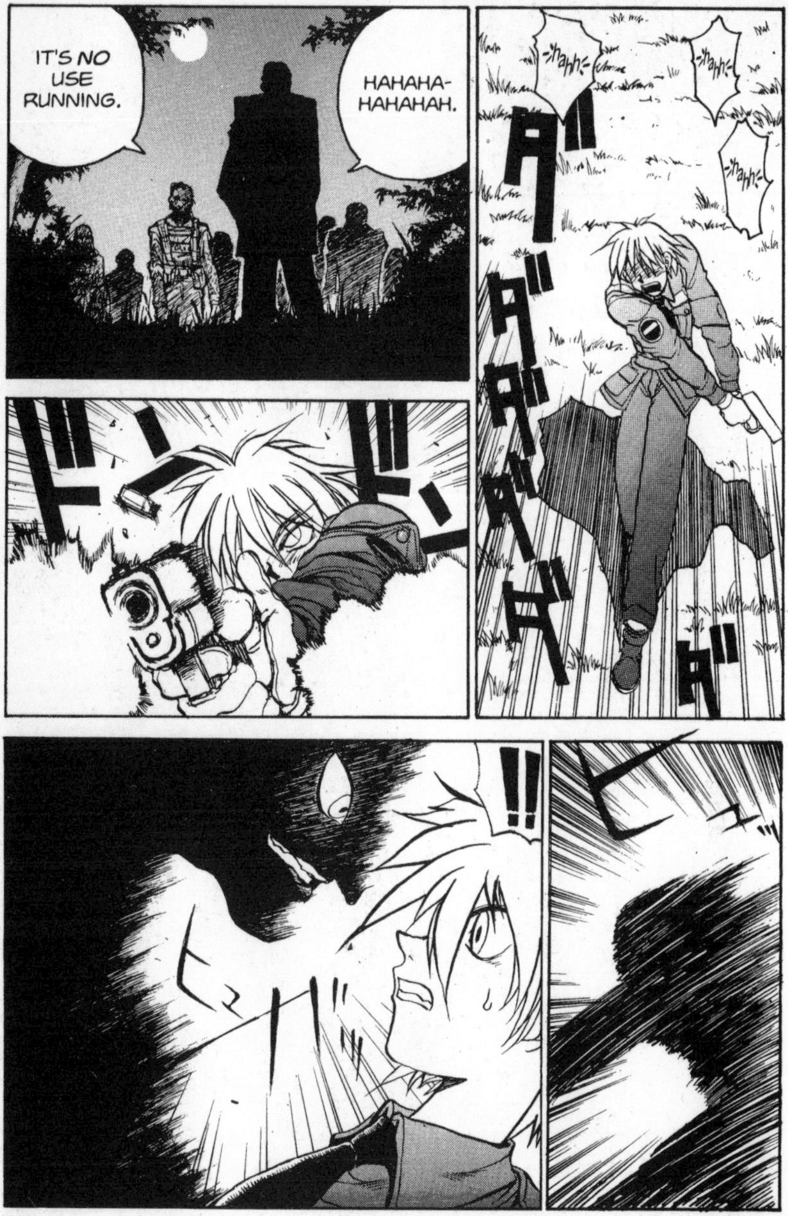
-hah-
-hah-
-hah-
IT'S NO USE RUNNING.
HAHAHA-HAHAHAH.
!!

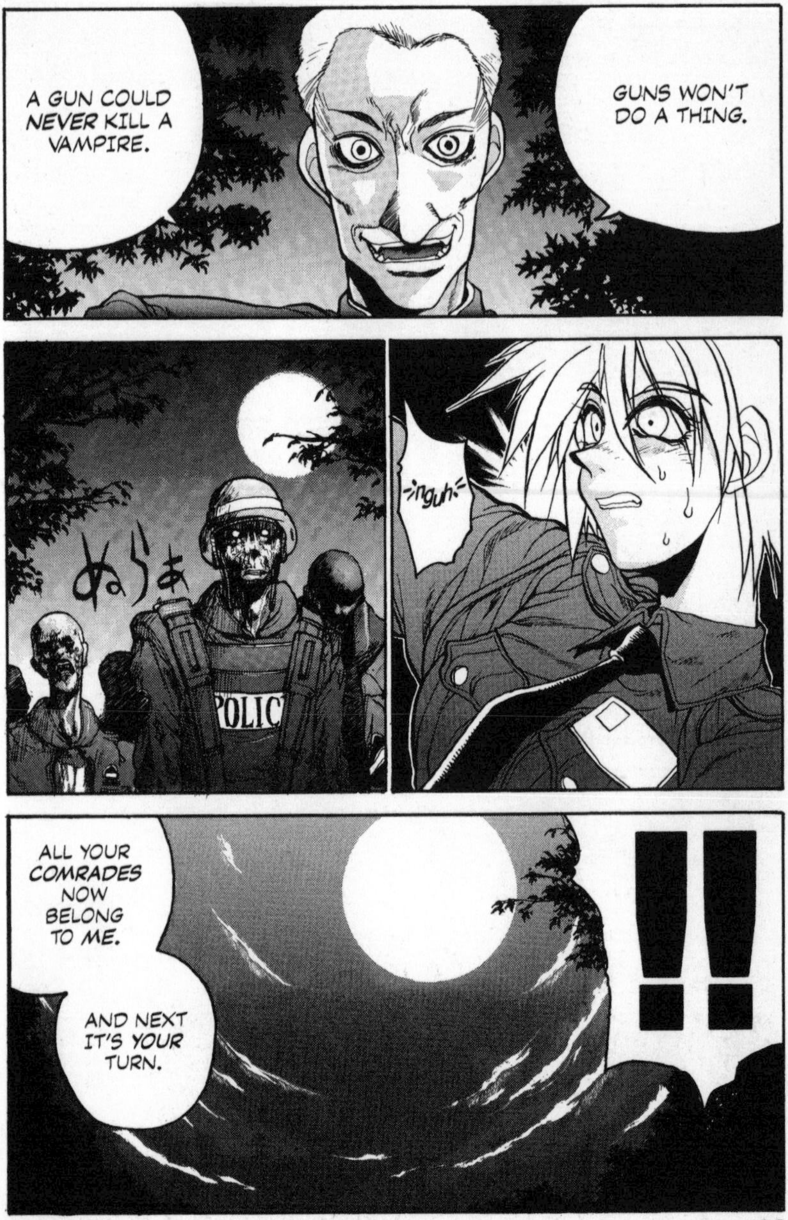
GUNS WON'T DO A THING.
A GUN COULD *NEVER* KILL A VAMPIRE.
-nguh-
ぬらあ
POLIC
!!
ALL YOUR *COMRADES* NOW BELONG TO *ME*.
AND NEXT IT'S *YOUR* TURN.

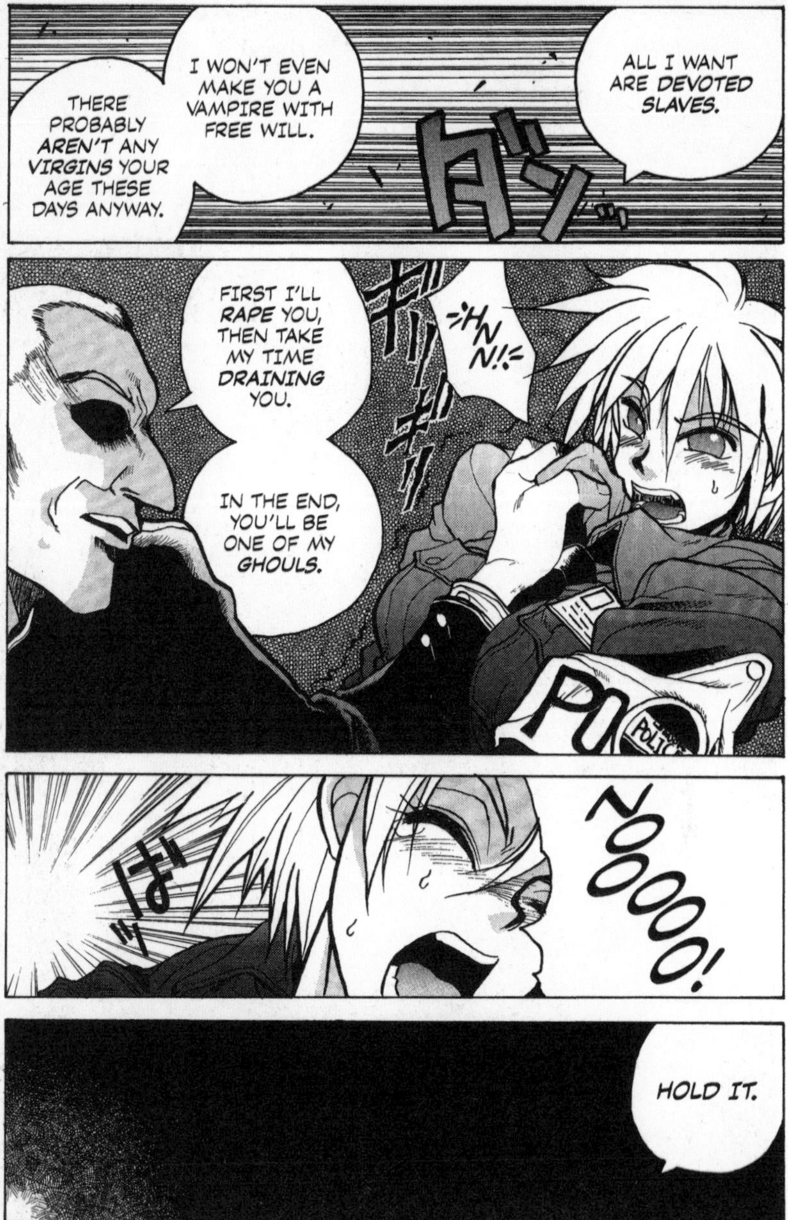
ALL I WANT ARE DEVOTED SLAVES.
I WON'T EVEN MAKE YOU A VAMPIRE WITH FREE WILL.
THERE PROBABLY AREN'T ANY VIRGINS YOUR AGE THESE DAYS ANYWAY.
HNN!
FIRST I'LL RAPE YOU, THEN TAKE MY TIME DRAINING YOU.
IN THE END, YOU'LL BE ONE OF MY GHOULS.
NOOOOO!
HOLD IT.

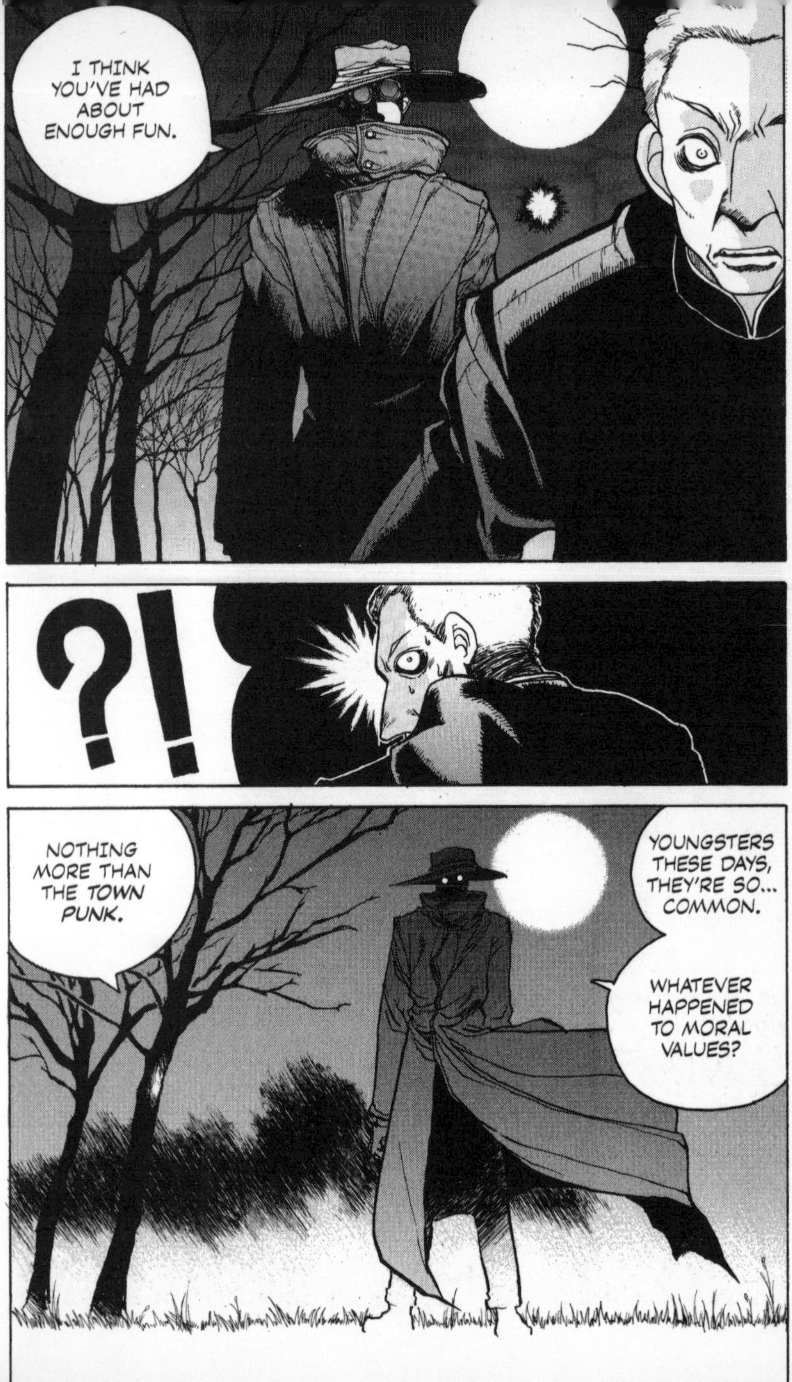
I THINK YOU'VE HAD ABOUT ENOUGH FUN.
?!
YOUNGSTERS THESE DAYS, THEY'RE SO... COMMON.
WHATEVER HAPPENED TO MORAL VALUES?
NOTHING MORE THAN THE *TOWN* PUNK.

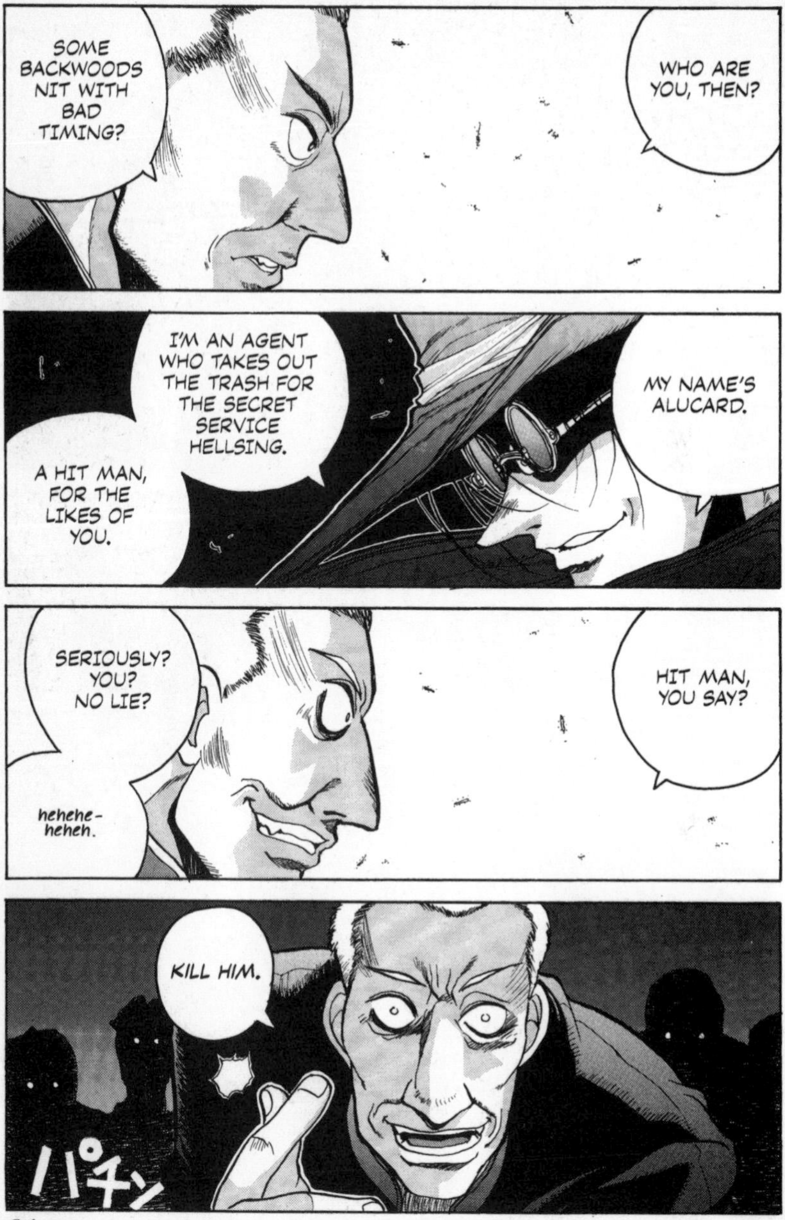
WHO ARE YOU, THEN?
SOME BACKWOODS NIT WITH BAD TIMING?
MY NAME'S ALUCARD.
I'M AN AGENT WHO TAKES OUT THE TRASH FOR THE SECRET SERVICE HELLSING.
A HIT MAN, FOR THE LIKES OF YOU.
HIT MAN, YOU SAY?
SERIOUSLY? YOU? NO LIE?
hehehe-heheh.
KILL HIM.
パチン

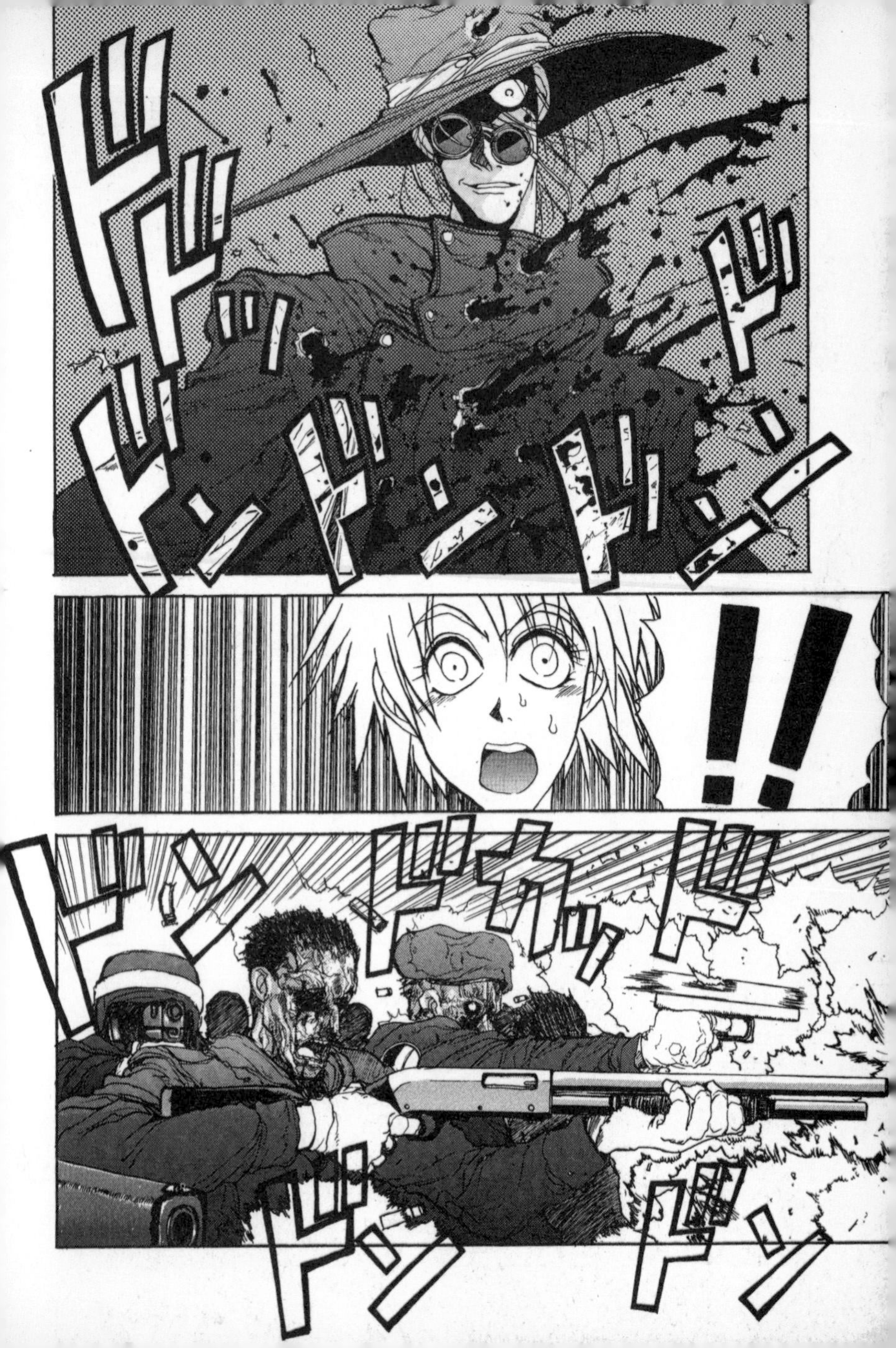
ドドドドッ
ドンドンドンドンッ
!!
ドカッドッ
ドンッ
ドンッ
ドッ

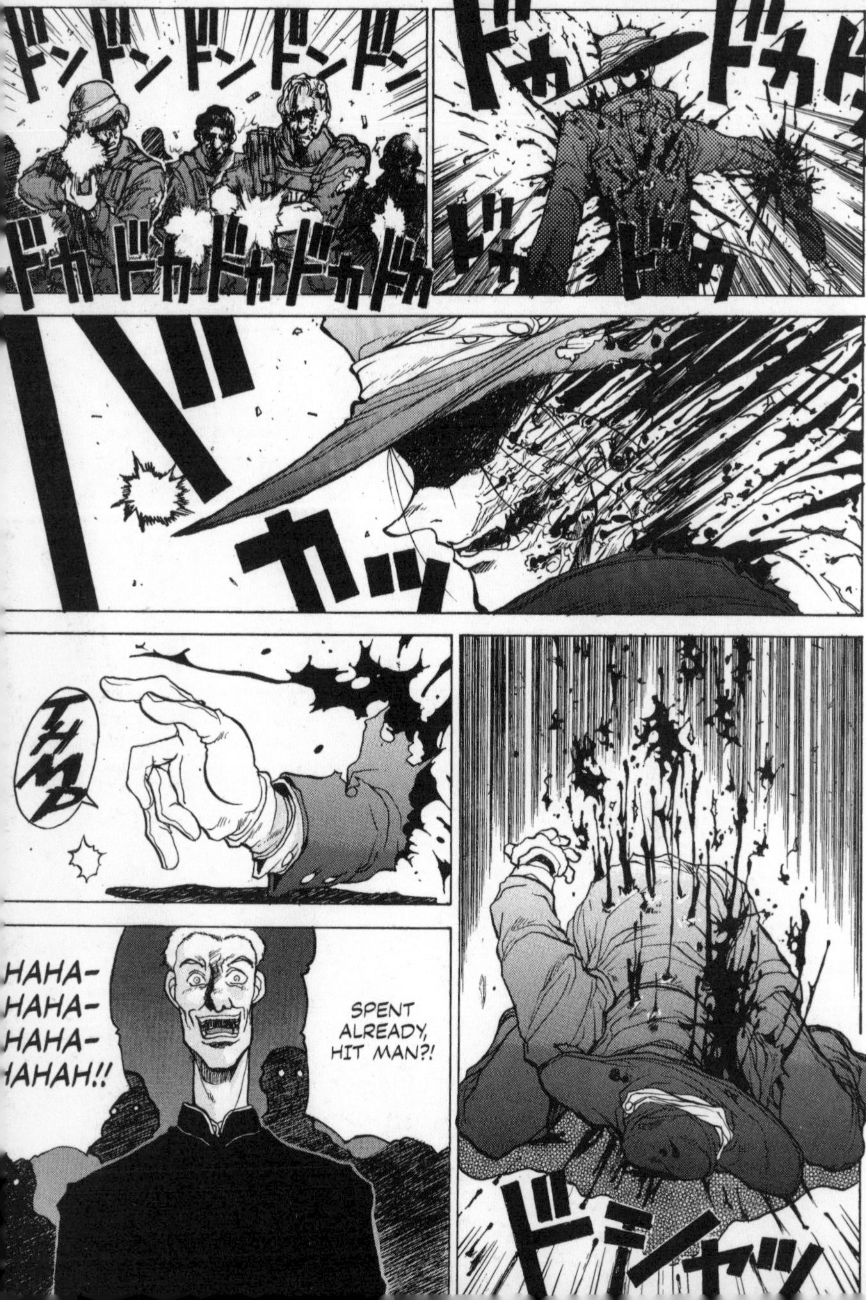
SPENT ALREADY, HIT MAN?!
HAHA-HAHA-HAHA-HAHAH!!

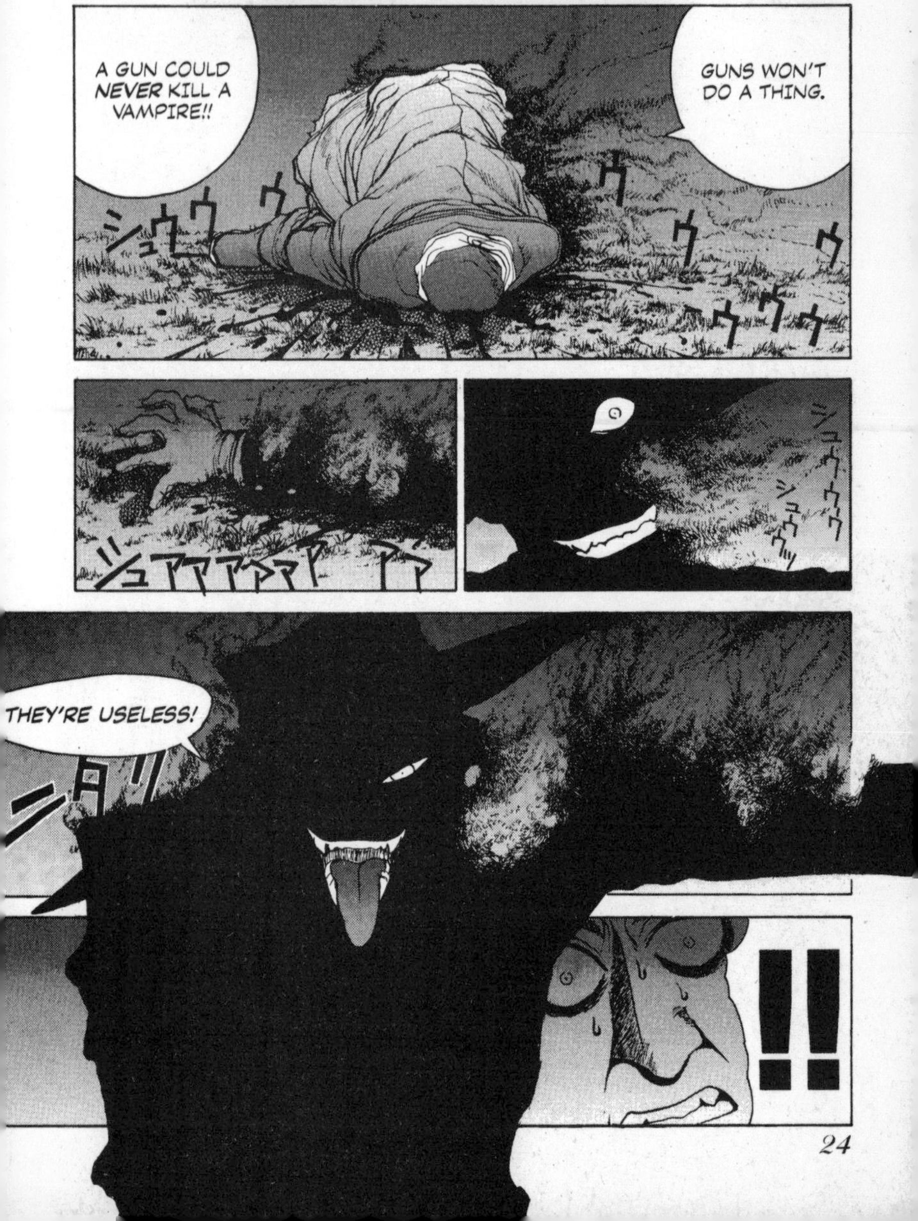
GUNS WON'T DO A THING.
A GUN COULD NEVER KILL A VAMPIRE!!
シュウウウ
ウウウウウウ
シュウウウ
シュウウッ
シュアアアアア アア
THEY'RE USELESS!
ニタリ
!!

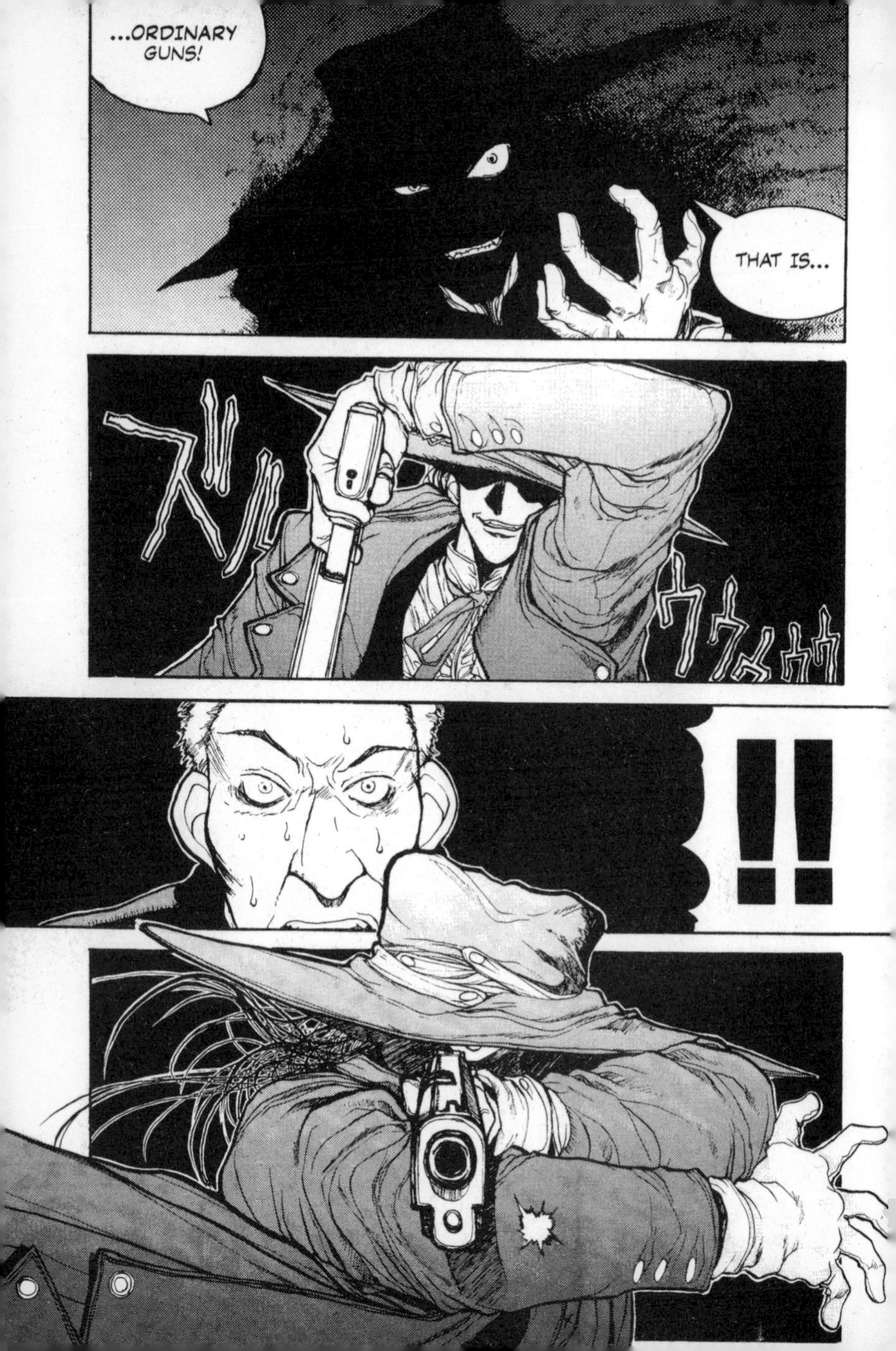
THAT IS...
...ORDINARY GUNS!
!!

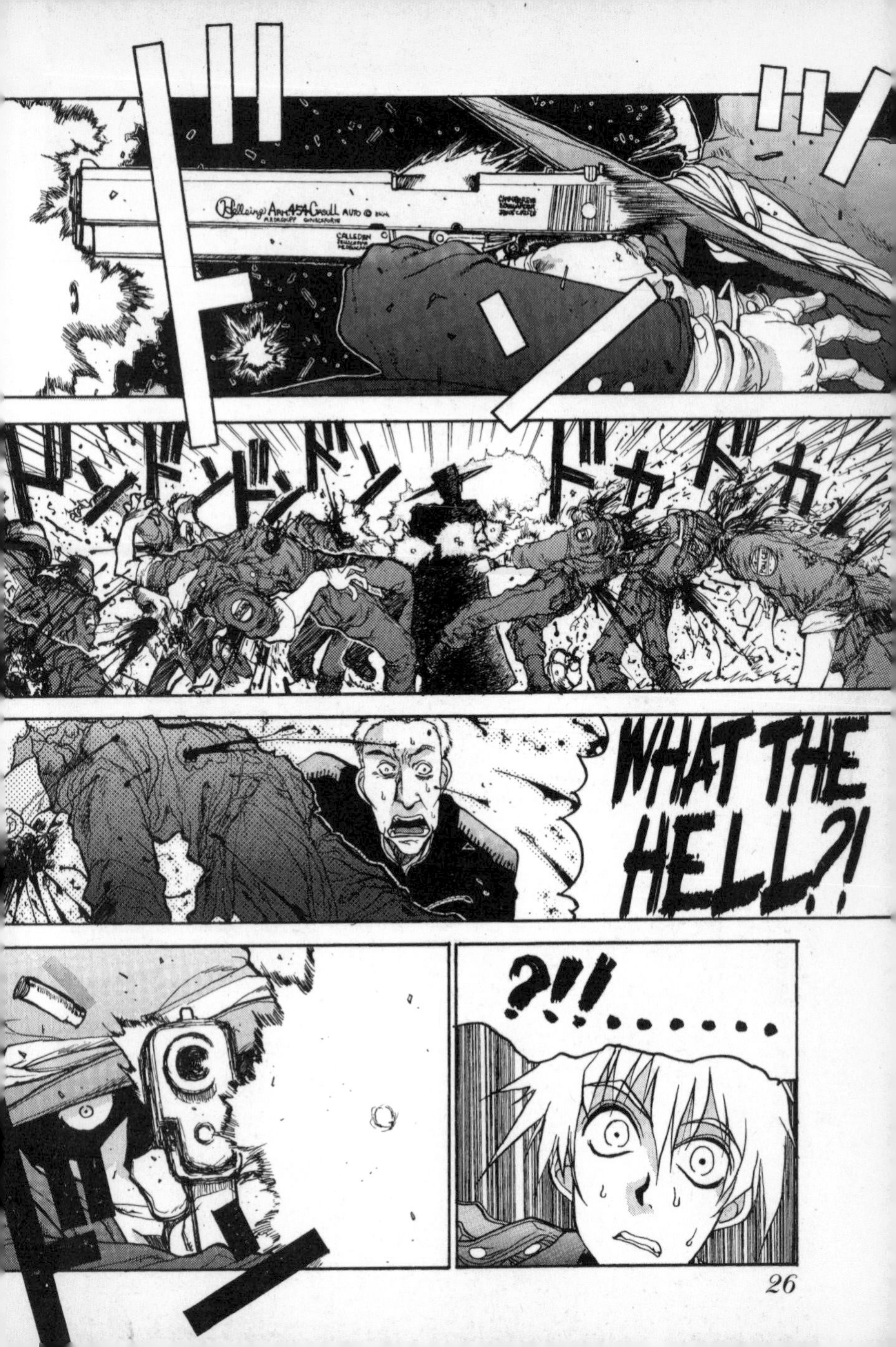
WHAT THE HELL?!
?!!......

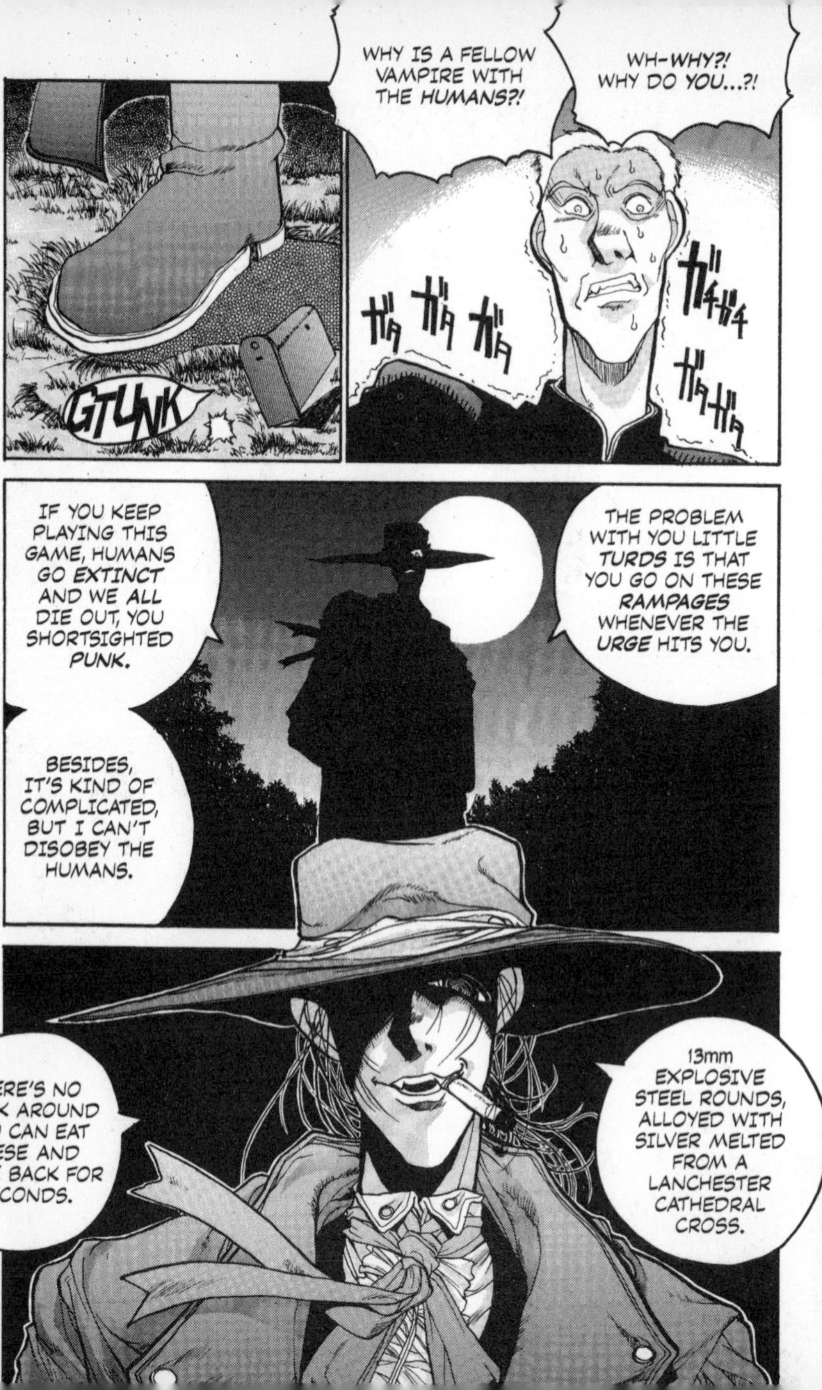
WH-WHY?! WHY DO YOU...?!
WHY IS A FELLOW VAMPIRE WITH THE HUMANS?!
ガチガチ
ガタガタ
ガタ ガタ ガタ
GTUNK
THE PROBLEM WITH YOU LITTLE TURDS IS THAT YOU GO ON THESE RAMPAGES WHENEVER THE URGE HITS YOU.
IF YOU KEEP PLAYING THIS GAME, HUMANS GO EXTINCT AND WE ALL DIE OUT, YOU SHORTSIGHTED PUNK.
BESIDES, IT'S KIND OF COMPLICATED, BUT I CAN'T DISOBEY THE HUMANS.
13mm EXPLOSIVE STEEL ROUNDS, ALLOYED WITH SILVER MELTED FROM A LANCHESTER CATHEDRAL CROSS.
THERE'S NO FREAK AROUND WHO CAN EAT THESE AND COME BACK FOR SECONDS.

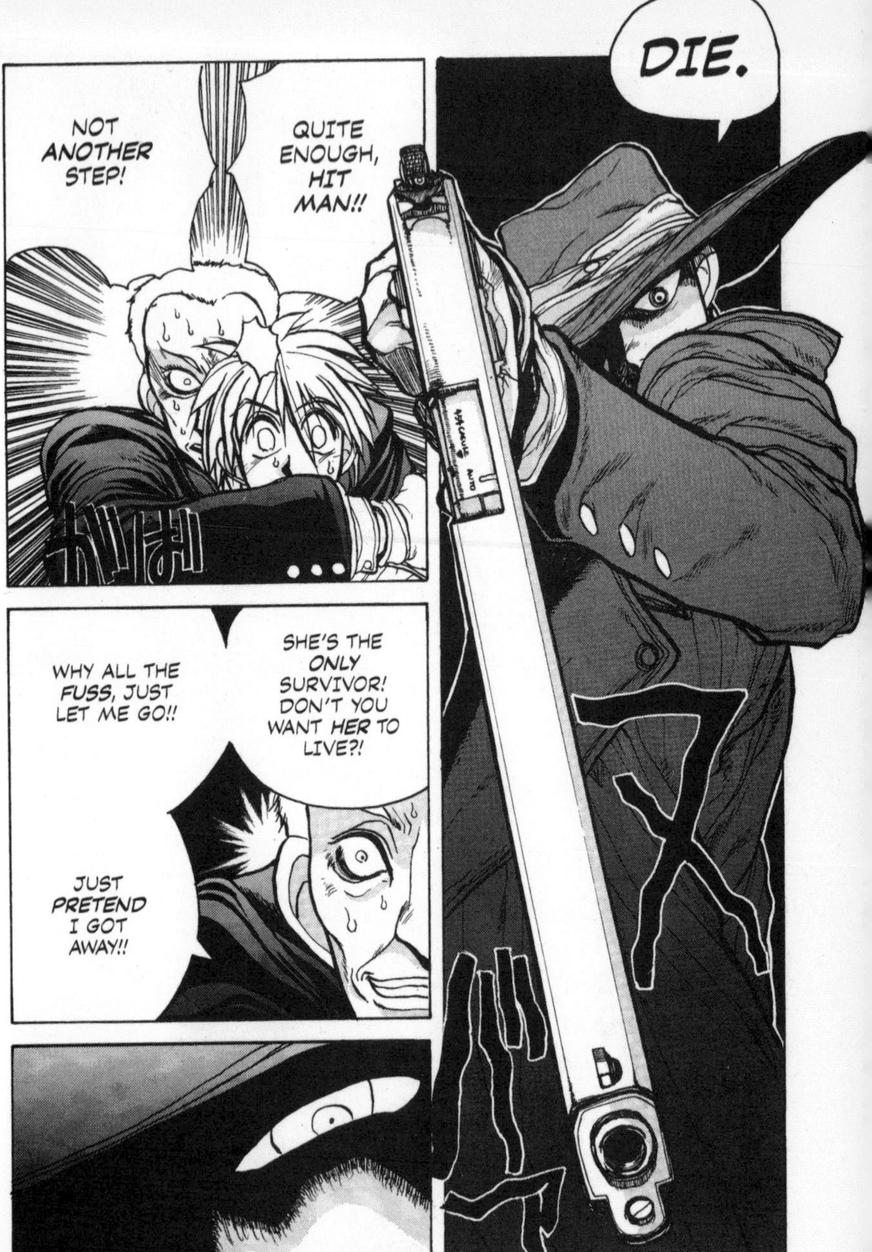
DIE.
QUITE ENOUGH, HIT MAN!!
NOT ANOTHER STEP!
SHE'S THE ONLY SURVIVOR! DON'T YOU WANT HER TO LIVE?!
WHY ALL THE FUSS, JUST LET ME GO!!
JUST PRETEND I GOT AWAY!!

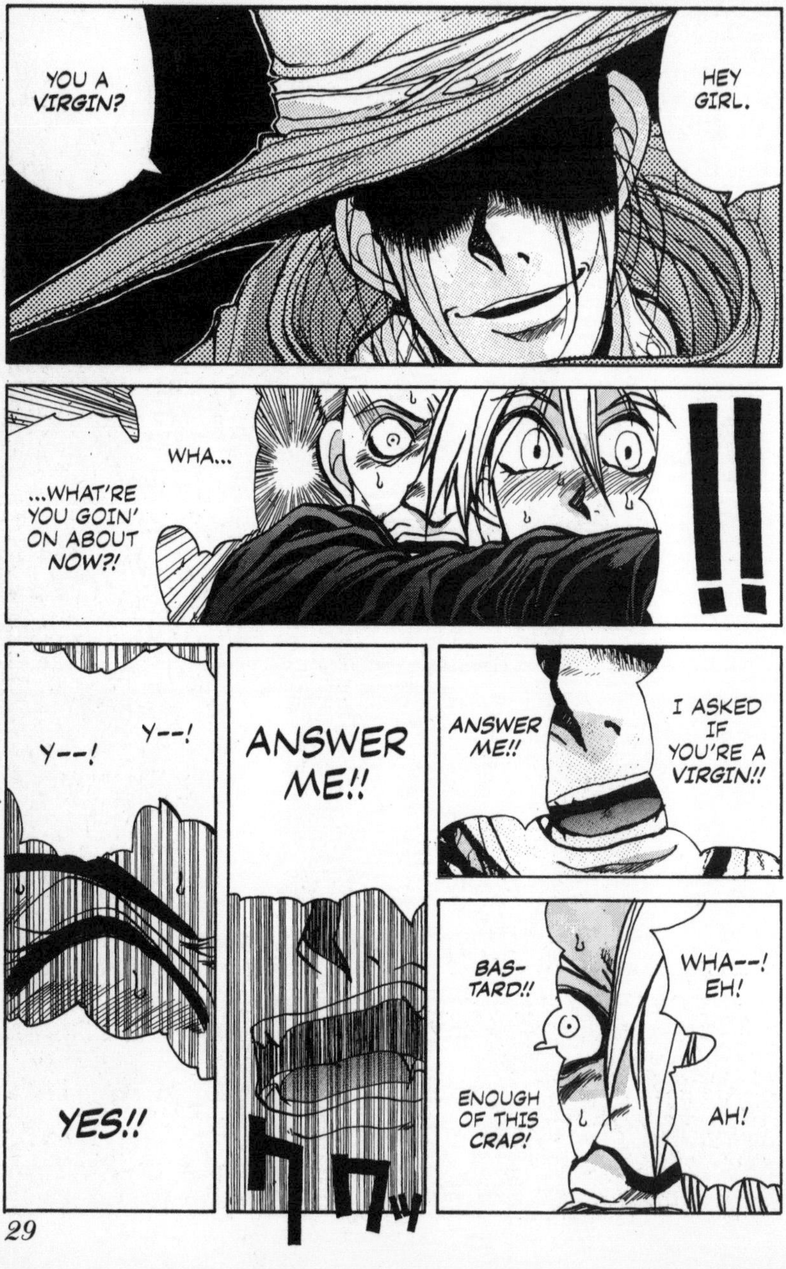
HEY GIRL.
YOU A VIRGIN?
!!
WHA...
...WHAT'RE YOU GOIN' ON ABOUT NOW?!
I ASKED IF YOU'RE A VIRGIN!!
ANSWER ME!!
WHA--! EH!
BAS-TARD!!
AH!
ENOUGH OF THIS CRAP!
ANSWER ME!!
Y--!
Y--!
YES!!

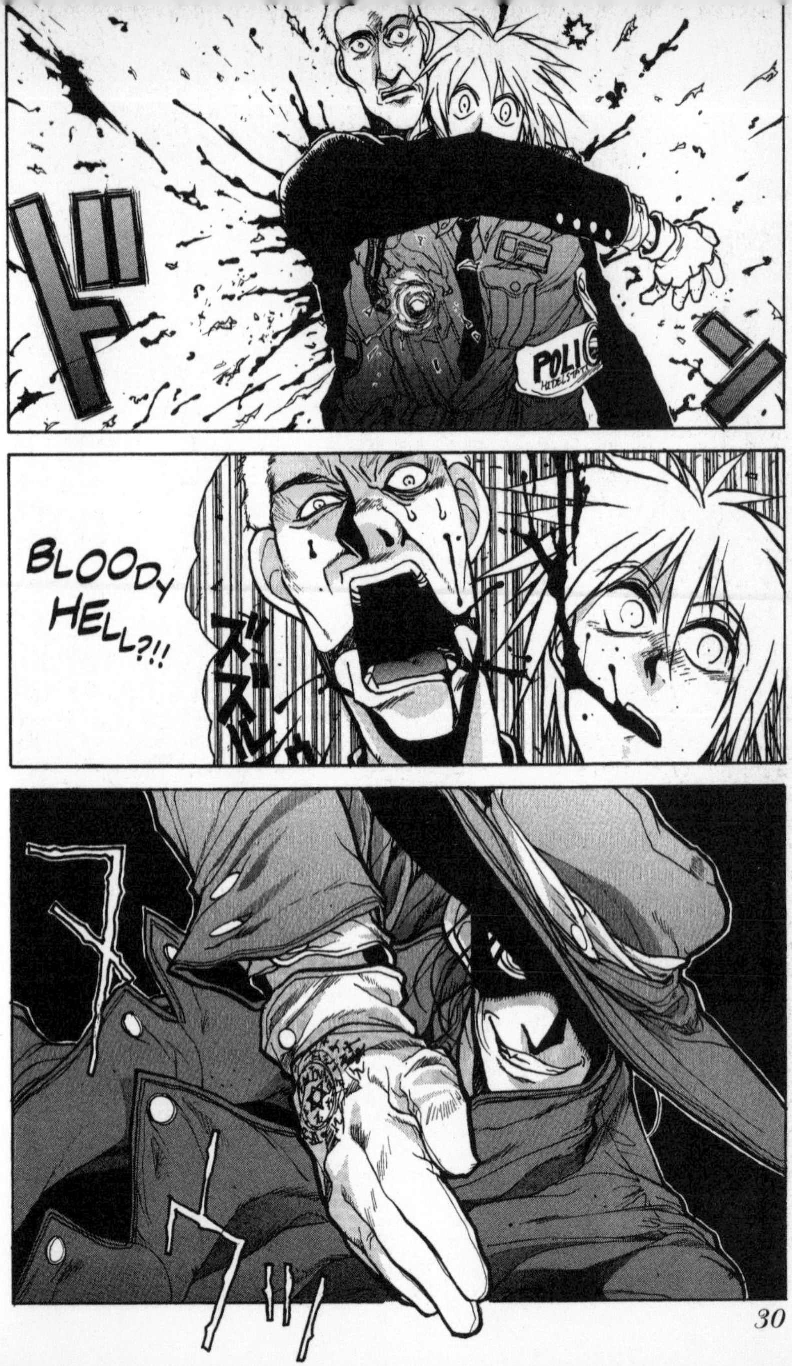
ドッ
POLI
BLOODY HELL?!!

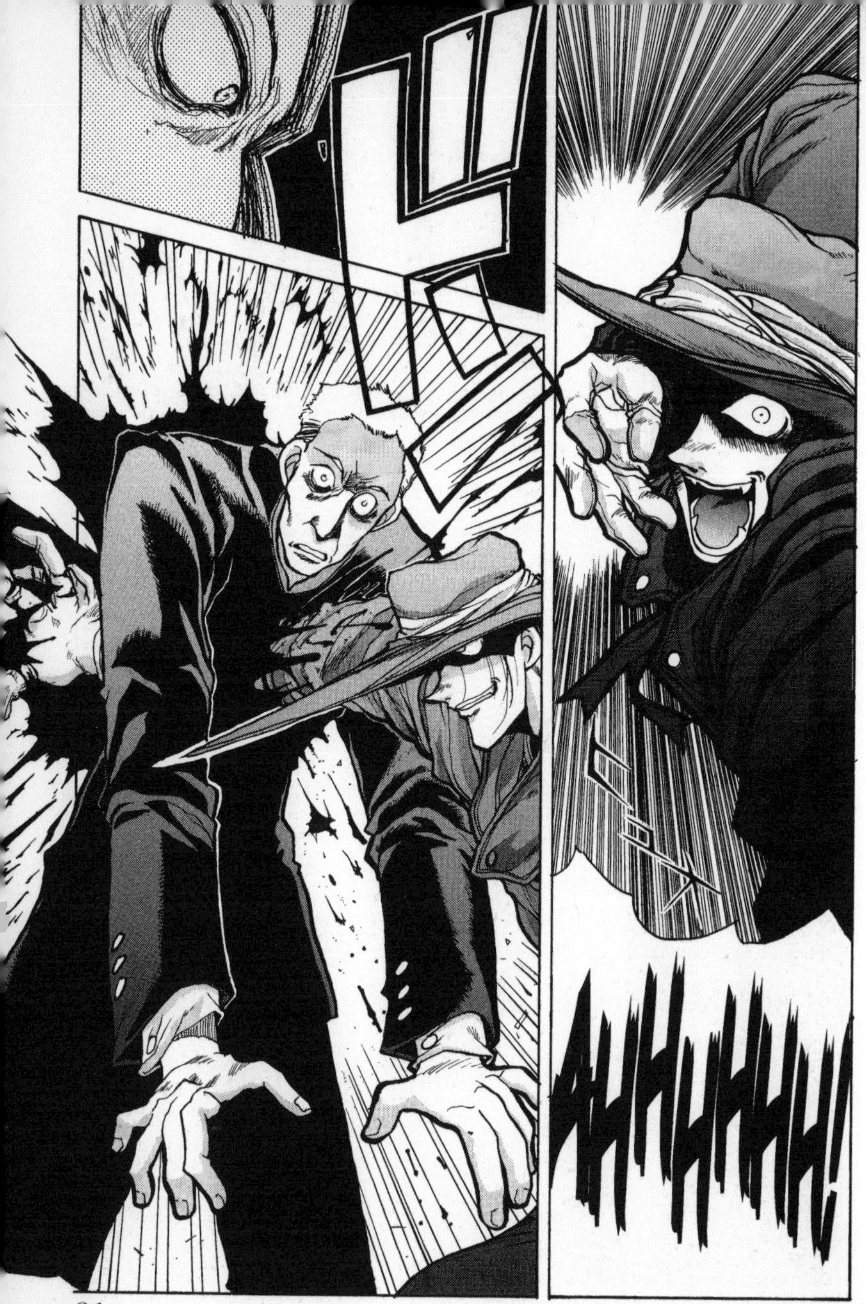
AHHHHHH!

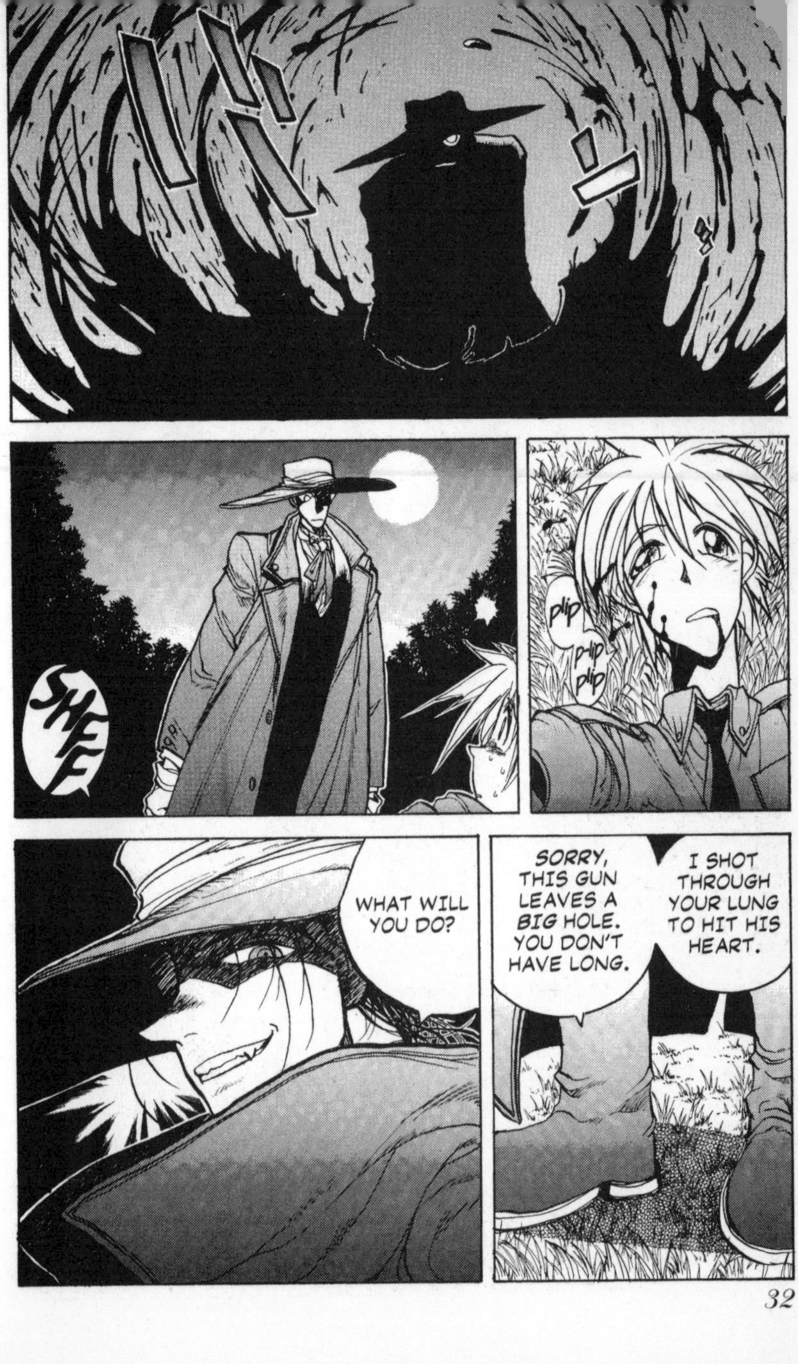
plip
p-lip
plip
SHFF
I SHOT THROUGH YOUR LUNG TO HIT HIS HEART.
SORRY, THIS GUN LEAVES A BIG HOLE. YOU DON'T HAVE LONG.
WHAT WILL YOU DO?

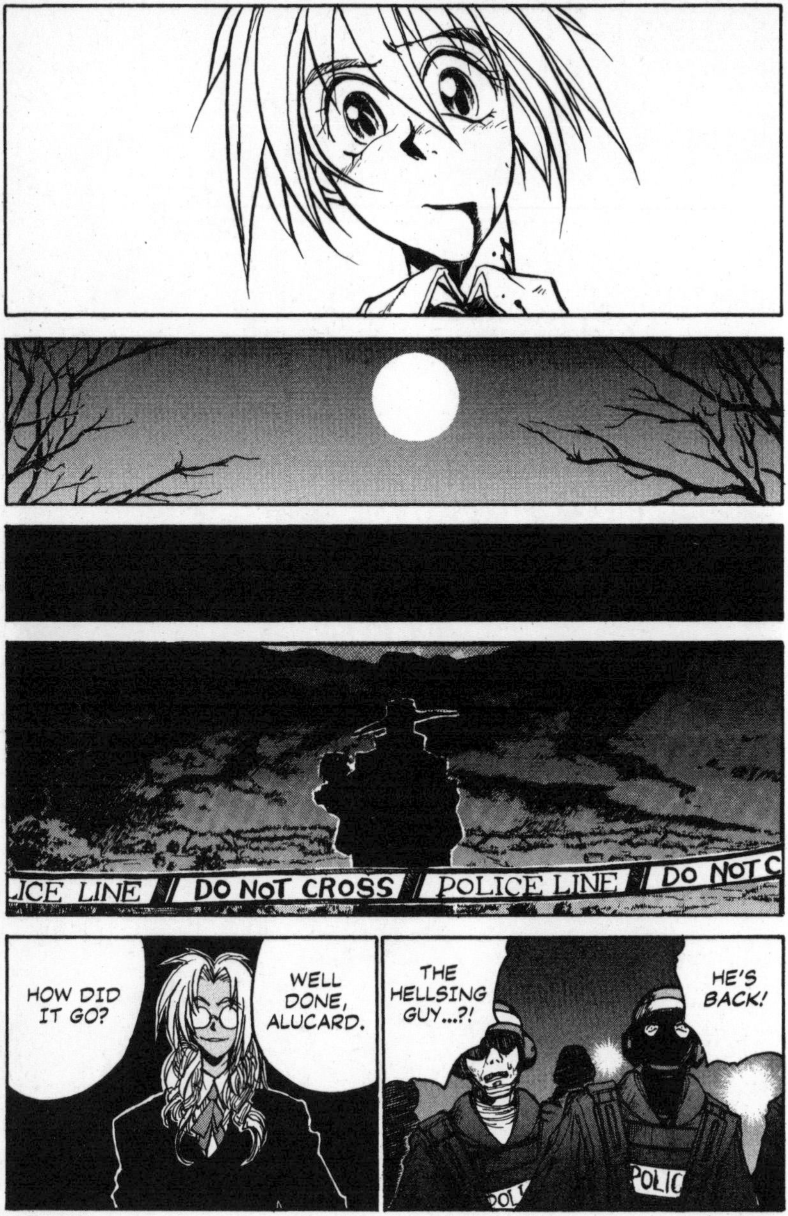
ICE LINE / DO NOT CROSS / POLICE LINE / DO NOT C
HE'S BACK!
THE HELLSING GUY...?!
WELL DONE, ALUCARD.
HOW DID IT GO?

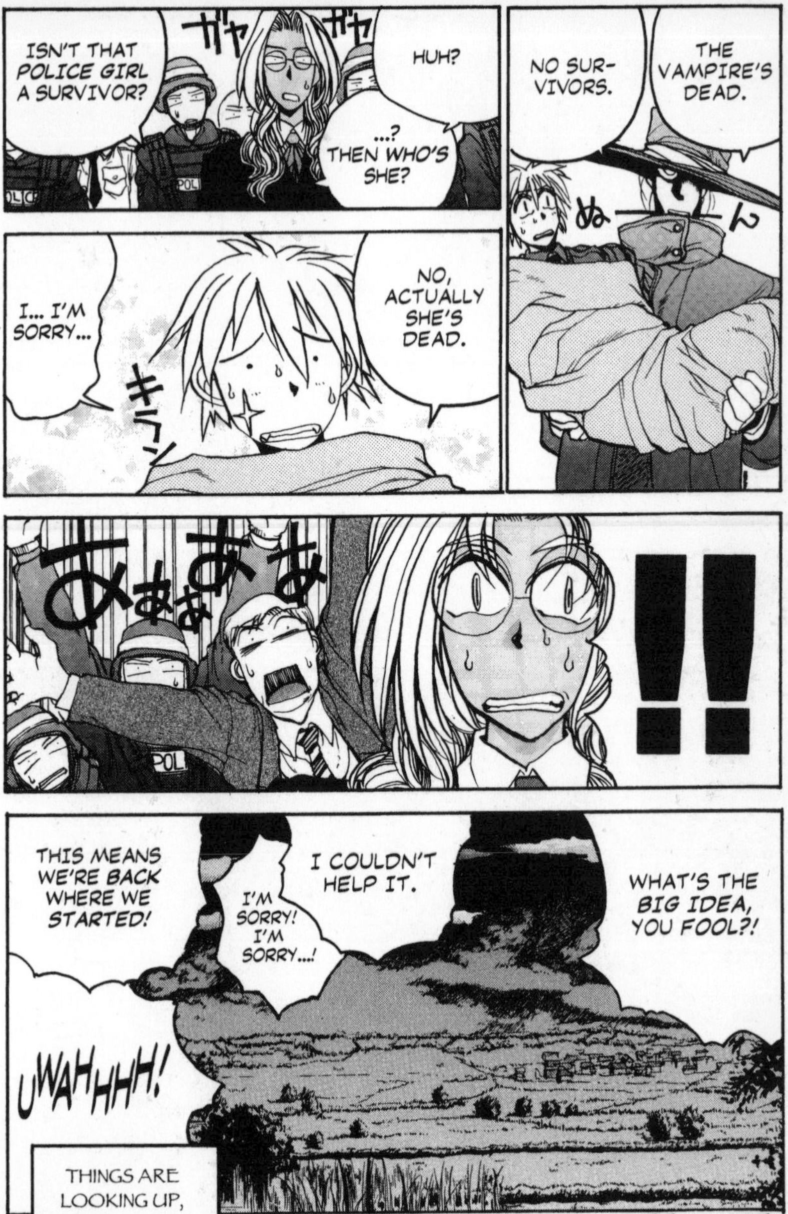
THE VAMPIRE'S DEAD.
NO SUR- VIVORS.
ぬーん
ガヤ ガヤ
HUH?
...? THEN WHO'S SHE?
ISN'T THAT POLICE GIRL A SURVIVOR?
NO, ACTUALLY SHE'S DEAD.
I... I'M SORRY...
キラン
!!
WHAT'S THE BIG IDEA, YOU FOOL?!
I COULDN'T HELP IT.
I'M SORRY! I'M SORRY...!
THIS MEANS WE'RE BACK WHERE WE STARTED!
UWAHHHH!
THINGS ARE LOOKING UP, LOOKING DOWN.

ORDER 01 / END

EHEH END

ORDER 02

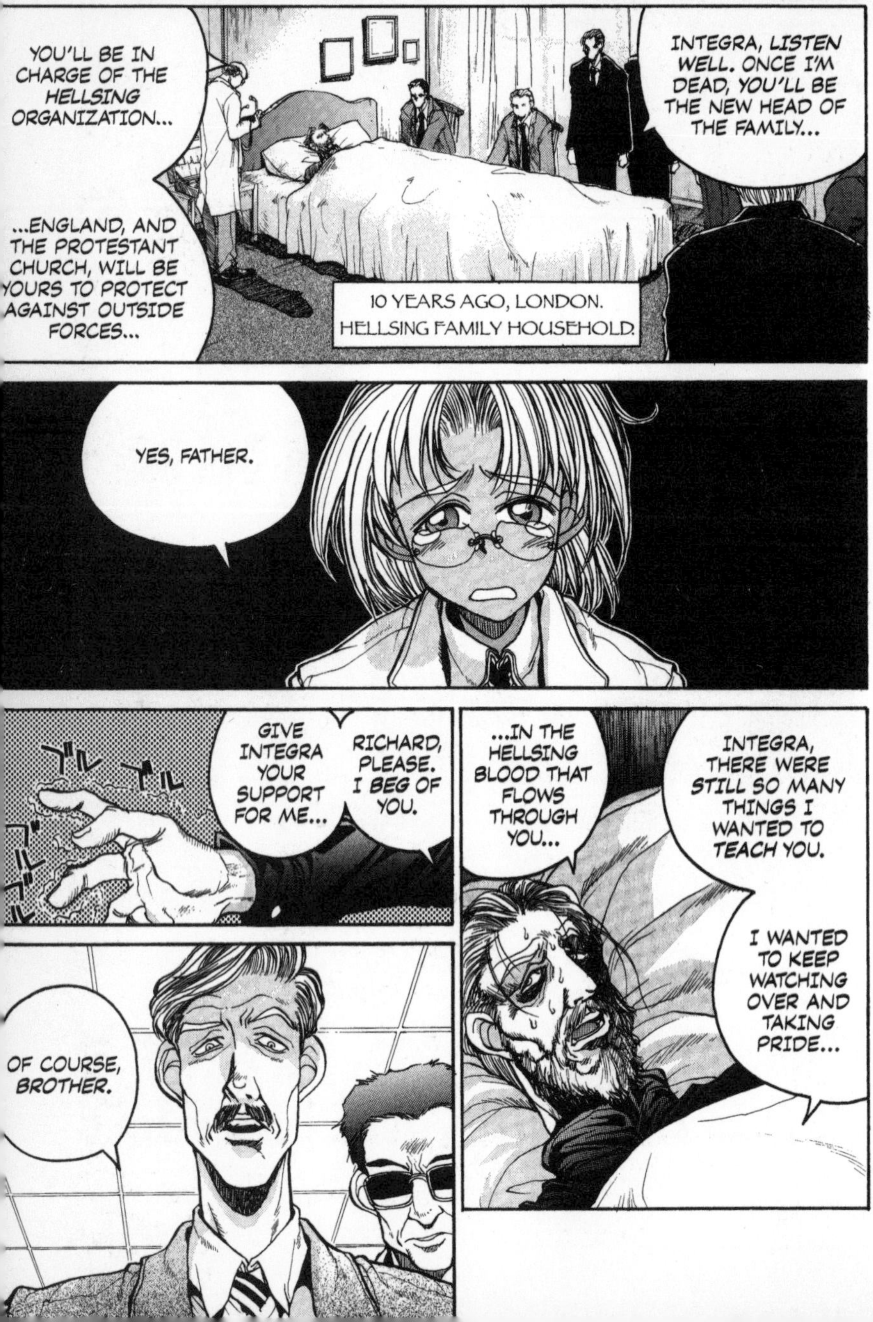

INTEGRA, LISTEN WELL. ONCE I'M DEAD, YOU'LL BE THE NEW HEAD OF THE FAMILY...
YOU'LL BE IN CHARGE OF THE HELLSING ORGANIZATION...
...ENGLAND, AND THE PROTESTANT CHURCH, WILL BE YOURS TO PROTECT AGAINST OUTSIDE FORCES...
10 YEARS AGO, LONDON. HELLSING FAMILY HOUSEHOLD.
YES, FATHER.
INTEGRA, THERE WERE STILL SO MANY THINGS I WANTED TO TEACH YOU.
I WANTED TO KEEP WATCHING OVER AND TAKING PRIDE...
...IN THE HELLSING BLOOD THAT FLOWS THROUGH YOU...
RICHARD, PLEASE. I BEG OF YOU.
GIVE INTEGRA YOUR SUPPORT FOR ME...
OF COURSE, BROTHER.

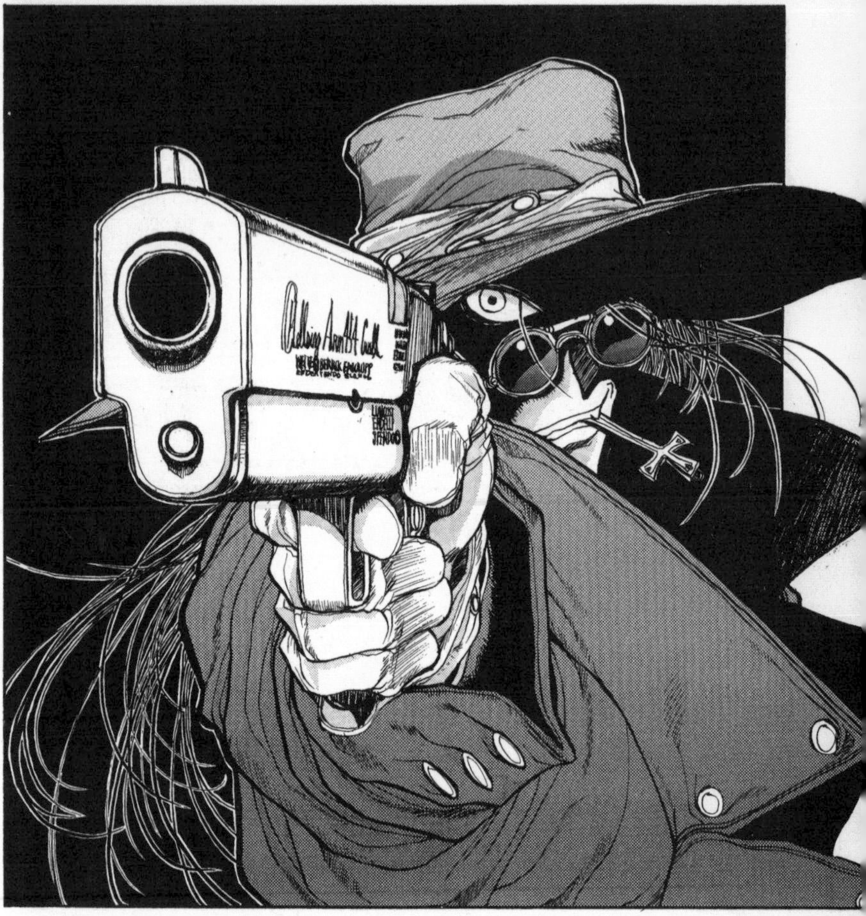

⚜ ORDER 02

マスター　オブ　モンスター
MASTER OF MONSTER

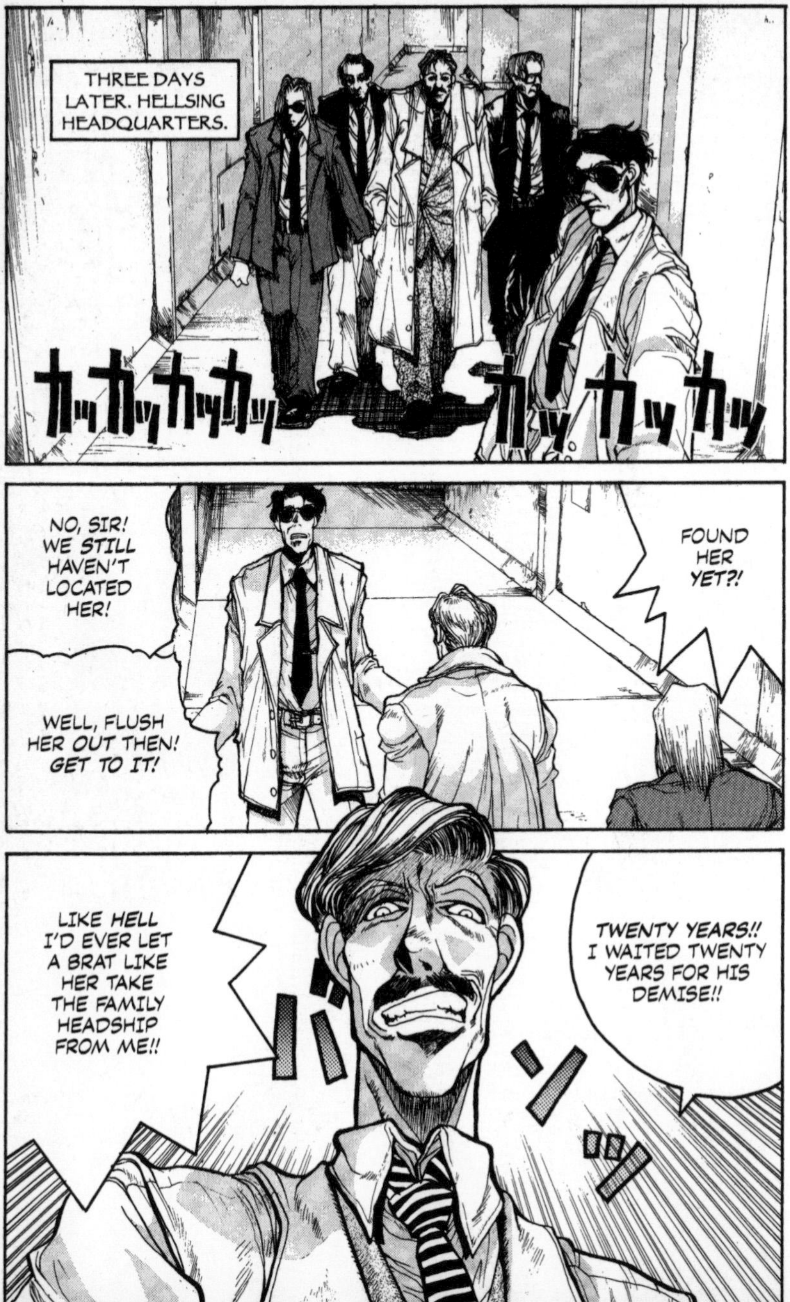
THREE DAYS LATER. HELLSING HEADQUARTERS.
カッカッカッ
カッカッカッカッ
FOUND HER YET?!
NO, SIR! WE STILL HAVEN'T LOCATED HER!
WELL, FLUSH HER OUT THEN! GET TO IT!
TWENTY YEARS!! I WAITED TWENTY YEARS FOR HIS DEMISE!!
LIKE HELL I'D EVER LET A BRAT LIKE HER TAKE THE FAMILY HEADSHIP FROM ME!!

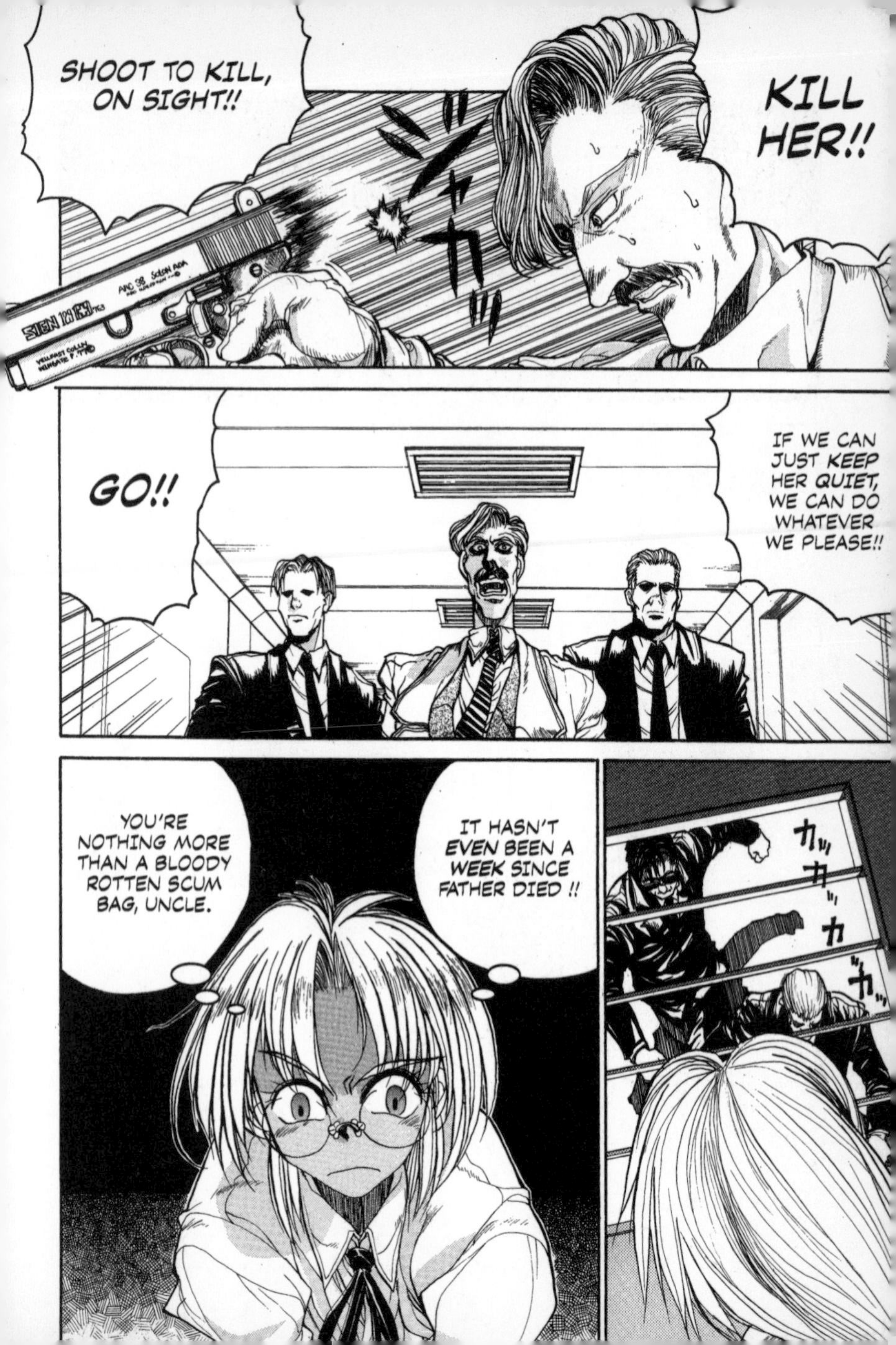
KILL HER!!
SHOOT TO KILL, ON SIGHT!!
IF WE CAN JUST KEEP HER QUIET, WE CAN DO WHATEVER WE PLEASE!!
GO!!
IT HASN'T EVEN BEEN A WEEK SINCE FATHER DIED !!
YOU'RE NOTHING MORE THAN A BLOODY ROTTEN SCUM BAG, UNCLE.

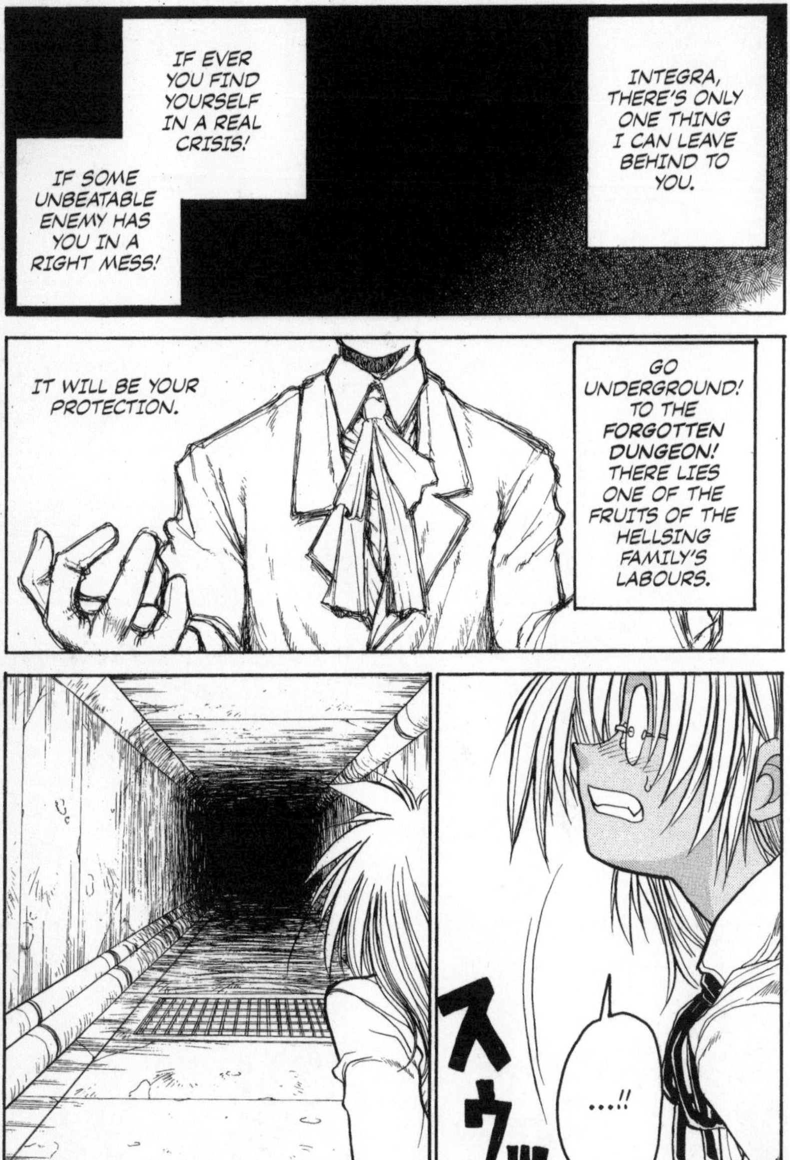
INTEGRA, THERE'S ONLY ONE THING I CAN LEAVE BEHIND TO YOU.
IF EVER YOU FIND YOURSELF IN A REAL CRISIS!
IF SOME UNBEATABLE ENEMY HAS YOU IN A RIGHT MESS!
GO UNDERGROUND! TO THE FORGOTTEN DUNGEON! THERE LIES ONE OF THE FRUITS OF THE HELLSING FAMILY'S LABOURS.
IT WILL BE YOUR PROTECTION.
...!!
スウッ

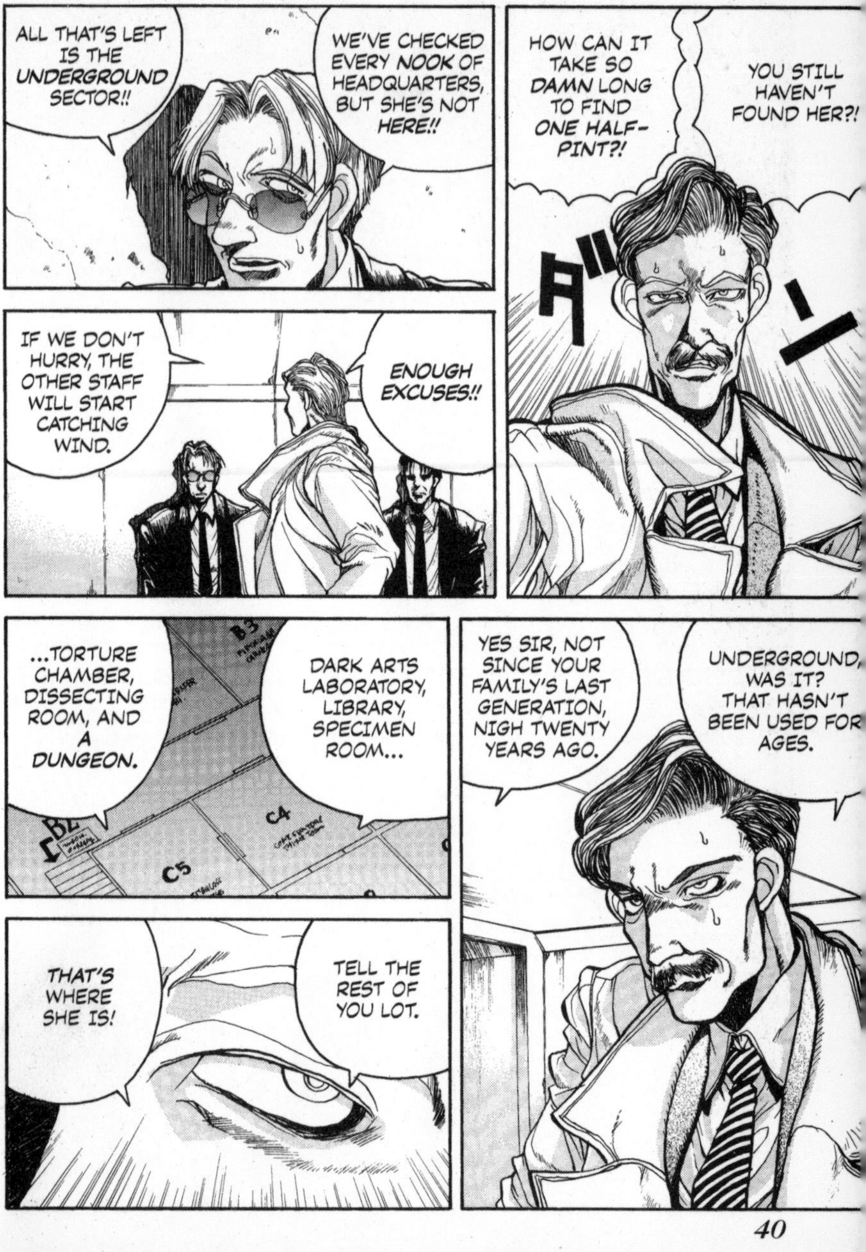
YOU STILL HAVEN'T FOUND HER?!
HOW CAN IT TAKE SO DAMN LONG TO FIND ONE HALF-PINT?!
WE'VE CHECKED EVERY NOOK OF HEADQUARTERS, BUT SHE'S NOT HERE!!
ALL THAT'S LEFT IS THE UNDERGROUND SECTOR!!
ENOUGH EXCUSES!!
IF WE DON'T HURRY, THE OTHER STAFF WILL START CATCHING WIND.
UNDERGROUND, WAS IT? THAT HASN'T BEEN USED FOR AGES.
YES SIR, NOT SINCE YOUR FAMILY'S LAST GENERATION, NIGH TWENTY YEARS AGO.
DARK ARTS LABORATORY, LIBRARY, SPECIMEN ROOM...
...TORTURE CHAMBER, DISSECTING ROOM, AND A DUNGEON.
B3
C4
C5
TELL THE REST OF YOU LOT.
THAT'S WHERE SHE IS!

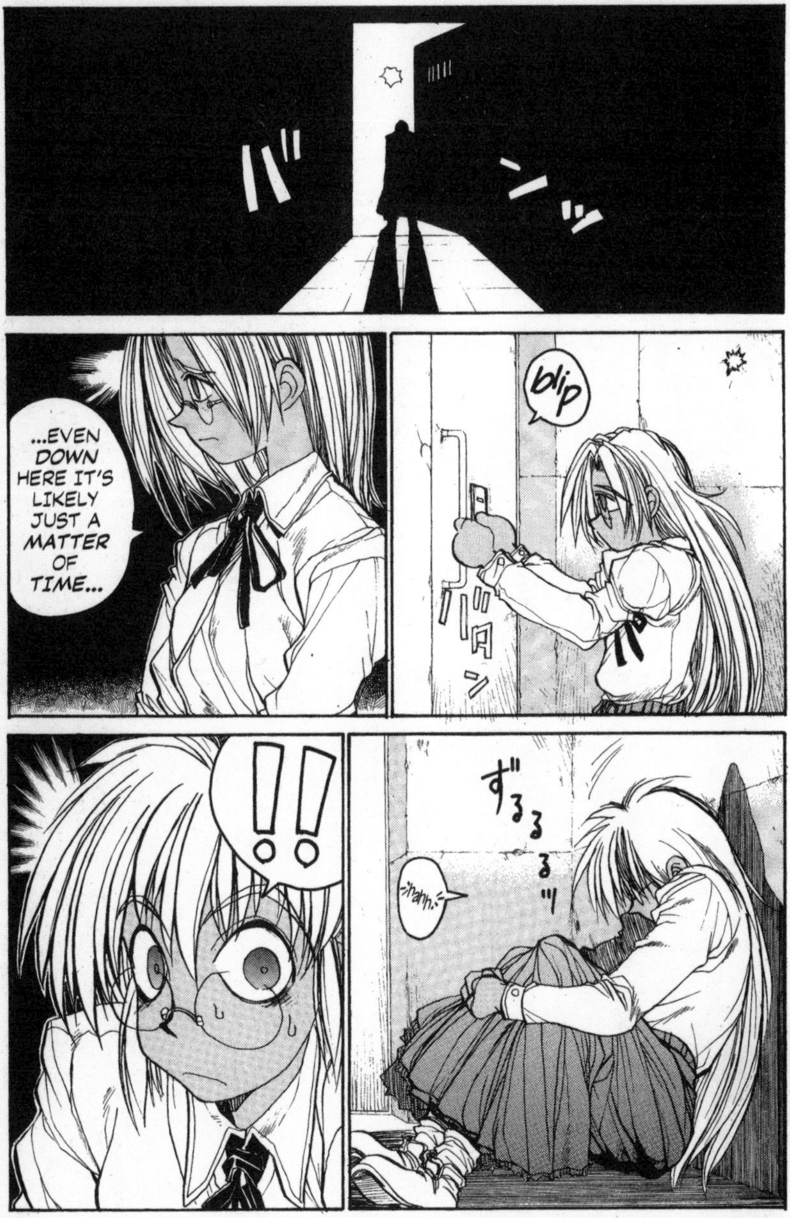
バンッ
blip
バタン
...EVEN DOWN HERE IT'S LIKELY JUST A MATTER OF TIME...
ずるるるッ
:nahh.:
!!

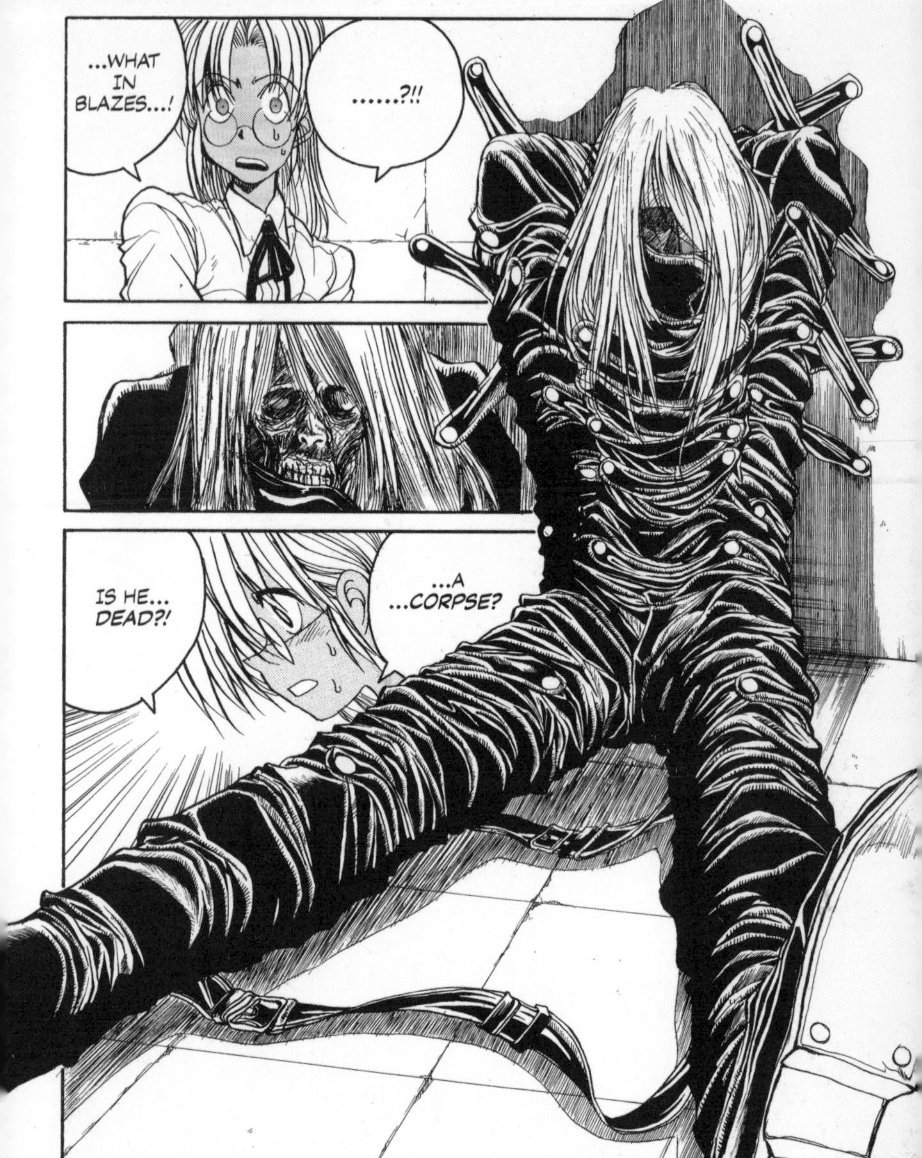
......?!!
...WHAT IN BLAZES...!
...A ...CORPSE?
IS HE... DEAD?!

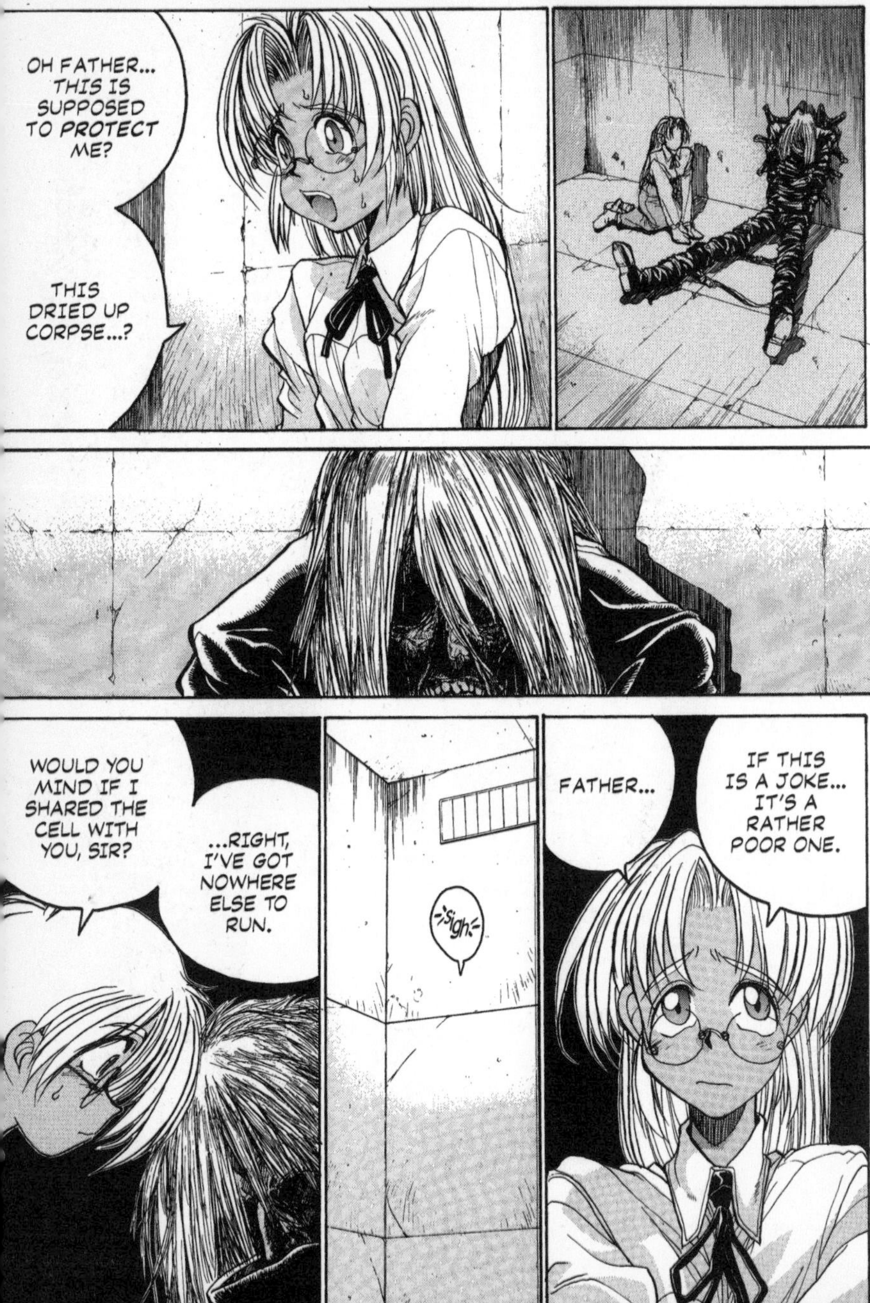
OH FATHER... THIS IS SUPPOSED TO PROTECT ME?
THIS DRIED UP CORPSE...?
IF THIS IS A JOKE... IT'S A RATHER POOR ONE.
FATHER...
Sigh
...RIGHT, I'VE GOT NOWHERE ELSE TO RUN.
WOULD YOU MIND IF I SHARED THE CELL WITH YOU, SIR?

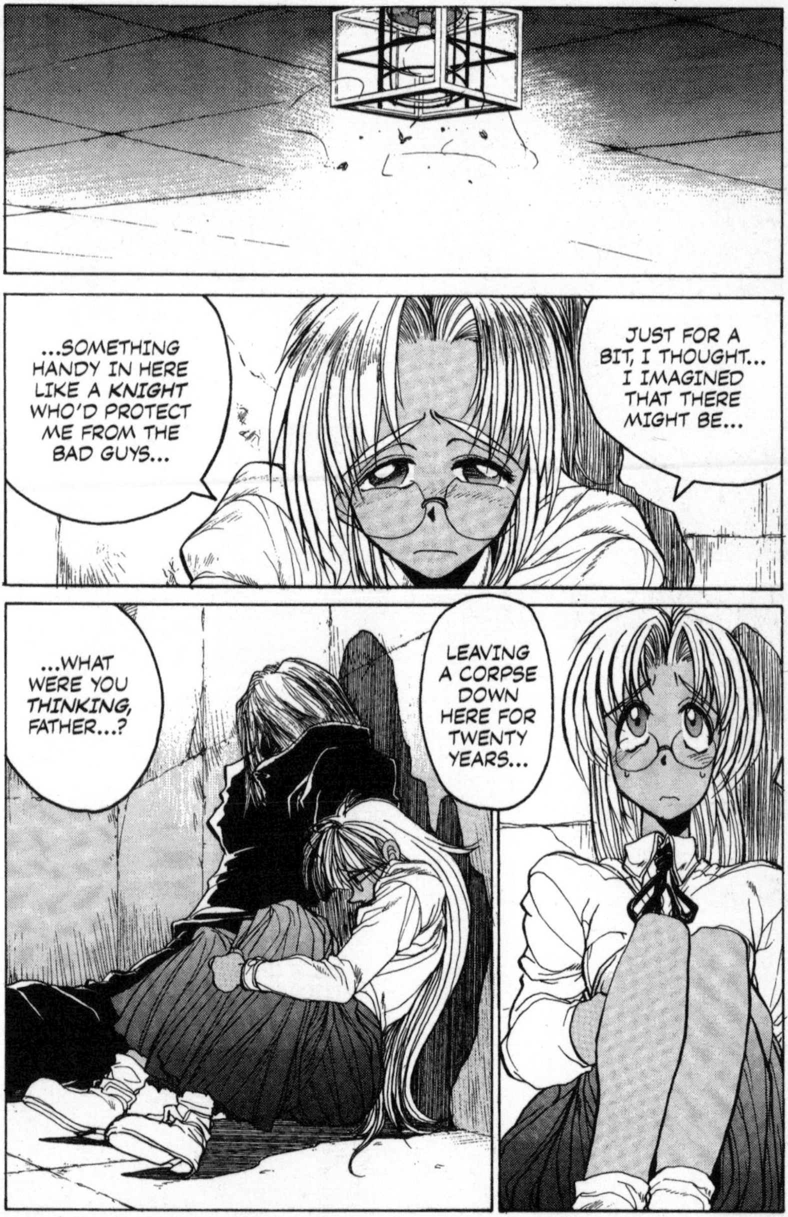

JUST FOR A BIT, I THOUGHT... I IMAGINED THAT THERE MIGHT BE...
...SOMETHING HANDY IN HERE LIKE A KNIGHT WHO'D PROTECT ME FROM THE BAD GUYS...
LEAVING A CORPSE DOWN HERE FOR TWENTY YEARS...
...WHAT WERE YOU THINKING, FATHER...?

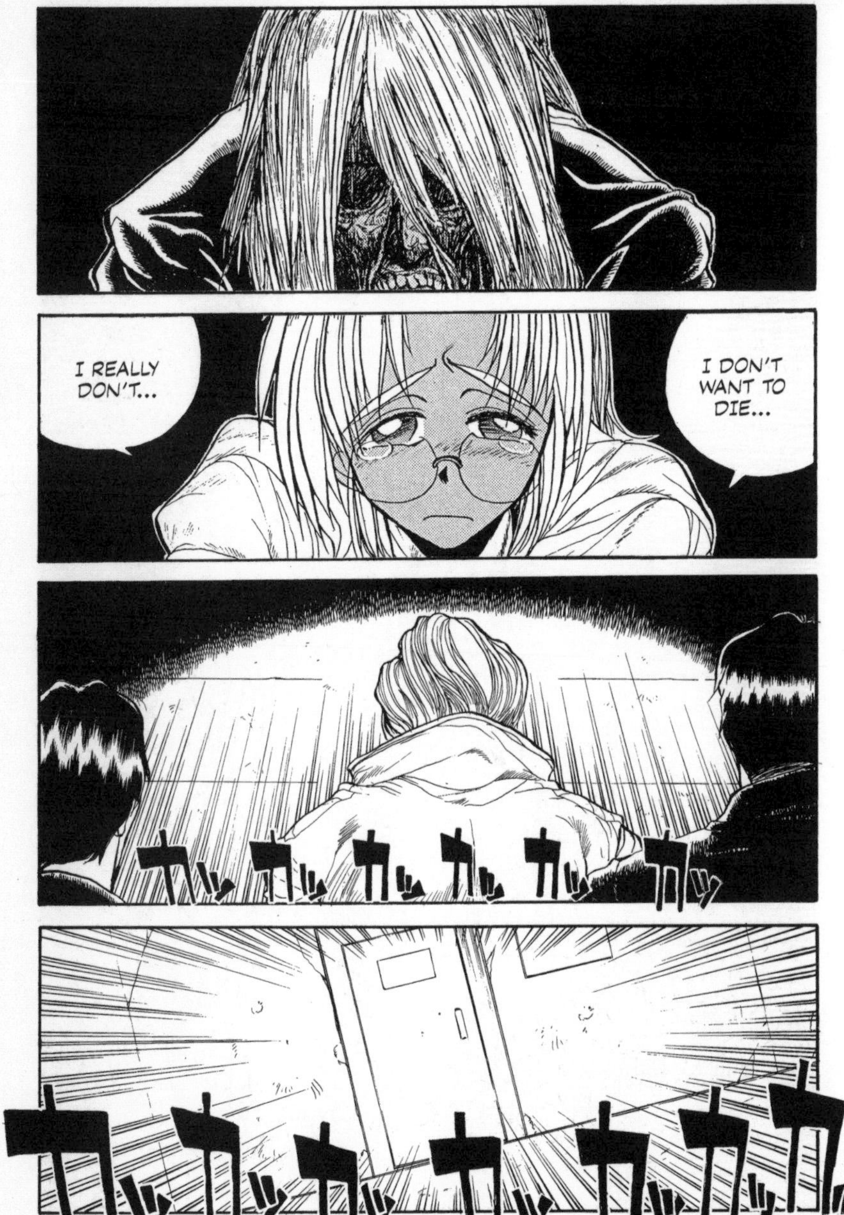
I DON'T WANT TO DIE...
I REALLY DON'T...
カッカッカッカッカッカッ
カッカッカッカッカッカッカッ

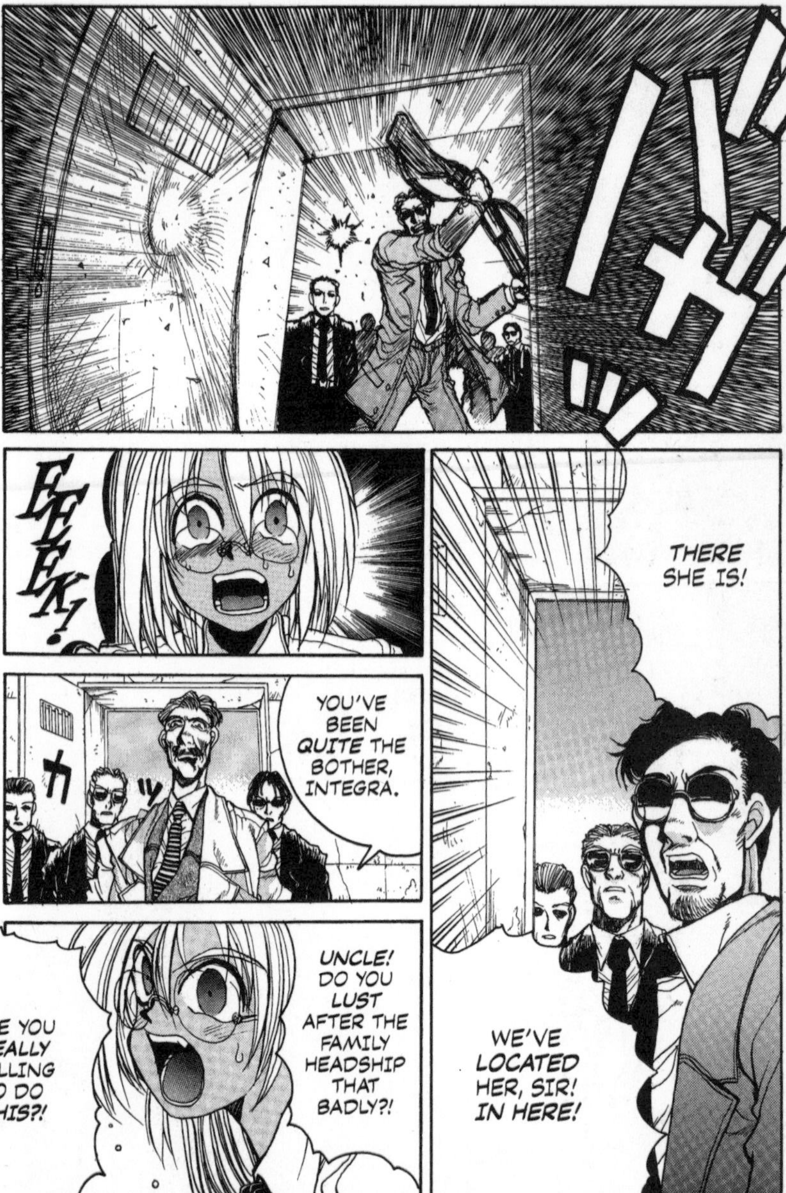
THERE SHE IS!
WE'VE LOCATED HER, SIR! IN HERE!
EEEK!
YOU'VE BEEN QUITE THE BOTHER, INTEGRA.
UNCLE! DO YOU LUST AFTER THE FAMILY HEADSHIP THAT BADLY?!
ARE YOU REALLY WILLING TO DO THIS?!

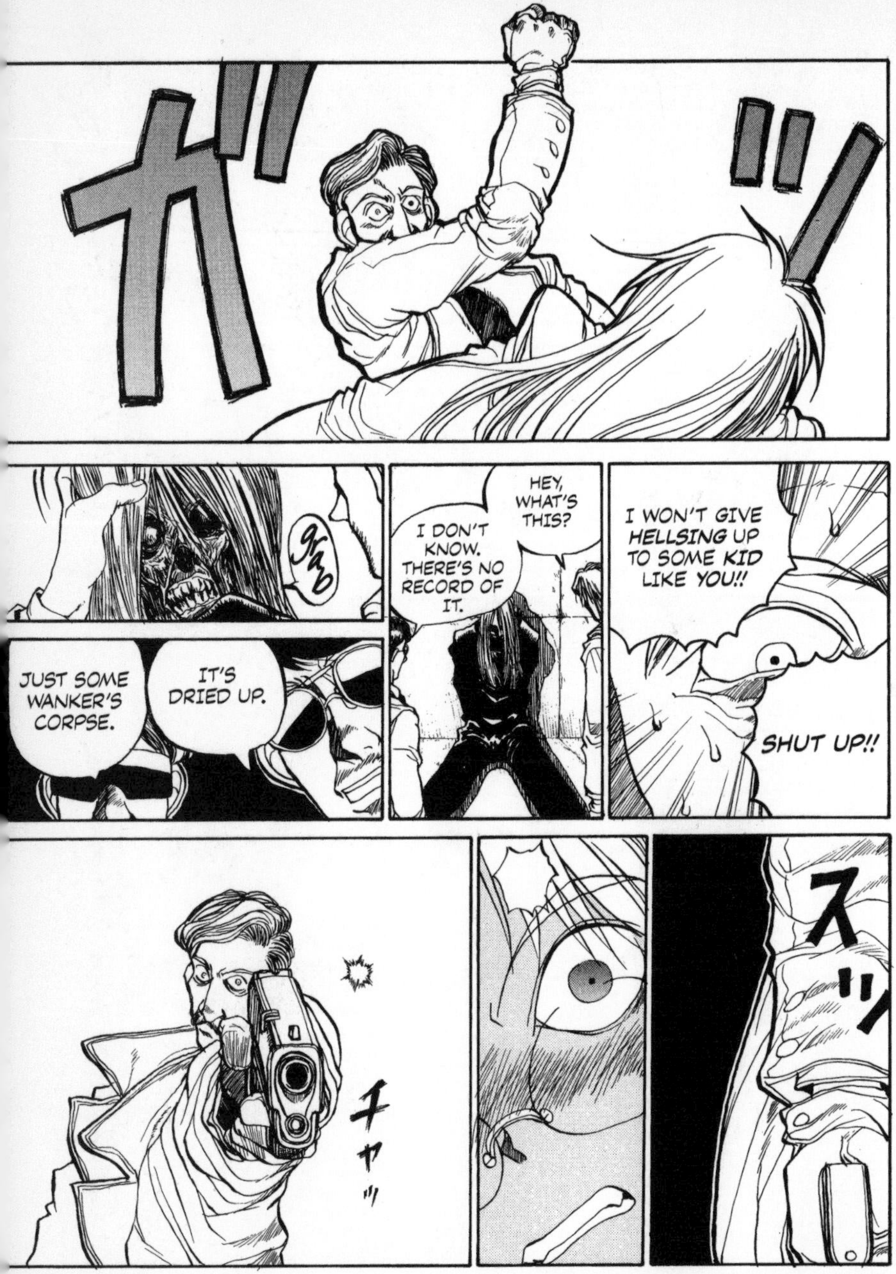
ガッ
I WON'T GIVE HELLSING UP TO SOME KID LIKE YOU!!
SHUT UP!!
HEY, WHAT'S THIS?
I DON'T KNOW. THERE'S NO RECORD OF IT.
IT'S DRIED UP.
JUST SOME WANKER'S CORPSE.
スッ
チャッ

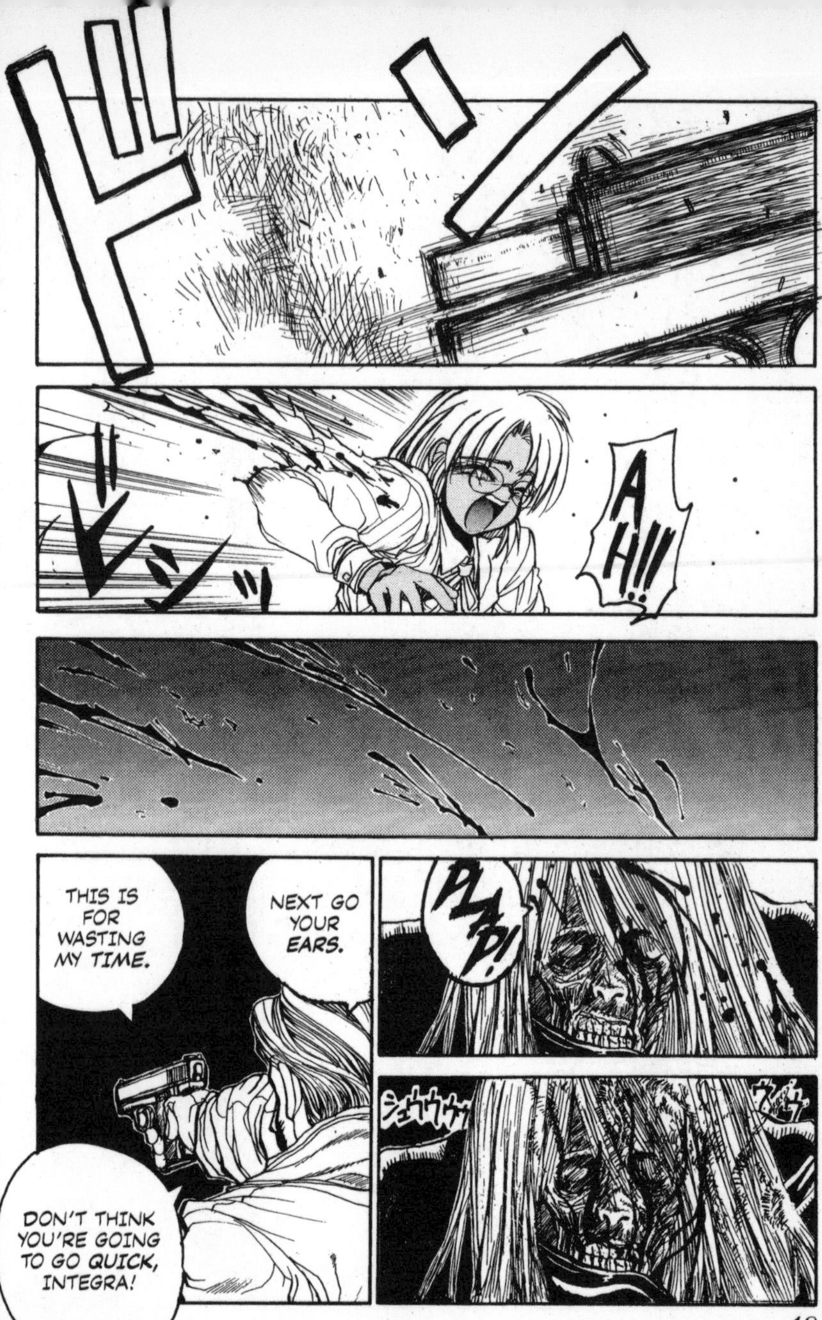
AH!!
PLAP!
NEXT GO YOUR EARS.
THIS IS FOR WASTING MY TIME.
DON'T THINK YOU'RE GOING TO GO QUICK, INTEGRA!

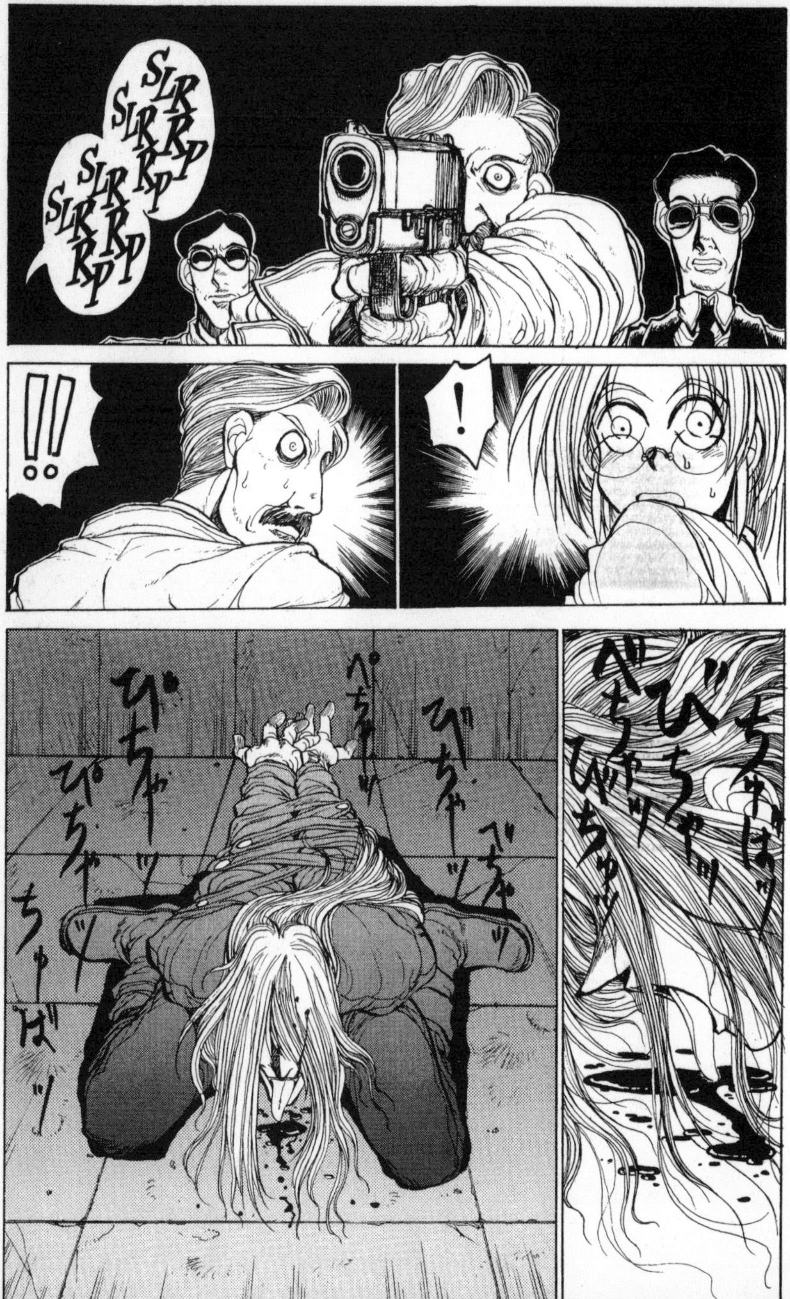
SLRRRP SLRRRP SLRRRP SLRRRP
!
!!
ちゅばッ
びちゃッ
べちゃッ
びちゅッ
ぺちゃッ
びちゃッ
ぴちゃッ
ぴちゃッ
ちゅばッ!
ぴちゃッ

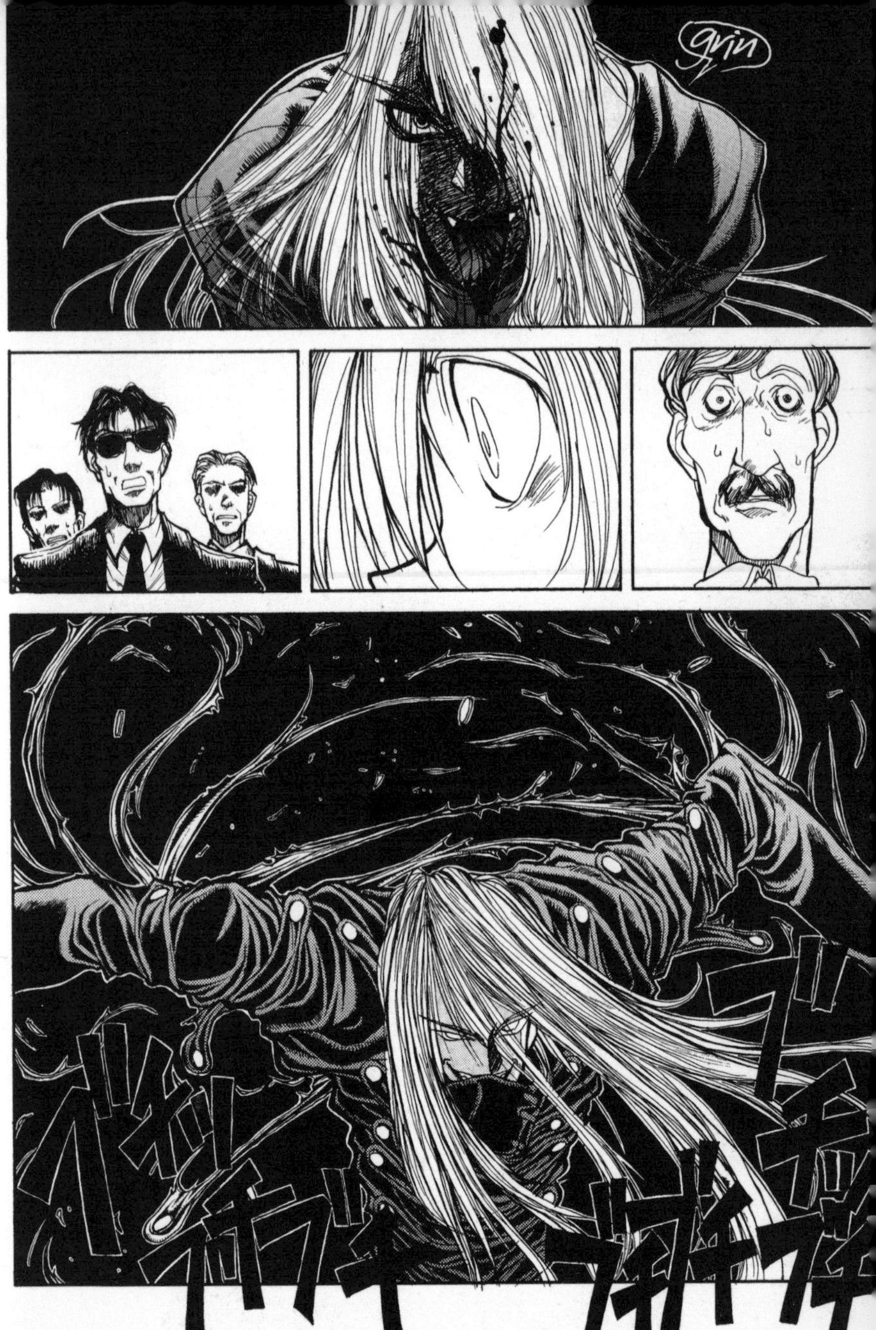
grin

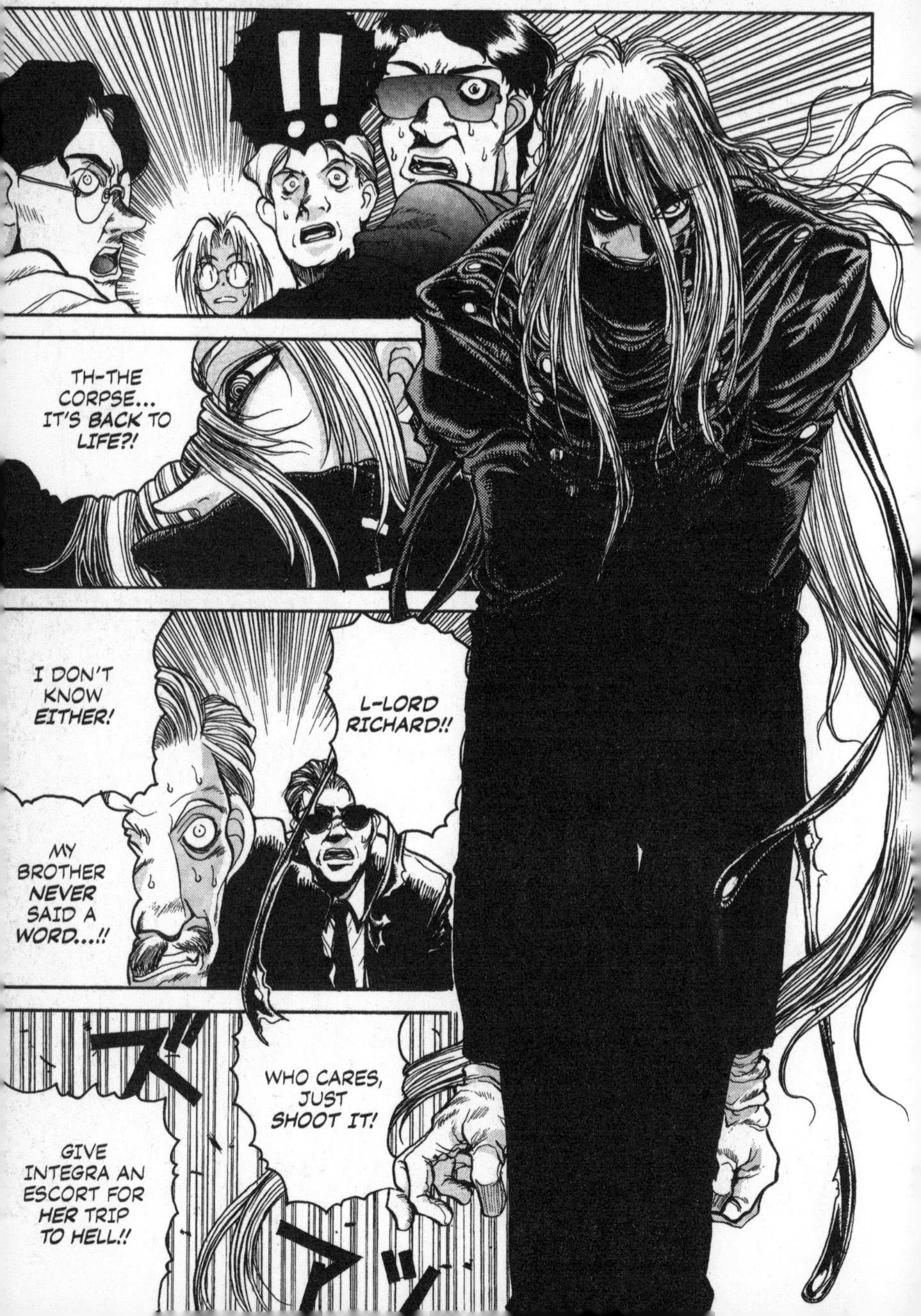
!!
TH-THE CORPSE... IT'S BACK TO LIFE?!
L-LORD RICHARD!!
I DON'T KNOW EITHER!
MY BROTHER NEVER SAID A WORD...!!
WHO CARES, JUST SHOOT IT!
GIVE INTEGRA AN ESCORT FOR HER TRIP TO HELL!!

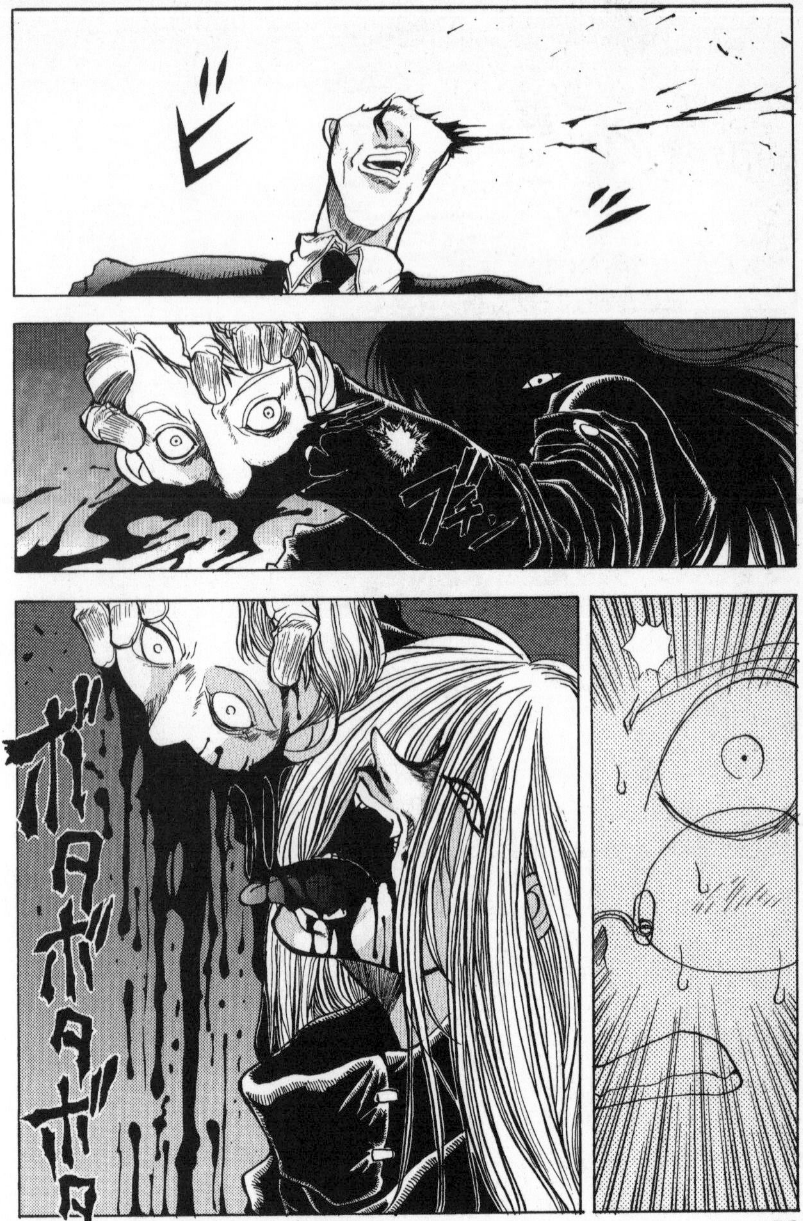
ビッ
ブチン
ボタボタボタボタ

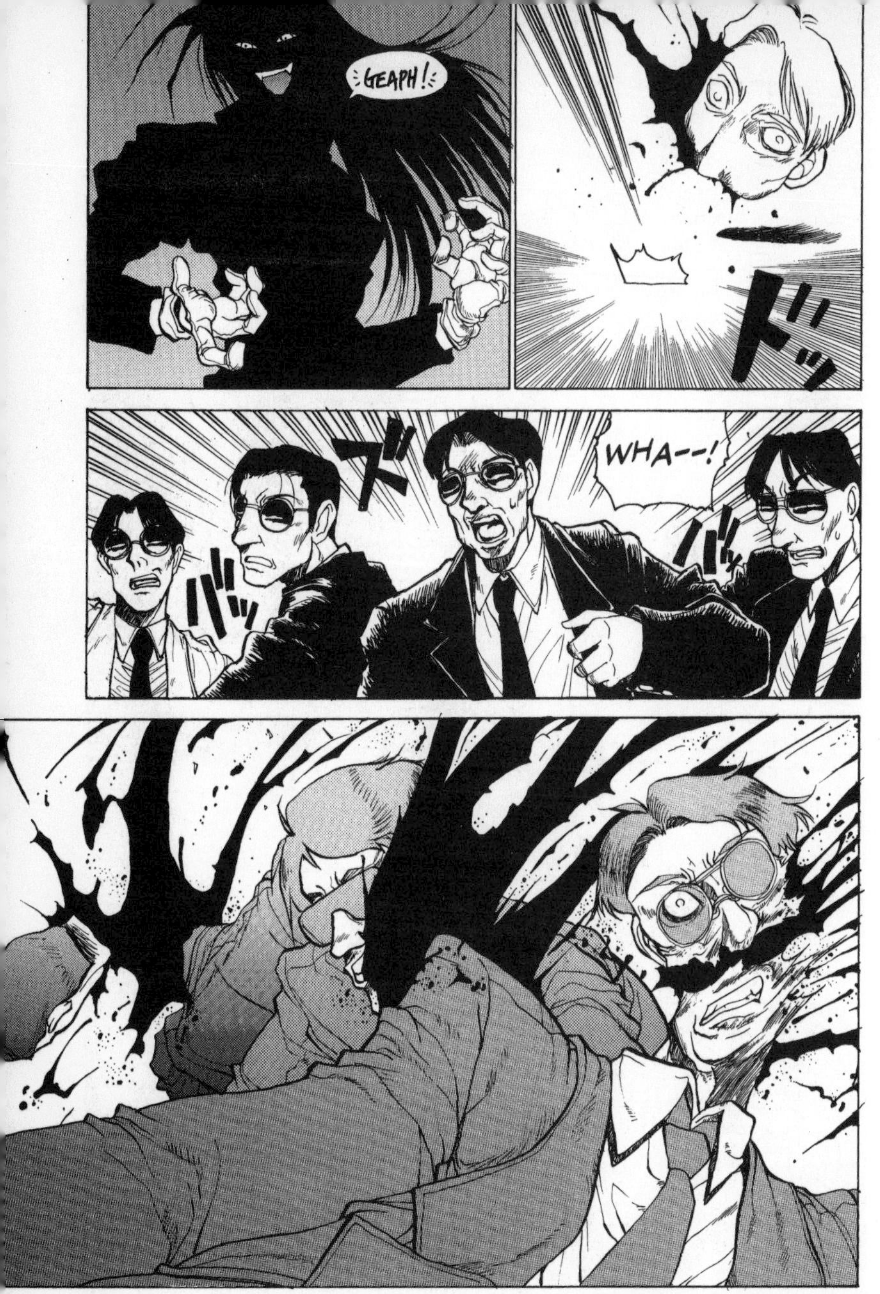

ドッ
GEAPH!
WHA--!
バッ
ズ
バッ

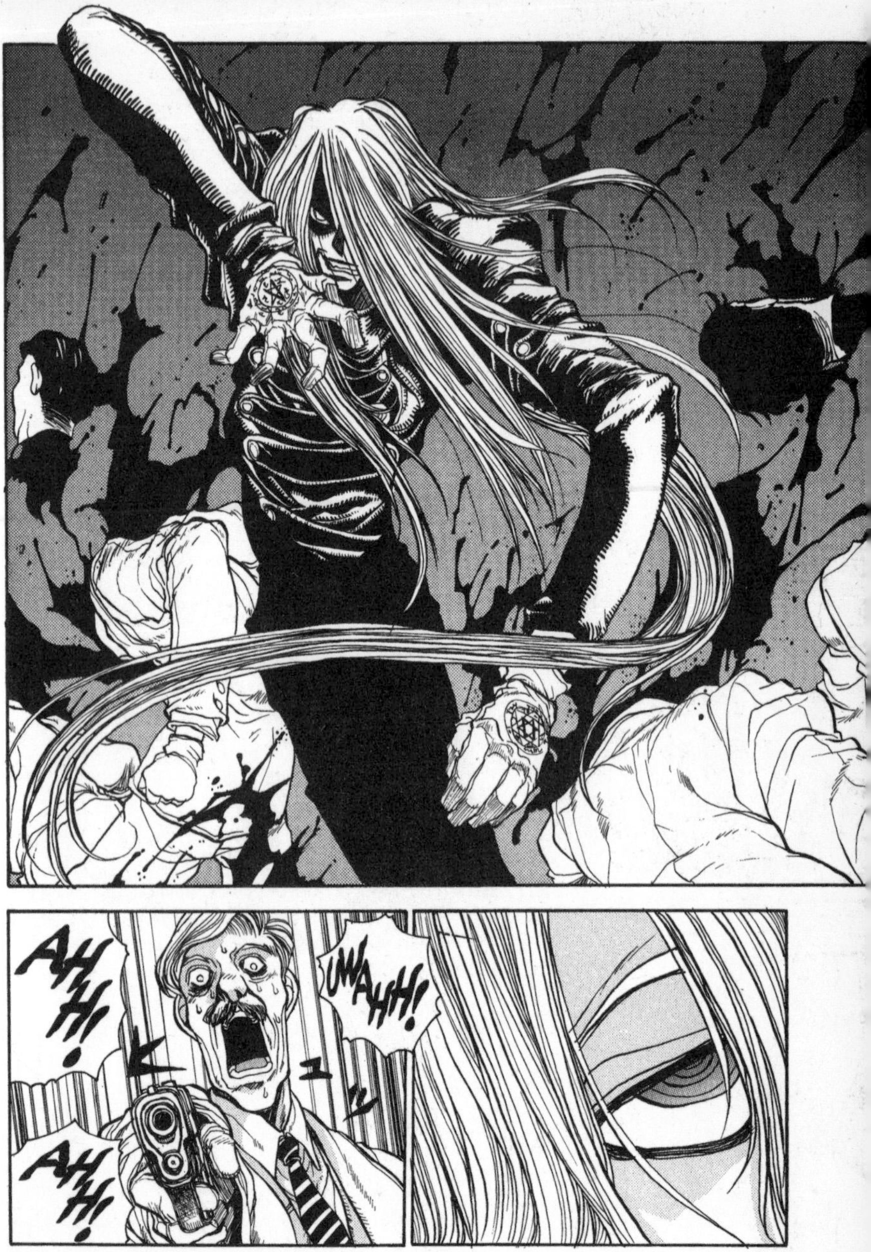
UWAHH!
AHHH!
AHHH!

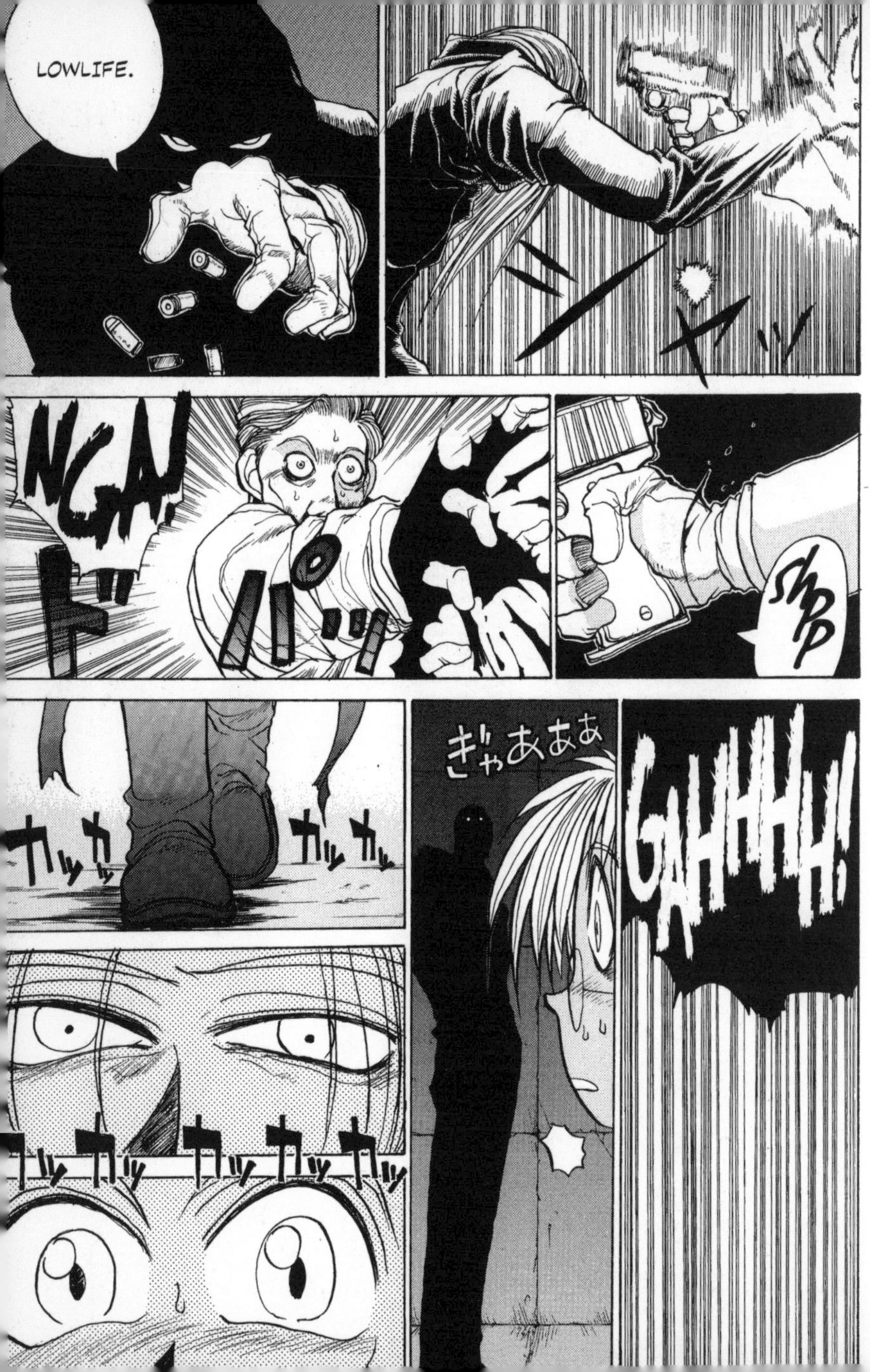
LOWLIFE.
shpp
NGA!
GAHHHH!
ぎゃあああ
カッカッ カッカッ
カッカッカッカッカッ

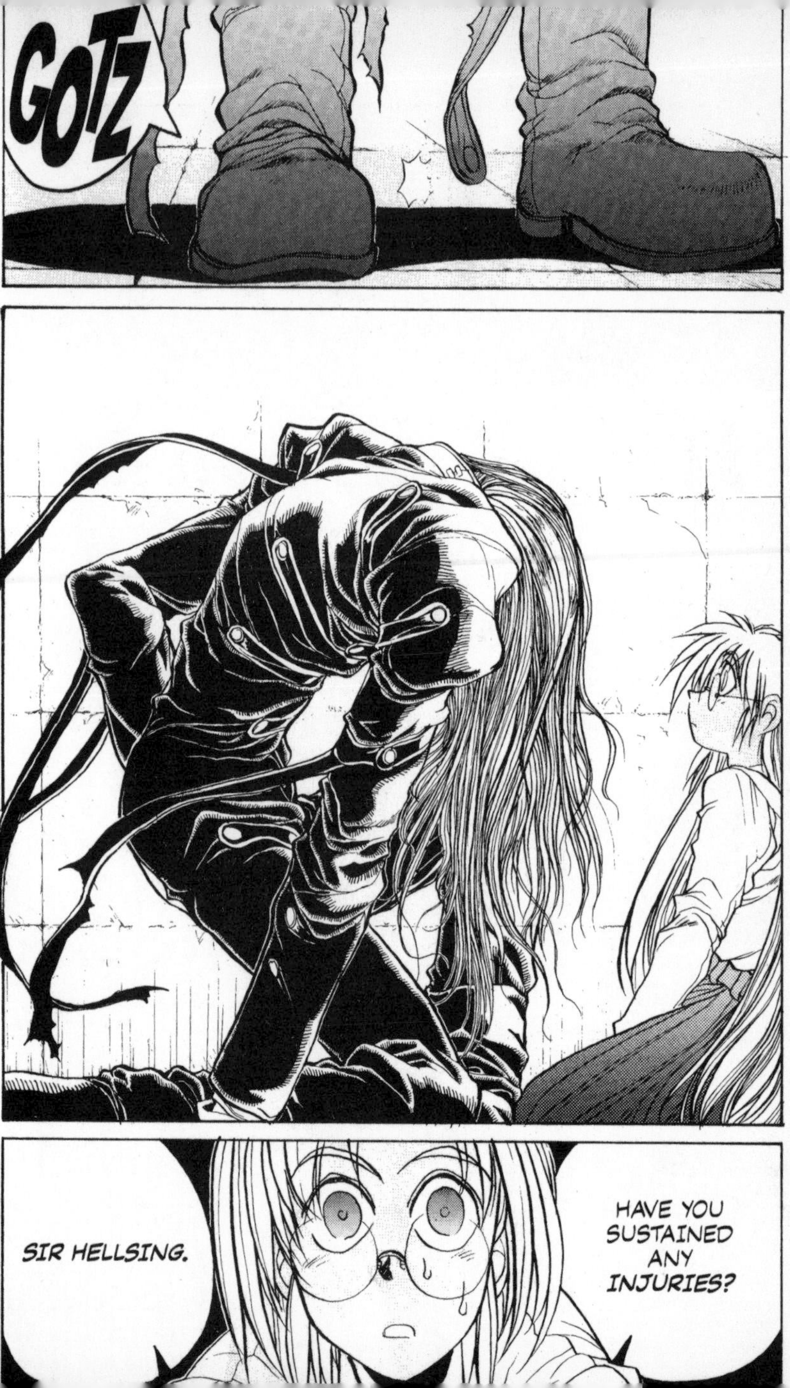
GOTZ
HAVE YOU SUSTAINED ANY INJURIES?
SIR HELLSING.

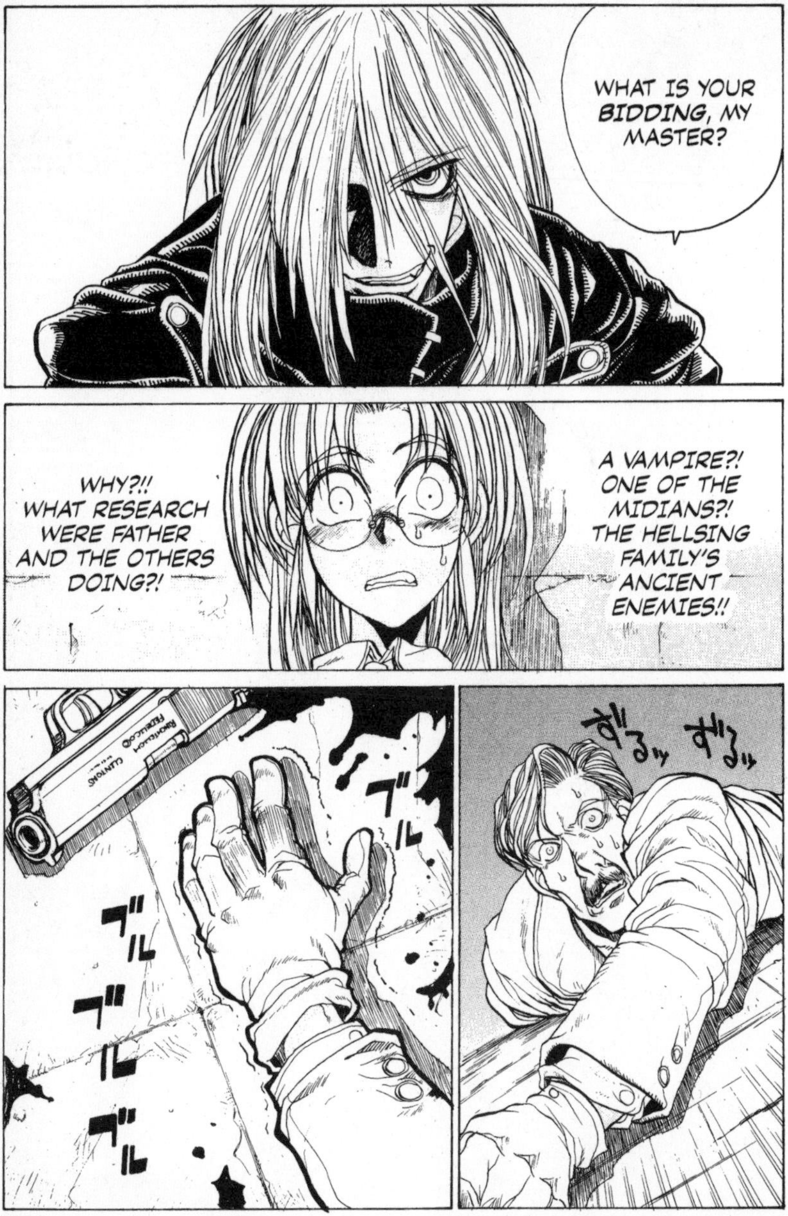
WHAT IS YOUR BIDDING, MY MASTER?
A VAMPIRE?! ONE OF THE MIDIANS?! THE HELLSING FAMILY'S ANCIENT ENEMIES!!
WHY?!! WHAT RESEARCH WERE FATHER AND THE OTHERS DOING?!
ずるッ ずるッ
ブル
ブル
ブル
ブル

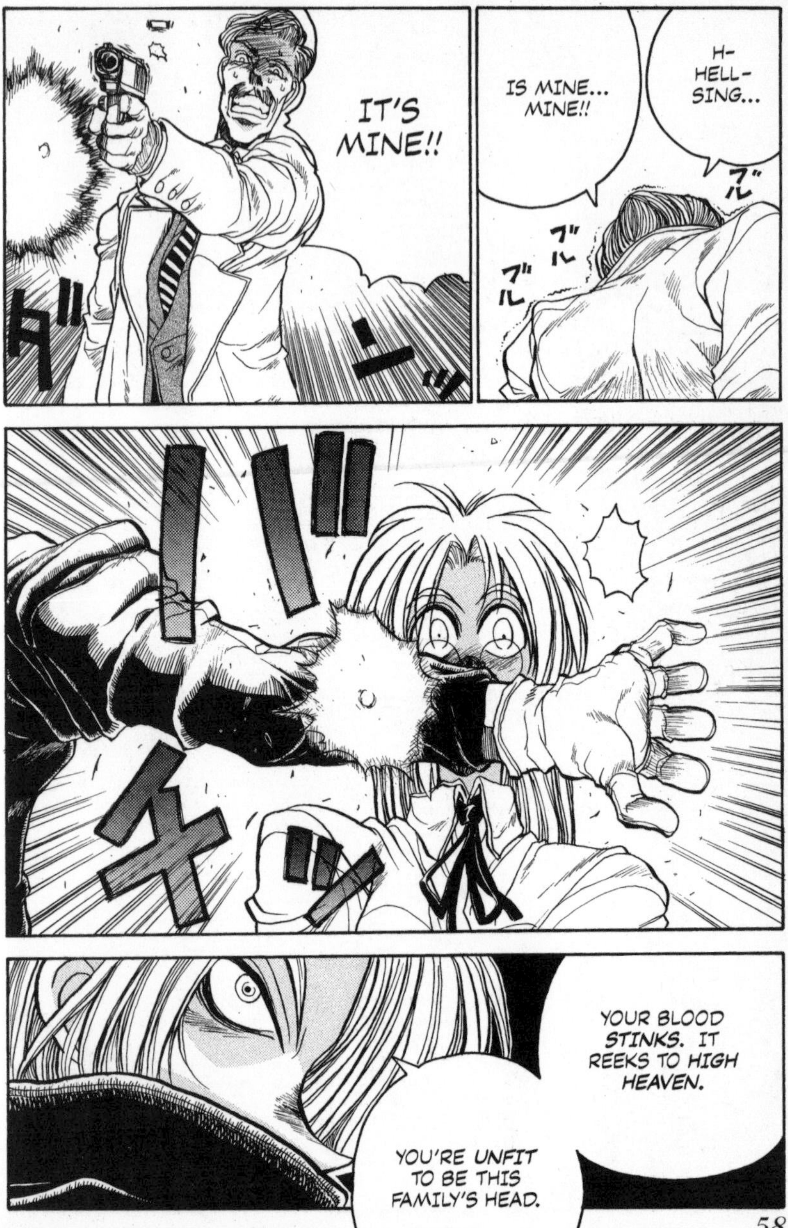
H-
HELL-
SING...
IS MINE...
MINE!!
ブル
ブル
ブル
IT'S
MINE!!
YOUR BLOOD STINKS. IT REEKS TO HIGH HEAVEN.
YOU'RE UNFIT TO BE THIS FAMILY'S HEAD.

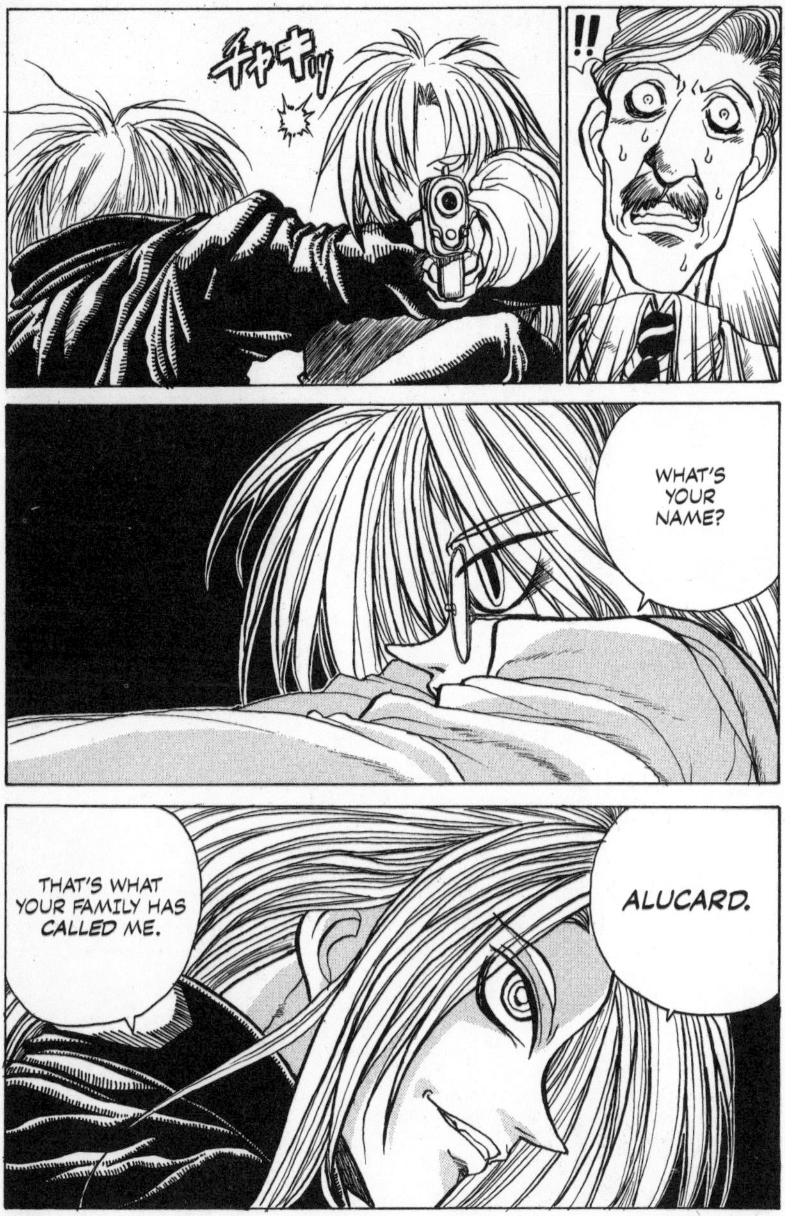
!!
チャキッ
WHAT'S YOUR NAME?
ALUCARD.
THAT'S WHAT YOUR FAMILY HAS CALLED ME.

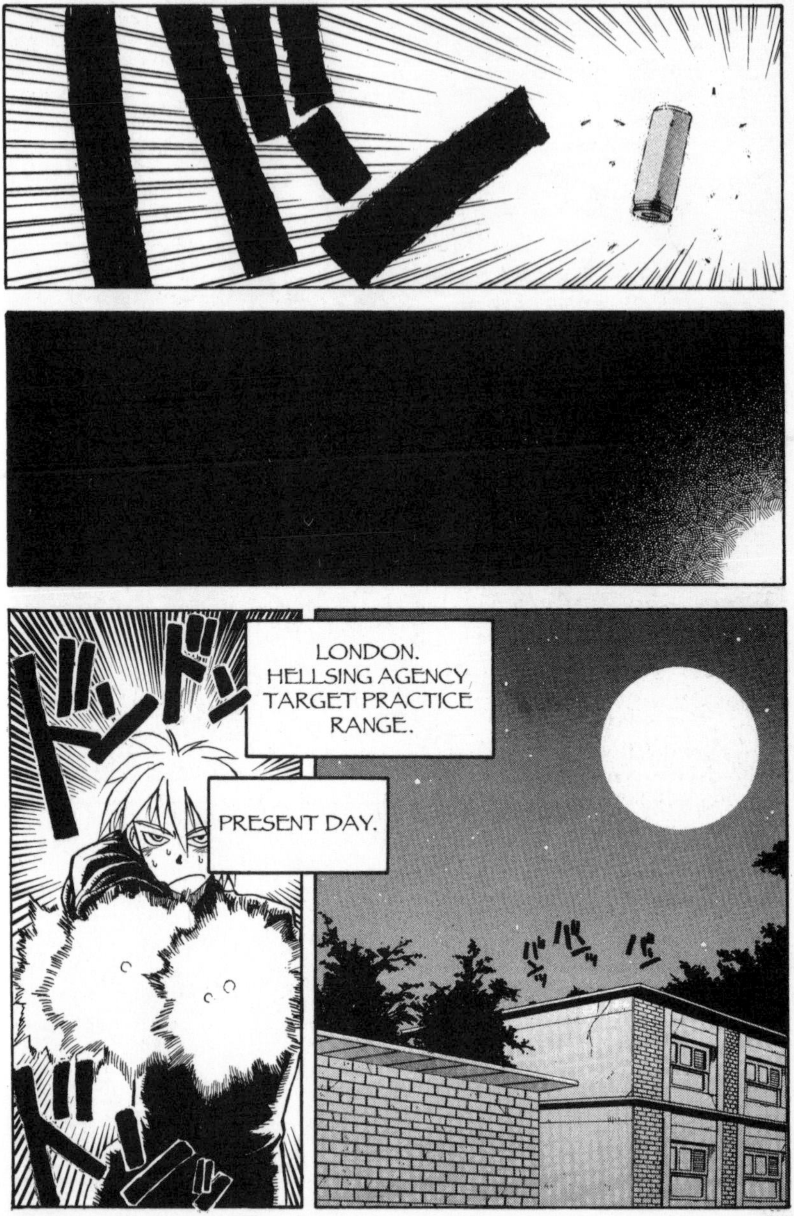
LONDON. HELLSING AGENCY TARGET PRACTICE RANGE.
PRESENT DAY.

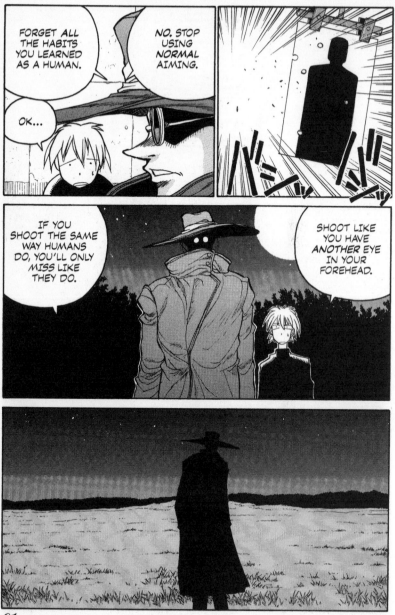

NO. STOP USING NORMAL AIMING.
FORGET ALL THE HABITS YOU LEARNED AS A HUMAN.
OK...
SHOOT LIKE YOU HAVE ANOTHER EYE IN YOUR FOREHEAD.
IF YOU SHOOT THE SAME WAY HUMANS DO, YOU'LL ONLY MISS LIKE THEY DO.

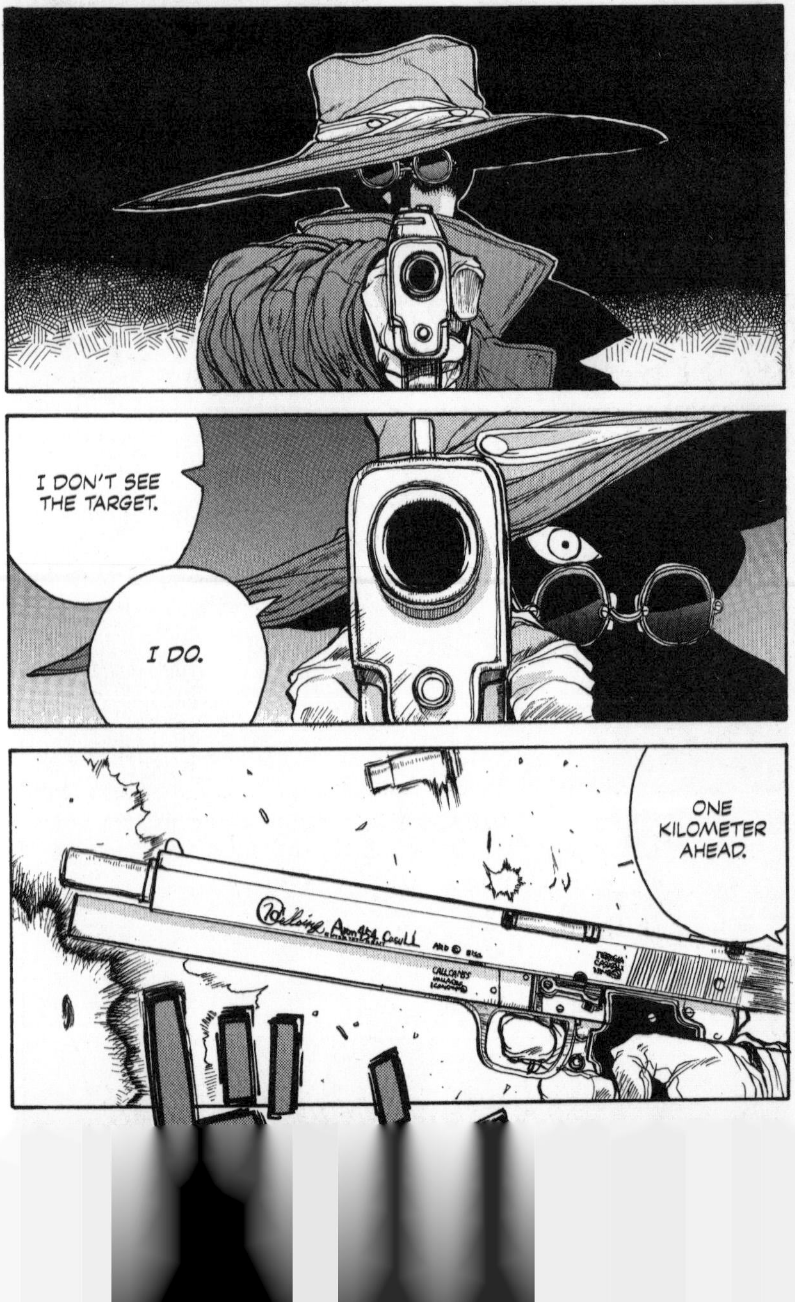
I DON'T SEE THE TARGET.
I DO.
ONE KILOMETER AHEAD.

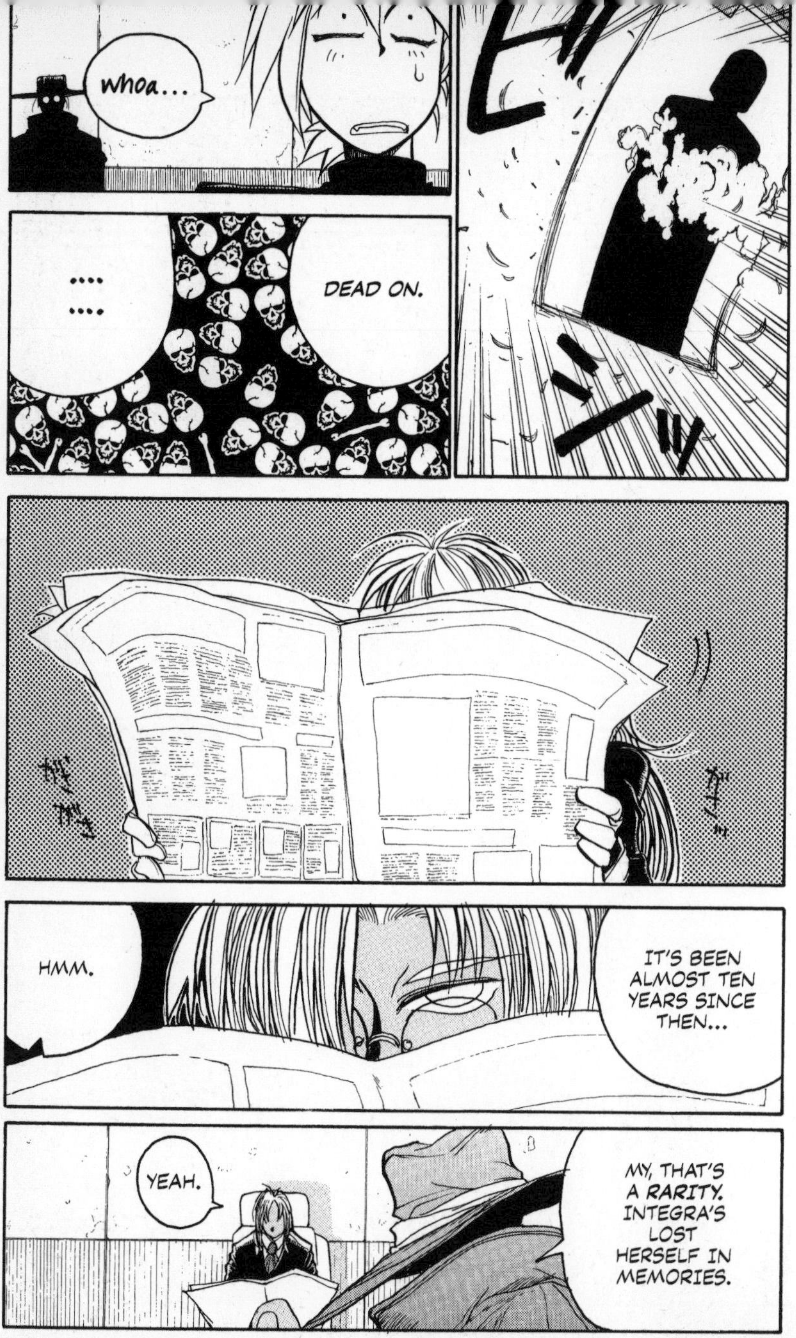
whoa...
DEAD ON.
....
....
IT'S BEEN ALMOST TEN YEARS SINCE THEN...
HMM.
MY, THAT'S A *RARITY.* INTEGRA'S LOST HERSELF IN MEMORIES.
YEAH.

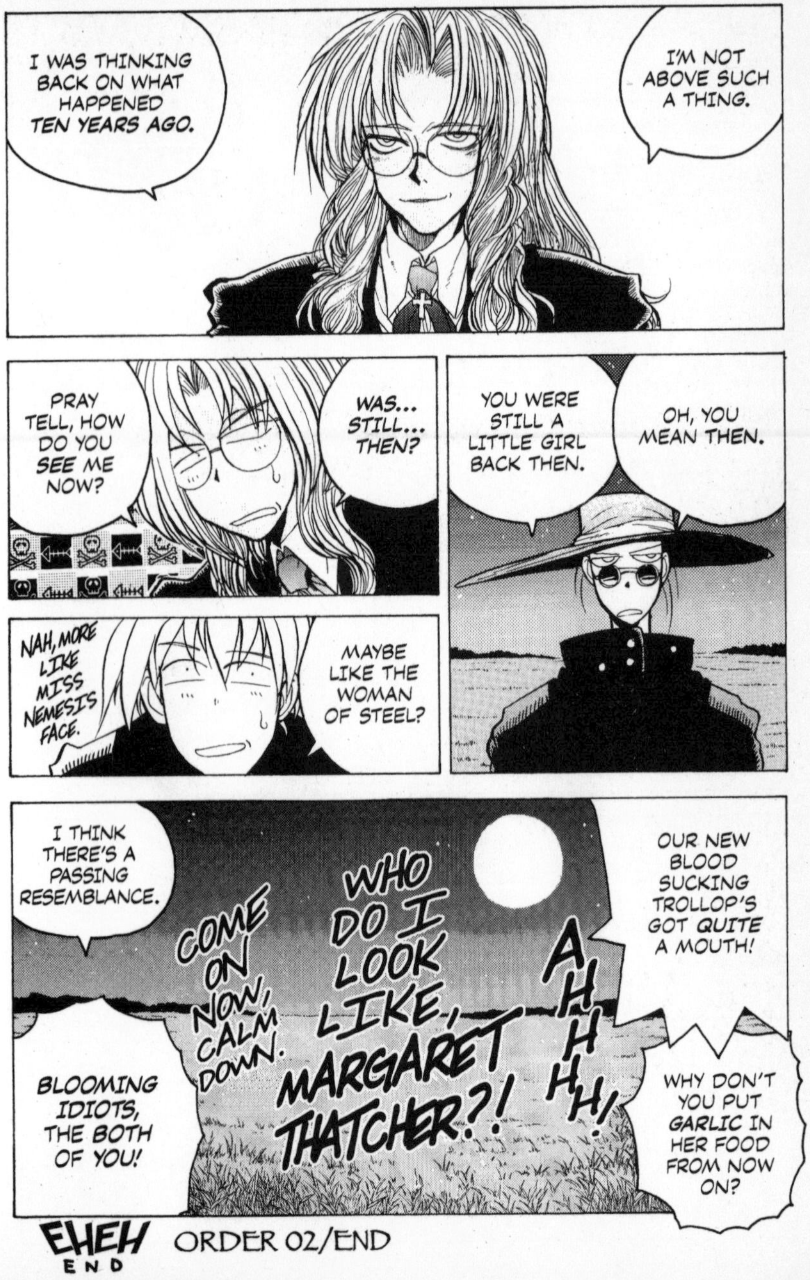
I'M NOT ABOVE SUCH A THING.
I WAS THINKING BACK ON WHAT HAPPENED TEN YEARS AGO.
OH, YOU MEAN THEN.
YOU WERE STILL A LITTLE GIRL BACK THEN.
WAS... STILL... THEN?
PRAY TELL, HOW DO YOU SEE ME NOW?
MAYBE LIKE THE WOMAN OF STEEL?
NAH, MORE LIKE MISS NEMESIS FACE.
OUR NEW BLOOD SUCKING TROLLOP'S GOT QUITE A MOUTH!
I THINK THERE'S A PASSING RESEMBLANCE.
AHHHHH!
WHO DO I LOOK LIKE, MARGARET THATCHER?!
COME ON NOW, CALM DOWN.
WHY DON'T YOU PUT GARLIC IN HER FOOD FROM NOW ON?
BLOOMING IDIOTS, THE BOTH OF YOU!

EHEH END ORDER 02/END

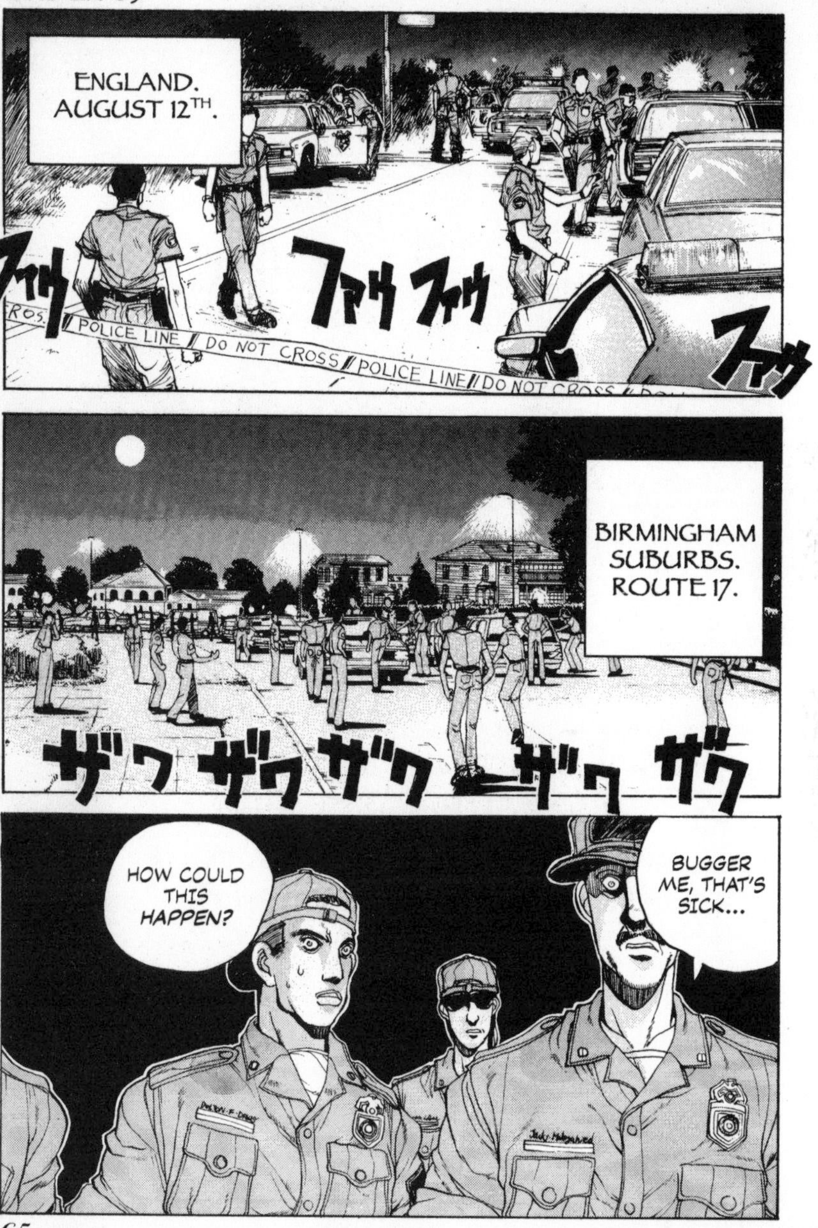
ENGLAND. AUGUST 12TH.
POLICE LINE
DO NOT CROSS
POLICE LINE
DO NOT CROSS
BIRMINGHAM SUBURBS. ROUTE 17.
BUGGER ME, THAT'S SICK...
HOW COULD THIS HAPPEN?

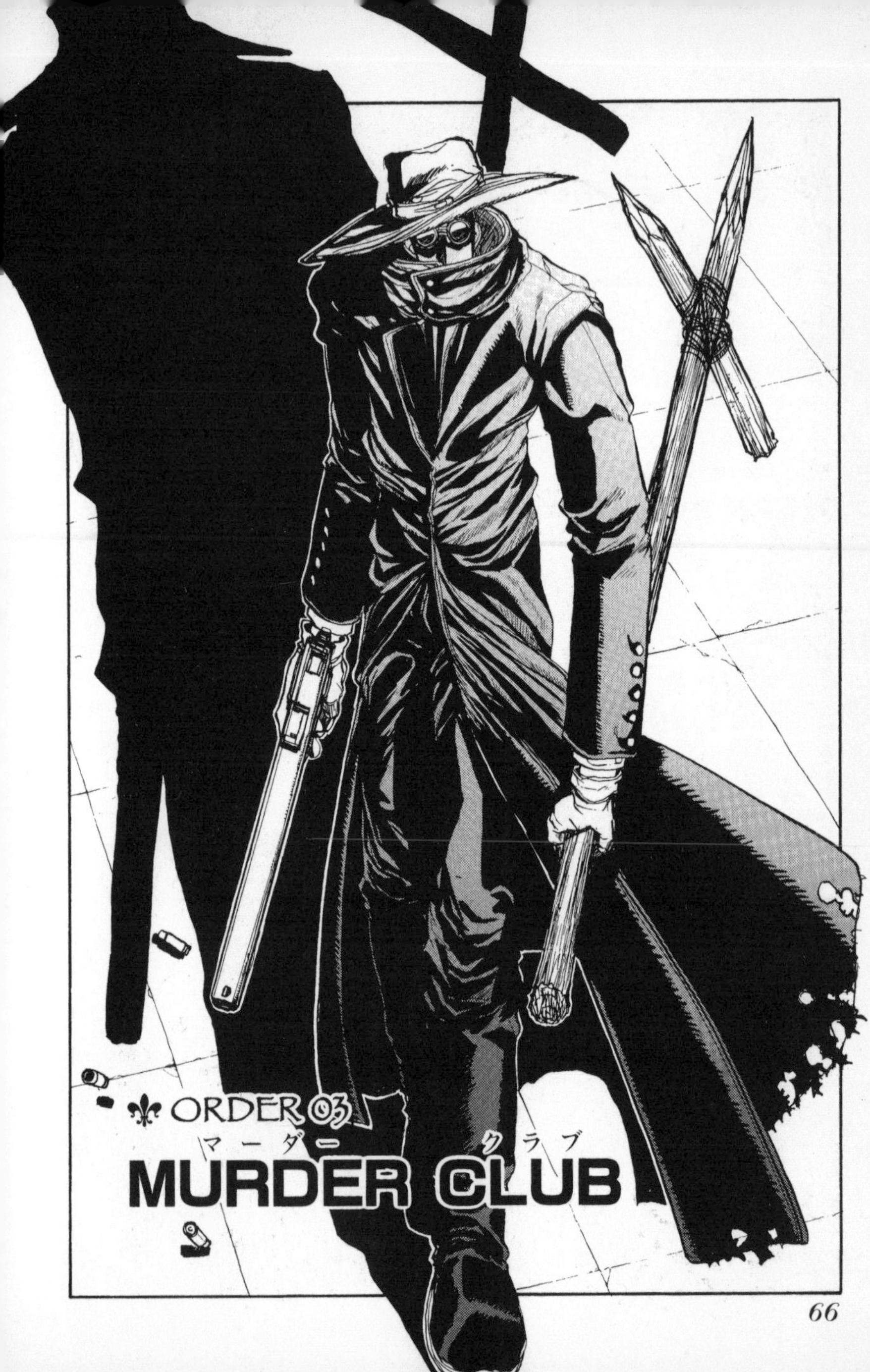
ORDER 03
マーダー クラブ
MURDER CLUB

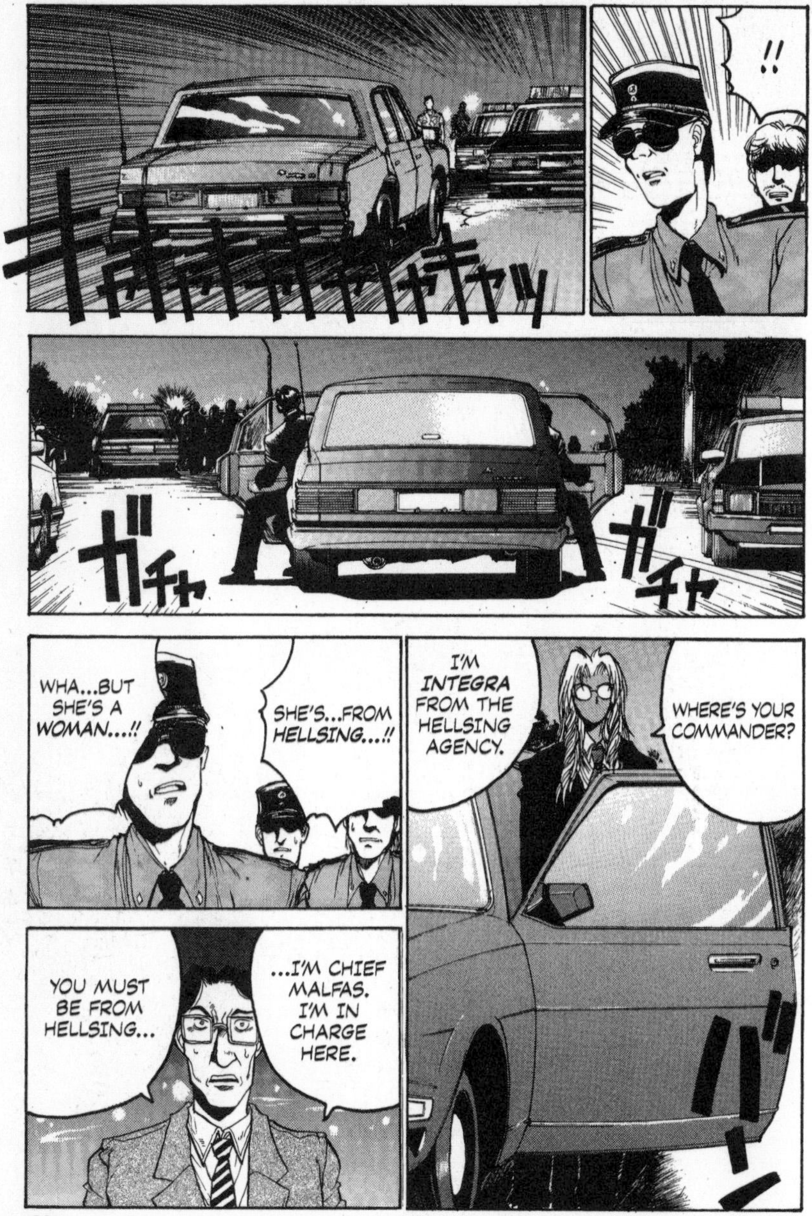
!!
ガチャ
ガチャ
WHERE'S YOUR COMMANDER?
I'M *INTEGRA* FROM THE HELLSING AGENCY.
SHE'S...FROM HELLSING...!!
WHA...BUT SHE'S A *WOMAN*...!!
...I'M CHIEF MALFAS. I'M IN CHARGE HERE.
YOU MUST BE FROM HELLSING...

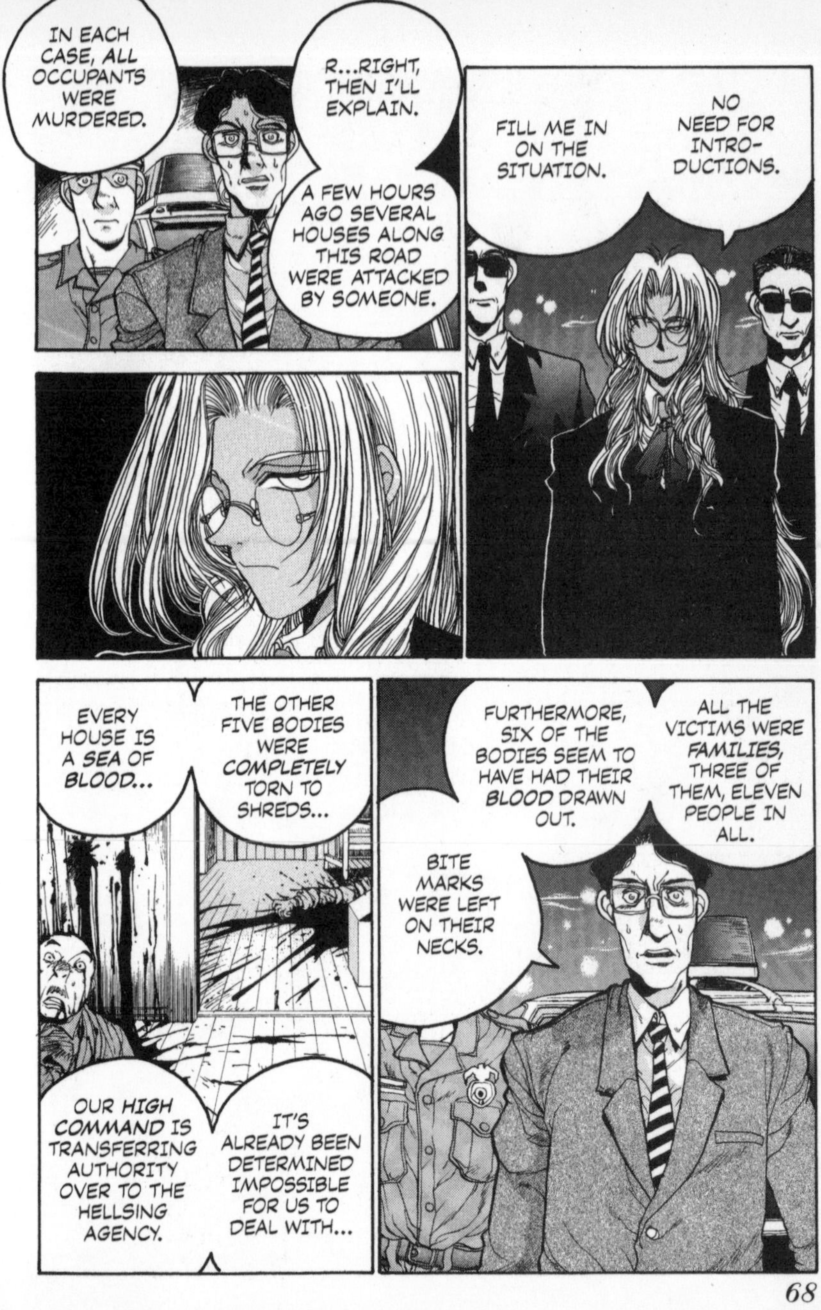
NO NEED FOR INTRO-DUCTIONS.
FILL ME IN ON THE SITUATION.
R...RIGHT, THEN I'LL EXPLAIN.
A FEW HOURS AGO SEVERAL HOUSES ALONG THIS ROAD WERE ATTACKED BY SOMEONE.
IN EACH CASE, ALL OCCUPANTS WERE MURDERED.
ALL THE VICTIMS WERE FAMILIES, THREE OF THEM, ELEVEN PEOPLE IN ALL.
FURTHERMORE, SIX OF THE BODIES SEEM TO HAVE HAD THEIR BLOOD DRAWN OUT.
BITE MARKS WERE LEFT ON THEIR NECKS.
THE OTHER FIVE BODIES WERE COMPLETELY TORN TO SHREDS...
EVERY HOUSE IS A SEA OF BLOOD...
IT'S ALREADY BEEN DETERMINED IMPOSSIBLE FOR US TO DEAL WITH...
OUR HIGH COMMAND IS TRANSFERRING AUTHORITY OVER TO THE HELLSING AGENCY.

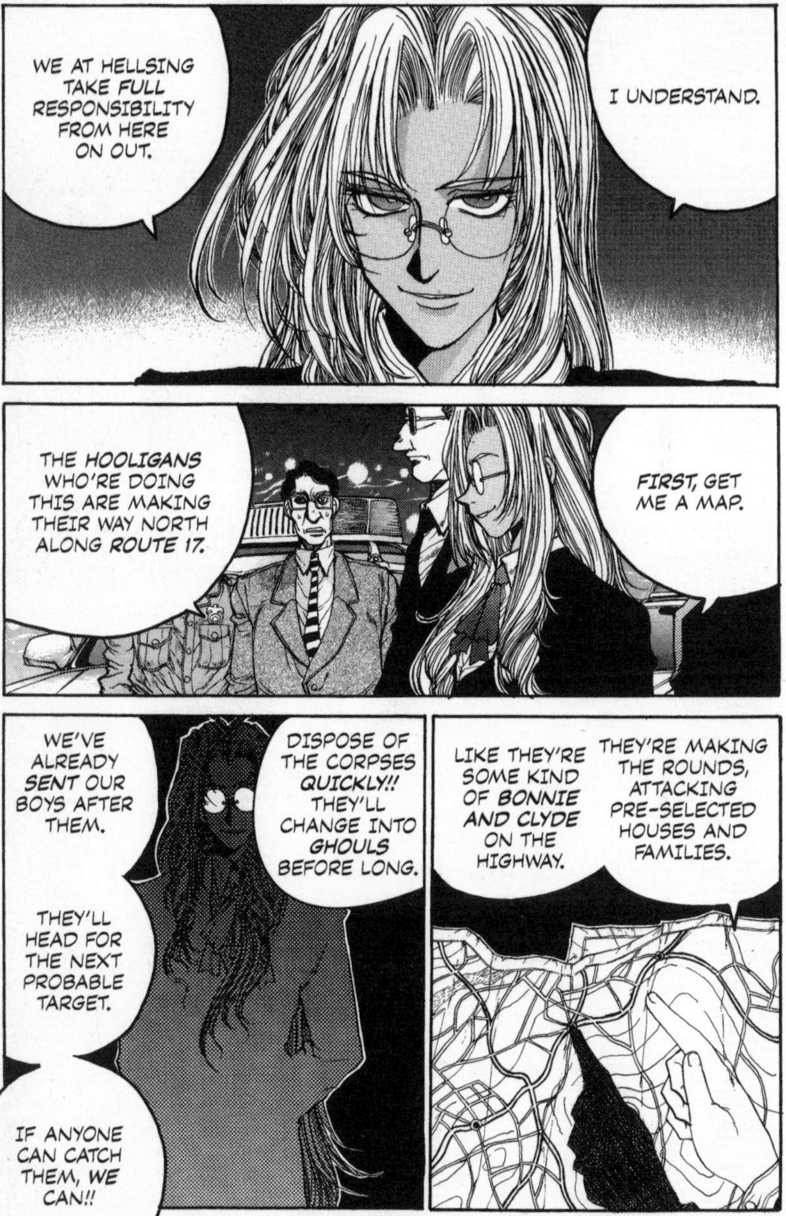
I UNDERSTAND.
WE AT HELLSING TAKE FULL RESPONSIBILITY FROM HERE ON OUT.
FIRST, GET ME A MAP.
THE HOOLIGANS WHO'RE DOING THIS ARE MAKING THEIR WAY NORTH ALONG ROUTE 17.
THEY'RE MAKING THE ROUNDS, ATTACKING PRE-SELECTED HOUSES AND FAMILIES.
LIKE THEY'RE SOME KIND OF BONNIE AND CLYDE ON THE HIGHWAY.
DISPOSE OF THE CORPSES QUICKLY!! THEY'LL CHANGE INTO GHOULS BEFORE LONG.
WE'VE ALREADY SENT OUR BOYS AFTER THEM.
THEY'LL HEAD FOR THE NEXT PROBABLE TARGET.
IF ANYONE CAN CATCH THEM, WE CAN!!

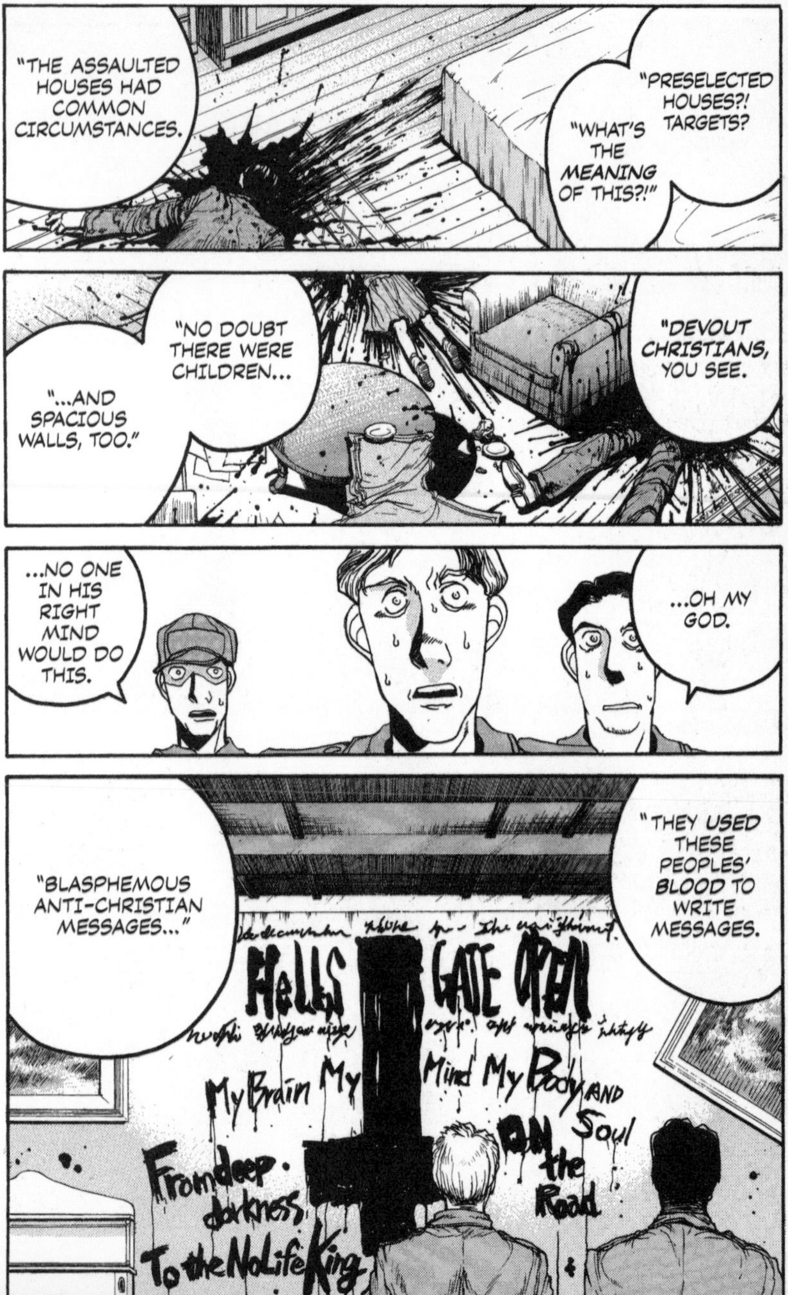
"PRESELECTED HOUSES?! TARGETS?
"WHAT'S THE MEANING OF THIS?!"
"THE ASSAULTED HOUSES HAD COMMON CIRCUMSTANCES.
"DEVOUT CHRISTIANS, YOU SEE.
"NO DOUBT THERE WERE CHILDREN...
"...AND SPACIOUS WALLS, TOO."
...OH MY GOD.
...NO ONE IN HIS RIGHT MIND WOULD DO THIS.
"THEY USED THESE PEOPLES' BLOOD TO WRITE MESSAGES.
"BLASPHEMOUS ANTI-CHRISTIAN MESSAGES..."
HELLS GATE OPEN
My Brain My Mind My Body AND Soul
ON the Road
From deep darkness
To the NoLife King

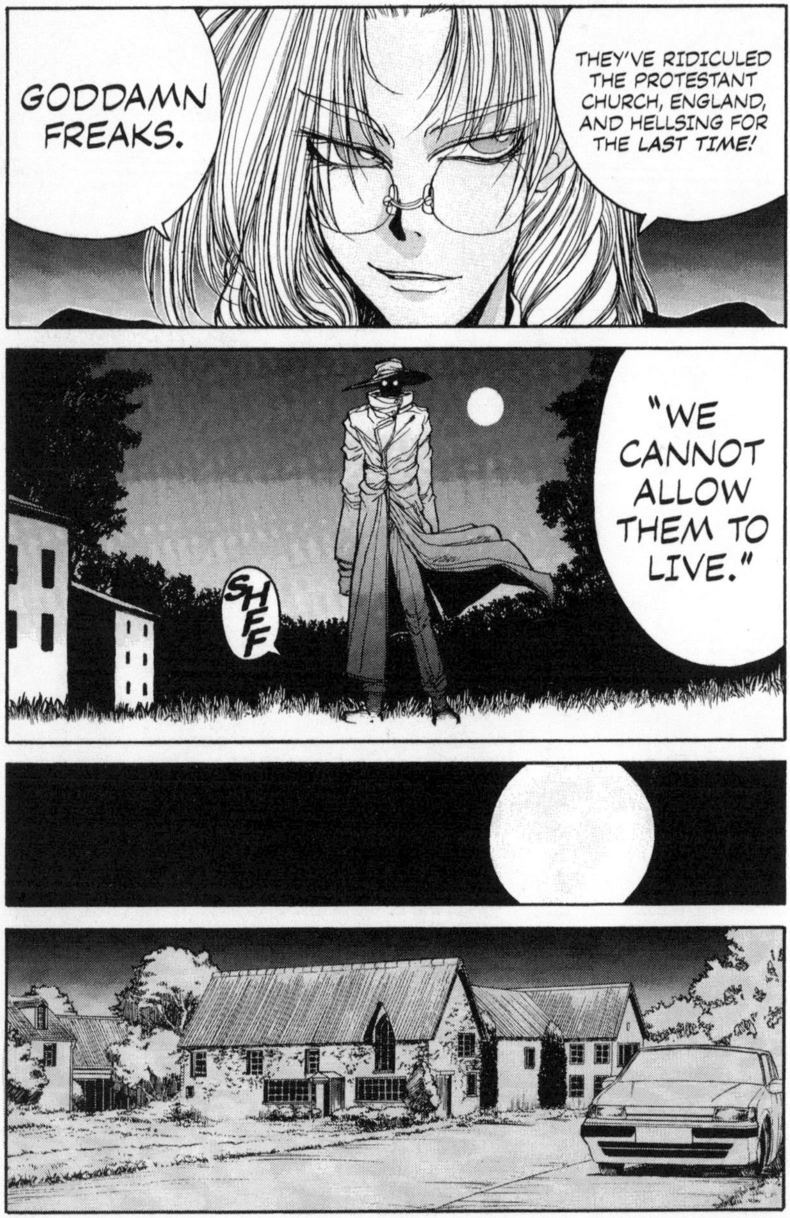
THEY'VE RIDICULED THE PROTESTANT CHURCH, ENGLAND, AND HELLSING FOR THE LAST TIME!
GODDAMN FREAKS.
"WE CANNOT ALLOW THEM TO LIVE."
SHFF

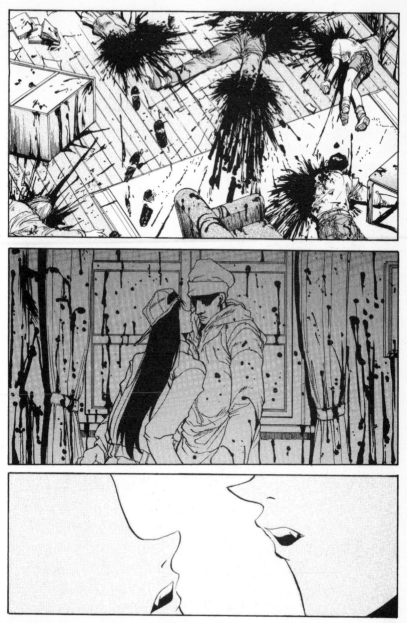

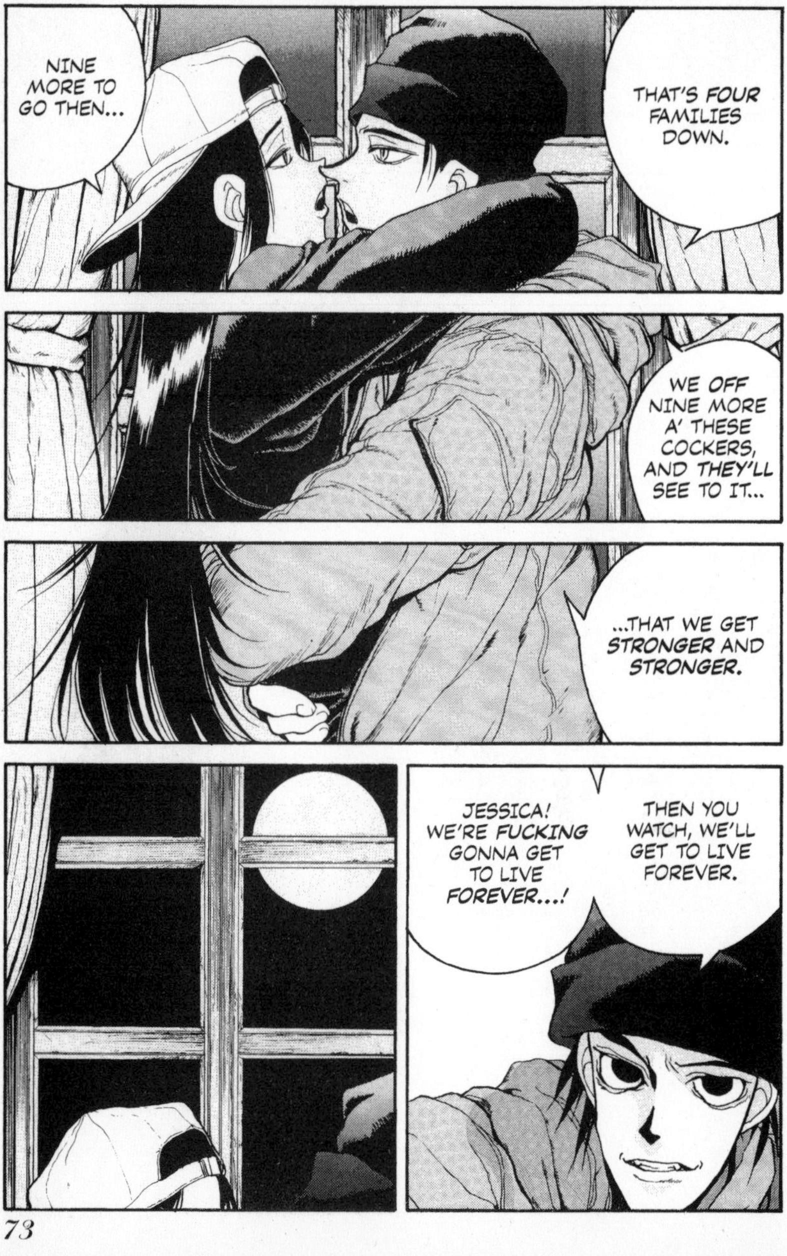
THAT'S FOUR FAMILIES DOWN.
NINE MORE TO GO THEN...
WE OFF NINE MORE A' THESE COCKERS, AND THEY'LL SEE TO IT...
...THAT WE GET STRONGER AND STRONGER.
THEN YOU WATCH, WE'LL GET TO LIVE FOREVER.
JESSICA! WE'RE FUCKING GONNA GET TO LIVE FOREVER...!

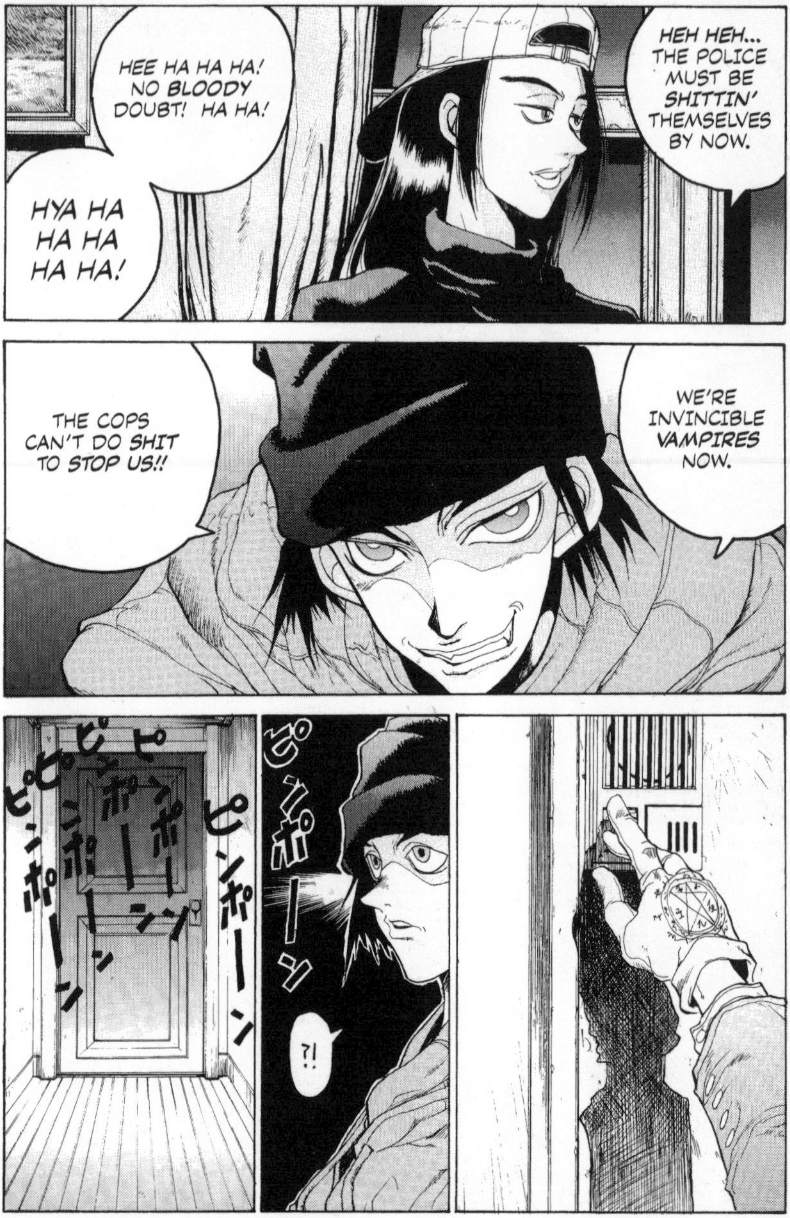
HEH HEH... THE POLICE MUST BE SHITTIN' THEMSELVES BY NOW.
HEE HA HA HA! NO BLOODY DOUBT! HA HA!
HYA HA HA HA HA HA!
WE'RE INVINCIBLE VAMPIRES NOW.
THE COPS CAN'T DO SHIT TO STOP US!!
ピンポーン
?!
ピンポーン
ピンポーン
ピンポーン
ピンポーン

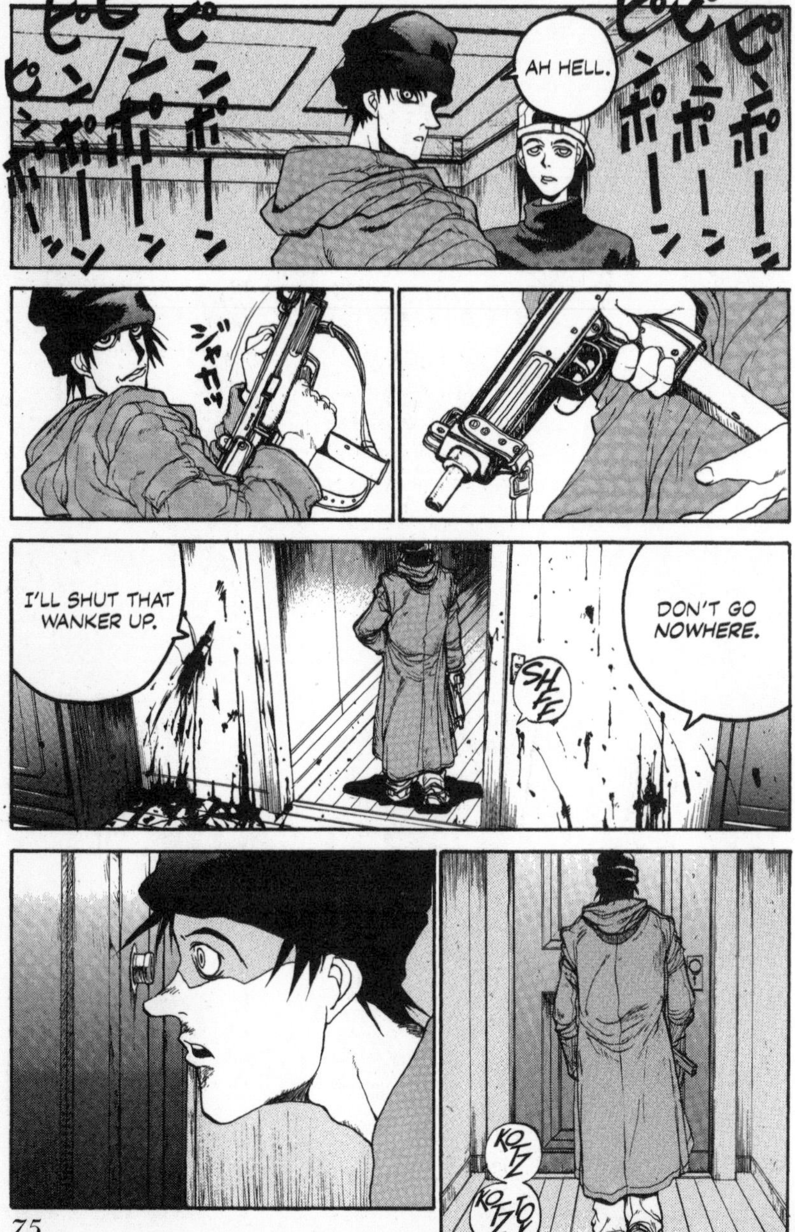
AH HELL.
ジャカッ
DON'T GO NOWHERE.
SHKK
I'LL SHUT THAT WANKER UP.
KOTZ
KOTZ TOK

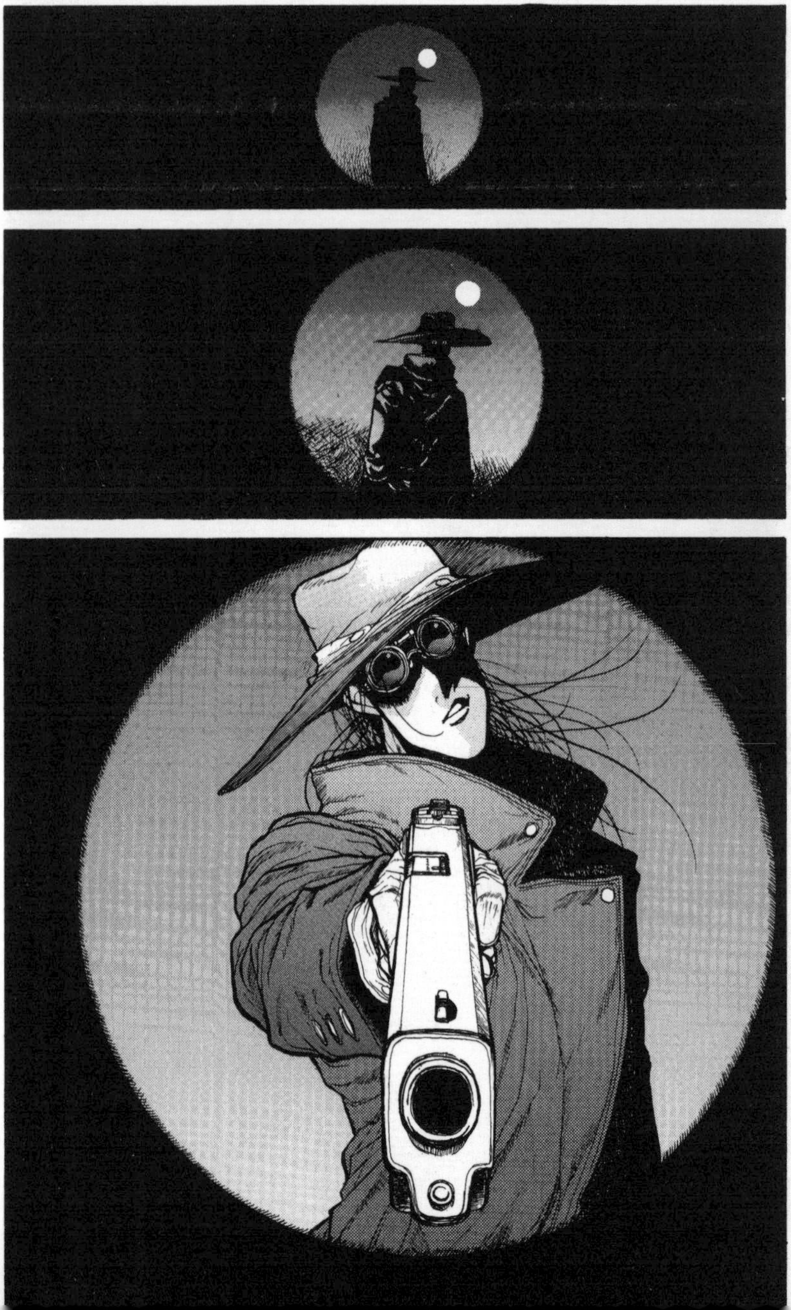

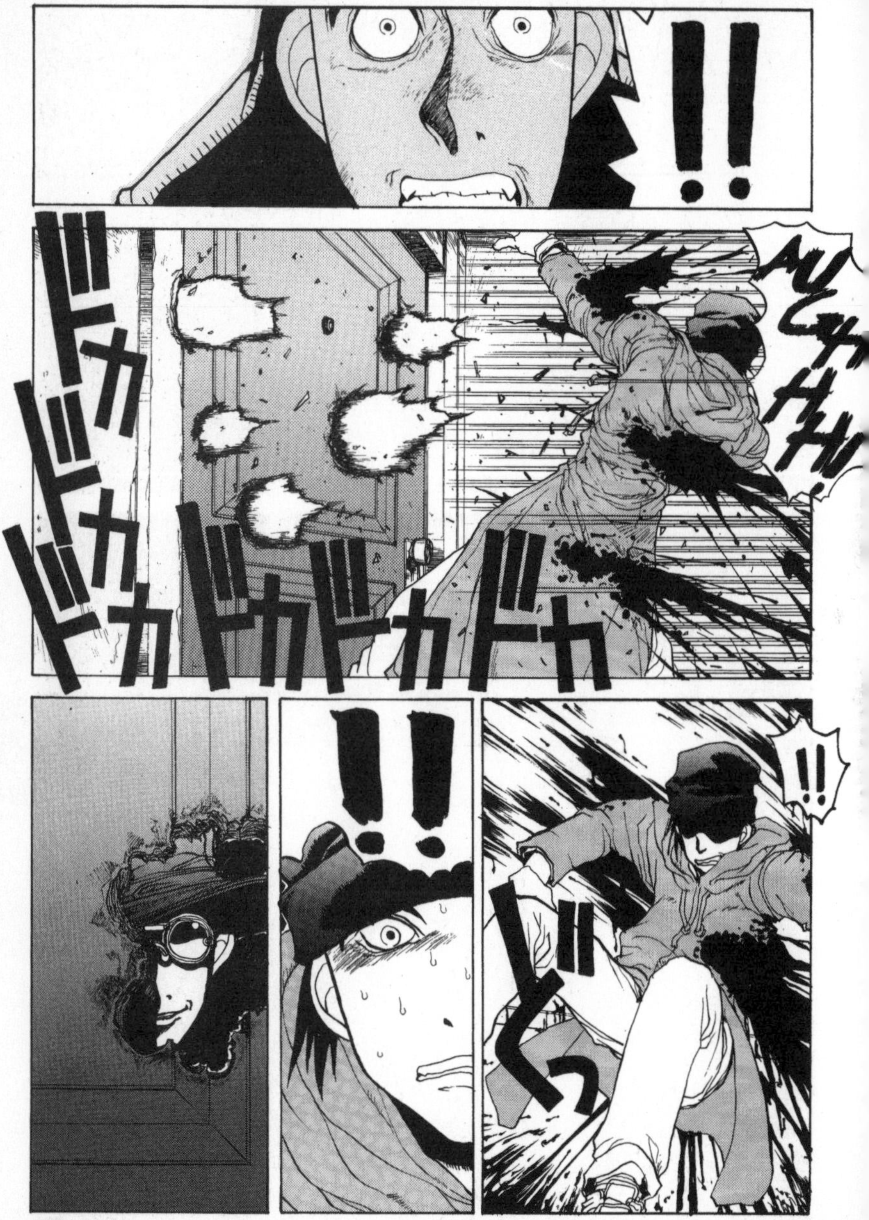
!!
AUGHHH!
ドカドカドカドカドカドカ
!!
ぐっ
!!

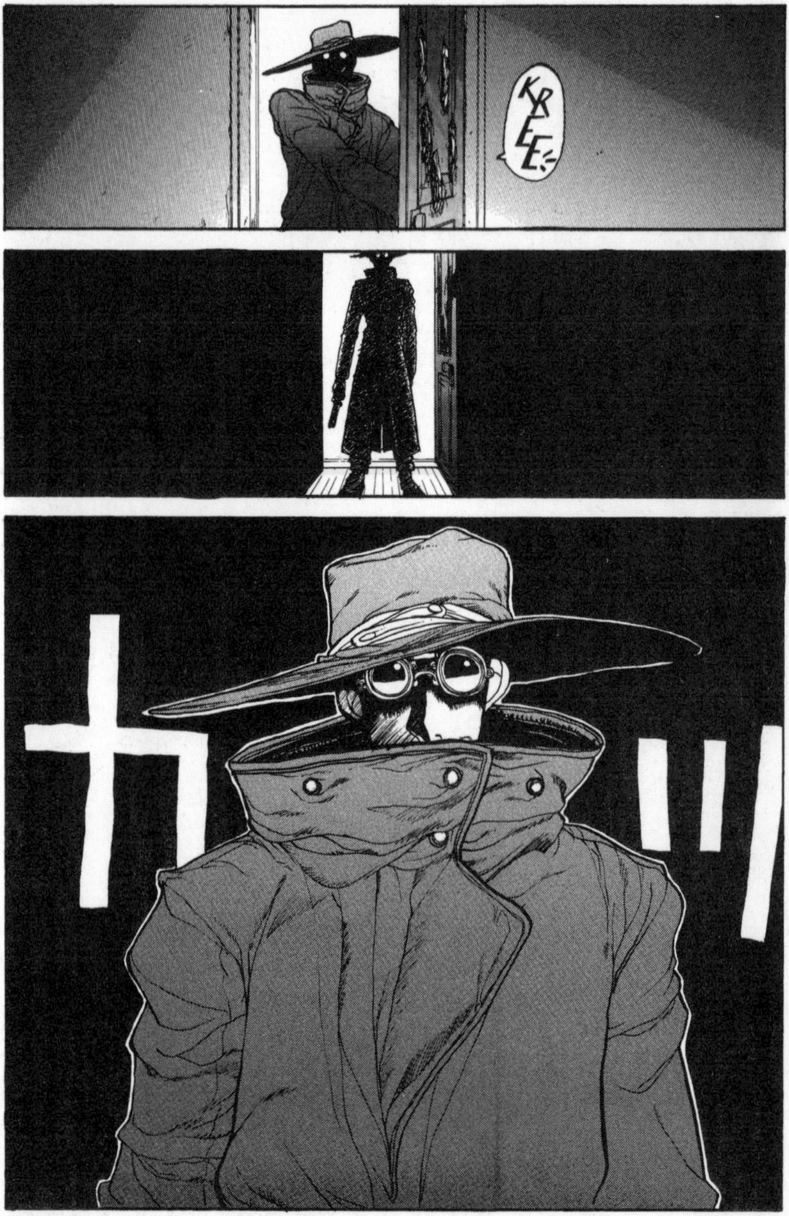
KREEE
カッ

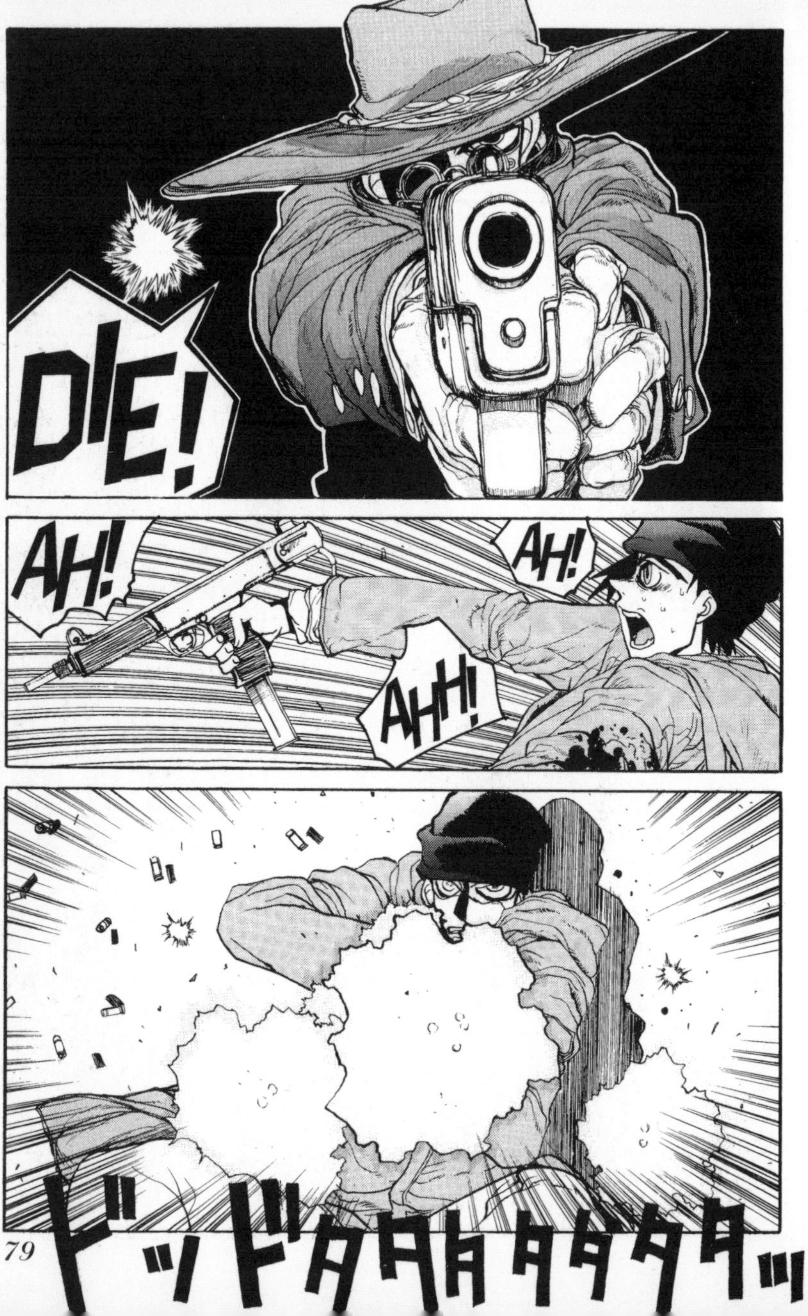
DIE!
AH!
AHH!
AH!
ドッドタタタタタタッ

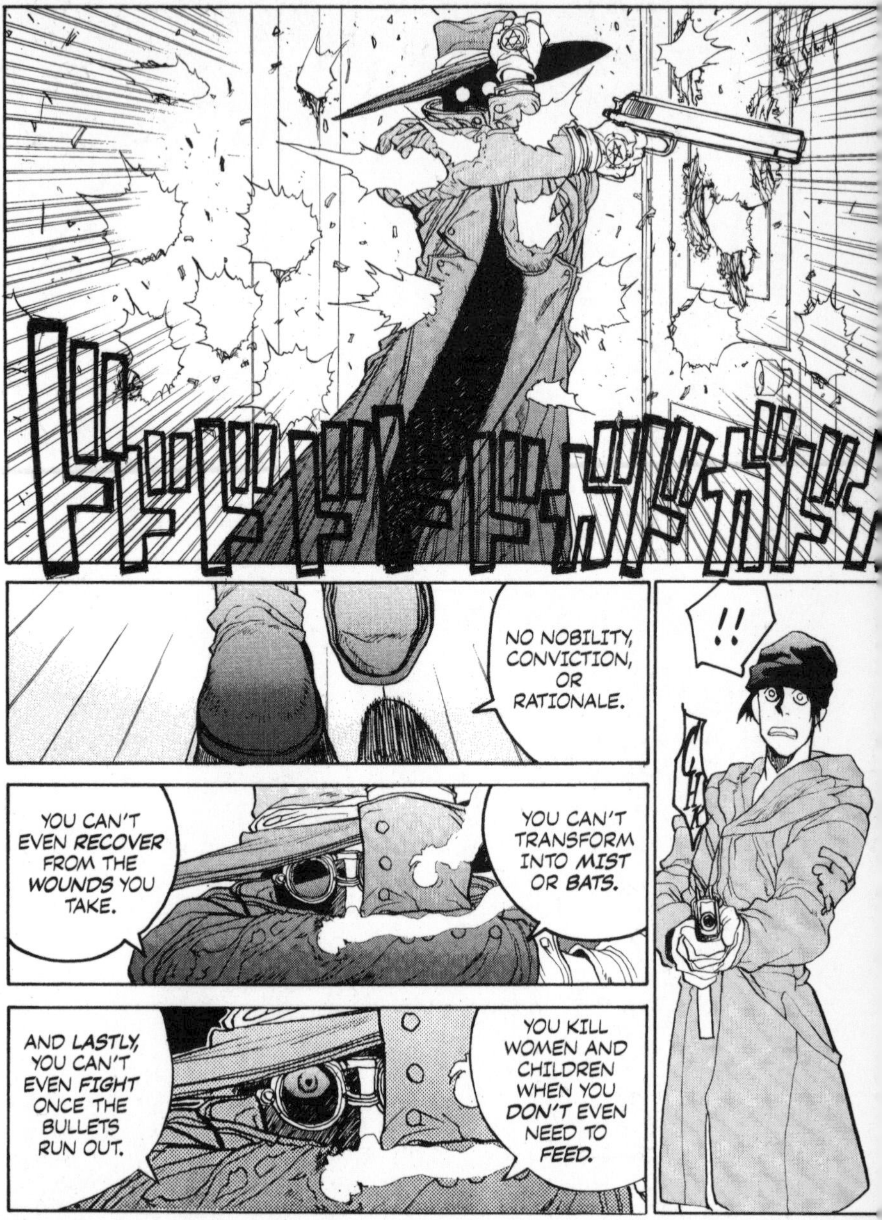
!!
NO NOBILITY, CONVICTION, OR RATIONALE.
YOU CAN'T TRANSFORM INTO *MIST* OR *BATS.*
YOU CAN'T EVEN *RECOVER* FROM THE *WOUNDS* YOU TAKE.
YOU KILL WOMEN AND CHILDREN WHEN YOU *DON'T* EVEN NEED TO *FEED.*
AND *LASTLY,* YOU CAN'T EVEN *FIGHT* ONCE THE BULLETS RUN OUT.

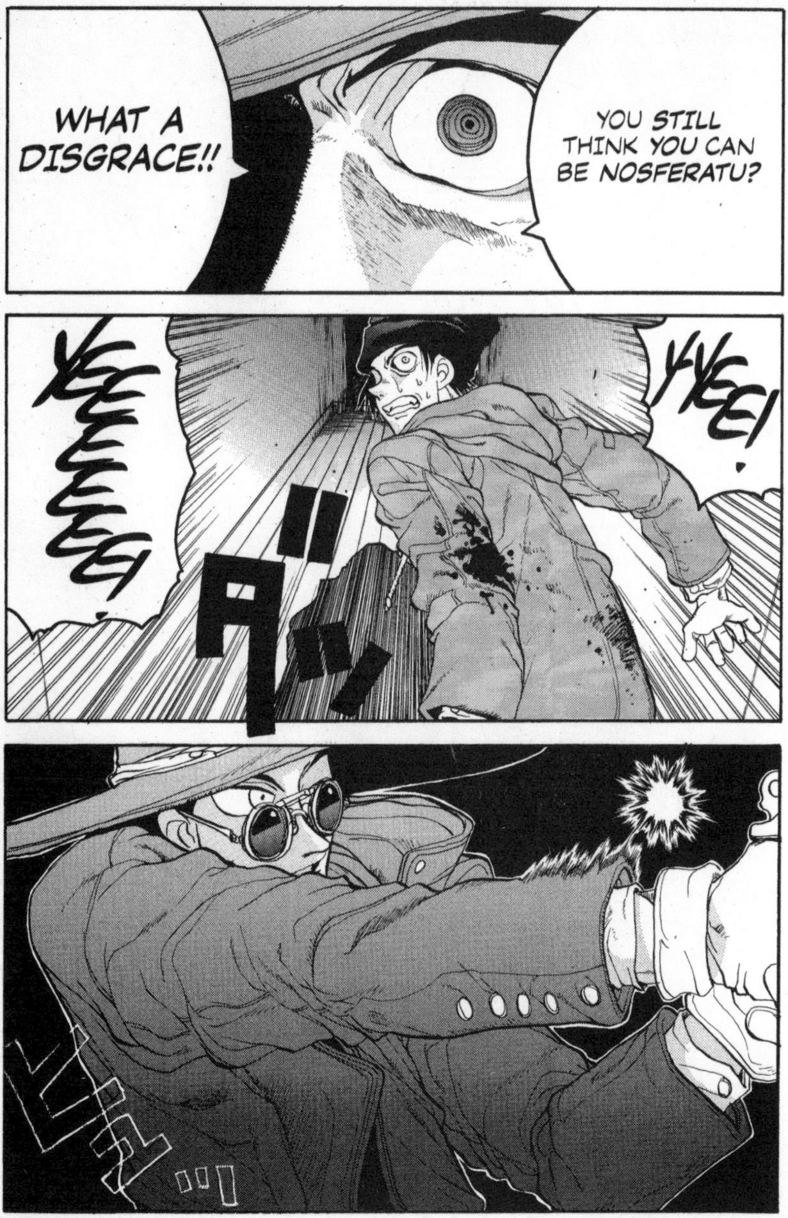
YOU STILL THINK YOU CAN BE NOSFERATU?
WHAT A DISGRACE!!
Y-YEE!
YEEEEEEEE!

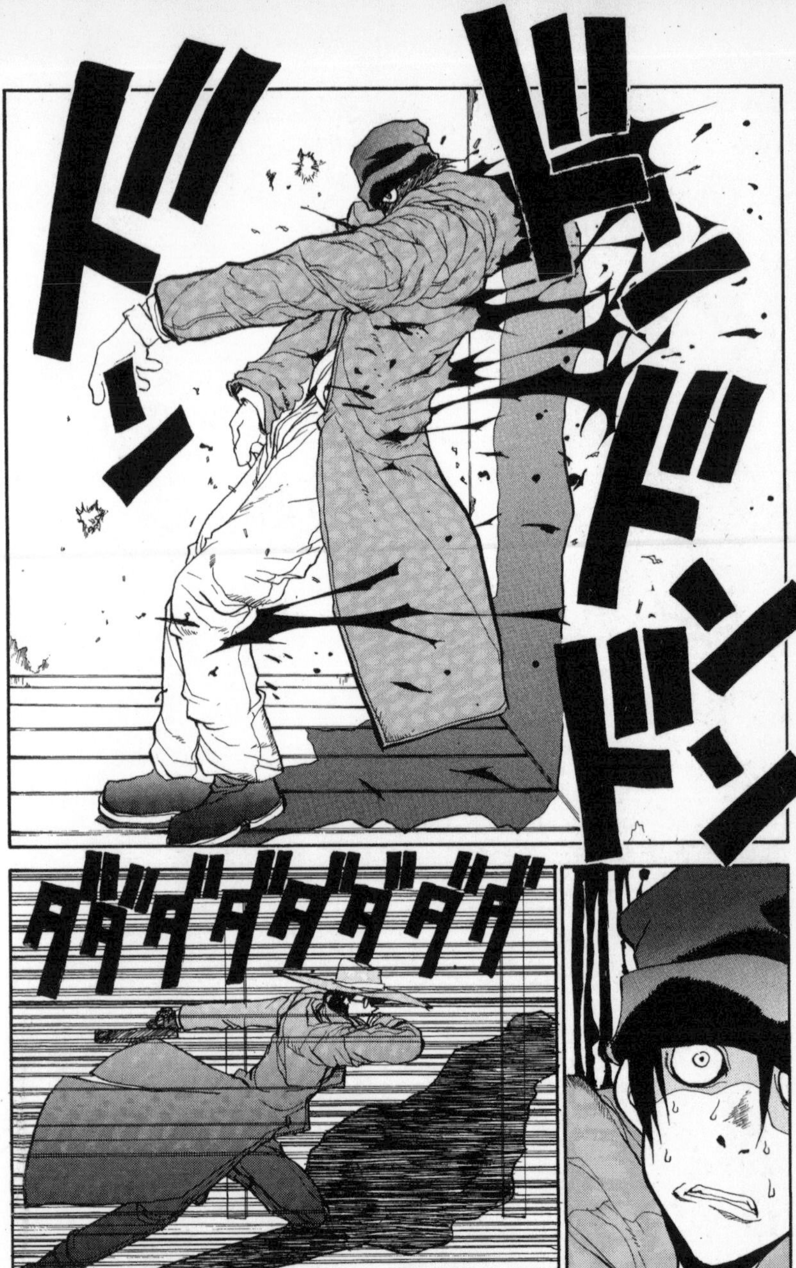
ドンドンドン
ドン
ダダダダダダダダ

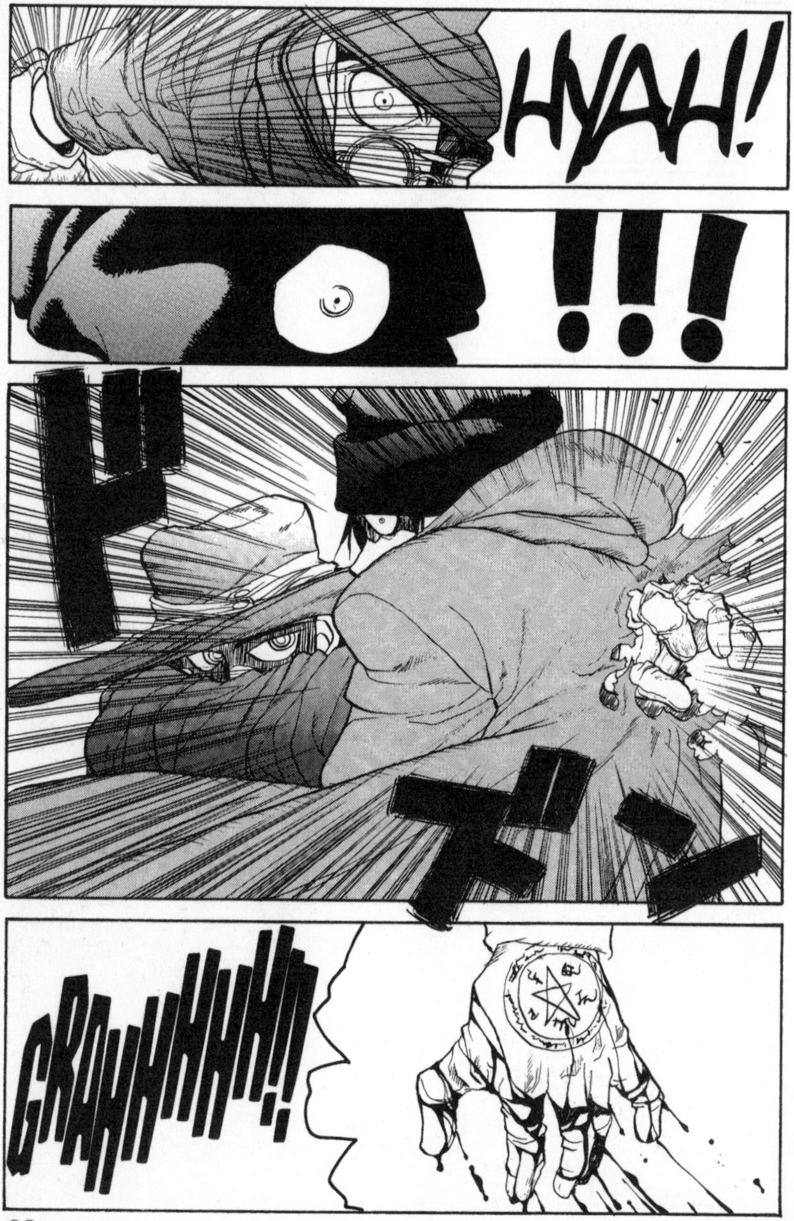
HYAH!
!!!
GRAHHHHHH!!

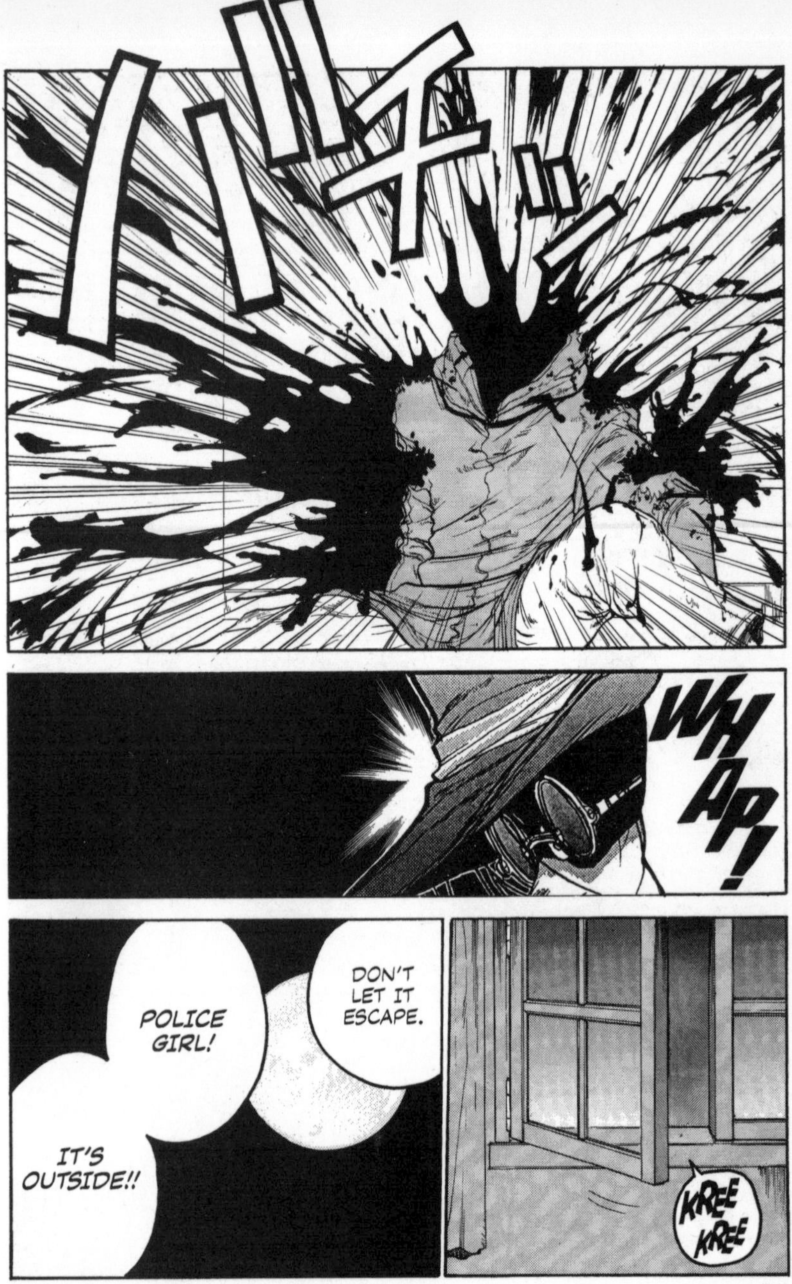
WHAP!
KREE KREE
DON'T LET IT ESCAPE.
POLICE GIRL!
IT'S OUTSIDE!!

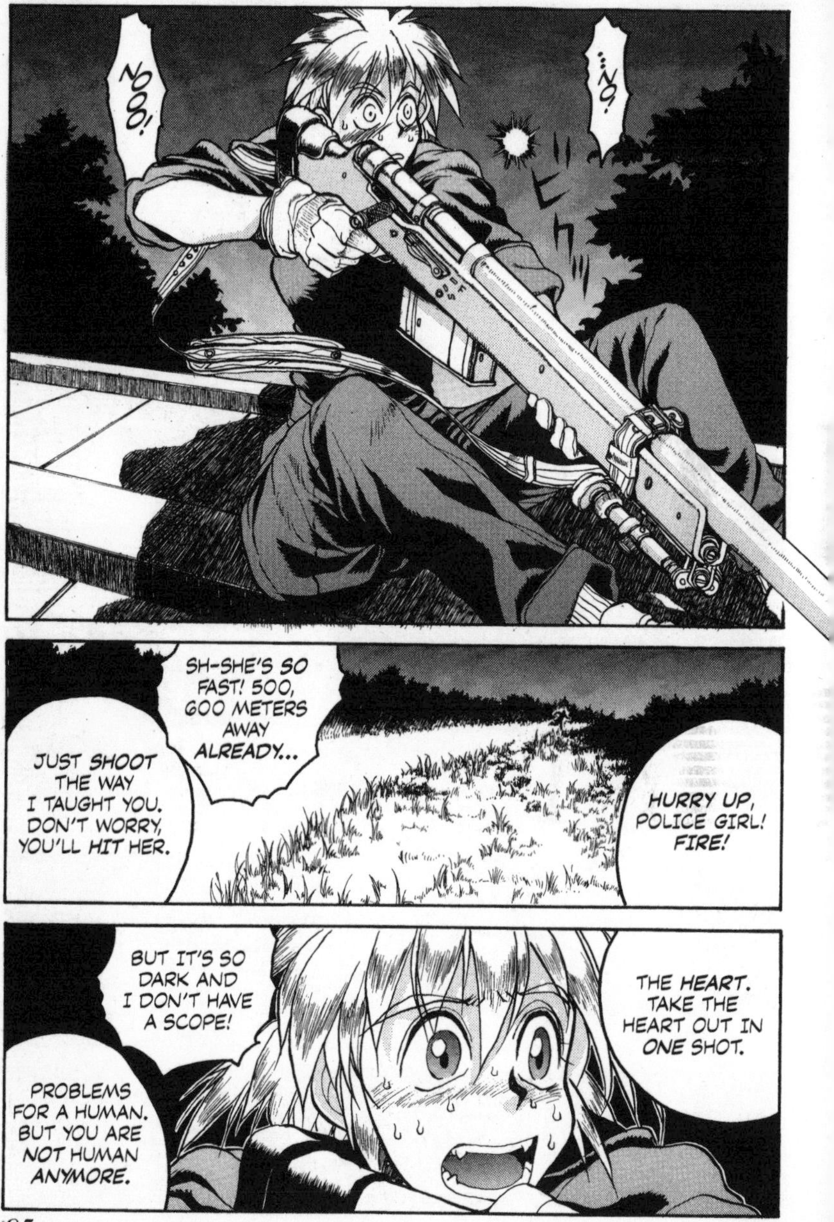
...NO.
NOOO!
HURRY UP, POLICE GIRL! FIRE!
SH-SHE'S SO FAST! 500, 600 METERS AWAY ALREADY...
JUST SHOOT THE WAY I TAUGHT YOU. DON'T WORRY, YOU'LL HIT HER.
BUT IT'S SO DARK AND I DON'T HAVE A SCOPE!
PROBLEMS FOR A HUMAN. BUT YOU ARE NOT HUMAN ANYMORE.
THE HEART. TAKE THE HEART OUT IN ONE SHOT.

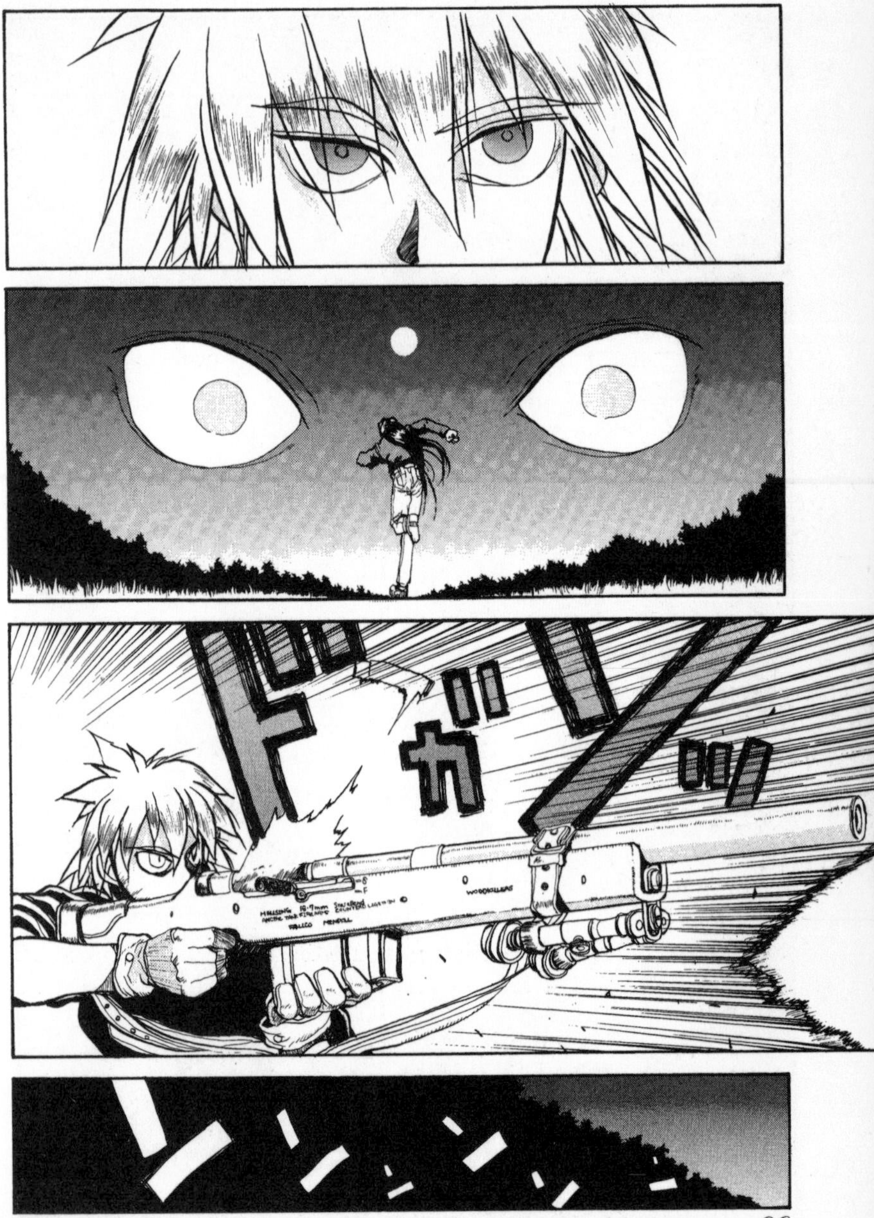
ドガッ
ンンン

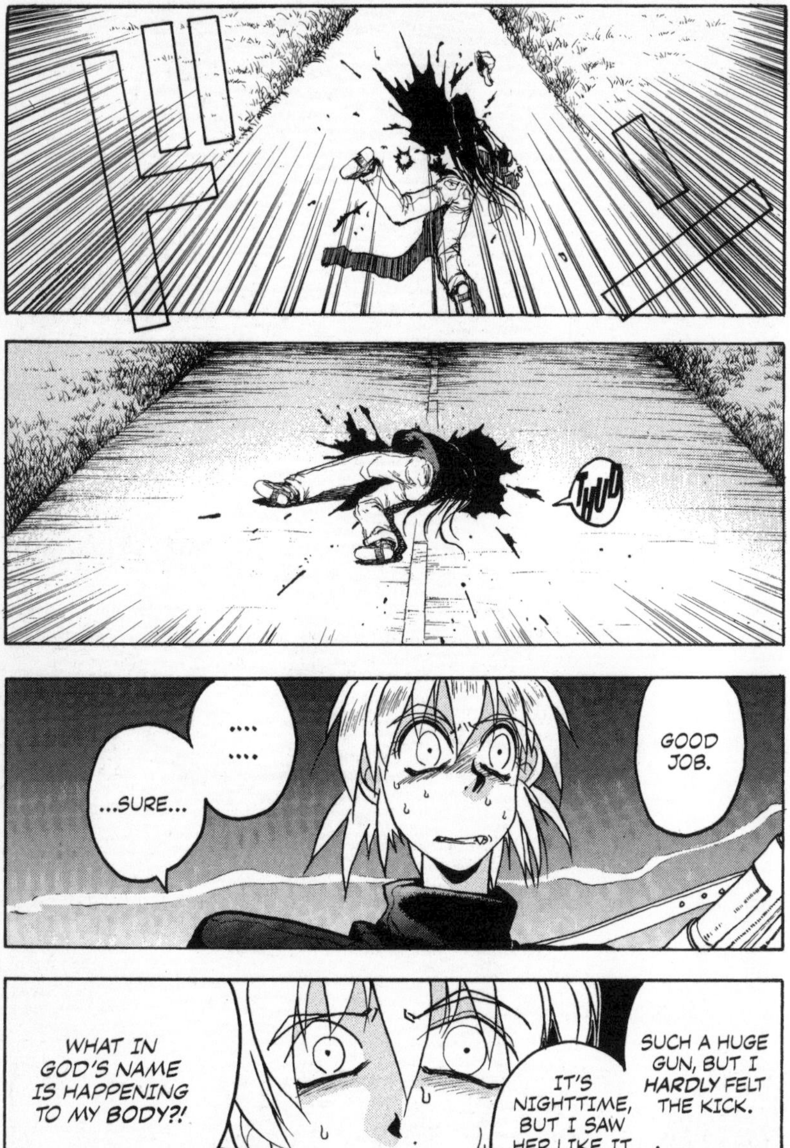
THUD
GOOD JOB.
....
....
...SURE...
SUCH A HUGE GUN, BUT I *HARDLY* FELT THE KICK.
IT'S NIGHTTIME, BUT I SAW HER LIKE IT WAS HIGH NOON.
WHAT IN GOD'S NAME IS HAPPENING TO MY BODY?!

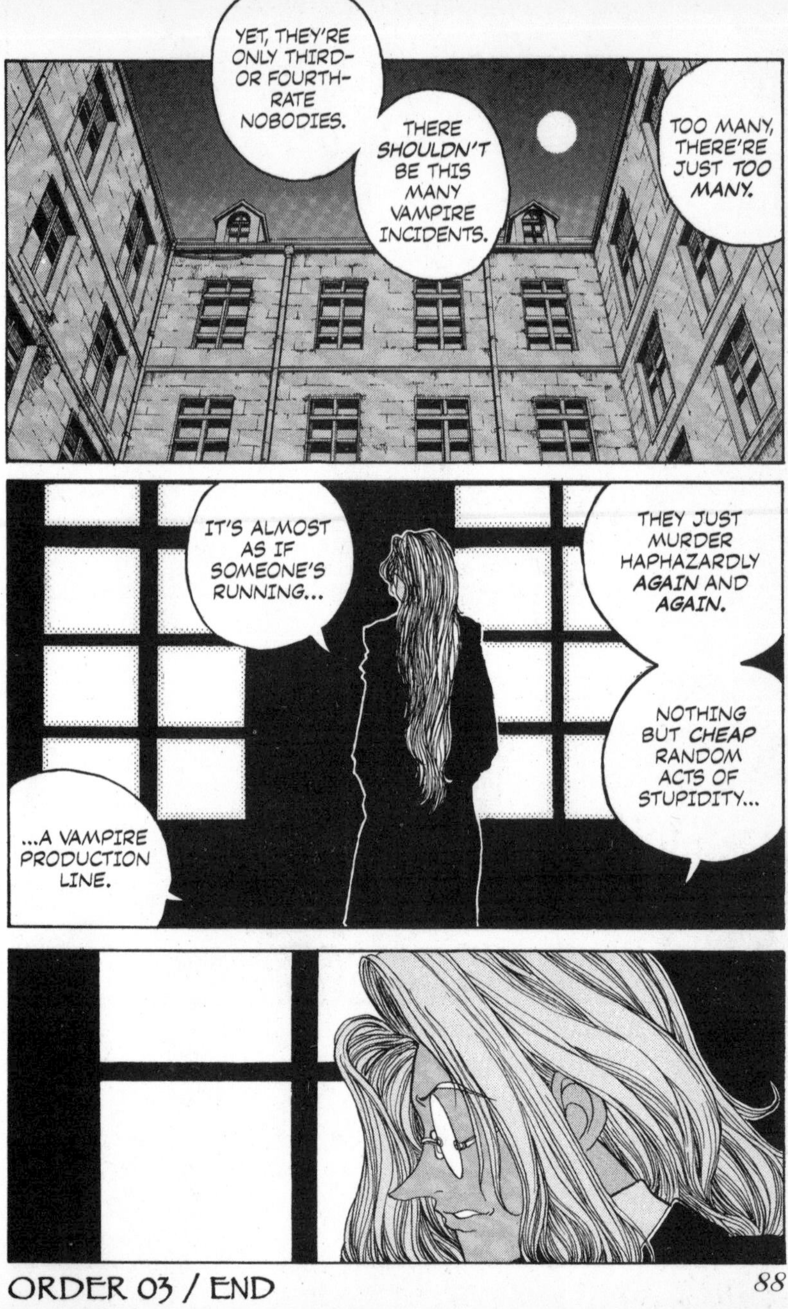
TOO MANY, THERE'RE JUST TOO MANY.
THERE SHOULDN'T BE THIS MANY VAMPIRE INCIDENTS.
YET, THEY'RE ONLY THIRD- OR FOURTH-RATE NOBODIES.
THEY JUST MURDER HAPHAZARDLY AGAIN AND AGAIN.
NOTHING BUT CHEAP RANDOM ACTS OF STUPIDITY...
IT'S ALMOST AS IF SOMEONE'S RUNNING...
...A VAMPIRE PRODUCTION LINE.

ORDER 03 / END

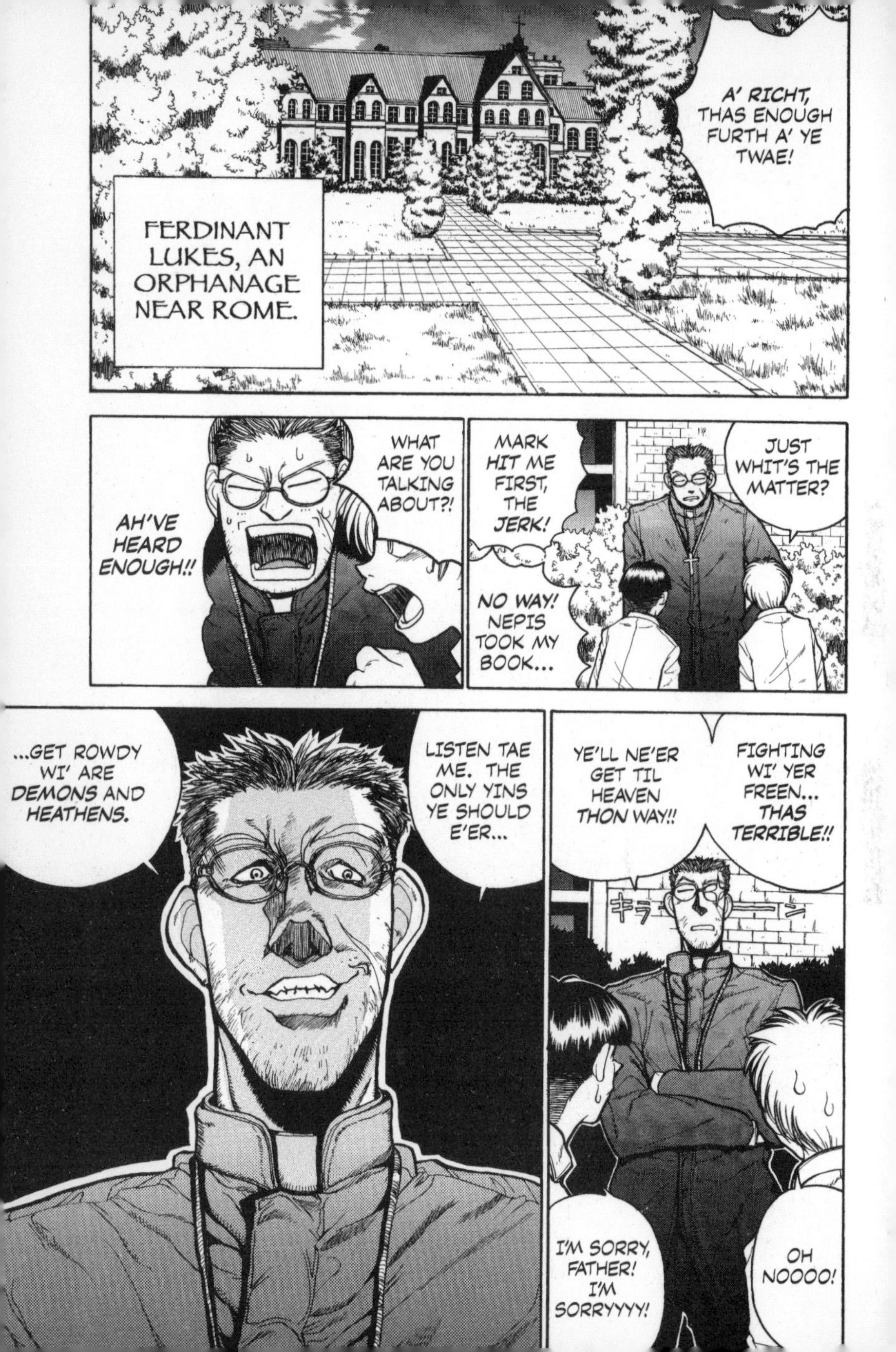
A' RICHT, THAS ENOUGH FURTH A' YE TWAE!
FERDINANT LUKES, AN ORPHANAGE NEAR ROME.
JUST WHIT'S THE MATTER?
MARK HIT ME FIRST, THE JERK!
NO WAY! NEPIS TOOK MY BOOK...
WHAT ARE YOU TALKING ABOUT?!
AH'VE HEARD ENOUGH!!
FIGHTING WI' YER FREEN... THAS TERRIBLE!!
YE'LL NE'ER GET TIL HEAVEN THON WAY!!
OH NOOOO!
I'M SORRY, FATHER! I'M SORRYYYY!
LISTEN TAE ME. THE ONLY YINS YE SHOULD E'ER...
...GET ROWDY WI' ARE DEMONS AND HEATHENS.

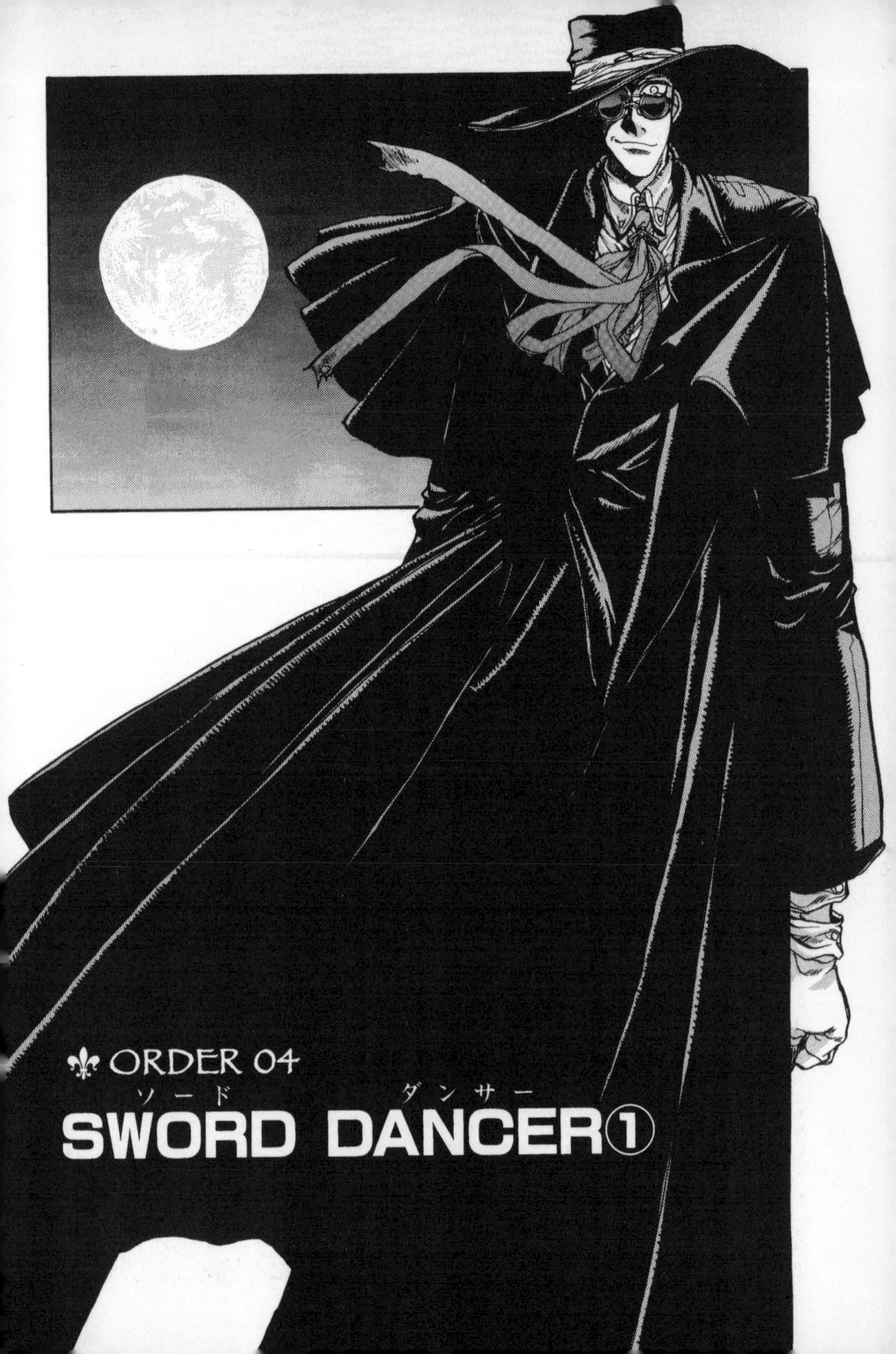
ORDER 04
ソード　ダンサー
SWORD DANCER①

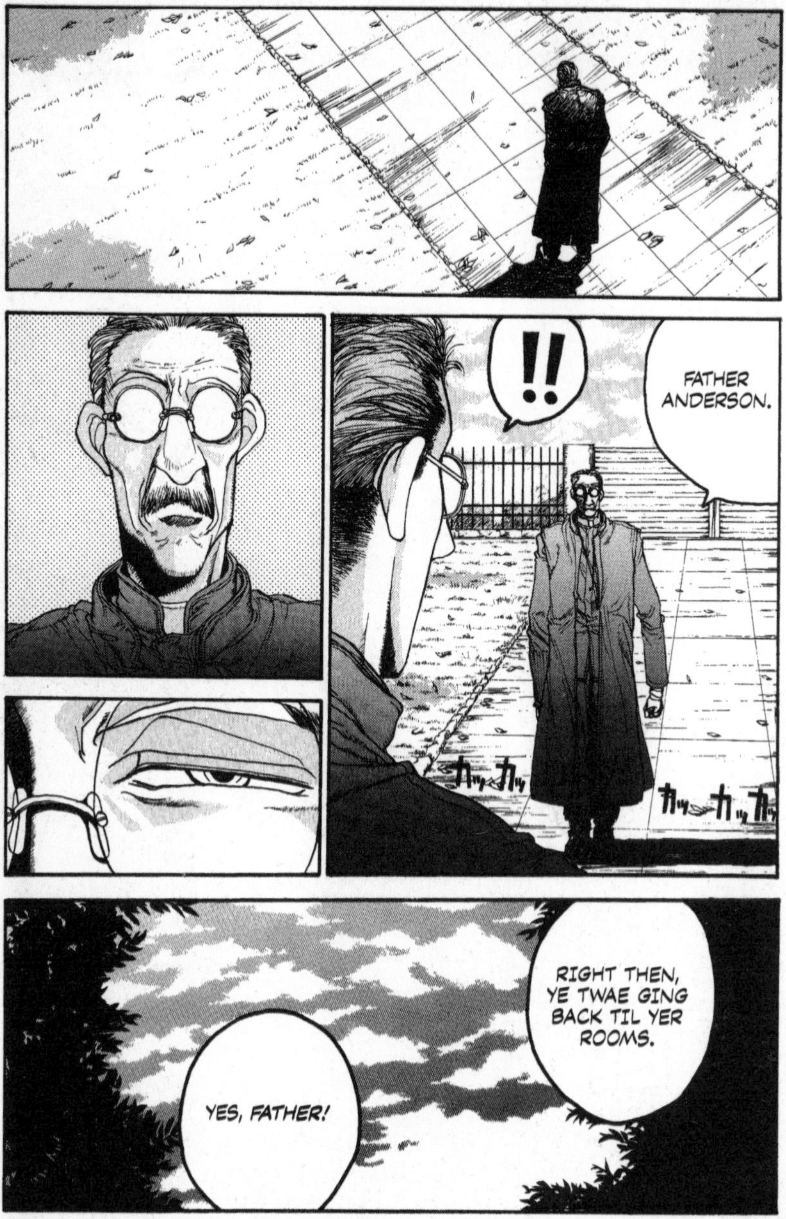
FATHER ANDERSON.
!!
カッ カッ
カッ カッ カッ
RIGHT THEN, YE TWAE GING BACK TIL YER ROOMS.
YES, FATHER!

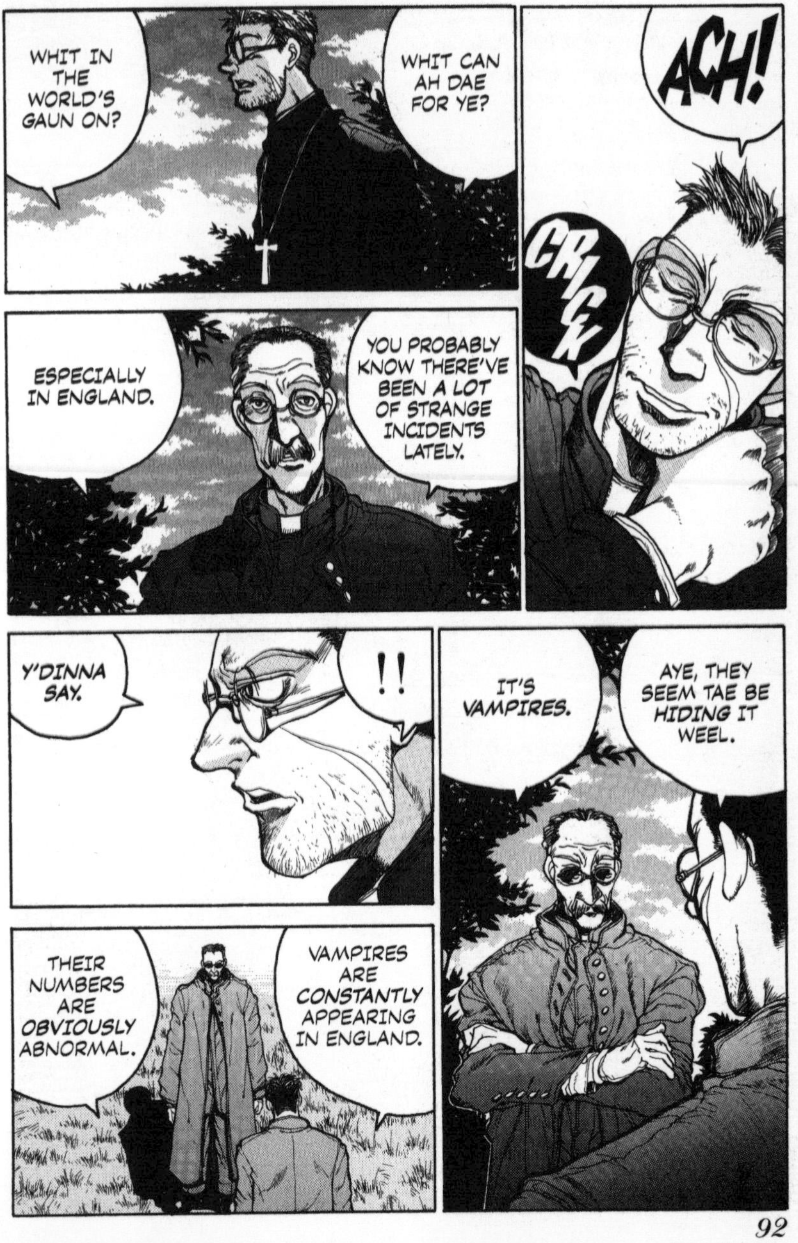
ACH!
CRICK
WHIT CAN AH DAE FOR YE?
WHIT IN THE WORLD'S GAUN ON?
YOU PROBABLY KNOW THERE'VE BEEN A LOT OF STRANGE INCIDENTS LATELY.
ESPECIALLY IN ENGLAND.
AYE, THEY SEEM TAE BE *HIDING* IT WEEL.
IT'S *VAMPIRES*.
!!
Y'DINNA SAY.
VAMPIRES ARE *CONSTANTLY* APPEARING IN ENGLAND.
THEIR NUMBERS ARE *OBVIOUSLY* ABNORMAL.

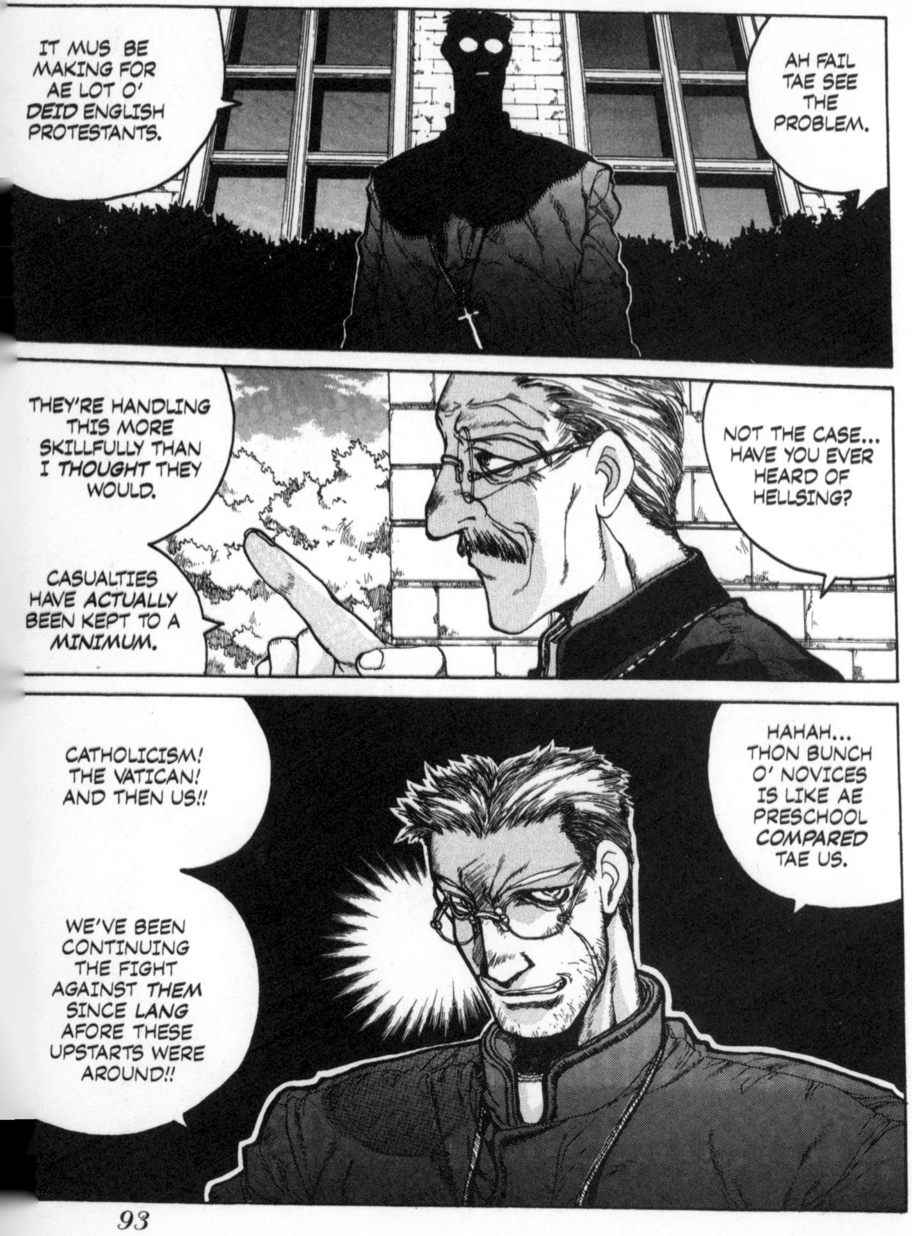
AH FAIL TAE SEE THE PROBLEM.
IT MUS BE MAKING FOR AE LOT O' DEID ENGLISH PROTESTANTS.
NOT THE CASE... HAVE YOU EVER HEARD OF HELLSING?
THEY'RE HANDLING THIS MORE SKILLFULLY THAN I THOUGHT THEY WOULD.
CASUALTIES HAVE ACTUALLY BEEN KEPT TO A MINIMUM.
HAHAH... THON BUNCH O' NOVICES IS LIKE AE PRESCHOOL COMPARED TAE US.
CATHOLICISM! THE VATICAN! AND THEN US!!
WE'VE BEEN CONTINUING THE FIGHT AGAINST THEM SINCE LANG AFORE THESE UPSTARTS WERE AROUND!!

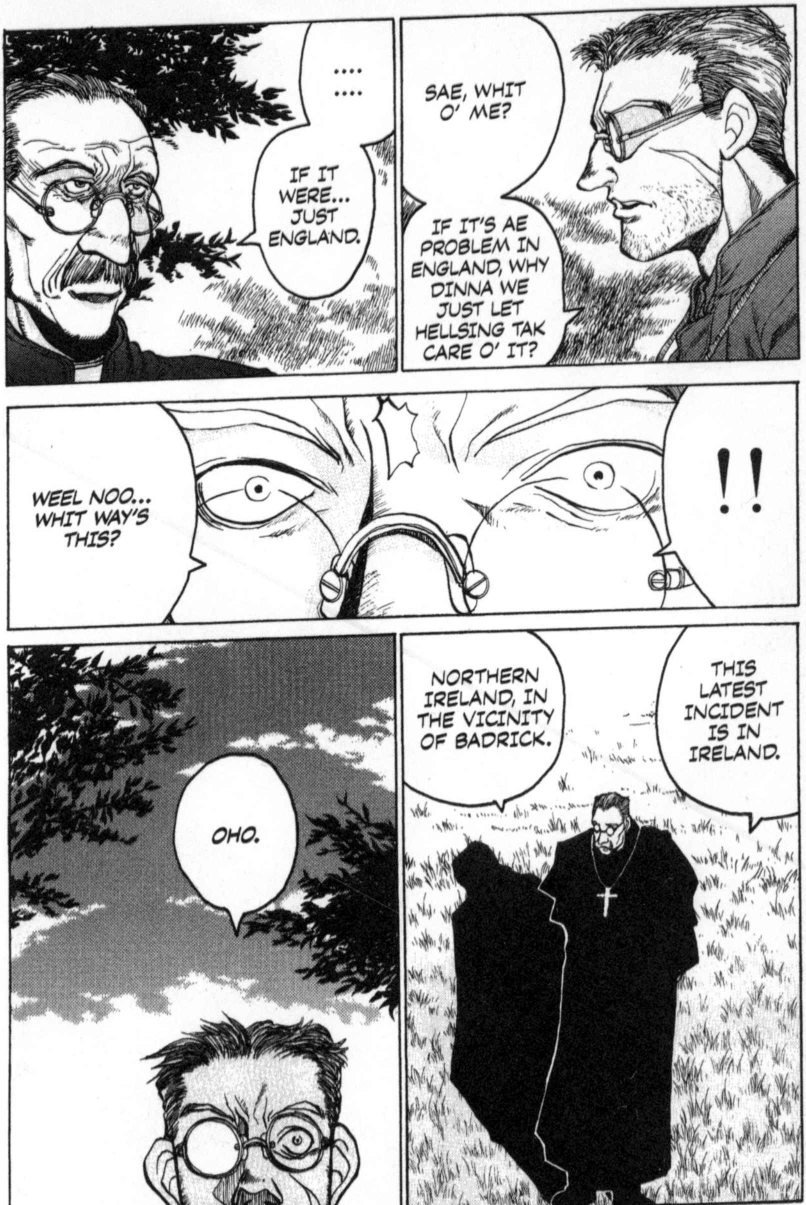
SAE, WHIT O' ME?
IF IT'S AE PROBLEM IN ENGLAND, WHY DINNA WE JUST LET HELLSING TAK CARE O' IT?
....
....
IF IT WERE... JUST ENGLAND.
!!
WEEL NOO... WHIT WAY'S THIS?
THIS LATEST INCIDENT IS IN IRELAND.
NORTHERN IRELAND, IN THE VICINITY OF BADRICK.
OHO.

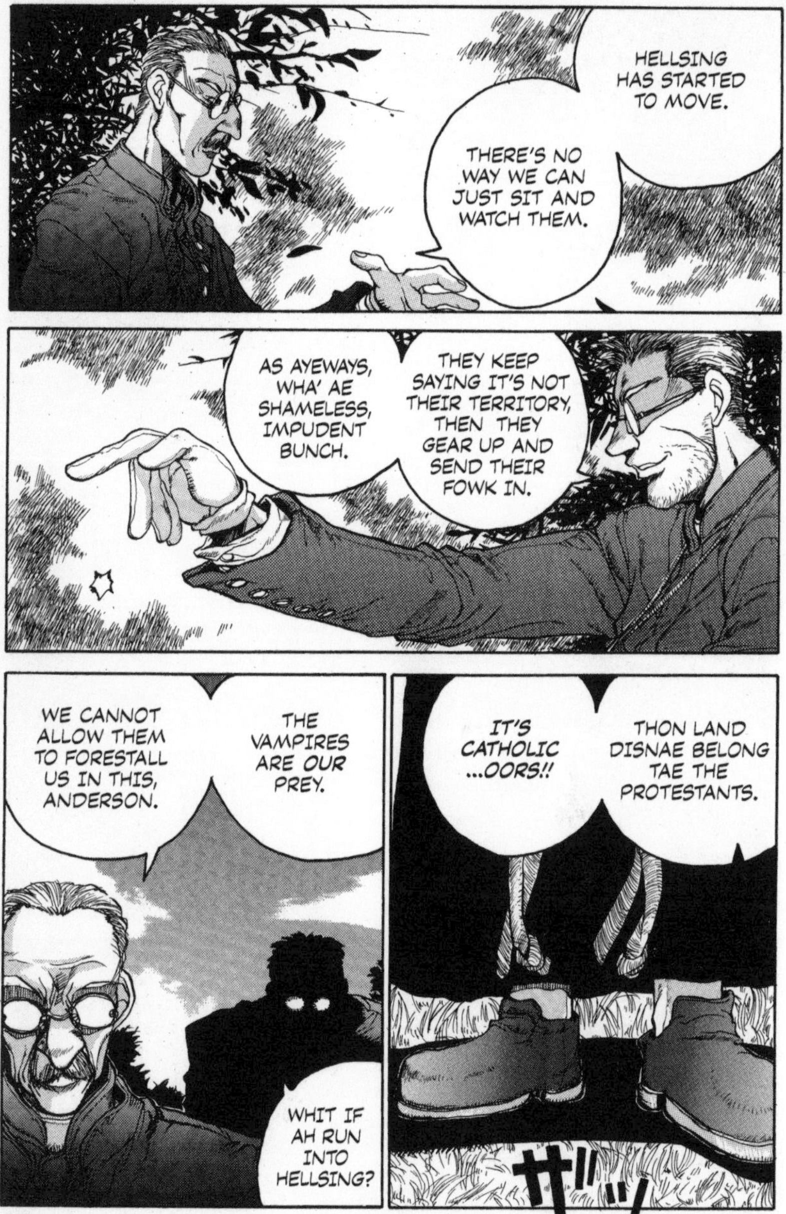
HELLSING HAS STARTED TO MOVE.
THERE'S NO WAY WE CAN JUST SIT AND WATCH THEM.
THEY KEEP SAYING IT'S NOT THEIR TERRITORY, THEN THEY GEAR UP AND SEND THEIR FOWK IN.
AS AYEWAYS, WHA' AE SHAMELESS, IMPUDENT BUNCH.
THON LAND DISNAE BELONG TAE THE PROTESTANTS.
IT'S CATHOLIC ...OORS!!
THE VAMPIRES ARE OUR PREY.
WE CANNOT ALLOW THEM TO FORESTALL US IN THIS, ANDERSON.
WHIT IF AH RUN INTO HELLSING?

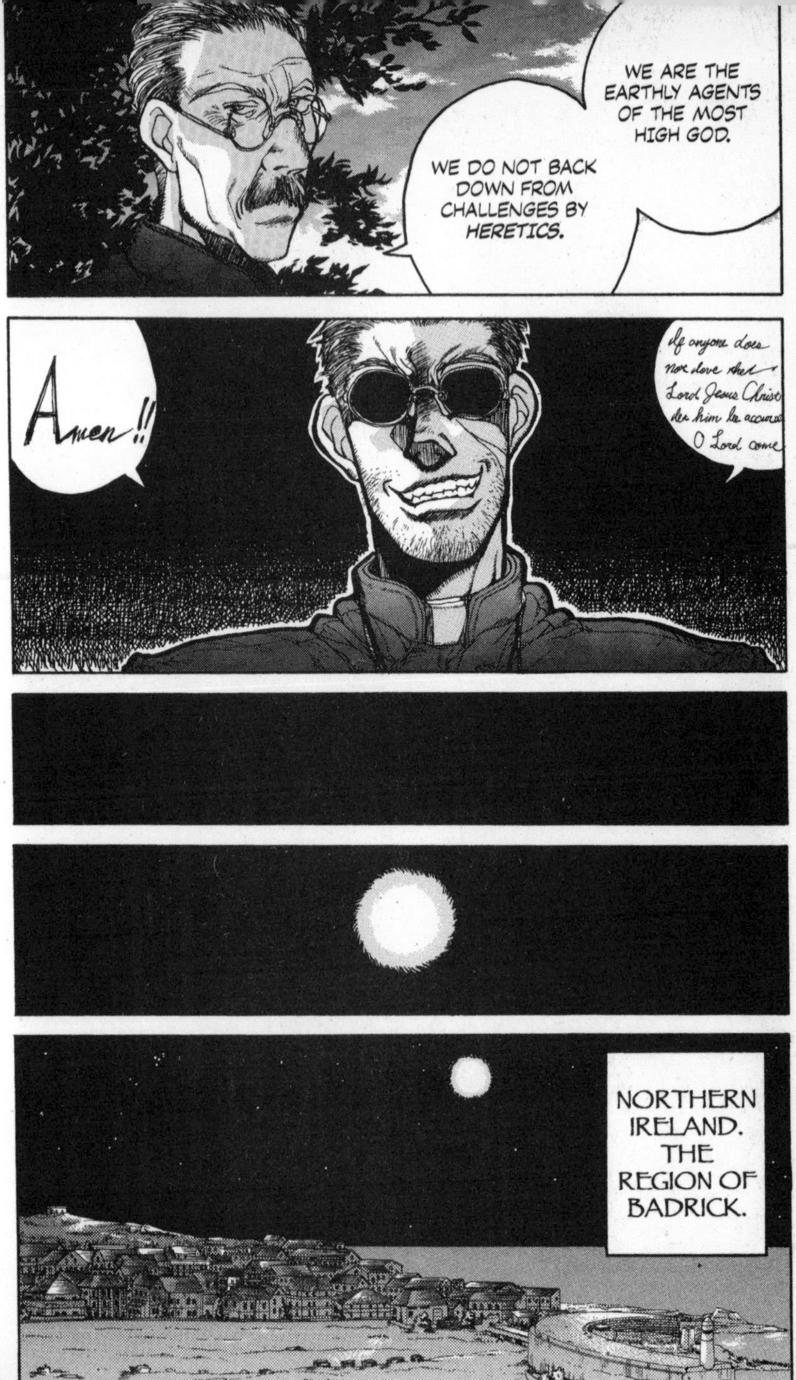
WE ARE THE EARTHLY AGENTS OF THE MOST HIGH GOD.
WE DO NOT BACK DOWN FROM CHALLENGES BY HERETICS.
If anyone does not love the Lord Jesus Christ let him be accursed O Lord come
Amen!!
NORTHERN IRELAND. THE REGION OF BADRICK.

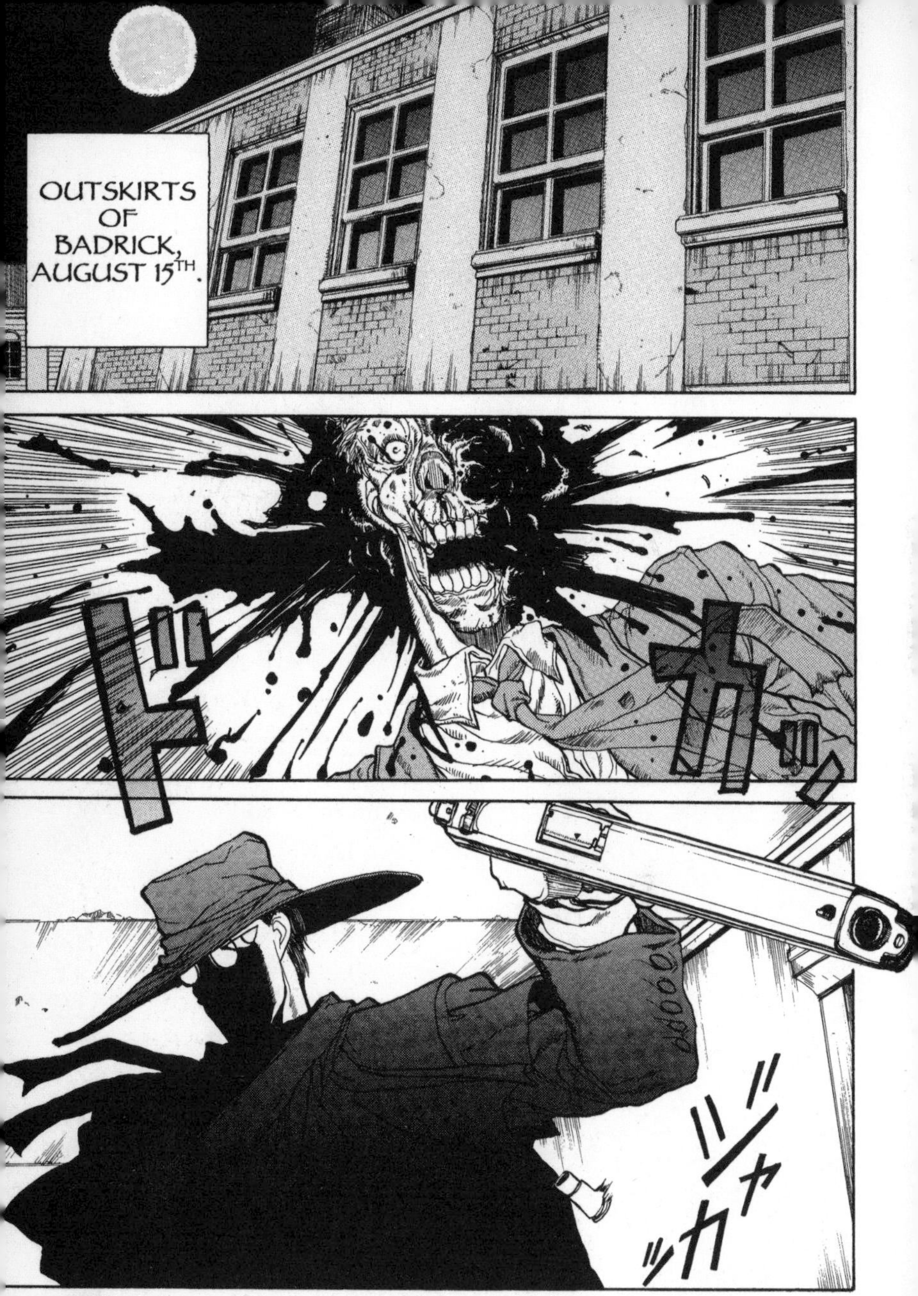
OUTSKIRTS OF BADRICK, AUGUST 15TH.
ジャカッ

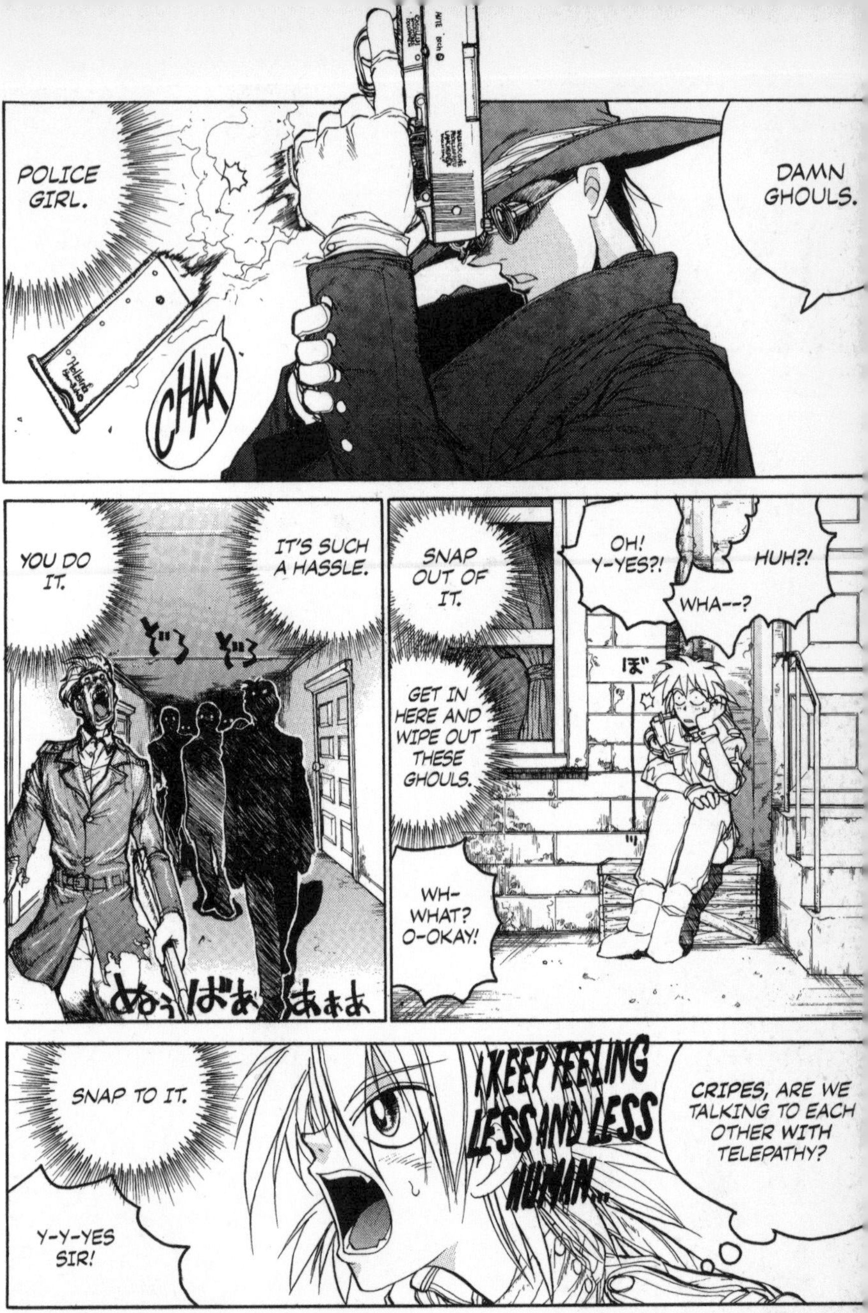
DAMN GHOULS.
POLICE GIRL.
CHAK
HUH?!
OH! Y-YES?!
WHA--?
ぼ
SNAP OUT OF IT.
GET IN HERE AND WIPE OUT THESE GHOULS.
WH- WHAT? O-OKAY!
IT'S SUCH A HASSLE.
YOU DO IT.
CRIPES, ARE WE TALKING TO EACH OTHER WITH TELEPATHY?
I KEEP FEELING LESS AND LESS HUMAN...
SNAP TO IT.
Y-Y-YES SIR!

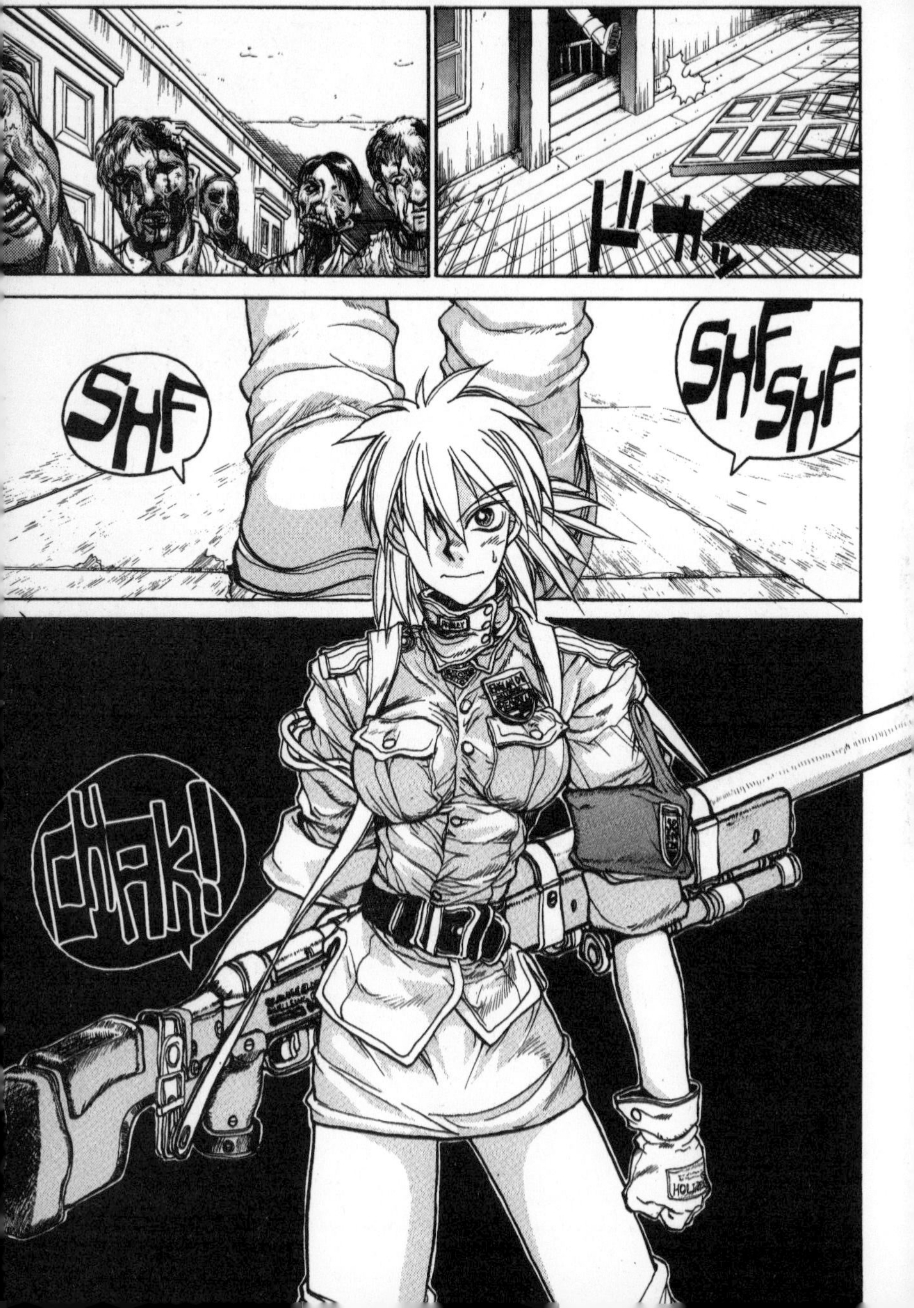
ドカッ
SHF SHF
SHF
CHAK!

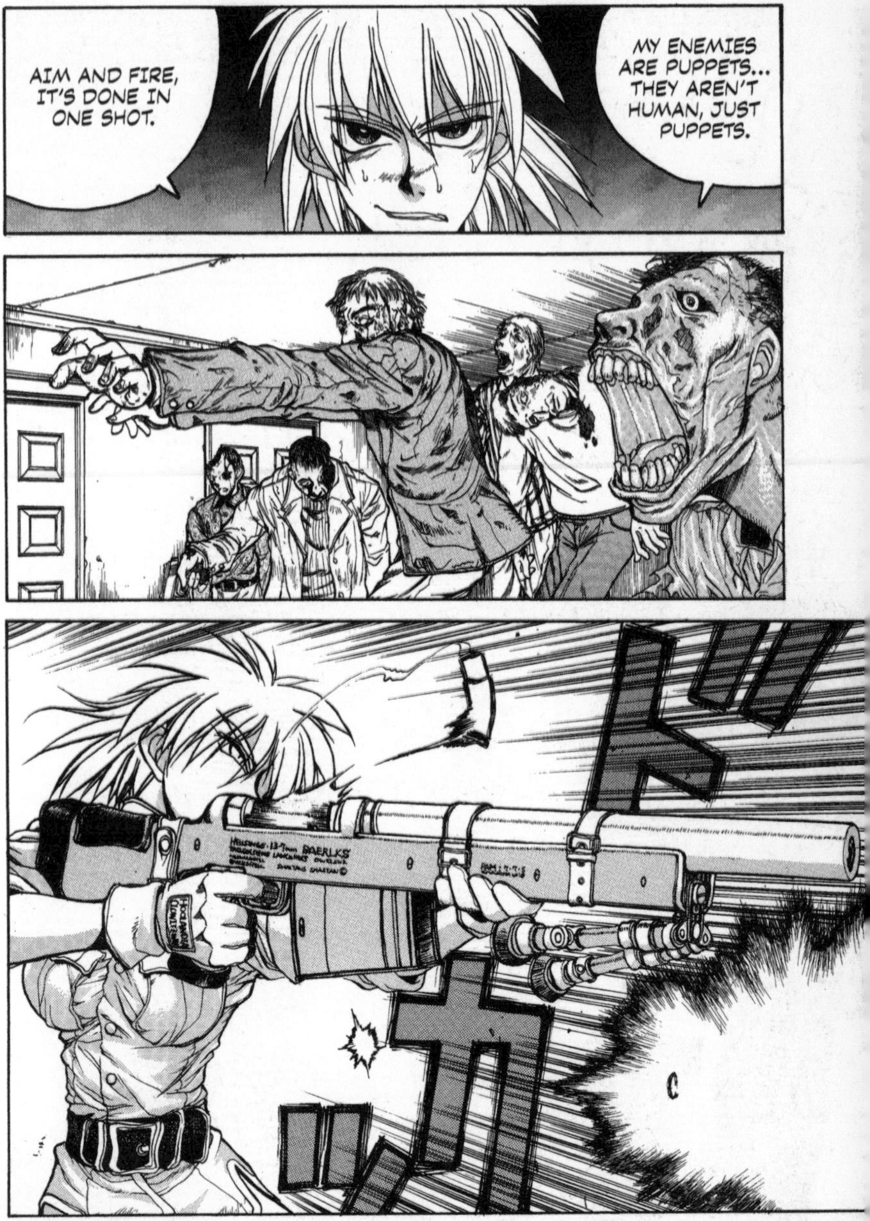
MY ENEMIES ARE PUPPETS... THEY AREN'T HUMAN, JUST PUPPETS.
AIM AND FIRE, IT'S DONE IN ONE SHOT.

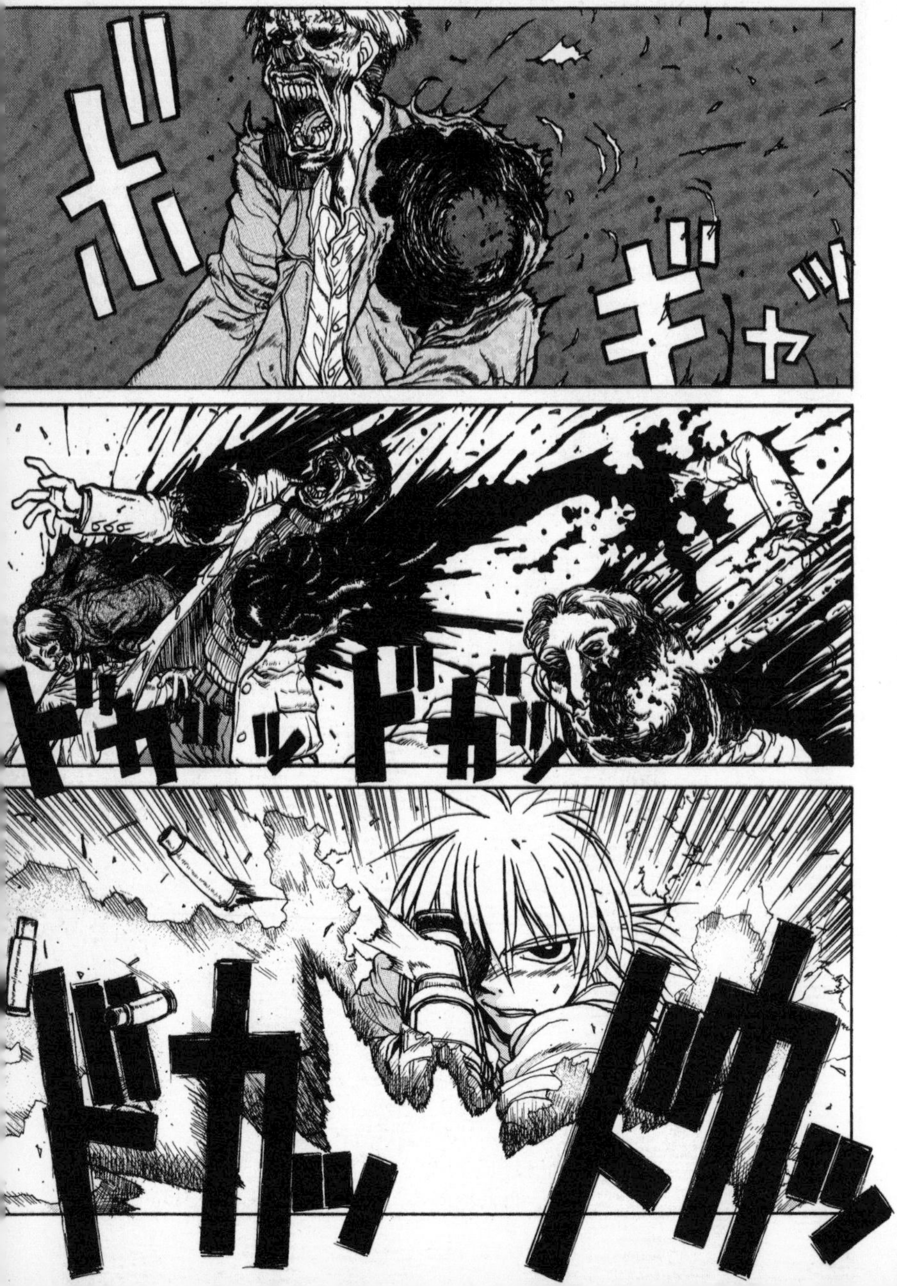
ギャッ
ボ
ドガッ
ドガッ
ドカッ
ドカッ

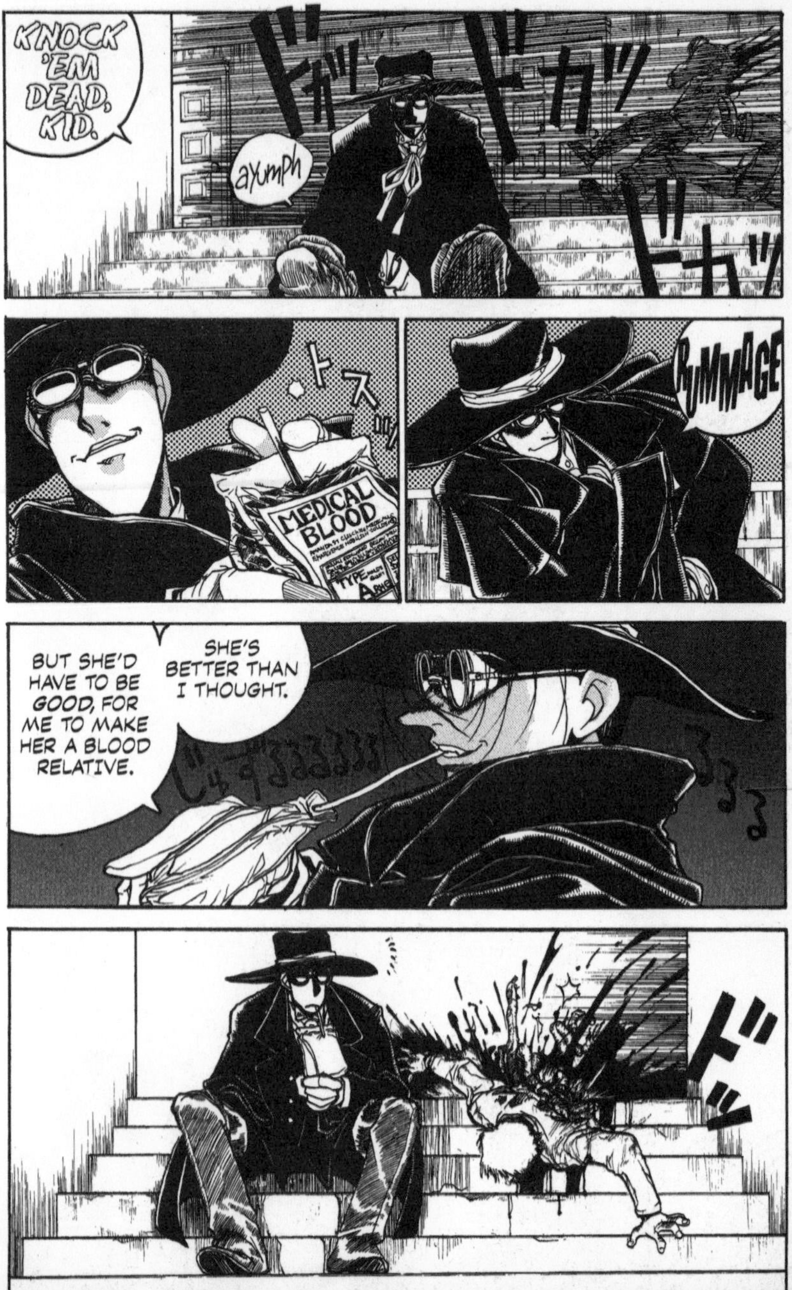
ドガッ
ドカッ
ドカッ
KNOCK 'EM DEAD, KID.
ayumph
RUMMAGE
トス
MEDICAL BLOOD
TYPE A
SHE'S BETTER THAN I THOUGHT.
BUT SHE'D HAVE TO BE GOOD, FOR ME TO MAKE HER A BLOOD RELATIVE.
ドドッ

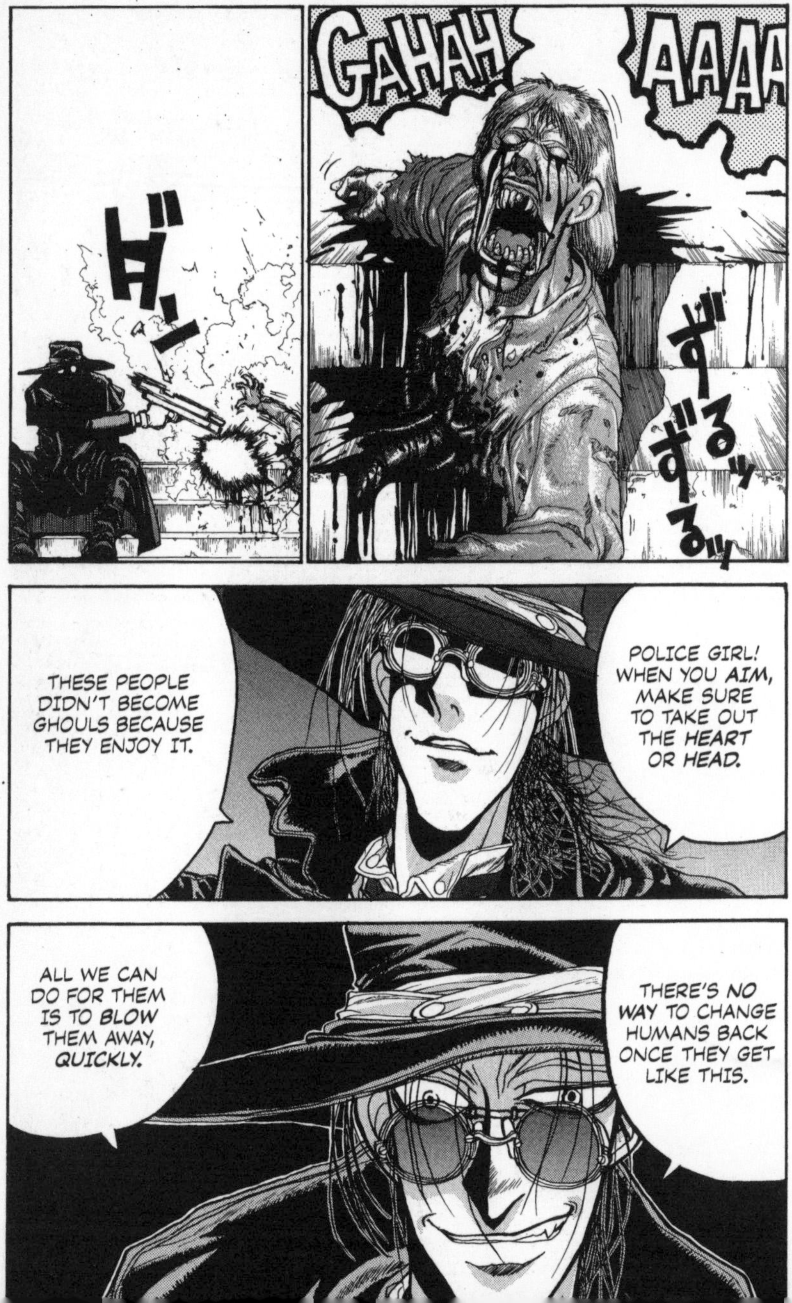
GAHAH
AAAA
ずるずるっ
ずるるっ
ダーン
POLICE GIRL! WHEN YOU *AIM*, MAKE SURE TO TAKE OUT THE *HEART* OR *HEAD*.
THESE PEOPLE DIDN'T BECOME GHOULS BECAUSE THEY ENJOY IT.
THERE'S *NO* WAY TO CHANGE HUMANS BACK ONCE THEY GET LIKE THIS.
ALL WE CAN DO FOR THEM IS TO *BLOW* THEM AWAY, *QUICKLY.*

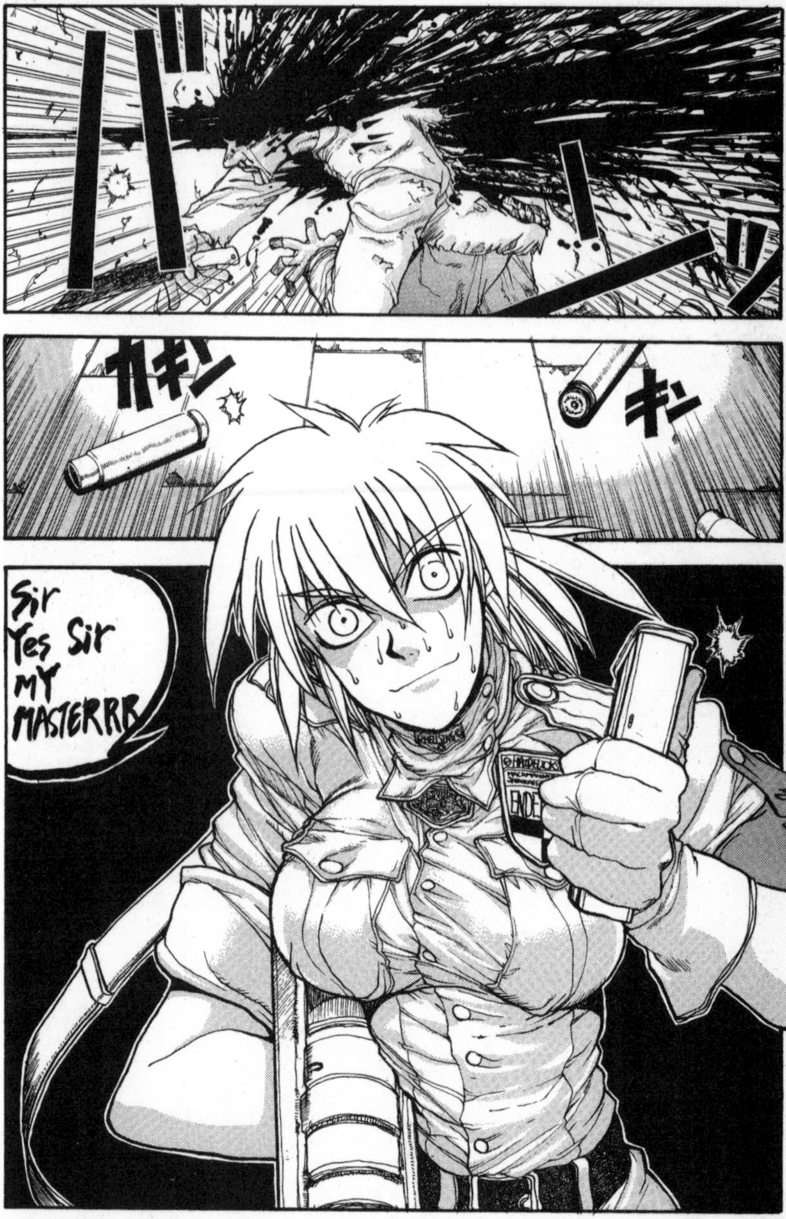
キン
カキン
Sir Yes Sir MY MASTERRR

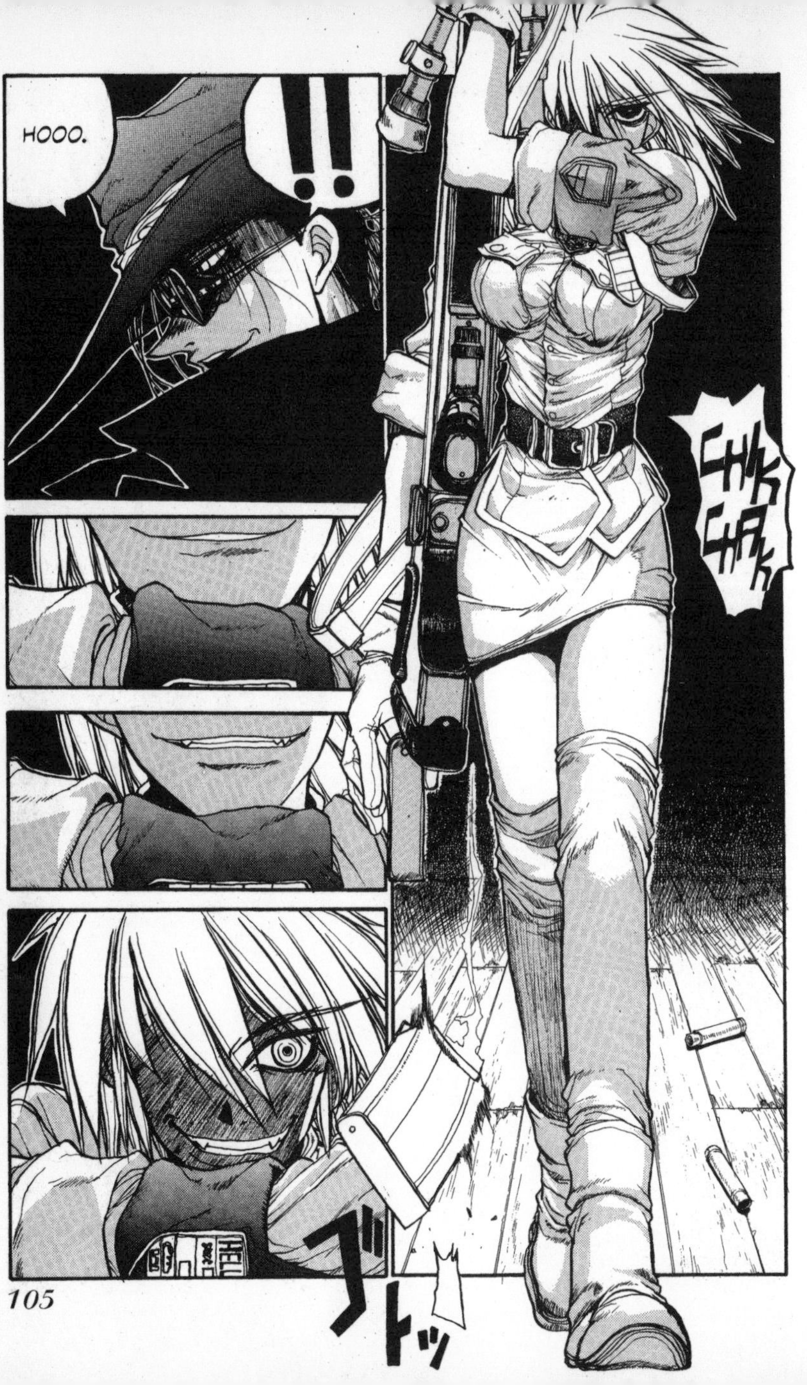
CHIK CHAK
ゴトッ
!!
HOOO.

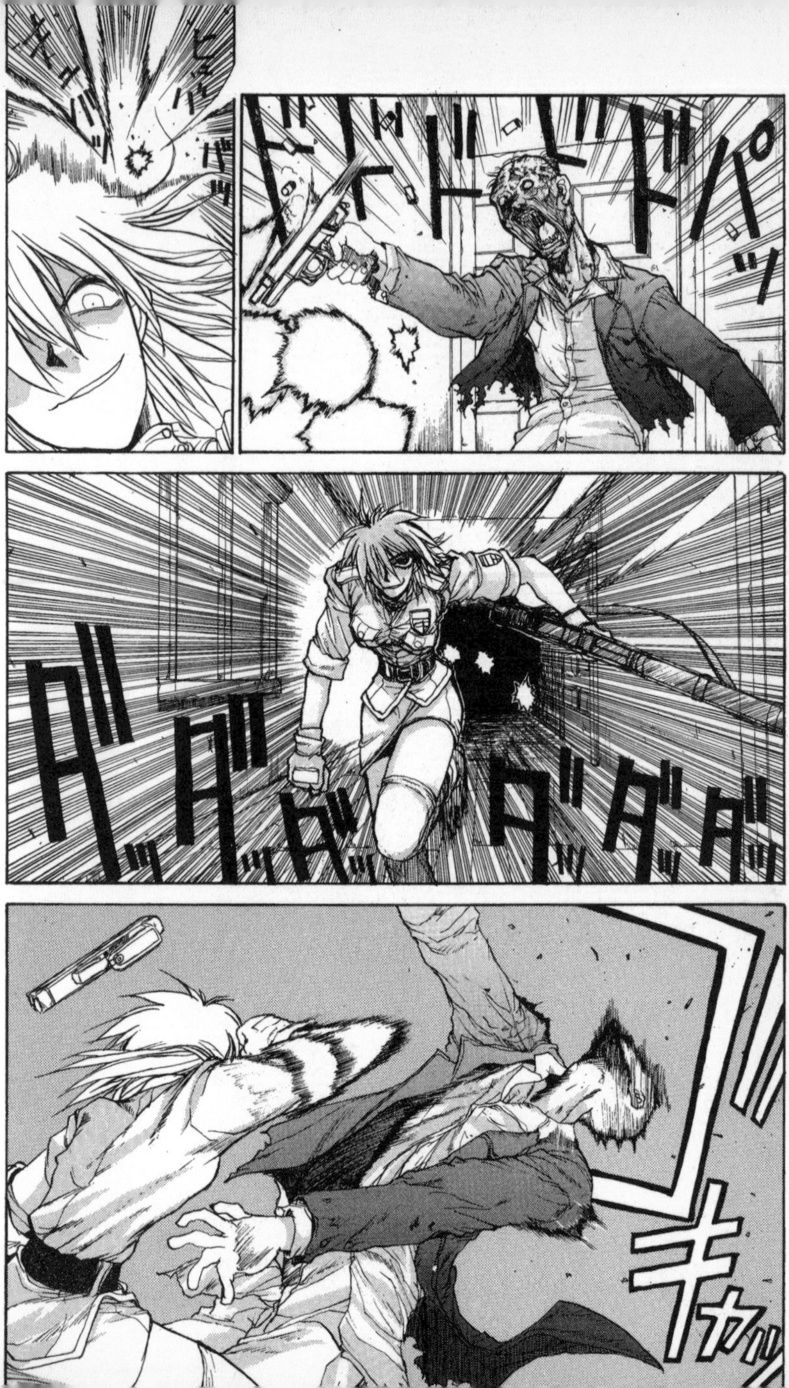

ドドドドドドパッ
キュババ
ヒュパバッ
ダッダッダッダダダダ
キャッ

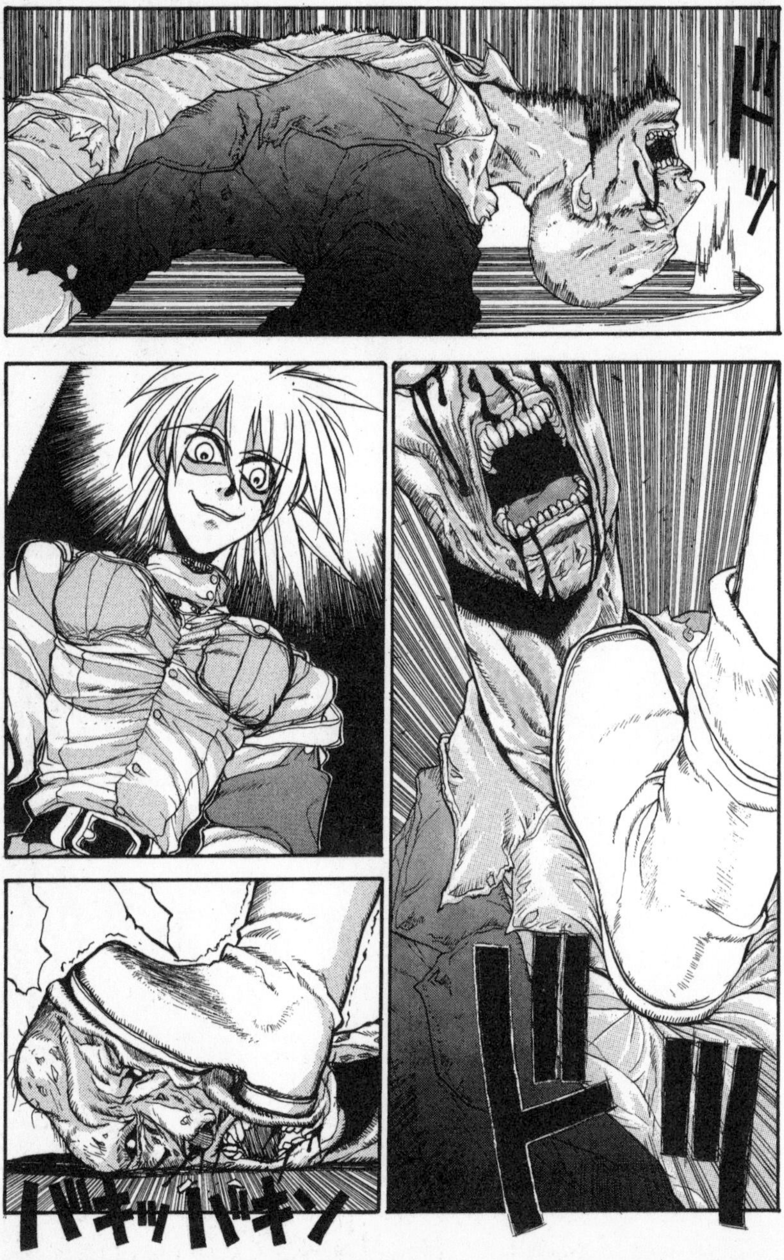
ドッ
ドッ
バギッバキン

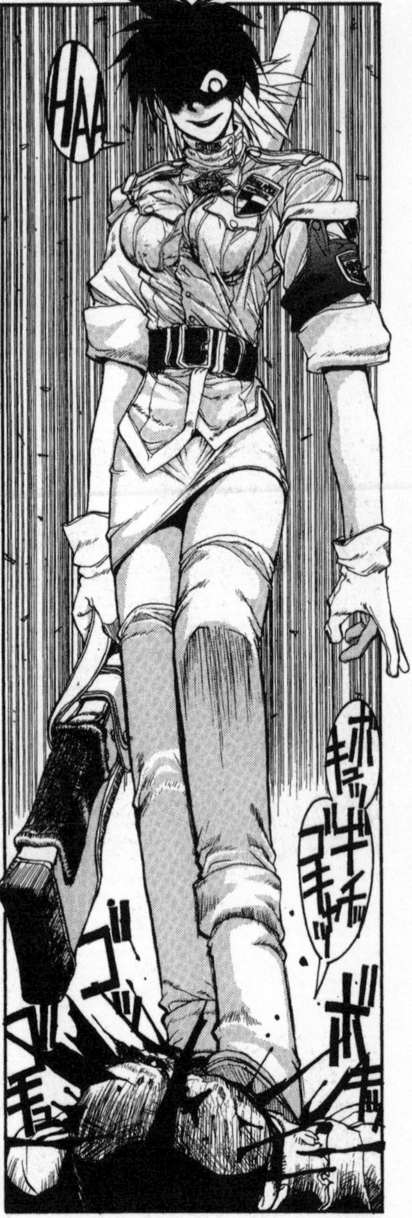
HAA

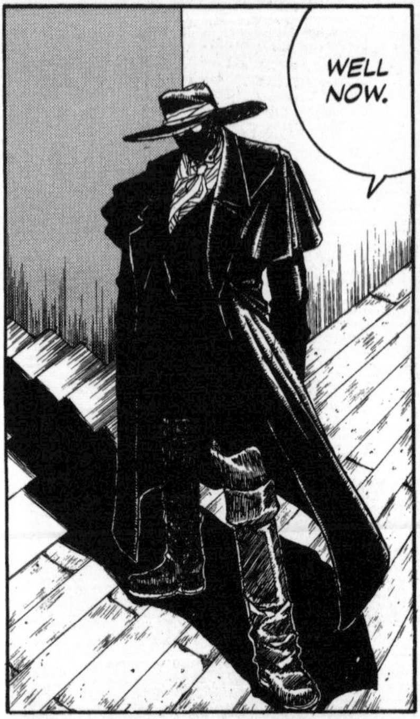
WELL NOW.

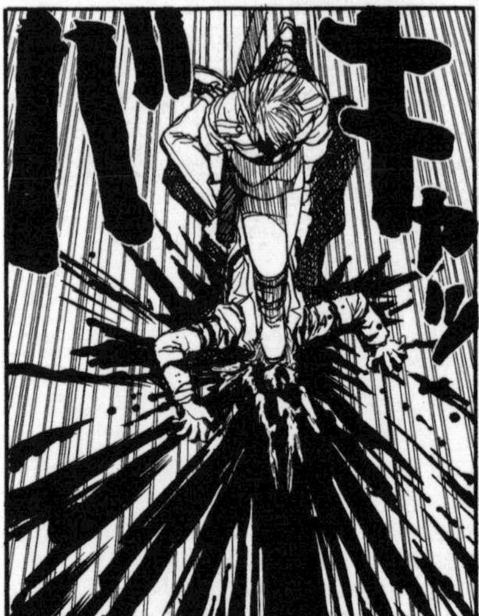
バキャッ

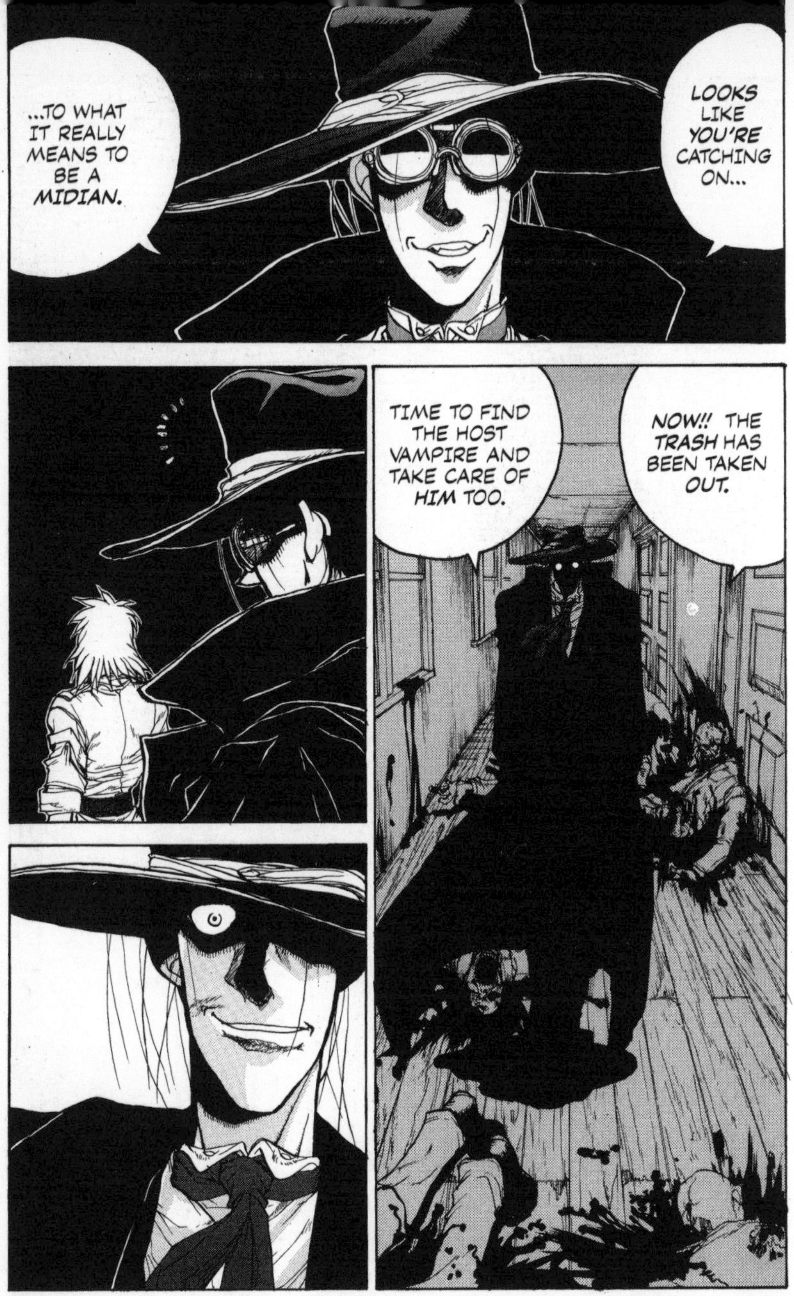
LOOKS LIKE YOU'RE CATCHING ON...
...TO WHAT IT REALLY MEANS TO BE A MIDIAN.
NOW!! THE TRASH HAS BEEN TAKEN OUT.
TIME TO FIND THE HOST VAMPIRE AND TAKE CARE OF HIM TOO.

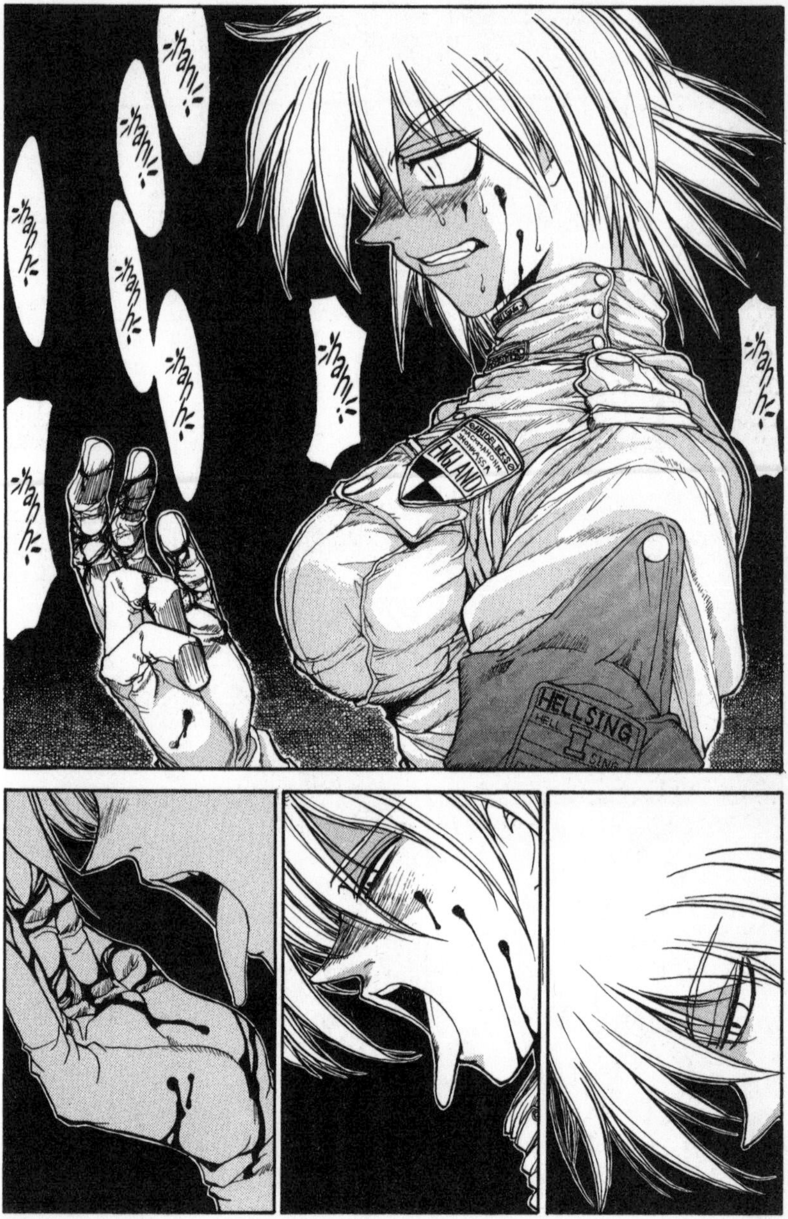
hahh!
hah!!
hah!!
hah!!
hahh!
hahh!
hahh!
hahh!
ENGLAND
HELLSING

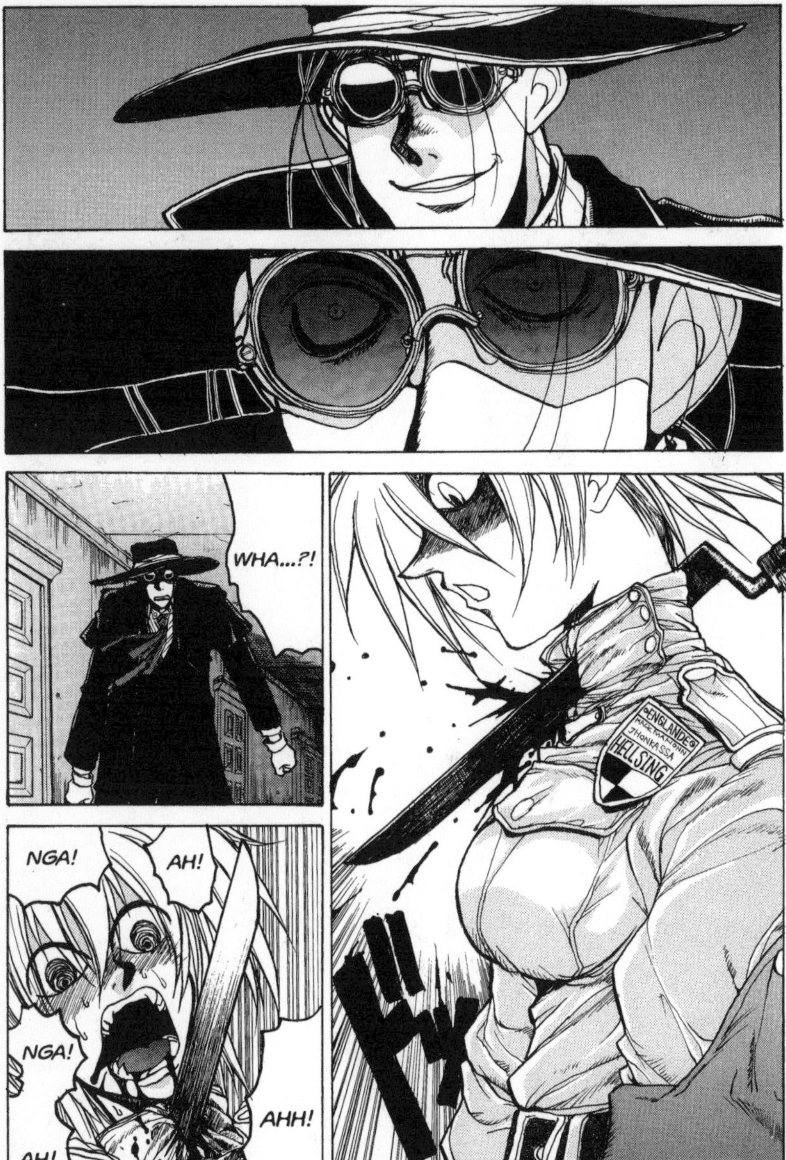
ENGLANDE
HELLSING
WHA...?!
AH!
NGA!
NGA!
AHH!
AH!

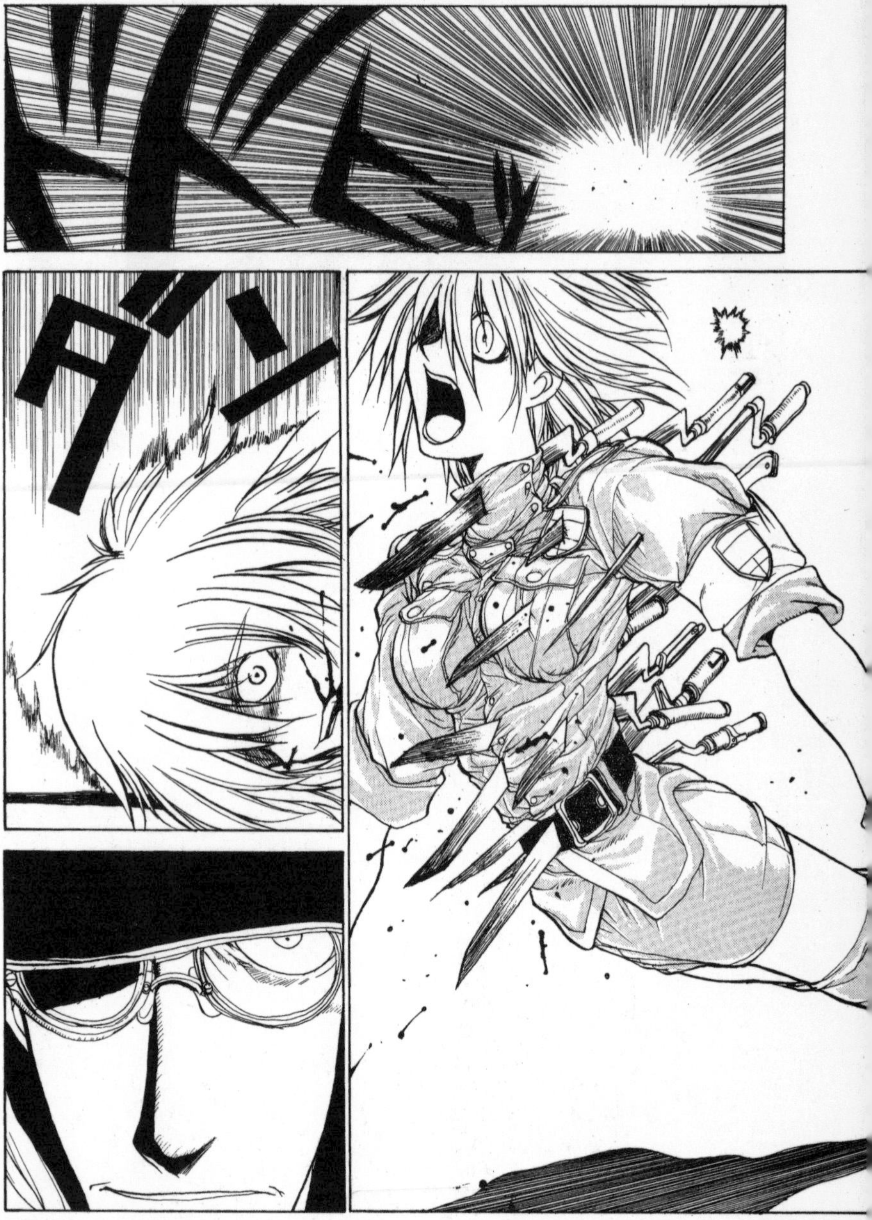
ドドドッ
ダン

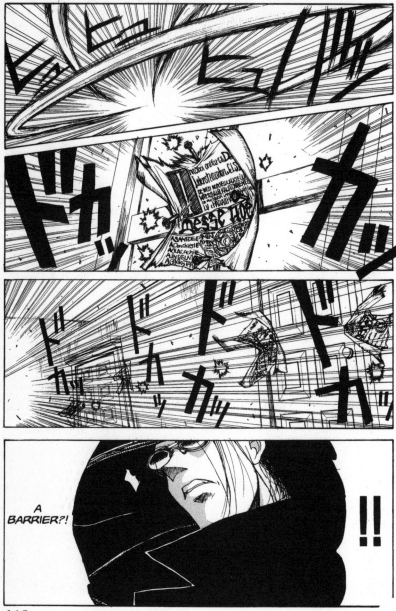

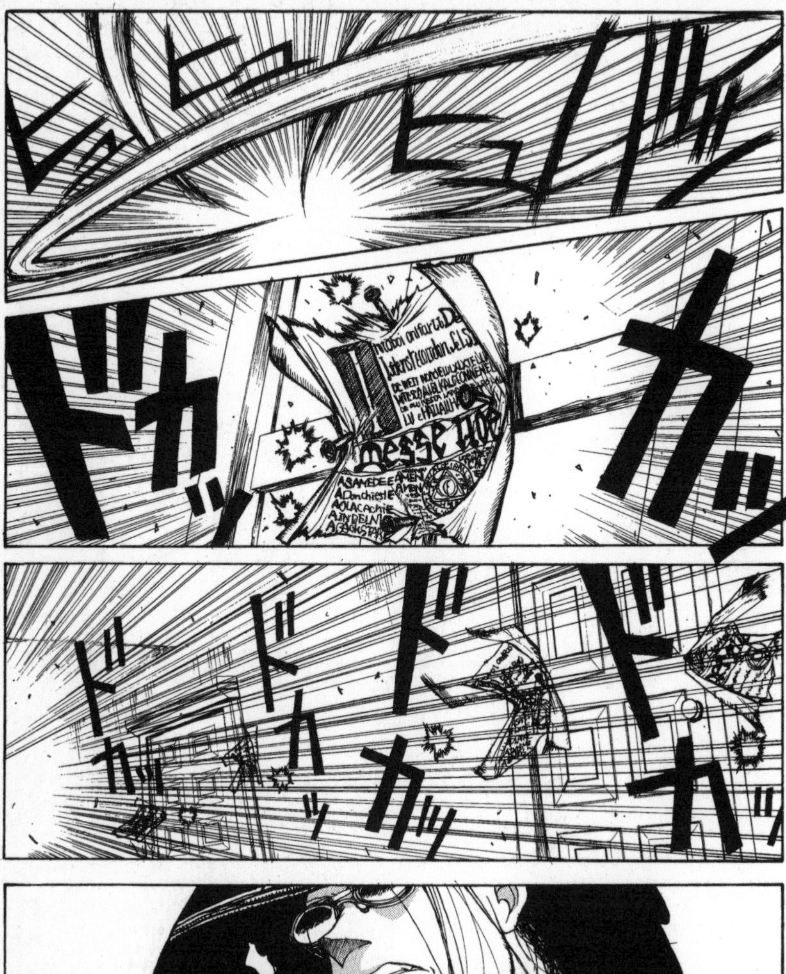
!!
A BARRIER?!

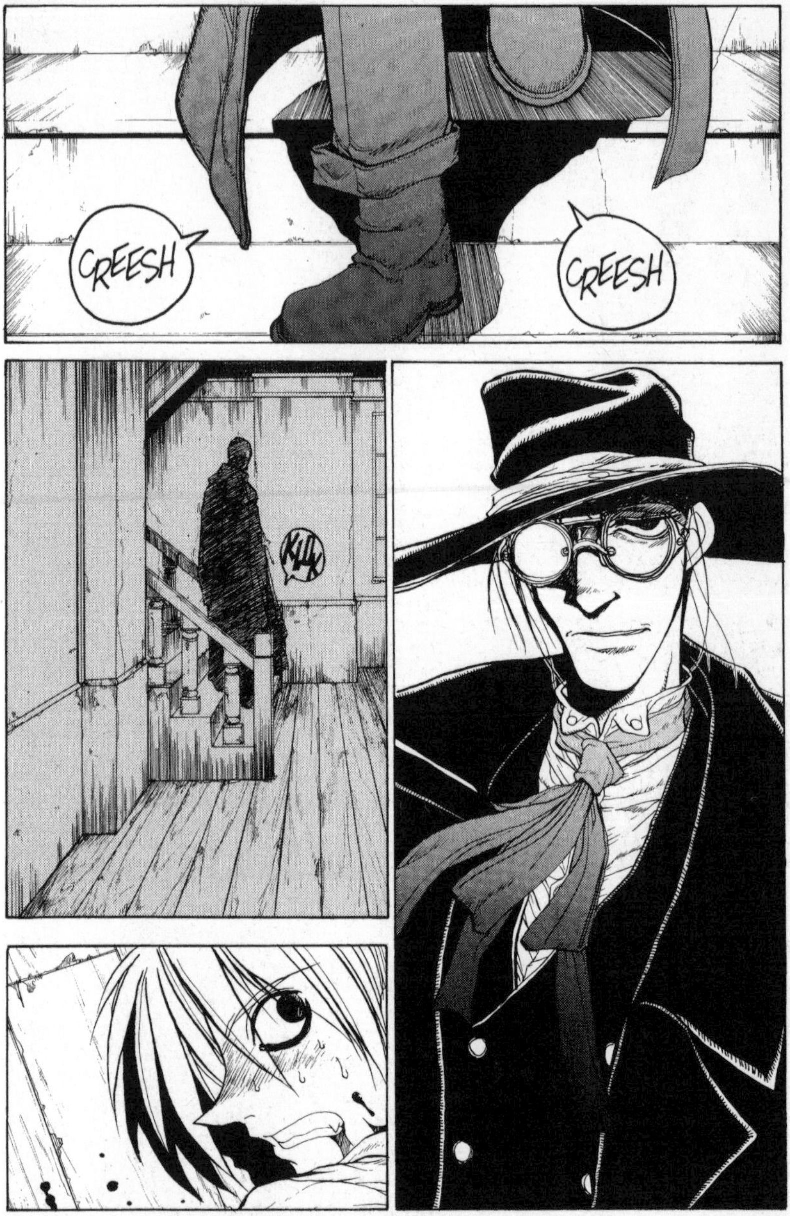
CREESH
CREESH
KLIK

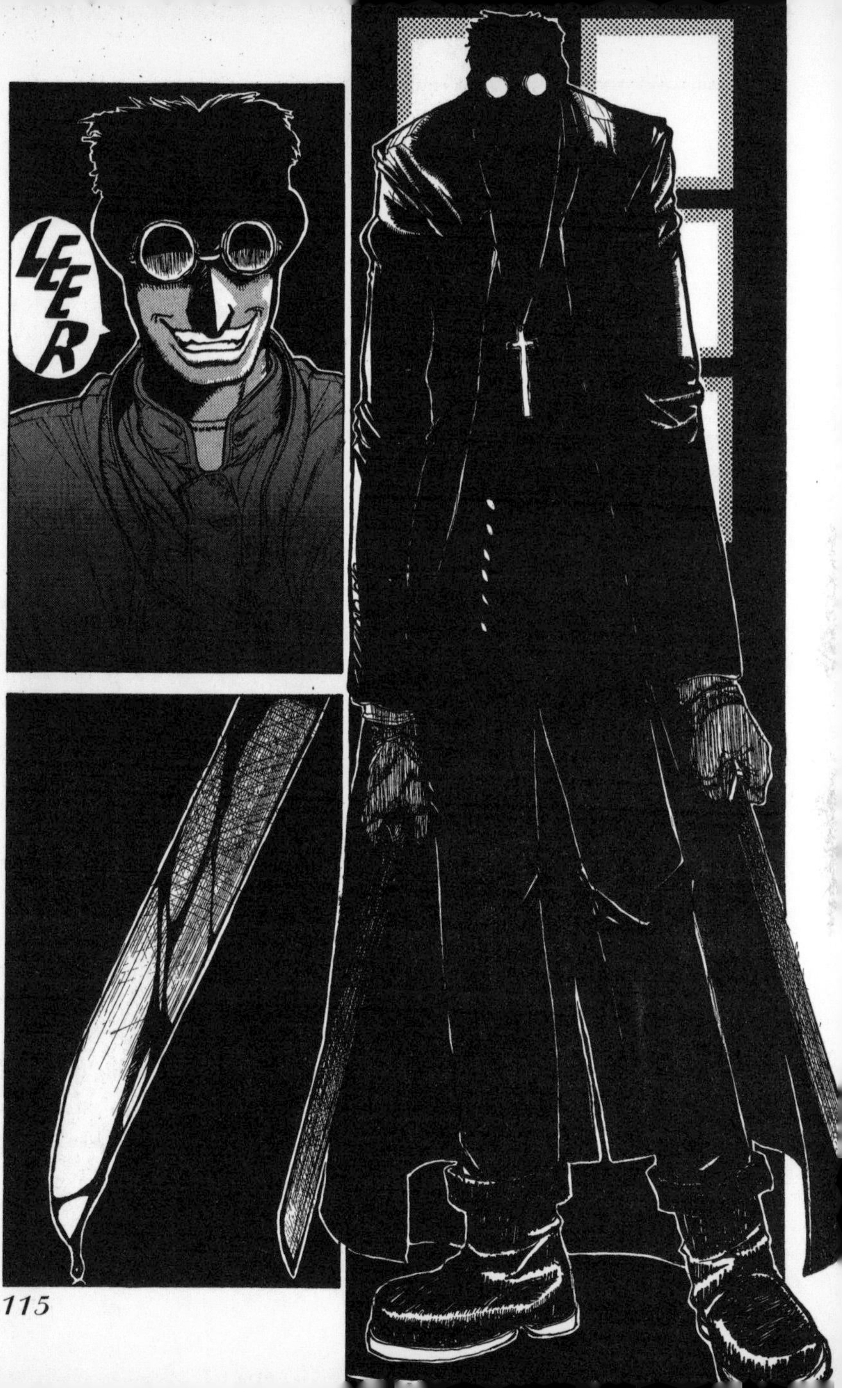
LEER

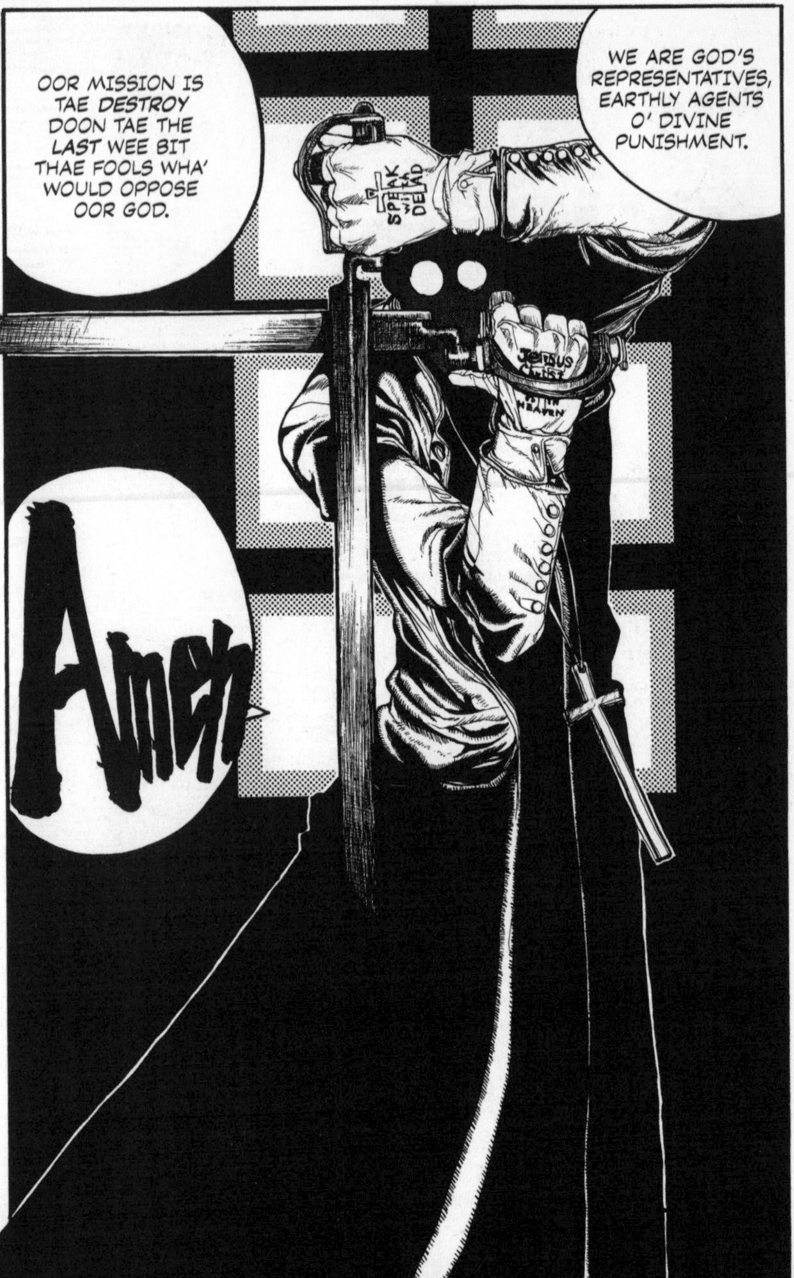
WE ARE GOD'S REPRESENTATIVES, EARTHLY AGENTS O' DIVINE PUNISHMENT.
OOR MISSION IS TAE *DESTROY* DOON TAE THE *LAST* WEE BIT THAE FOOLS WHA' WOULD OPPOSE OOR GOD.
Amen

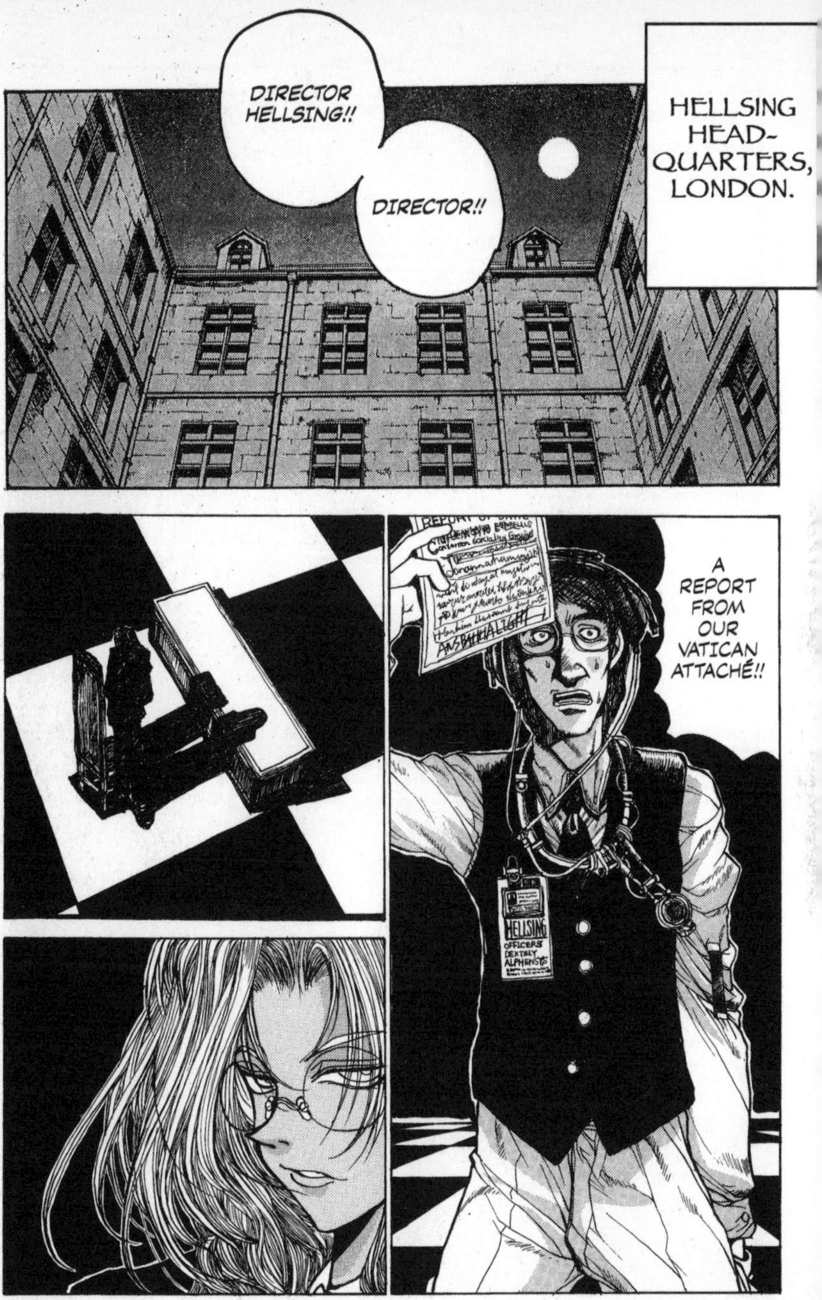
HELLSING HEAD-QUARTERS, LONDON.
DIRECTOR HELLSING!!
DIRECTOR!!
A REPORT FROM OUR VATICAN ATTACHÉ!!
HELLSING

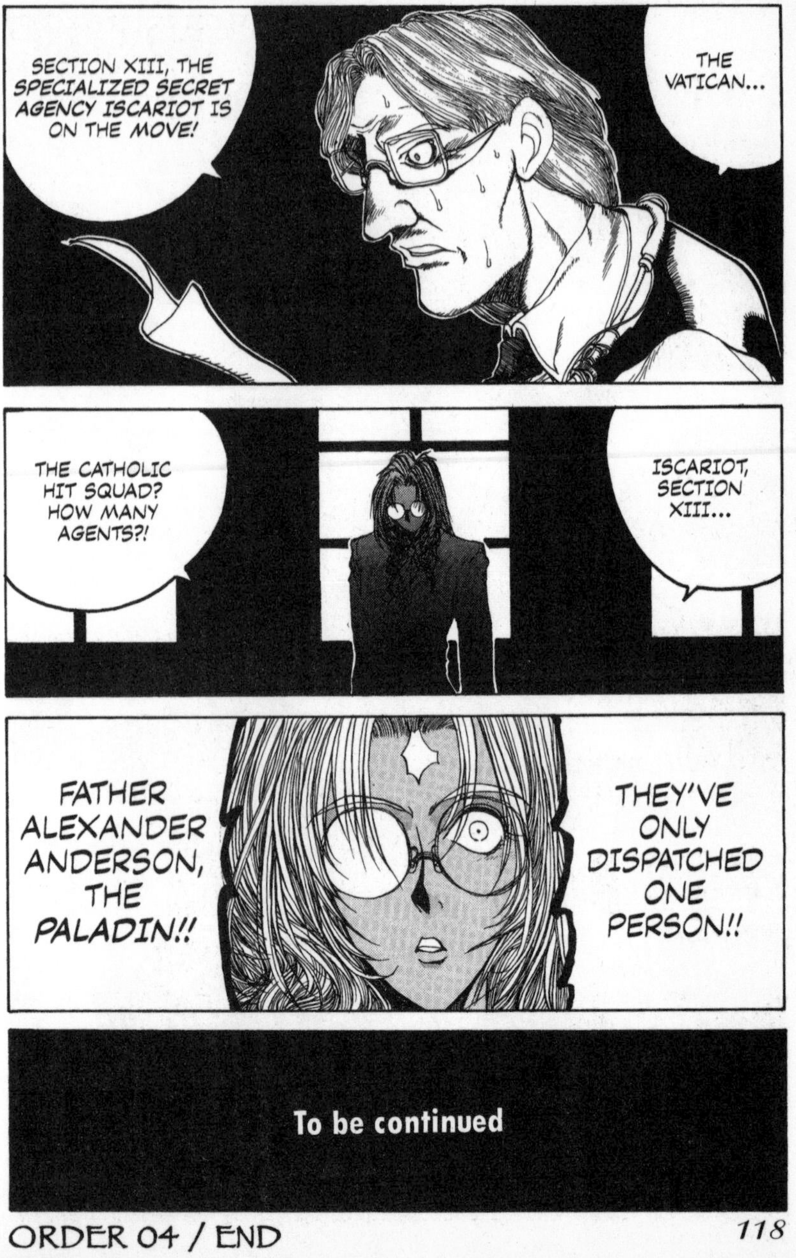
THE VATICAN...
SECTION XIII, THE SPECIALIZED SECRET AGENCY ISCARIOT IS ON THE MOVE!
ISCARIOT, SECTION XIII...
THE CATHOLIC HIT SQUAD? HOW MANY AGENTS?!
THEY'VE ONLY DISPATCHED ONE PERSON!!
FATHER ALEXANDER ANDERSON, THE PALADIN!!
To be continued

ORDER 04 / END

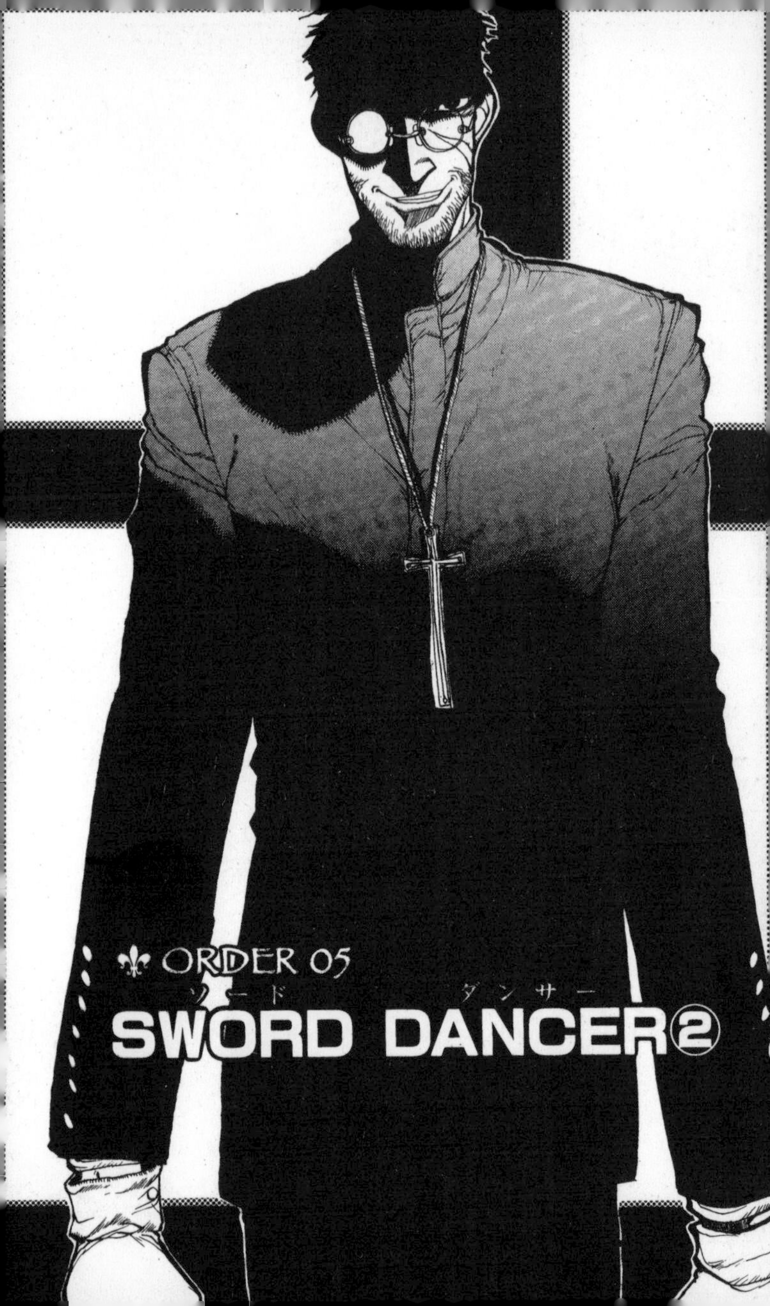
ORDER 05
ソード ダンサー
SWORD DANCER②

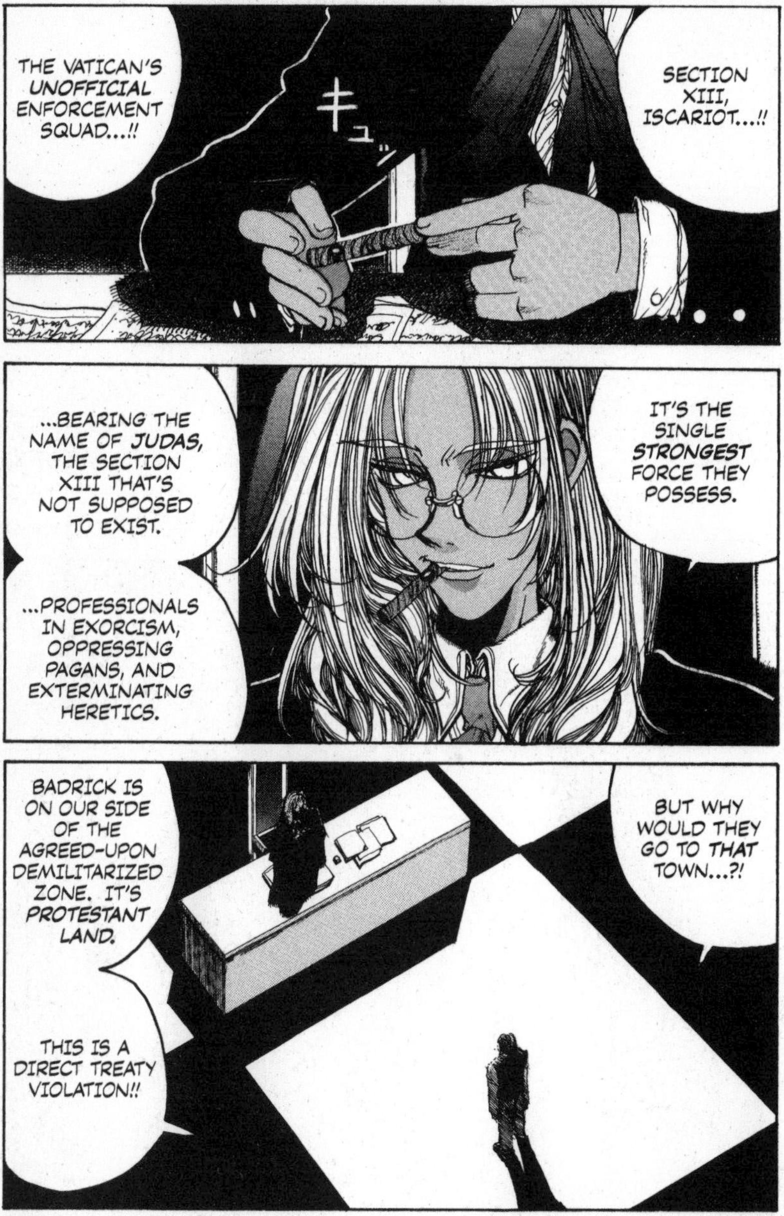
SECTION XIII, ISCARIOT...!!
THE VATICAN'S UNOFFICIAL ENFORCEMENT SQUAD...!!
キュッ
!!
...
IT'S THE SINGLE STRONGEST FORCE THEY POSSESS.
...BEARING THE NAME OF JUDAS, THE SECTION XIII THAT'S NOT SUPPOSED TO EXIST.
...PROFESSIONALS IN EXORCISM, OPPRESSING PAGANS, AND EXTERMINATING HERETICS.
BUT WHY WOULD THEY GO TO THAT TOWN...?!
BADRICK IS ON OUR SIDE OF THE AGREED-UPON DEMILITARIZED ZONE. IT'S PROTESTANT LAND.
THIS IS A DIRECT TREATY VIOLATION!!

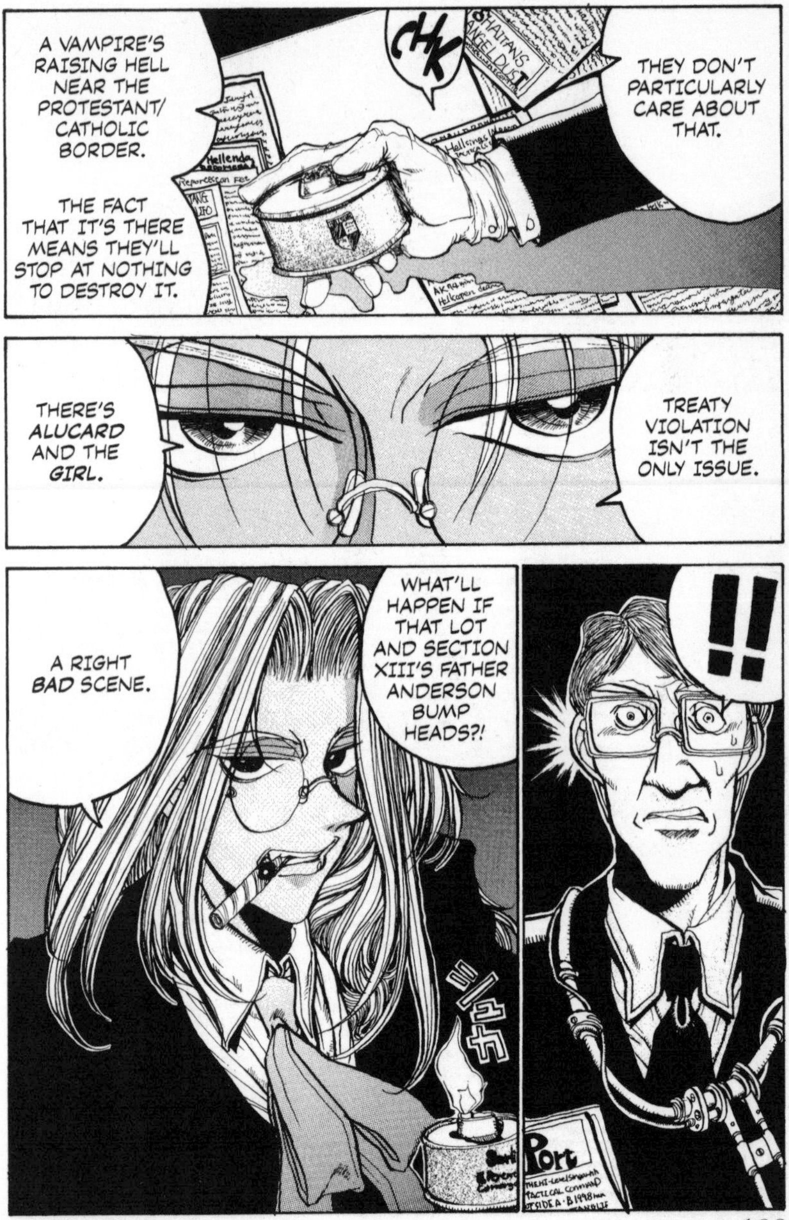
THEY DON'T PARTICULARLY CARE ABOUT THAT.
CHK
A VAMPIRE'S RAISING HELL NEAR THE PROTESTANT/ CATHOLIC BORDER.
THE FACT THAT IT'S THERE MEANS THEY'LL STOP AT NOTHING TO DESTROY IT.
TREATY VIOLATION ISN'T THE ONLY ISSUE.
THERE'S *ALUCARD* AND THE *GIRL*.
!!
WHAT'LL HAPPEN IF THAT LOT AND SECTION XIII'S FATHER ANDERSON BUMP HEADS?!
A RIGHT BAD SCENE.

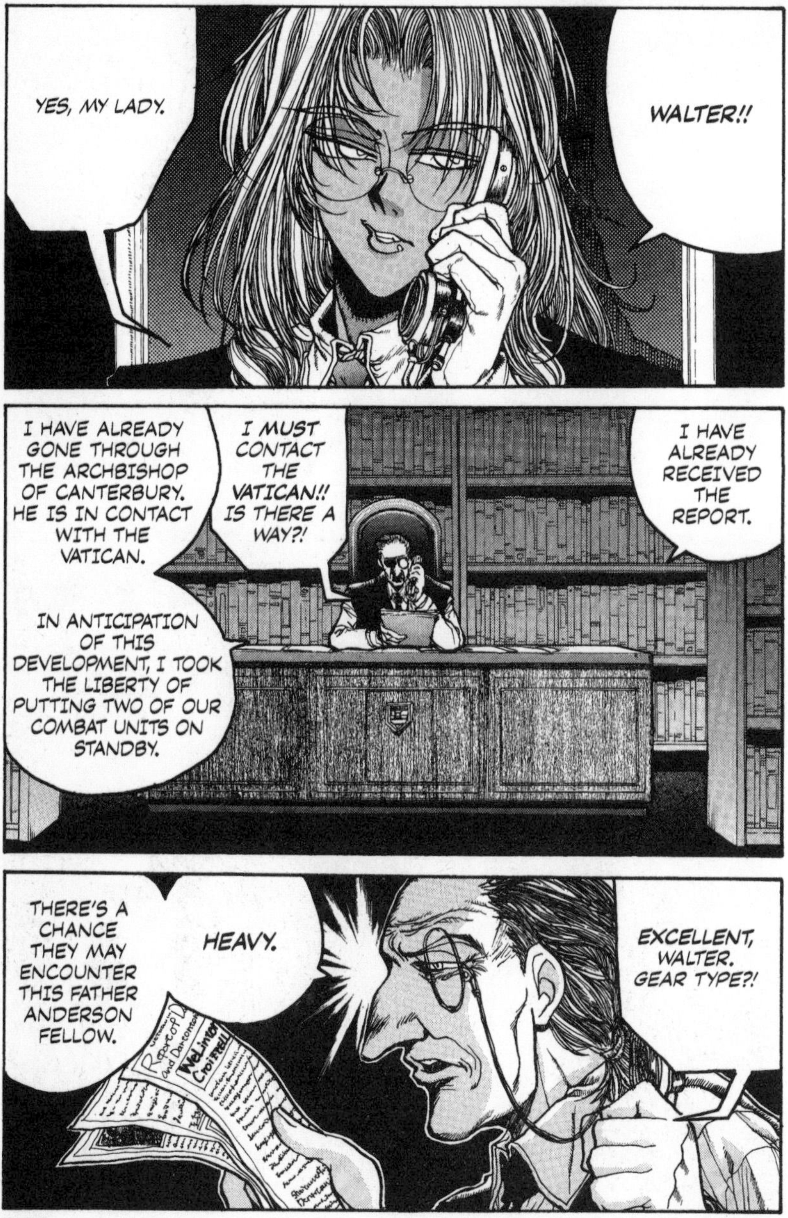
WALTER!!
YES, MY LADY.
I HAVE ALREADY RECEIVED THE REPORT.
I MUST CONTACT THE VATICAN!! IS THERE A WAY?!
I HAVE ALREADY GONE THROUGH THE ARCHBISHOP OF CANTERBURY. HE IS IN CONTACT WITH THE VATICAN.
IN ANTICIPATION OF THIS DEVELOPMENT, I TOOK THE LIBERTY OF PUTTING TWO OF OUR COMBAT UNITS ON STANDBY.
EXCELLENT, WALTER. GEAR TYPE?!
HEAVY.
THERE'S A CHANCE THEY MAY ENCOUNTER THIS FATHER ANDERSON FELLOW.

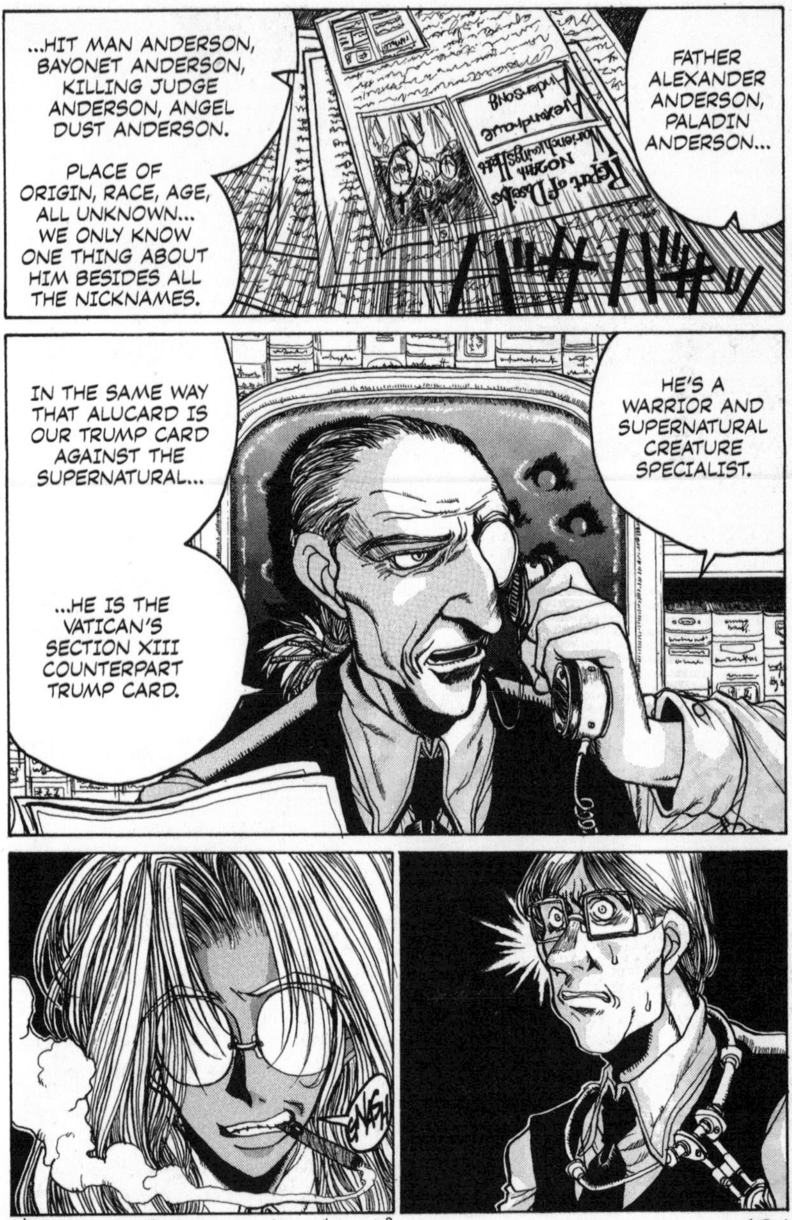
FATHER ALEXANDER ANDERSON, PALADIN ANDERSON...
...HIT MAN ANDERSON, BAYONET ANDERSON, KILLING JUDGE ANDERSON, ANGEL DUST ANDERSON.
PLACE OF ORIGIN, RACE, AGE, ALL UNKNOWN... WE ONLY KNOW ONE THING ABOUT HIM BESIDES ALL THE NICKNAMES.
バサバサッ
HE'S A WARRIOR AND SUPERNATURAL CREATURE SPECIALIST.
IN THE SAME WAY THAT ALUCARD IS OUR TRUMP CARD AGAINST THE SUPERNATURAL...
...HE IS THE VATICAN'S SECTION XIII COUNTERPART TRUMP CARD.
GNASH

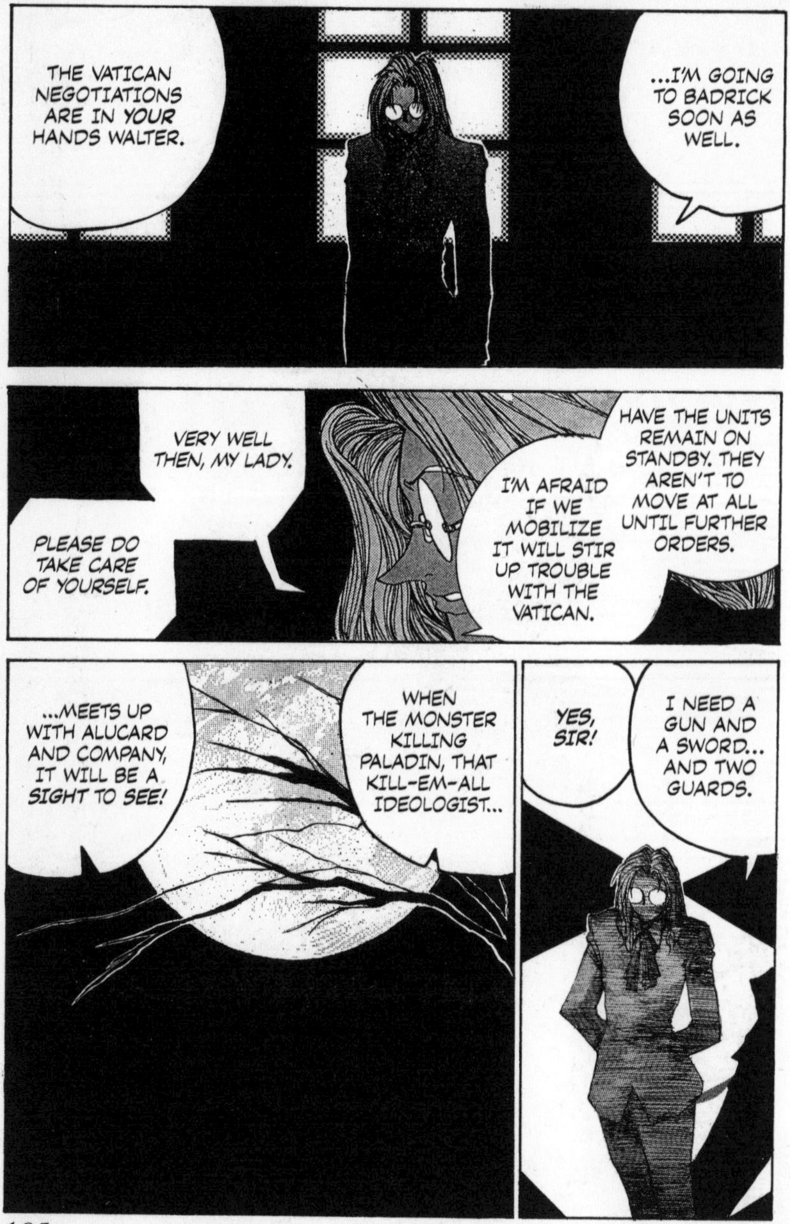
...I'M GOING TO BADRICK SOON AS WELL.
THE VATICAN NEGOTIATIONS ARE IN YOUR HANDS WALTER.
HAVE THE UNITS REMAIN ON STANDBY. THEY AREN'T TO MOVE AT ALL UNTIL FURTHER ORDERS.
I'M AFRAID IF WE MOBILIZE IT WILL STIR UP TROUBLE WITH THE VATICAN.
VERY WELL THEN, MY LADY.
PLEASE DO TAKE CARE OF YOURSELF.
I NEED A GUN AND A SWORD... AND TWO GUARDS.
YES, SIR!
WHEN THE MONSTER KILLING PALADIN, THAT KILL-EM-ALL IDEOLOGIST...
...MEETS UP WITH ALUCARD AND COMPANY, IT WILL BE A SIGHT TO SEE!

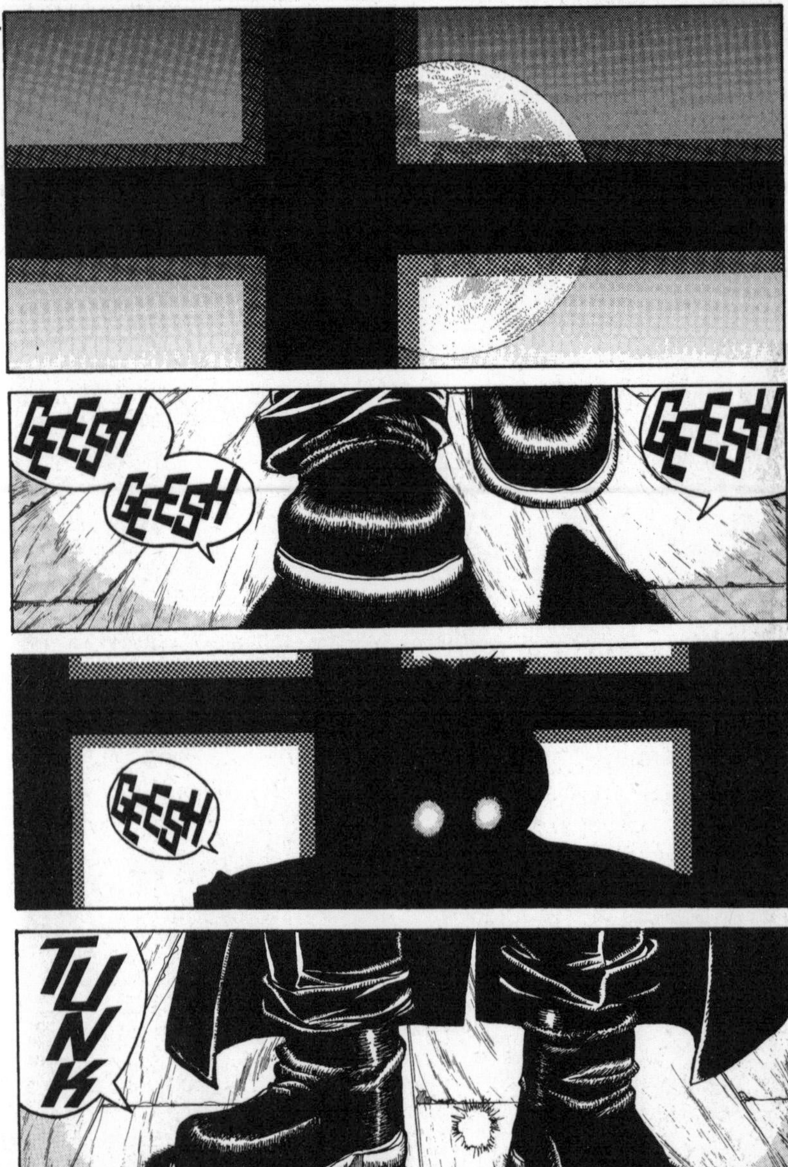
GEESH
GEESH
GEESH
GEESH
TUNK

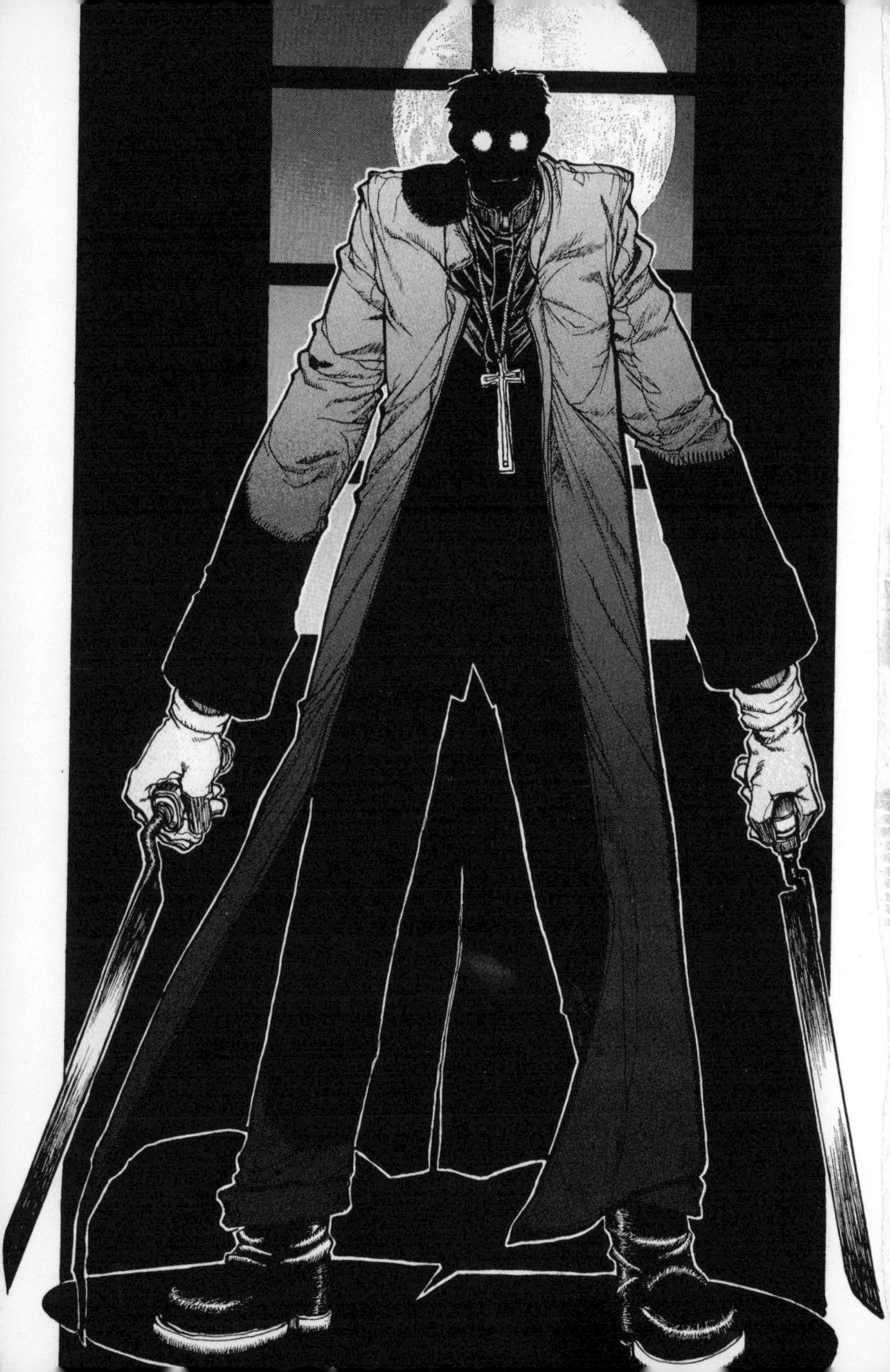

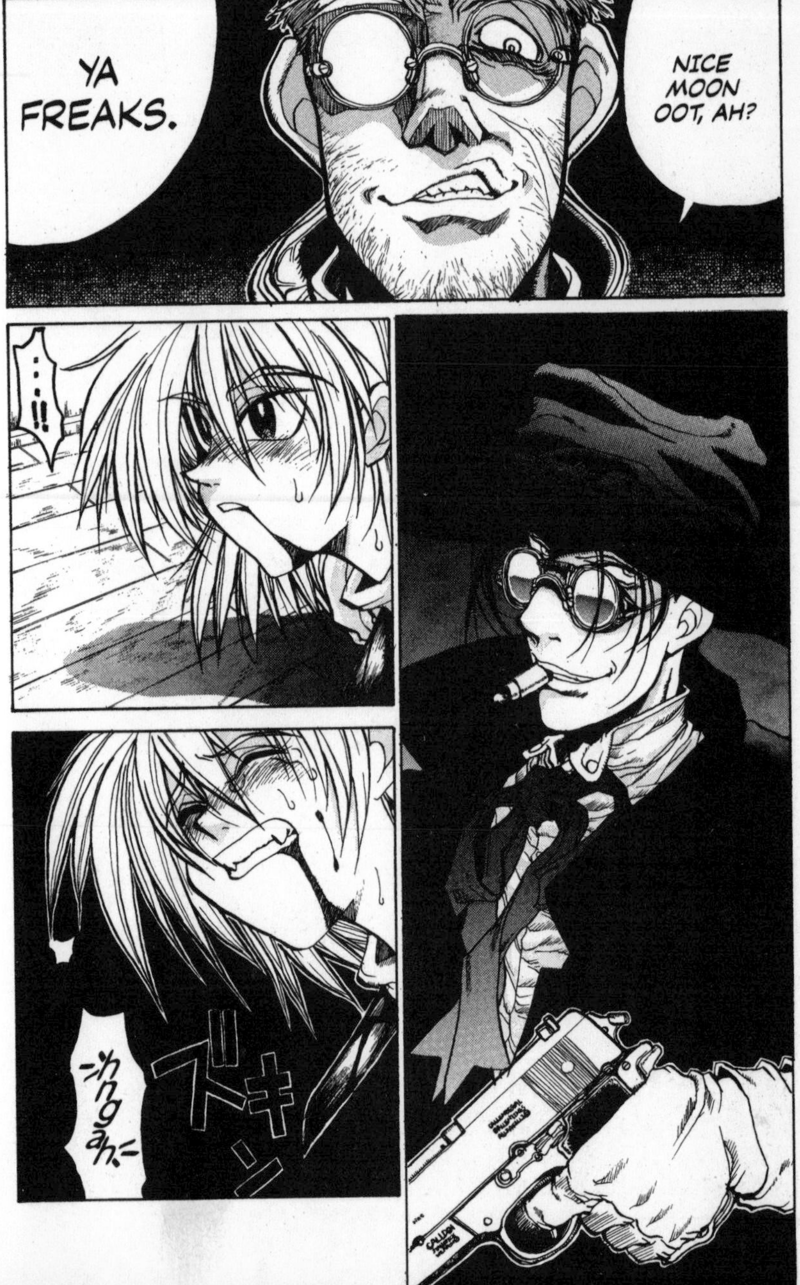
NICE MOON OOT, AH?
YA FREAKS.
...!!
ズキン
nngah

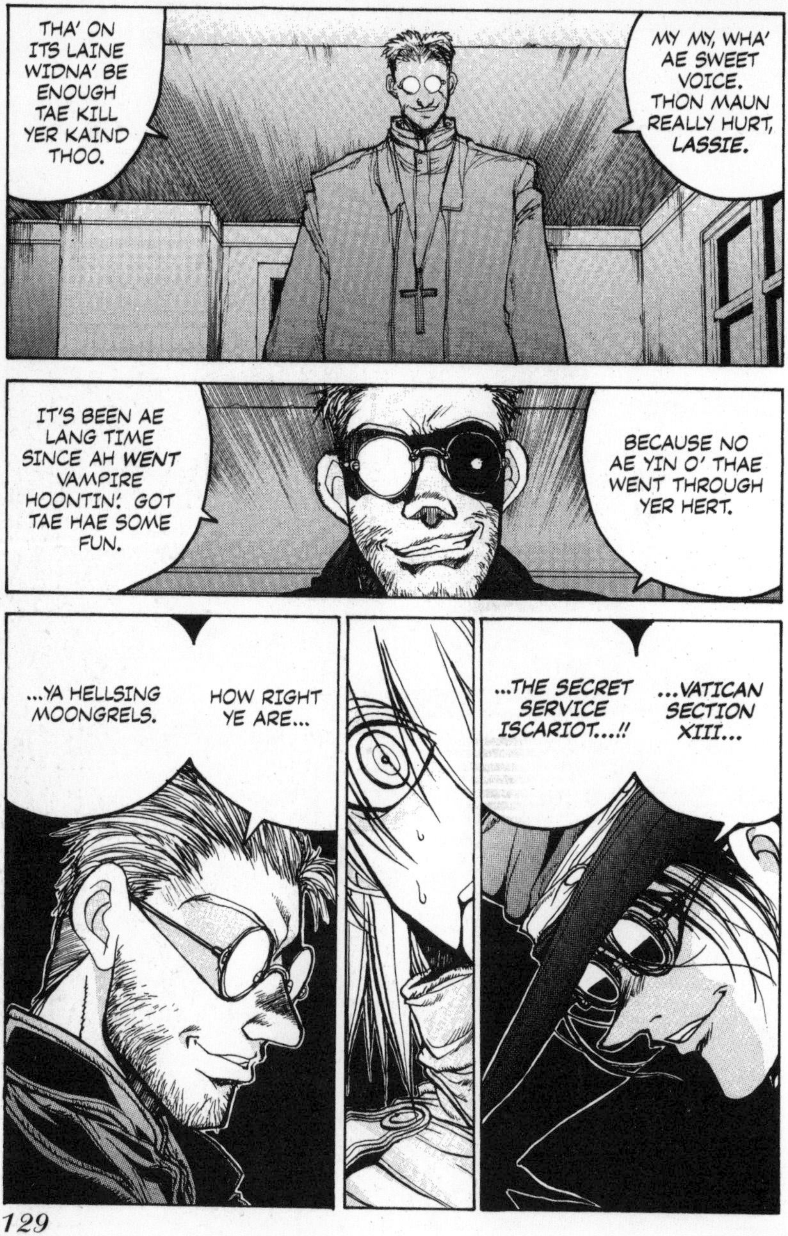

MY MY, WHA' AE SWEET VOICE. THON MAUN REALLY HURT, LASSIE.
THA' ON ITS LAINE WIDNA' BE ENOUGH TAE KILL YER KAIND THOO.
BECAUSE NO AE YIN O' THAE WENT THROUGH YER HERT.
IT'S BEEN AE LANG TIME SINCE AH WENT VAMPIRE HOONTIN'. GOT TAE HAE SOME FUN.
...VATICAN SECTION XIII...
...THE SECRET SERVICE ISCARIOT...!!
HOW RIGHT YE ARE...
...YA HELLSING MOONGRELS.

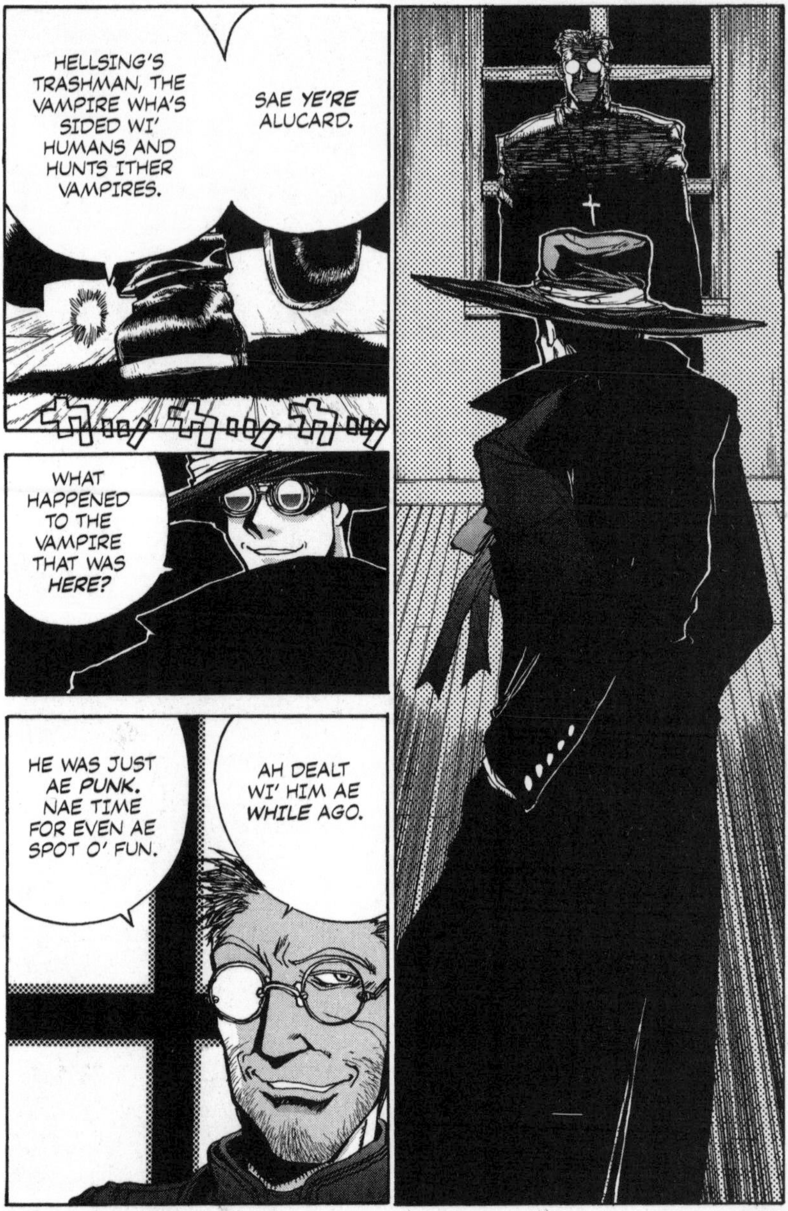
SAE *YE'RE* ALUCARD.
HELLSING'S TRASHMAN, THE VAMPIRE WHA'S SIDED WI' HUMANS AND HUNTS ITHER VAMPIRES.
WHAT HAPPENED TO THE VAMPIRE THAT WAS *HERE?*
AH DEALT WI' HIM AE *WHILE AGO.*
HE WAS JUST AE *PUNK.* NAE TIME FOR EVEN AE SPOT O' FUN.

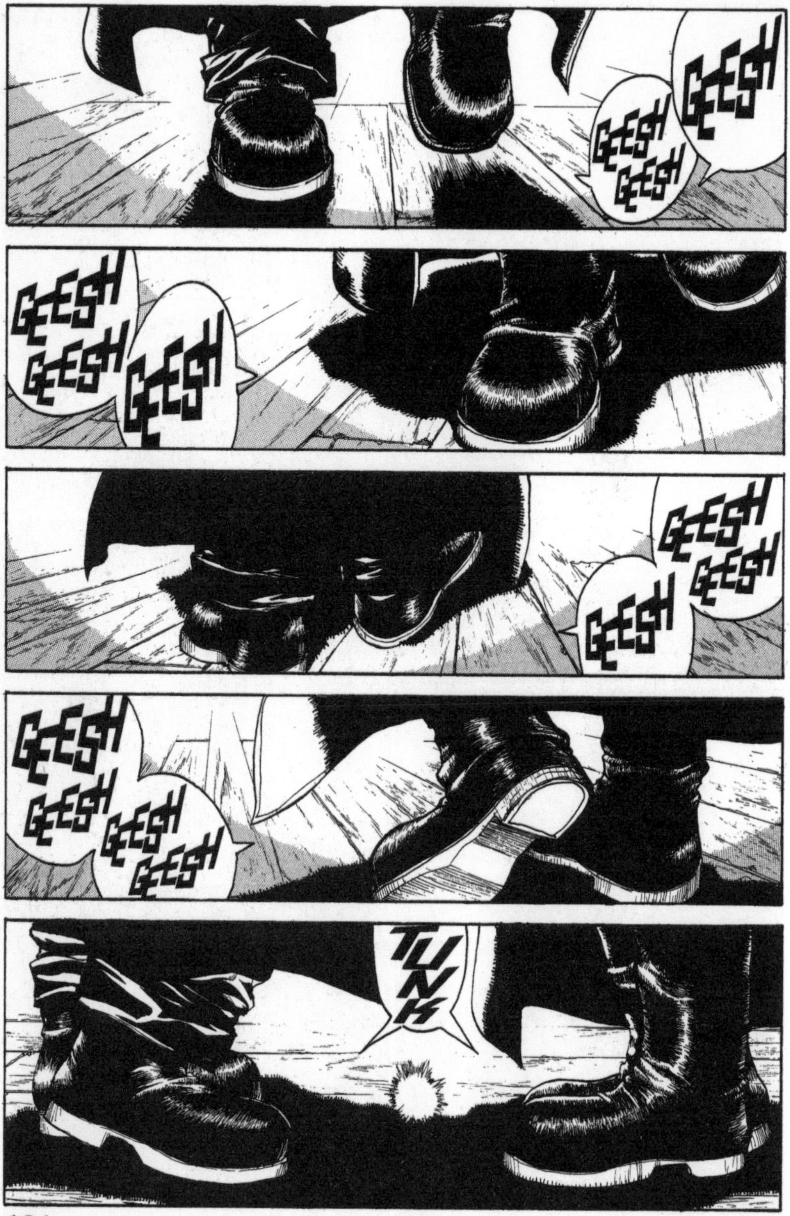
GEESH
GEESH GEESH
GEESH
GEESH GEESH
GEESH GEESH
GEESH
GEESH GEESH
GEESH GEESH
TUNK

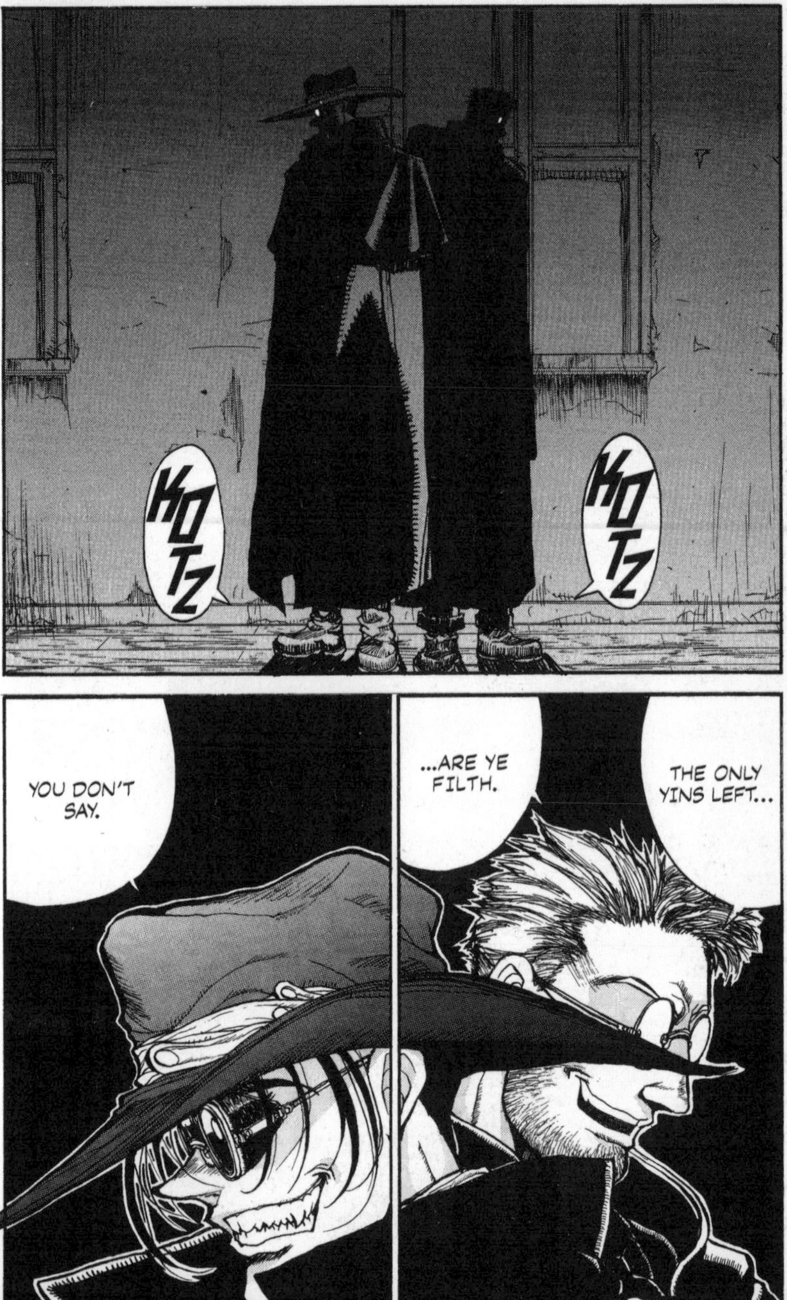
KOTZ
KOTZ
THE ONLY YINS LEFT...
...ARE YE FILTH.
YOU DON'T SAY.

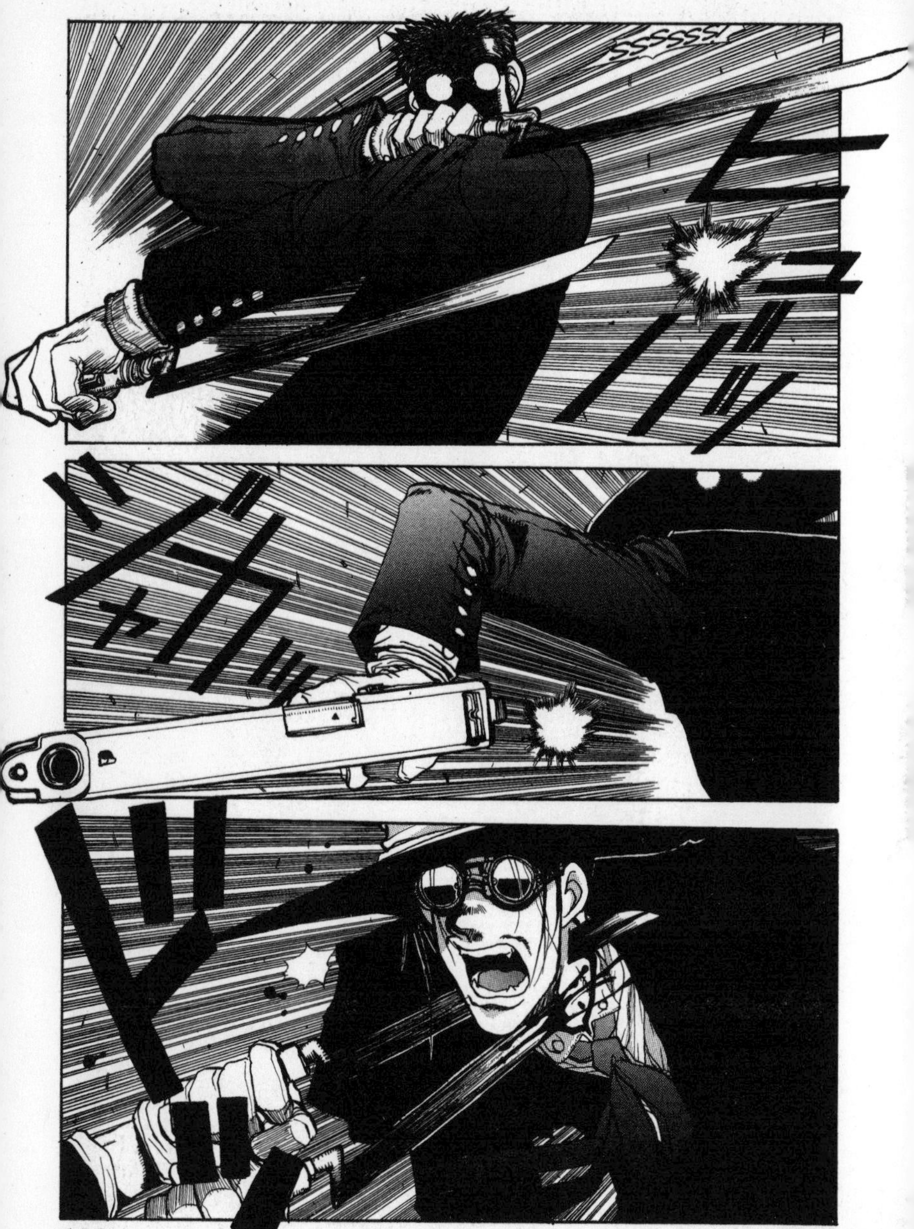
SSSSSS!

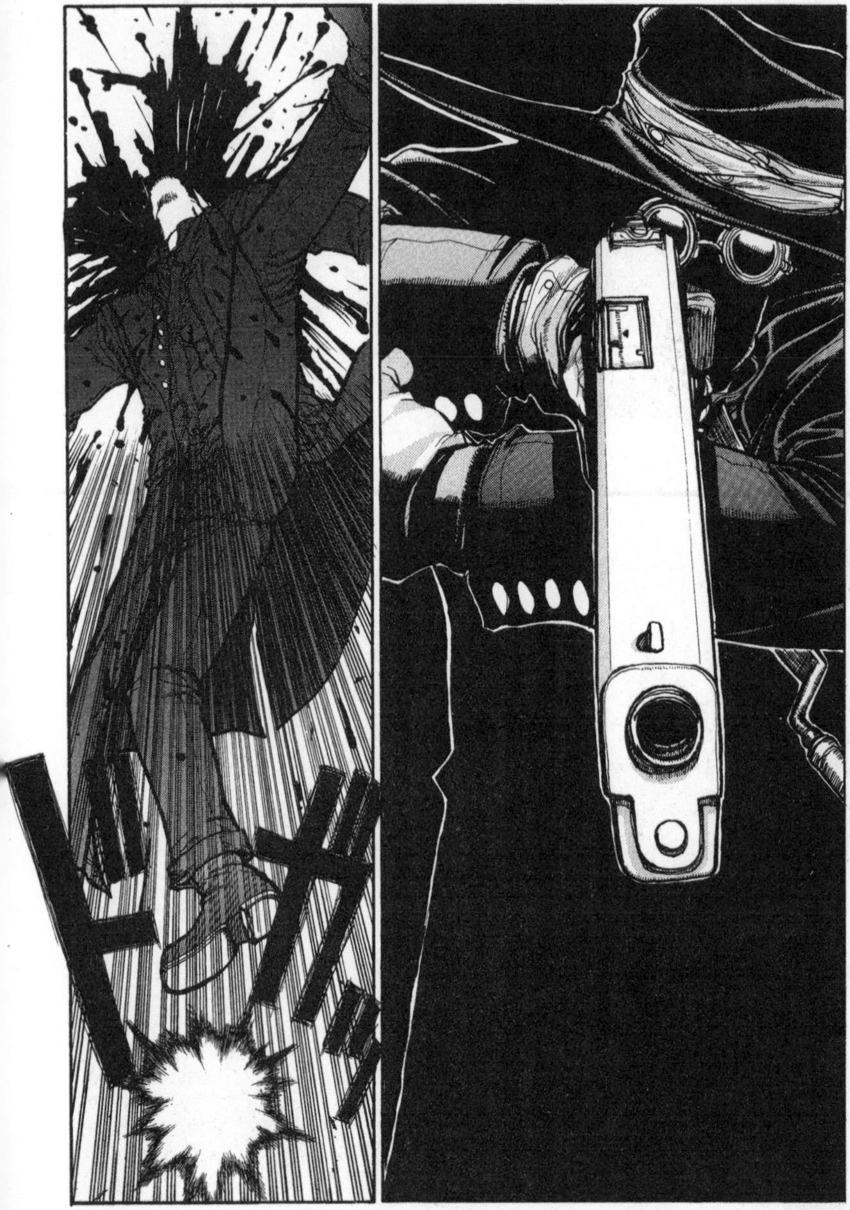

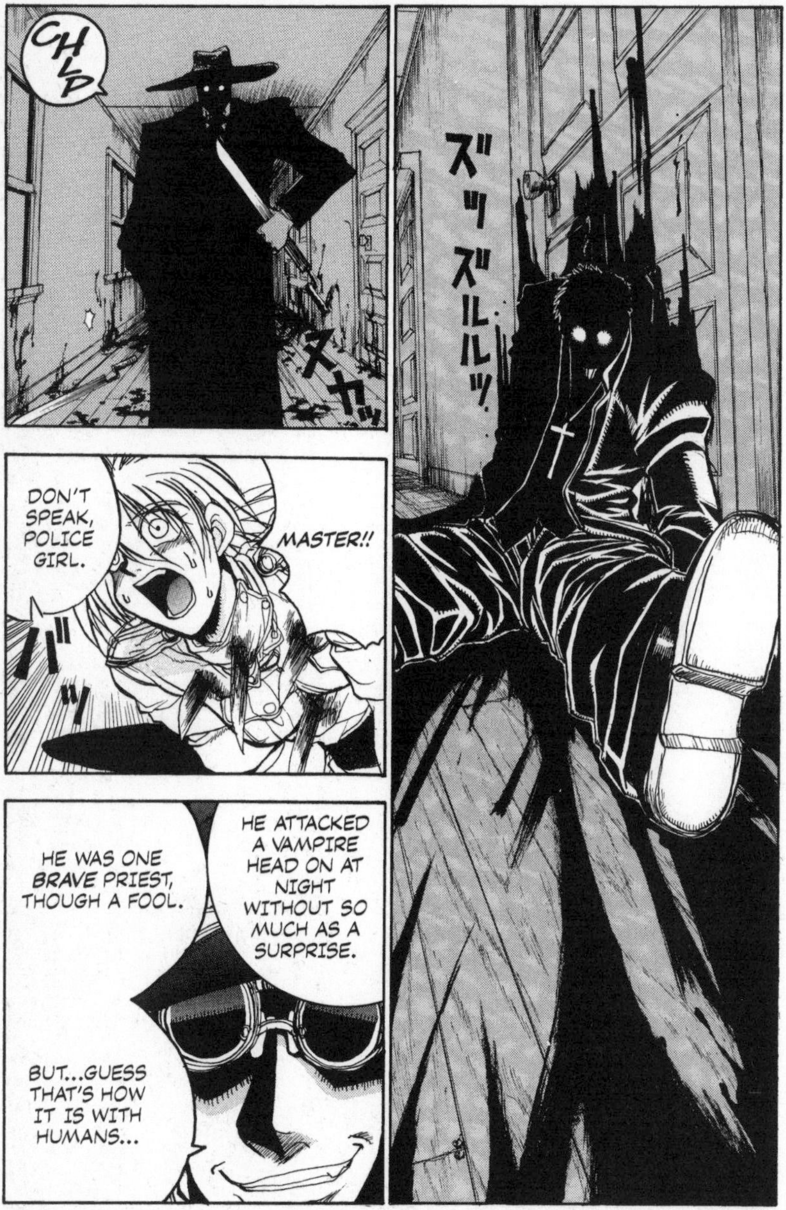

ズッ
ズルルッ
CHLP
MASTER!!
DON'T SPEAK, POLICE GIRL.
バッ
HE ATTACKED A VAMPIRE HEAD ON AT NIGHT WITHOUT SO MUCH AS A SURPRISE.
HE WAS ONE *BRAVE* PRIEST, THOUGH A FOOL.
BUT...GUESS THAT'S HOW IT IS WITH HUMANS...

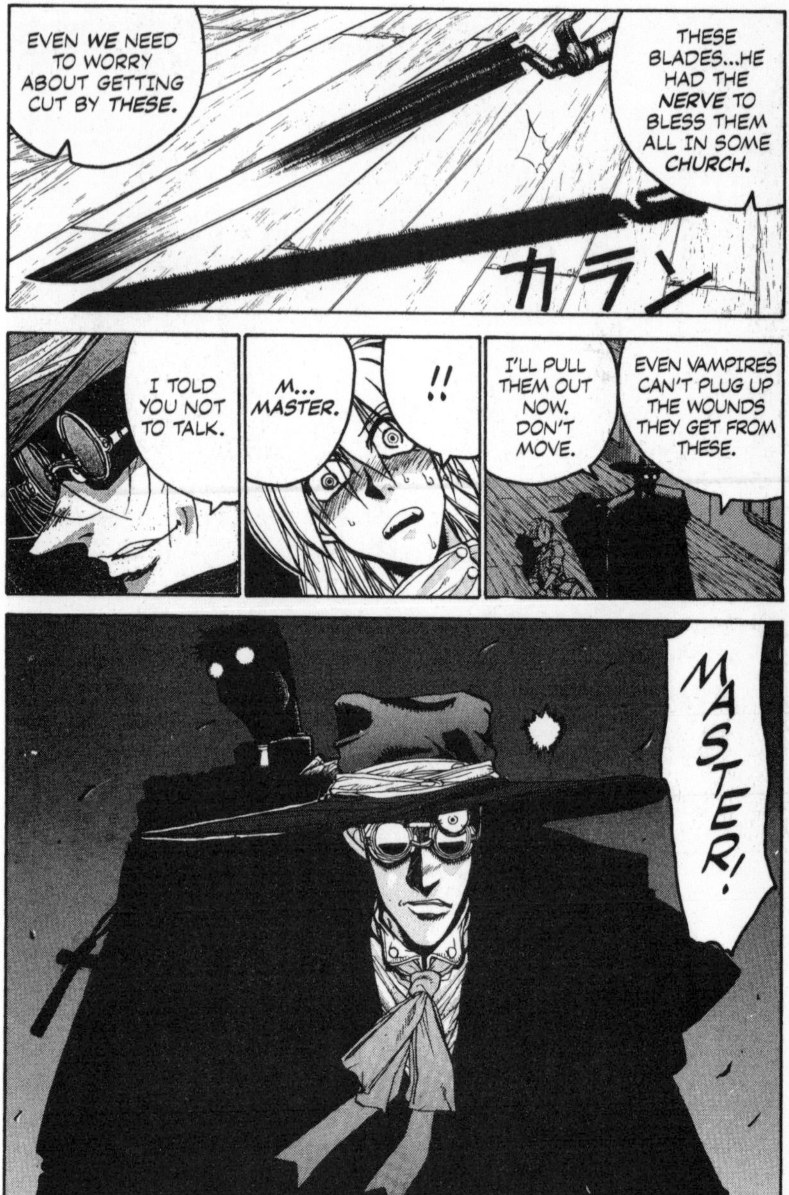

THESE BLADES...HE HAD THE NERVE TO BLESS THEM ALL IN SOME CHURCH.
EVEN WE NEED TO WORRY ABOUT GETTING CUT BY THESE.
カラン
EVEN VAMPIRES CAN'T PLUG UP THE WOUNDS THEY GET FROM THESE.
I'LL PULL THEM OUT NOW. DON'T MOVE.
!!
M... MASTER.
I TOLD YOU NOT TO TALK.
MASTER!

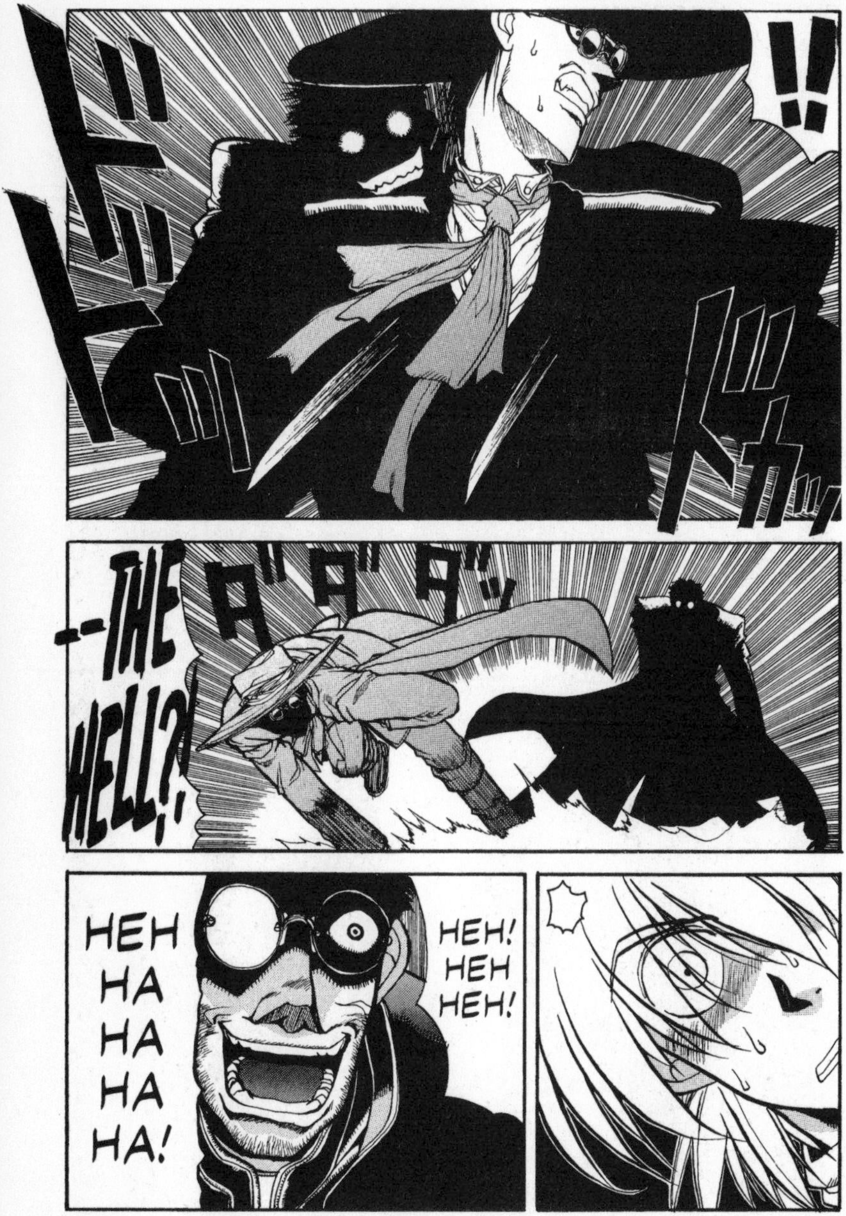
ドカッ
--THE HELL?!
HEH! HEH HEH!
HEH HA HA HA HA HA!

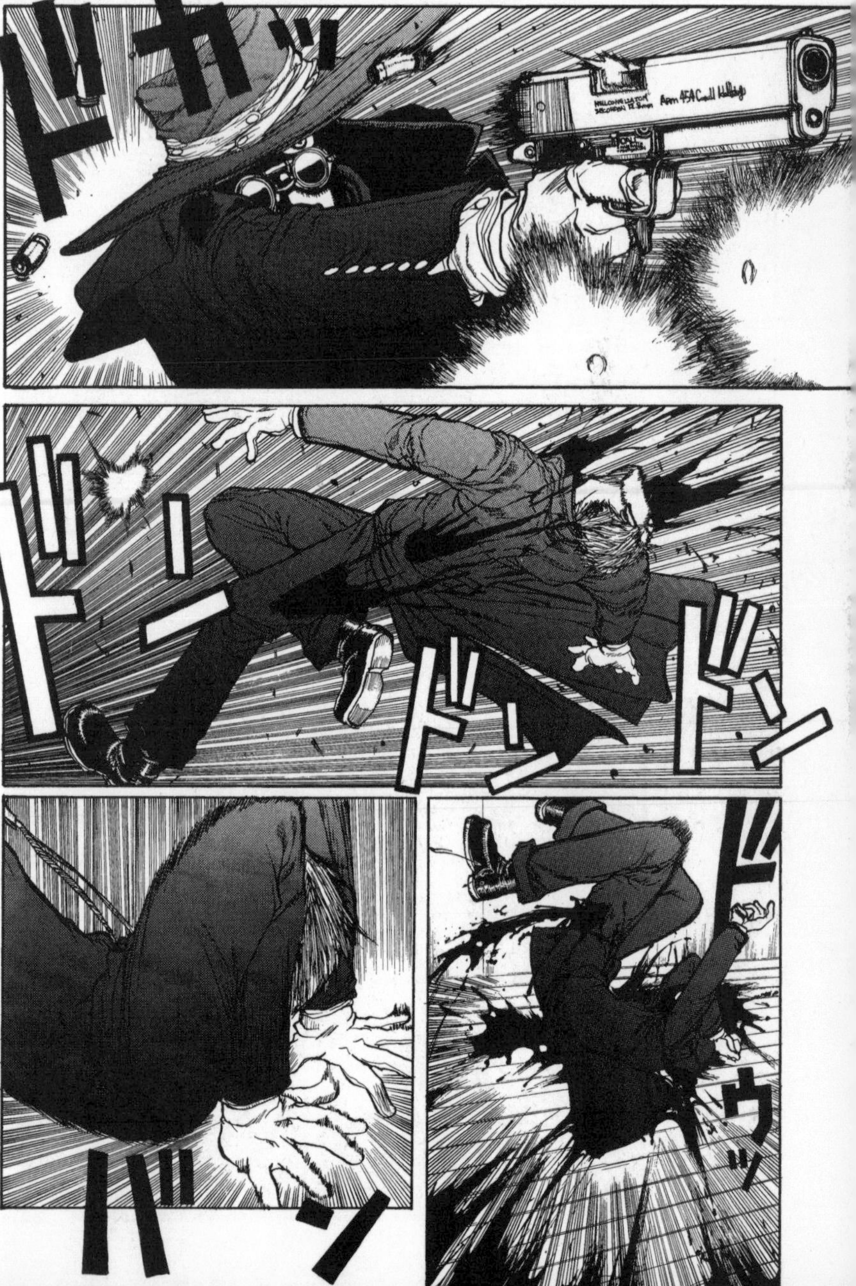
ドカッ
ドンッ
ドンッ
ドー
ド
ウッ
バッ

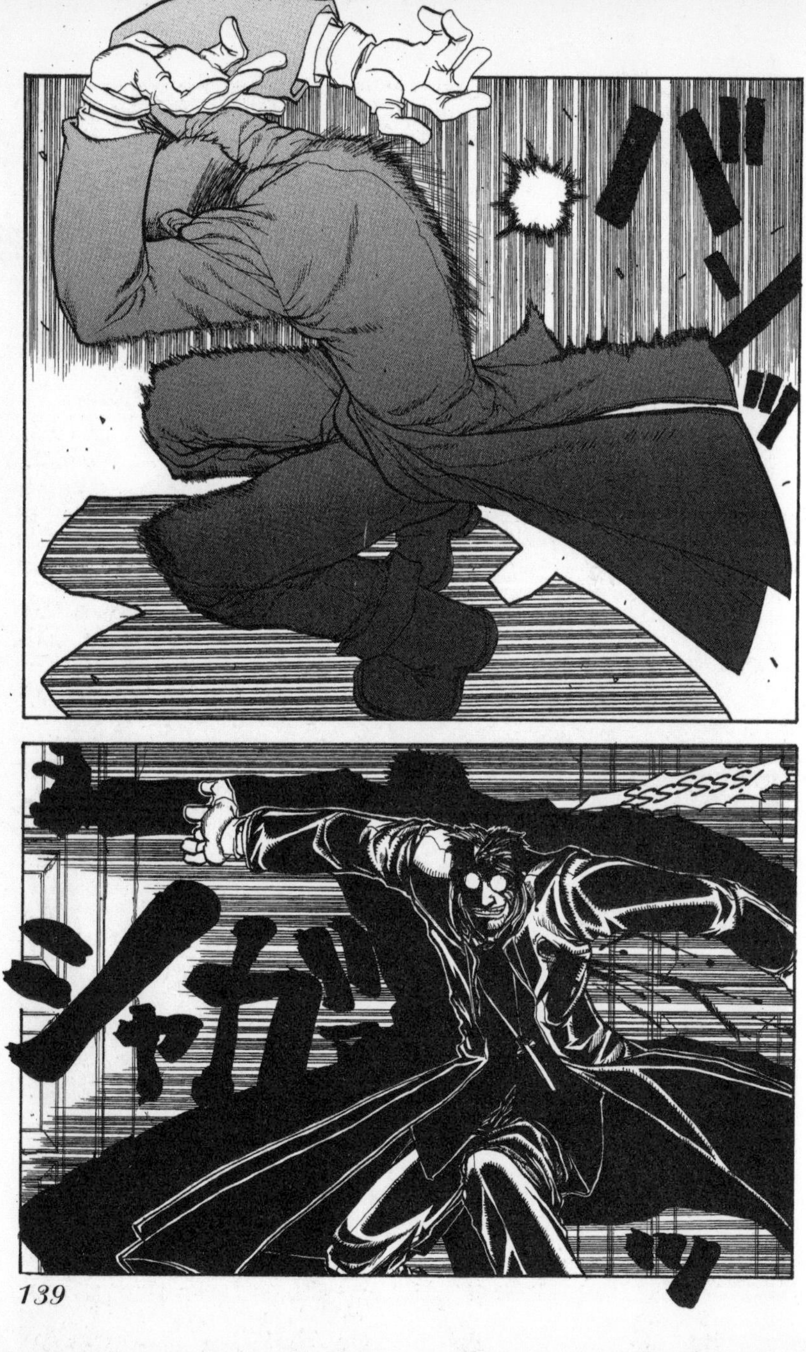
SSSSSSS!

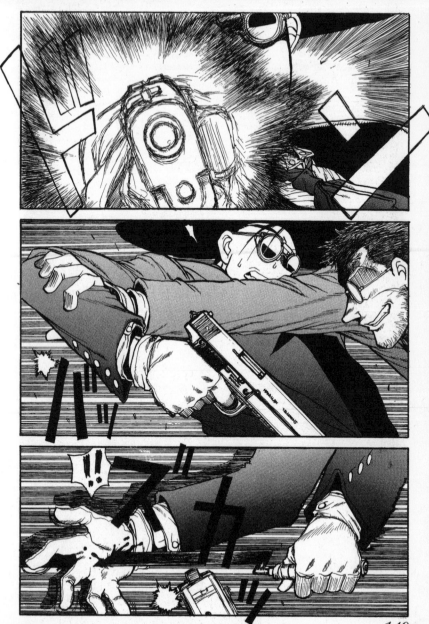

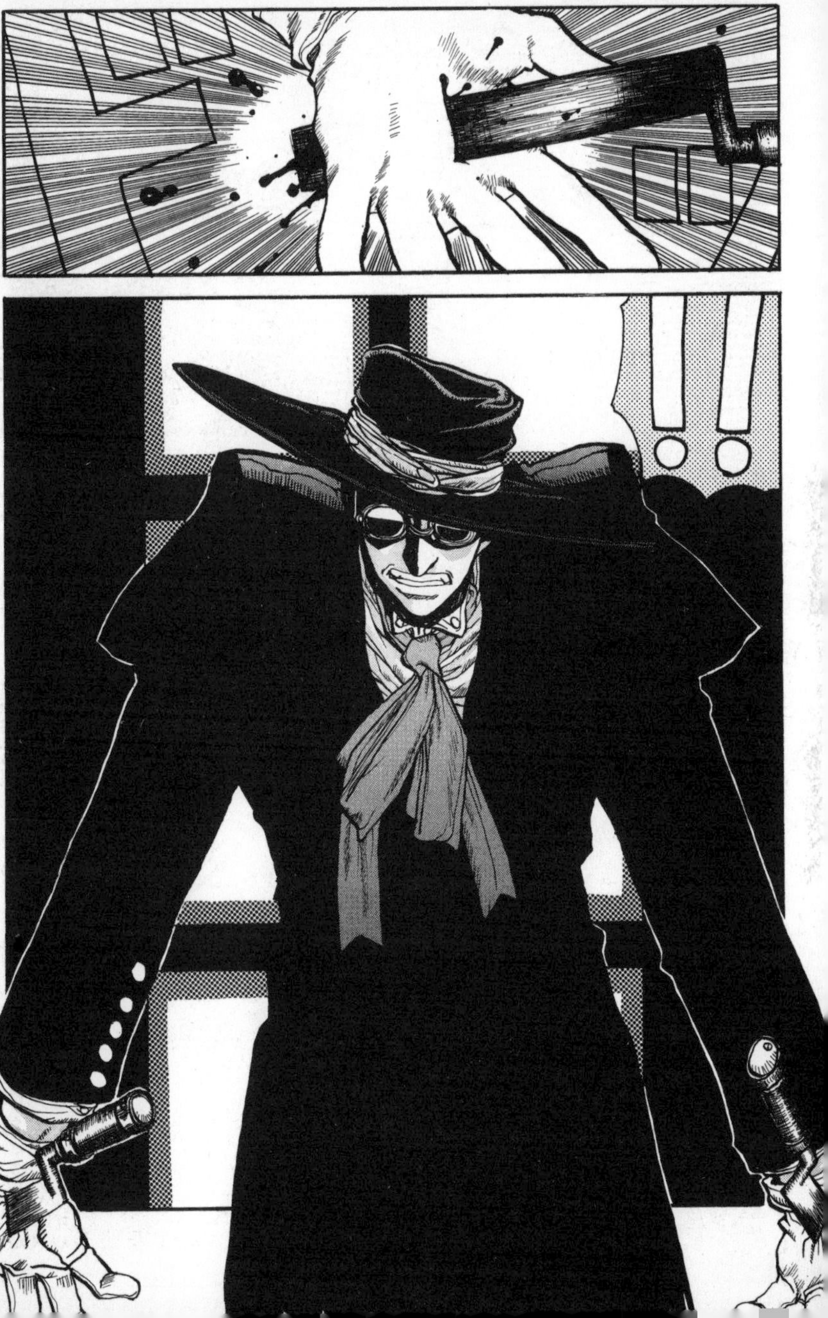
!!

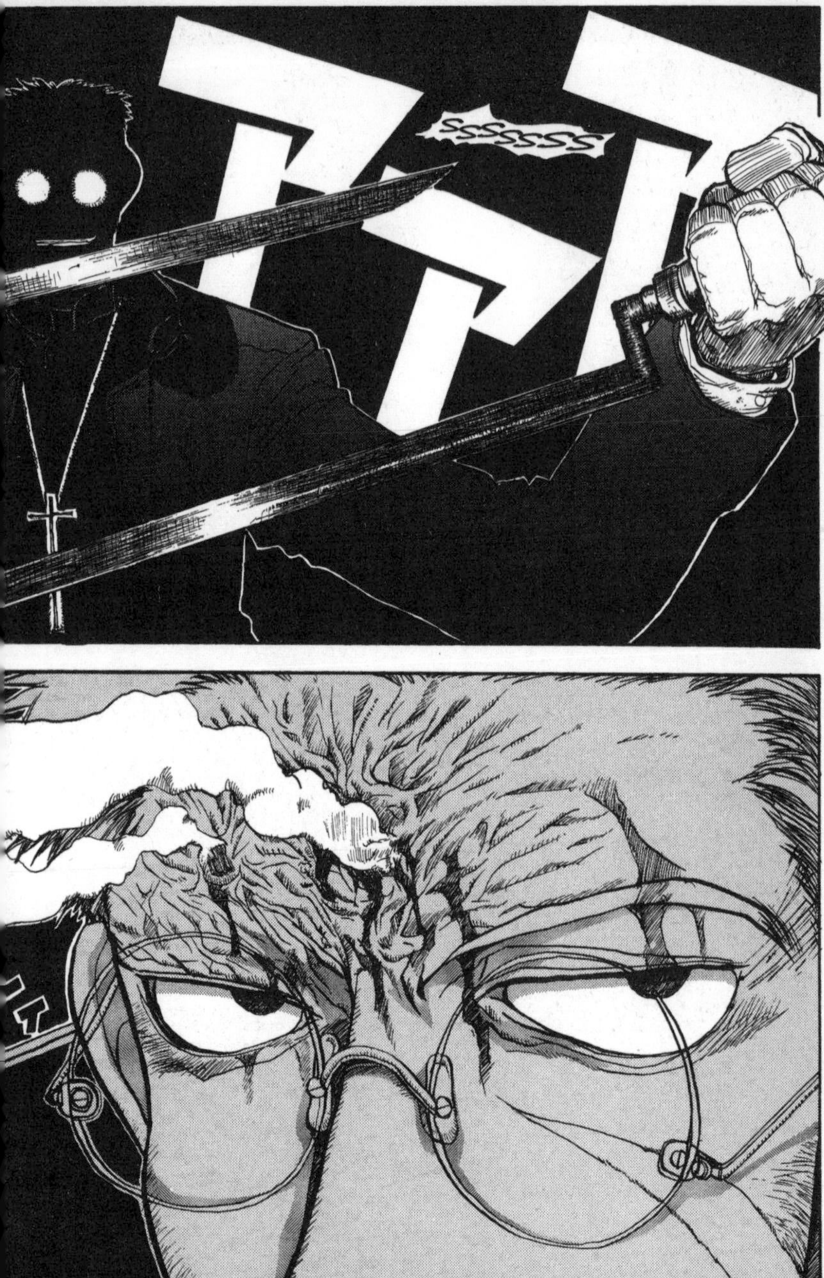
SSSSSSSS

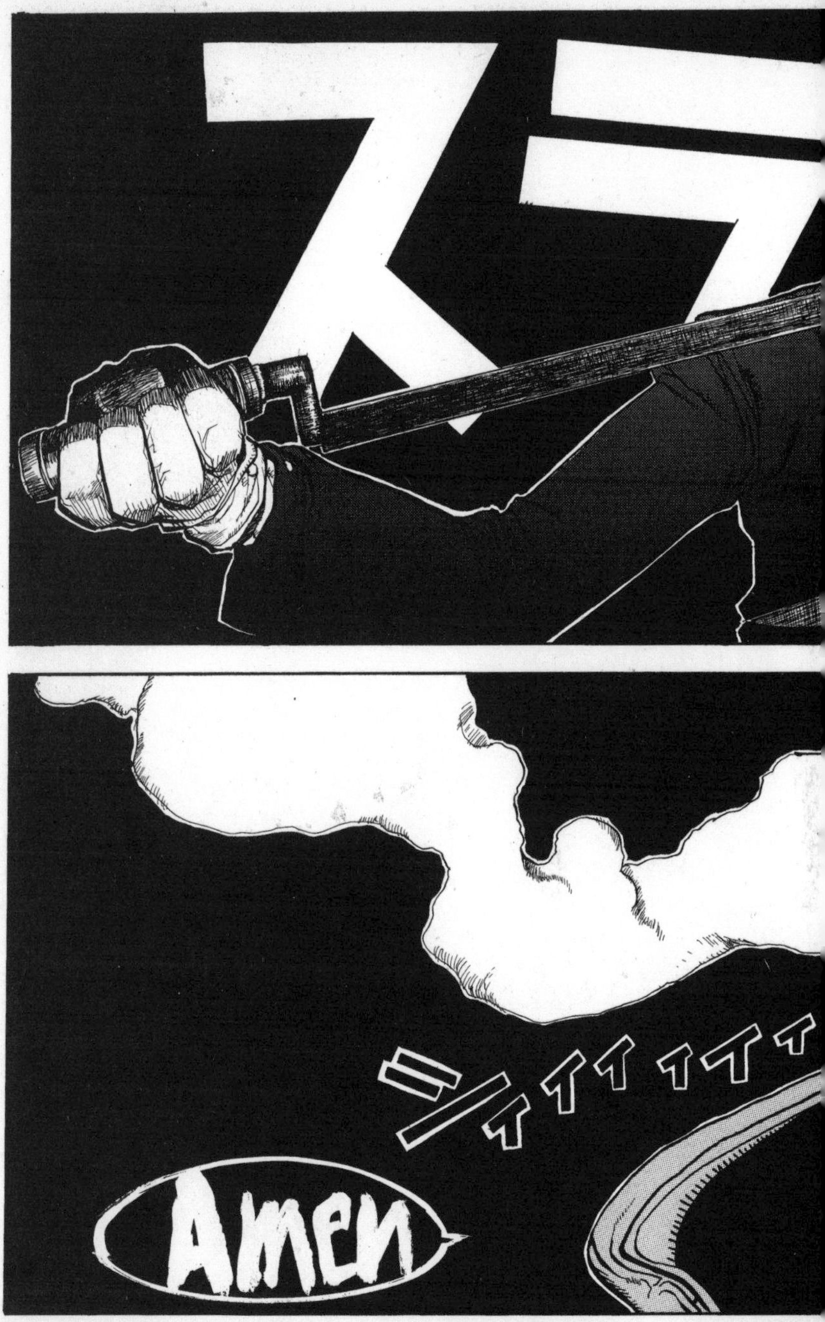
Amen

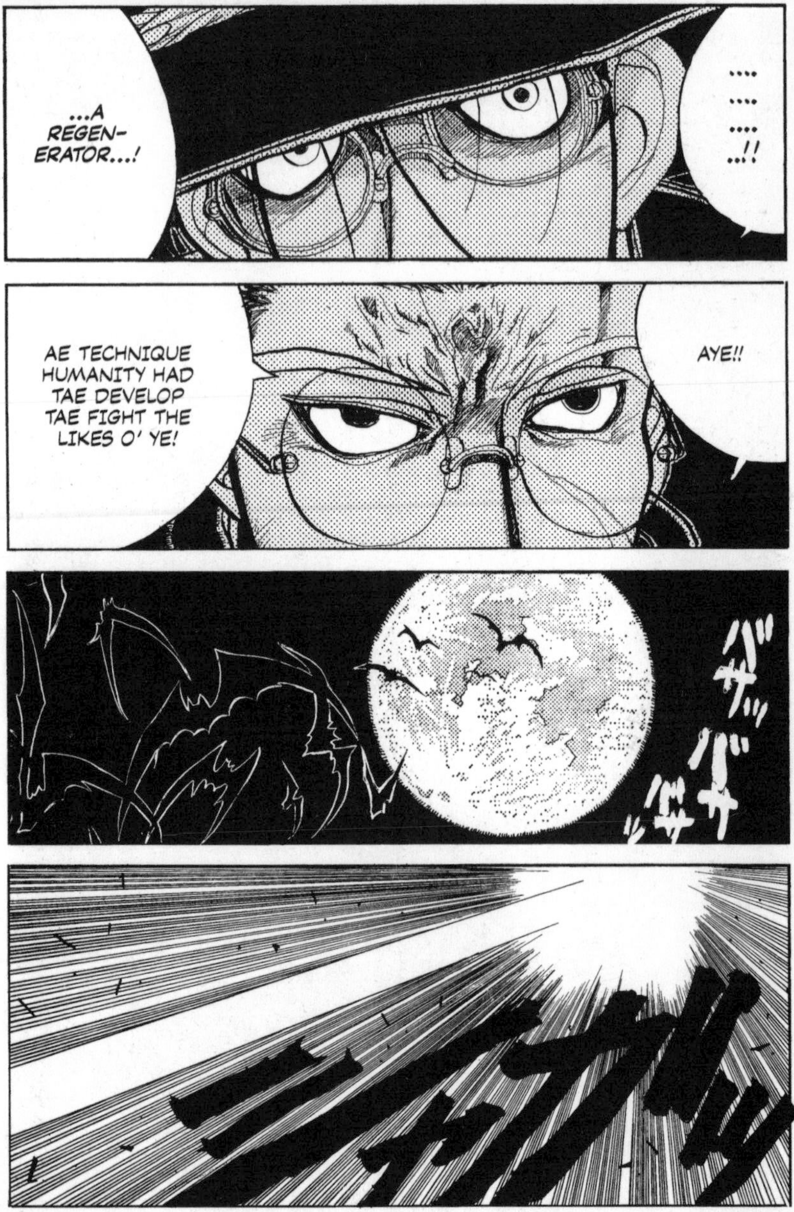
....
....
....
...!!
...A REGEN-
ERATOR...!
AYE!!
AE TECHNIQUE
HUMANITY HAD
TAE DEVELOP
TAE FIGHT THE
LIKES O' YE!

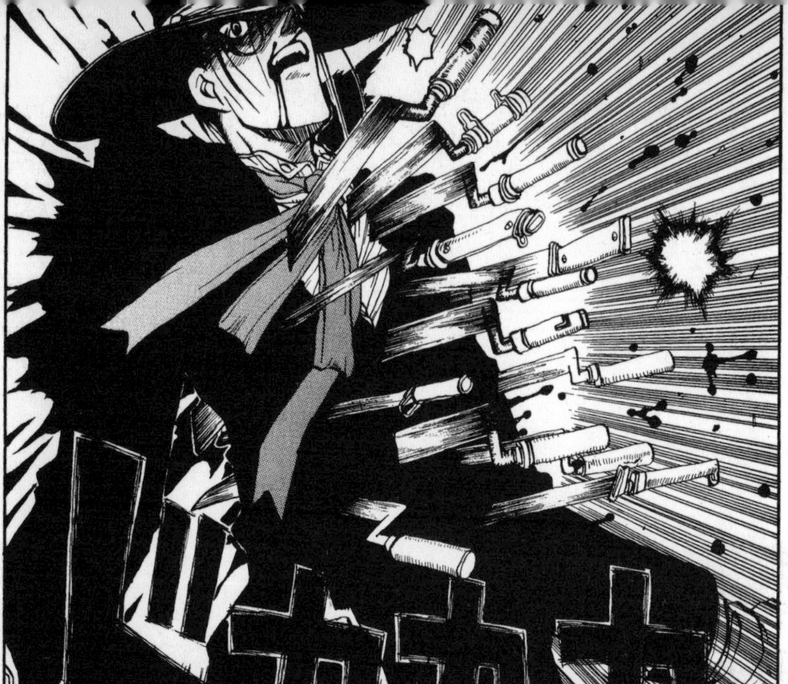

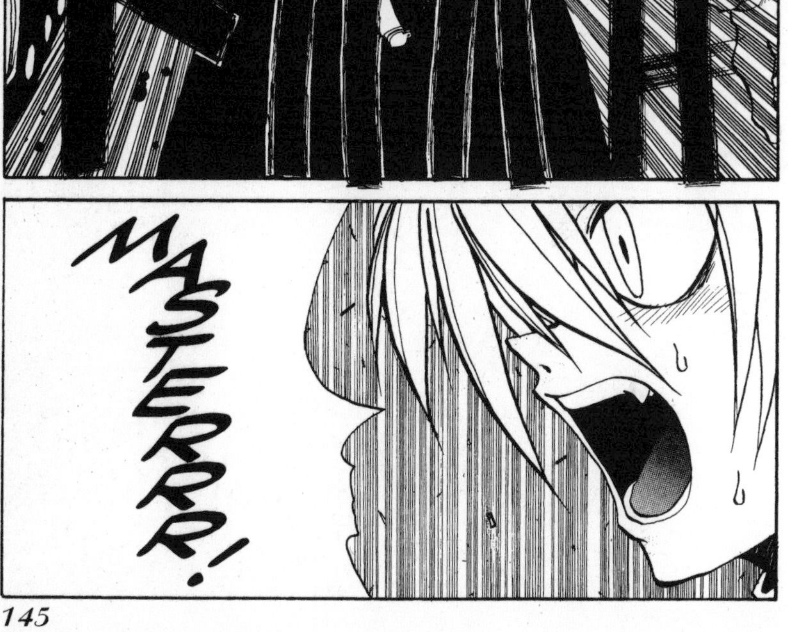
MASTERRR!

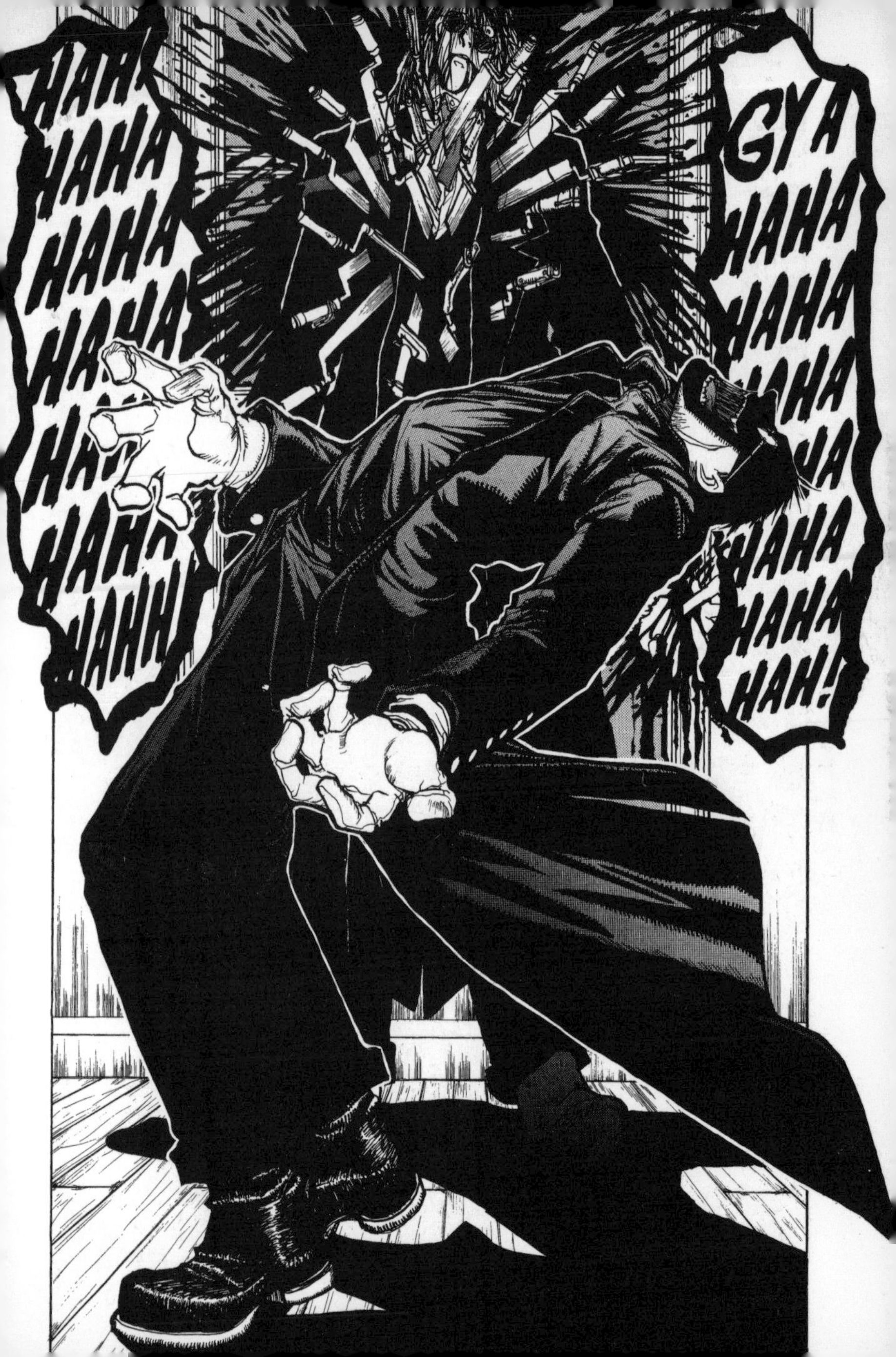
GYA HAHA HAHA HAHA HAHA HAHA HAHA HAHA HAH!
HAH HAHA HAHA HAHA HAHA HAHA HAHA HAHA HAHH!

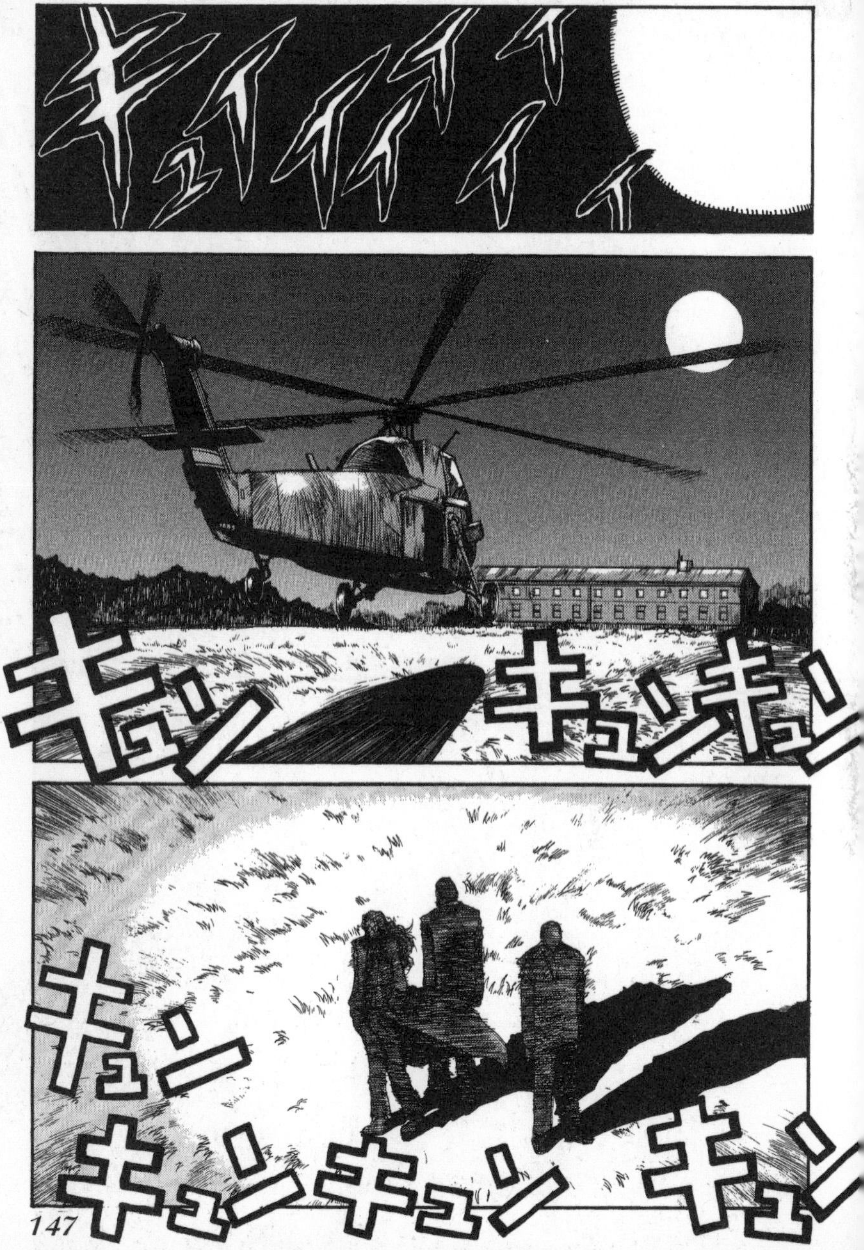
キュイイイイイイ
キュン
キュンキュン
キュン
キュンキュンキュン

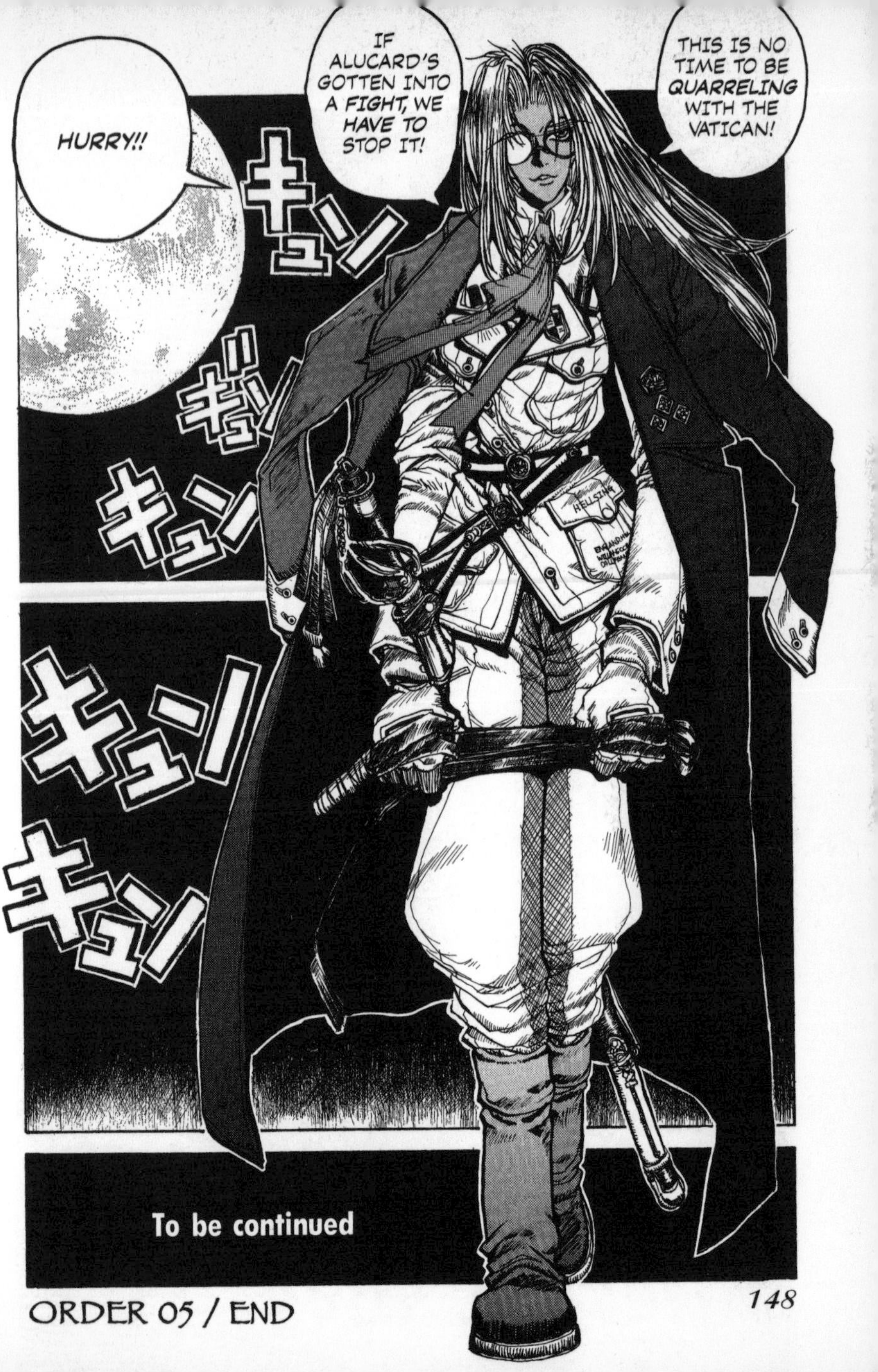
THIS IS NO TIME TO BE *QUARRELING* WITH THE VATICAN!
IF ALUCARD'S GOTTEN INTO A *FIGHT*, WE *HAVE* TO STOP IT!
HURRY!!
キュン
ギュン
キュン
キューン
キュン
To be continued

ORDER 05 / END

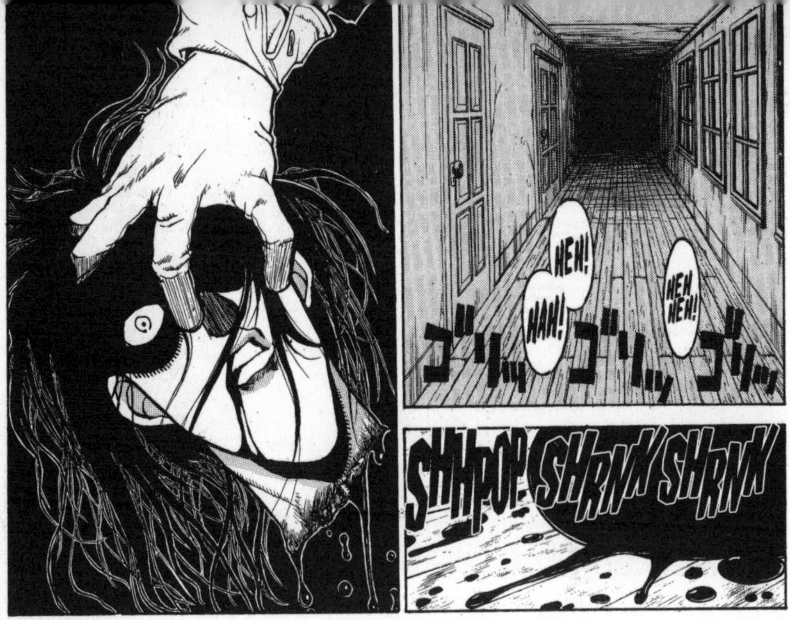
HEH HEH!
HEH! HAH!
SHHPOP SHRNK SHRNK

❧ ORDER 07

SWORD DANCER③

ソード　ダンサー

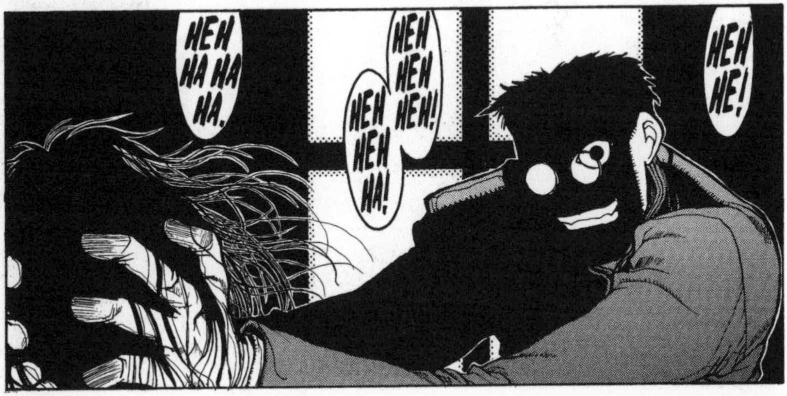
HEH HE!
HEH HEH HEH!
HEH HEH HEH HA!
HEH HA HA HA HA.

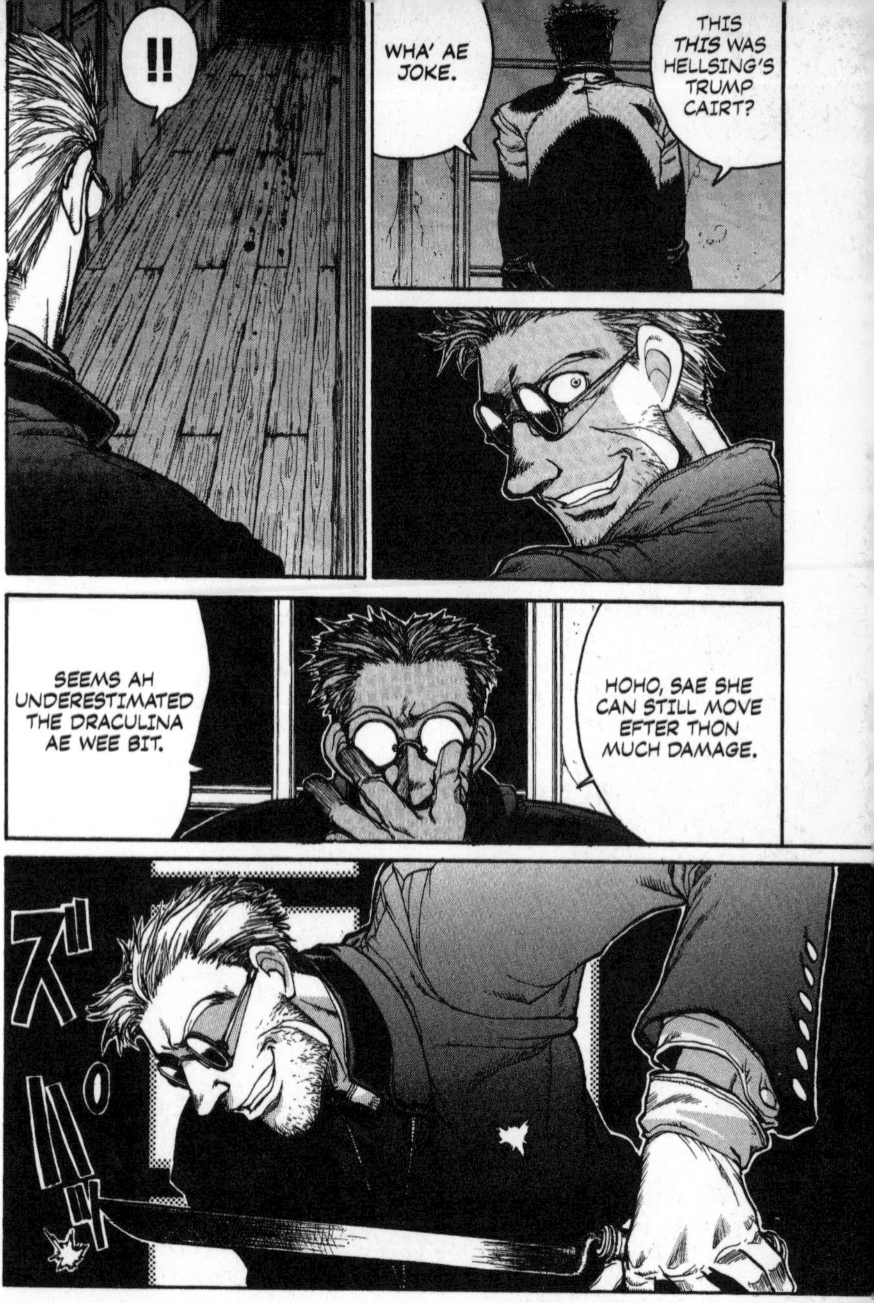
THIS THIS WAS HELLSING'S TRUMP CAIRT?
WHA' AE JOKE.
!!
HOHO, SAE SHE CAN STILL MOVE EFTER THON MUCH DAMAGE.
SEEMS AH UNDERESTIMATED THE DRACULINA AE WEE BIT.
ズパッ

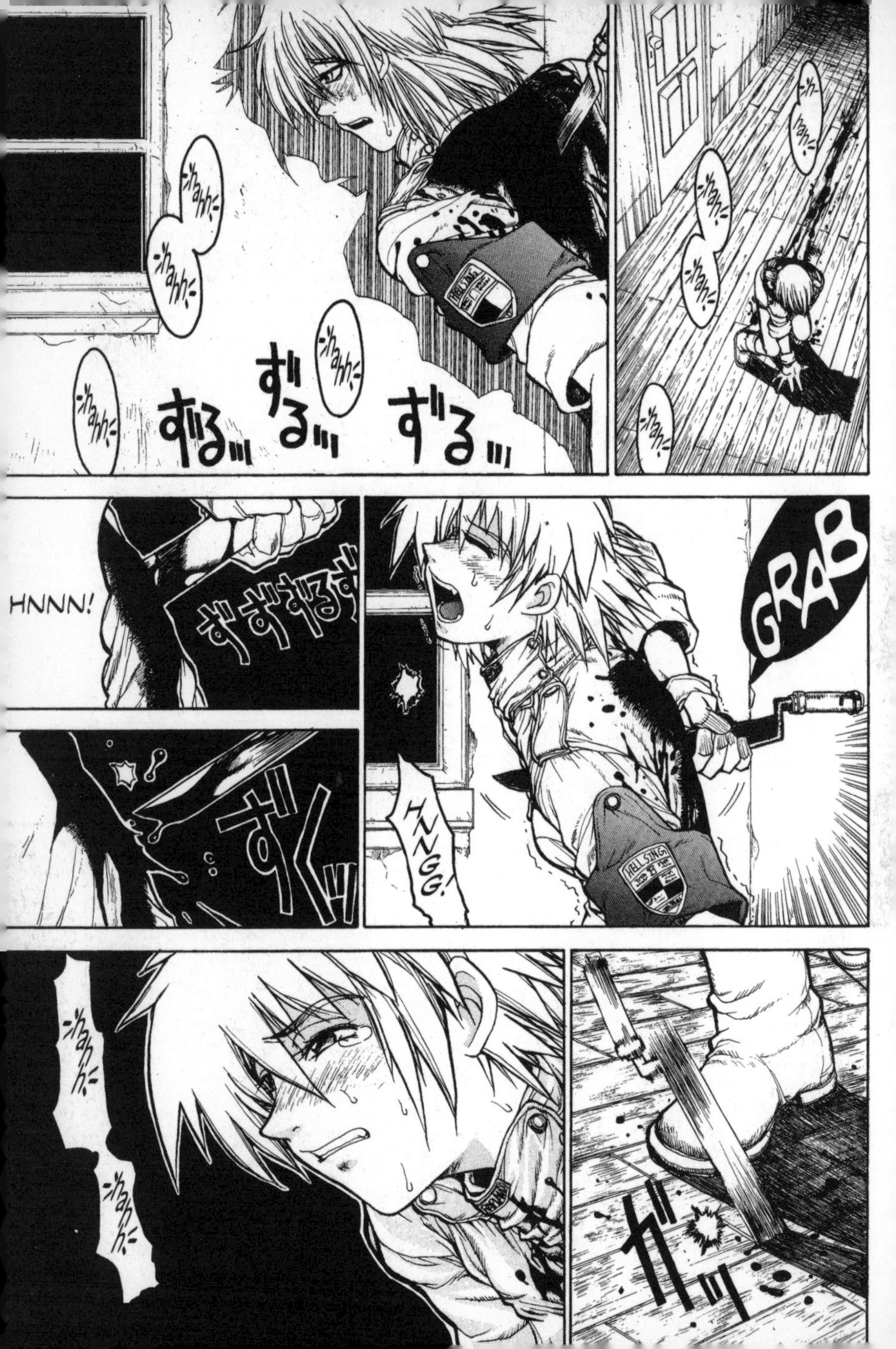

hah
hah
hah
hah
hah
hahh
hahh
hahh
hahh
ずる
ずる
ずる
GRAB
HNNGG!
HNNN!
ずずずるず
ずくッ
ガッ
hah
hah

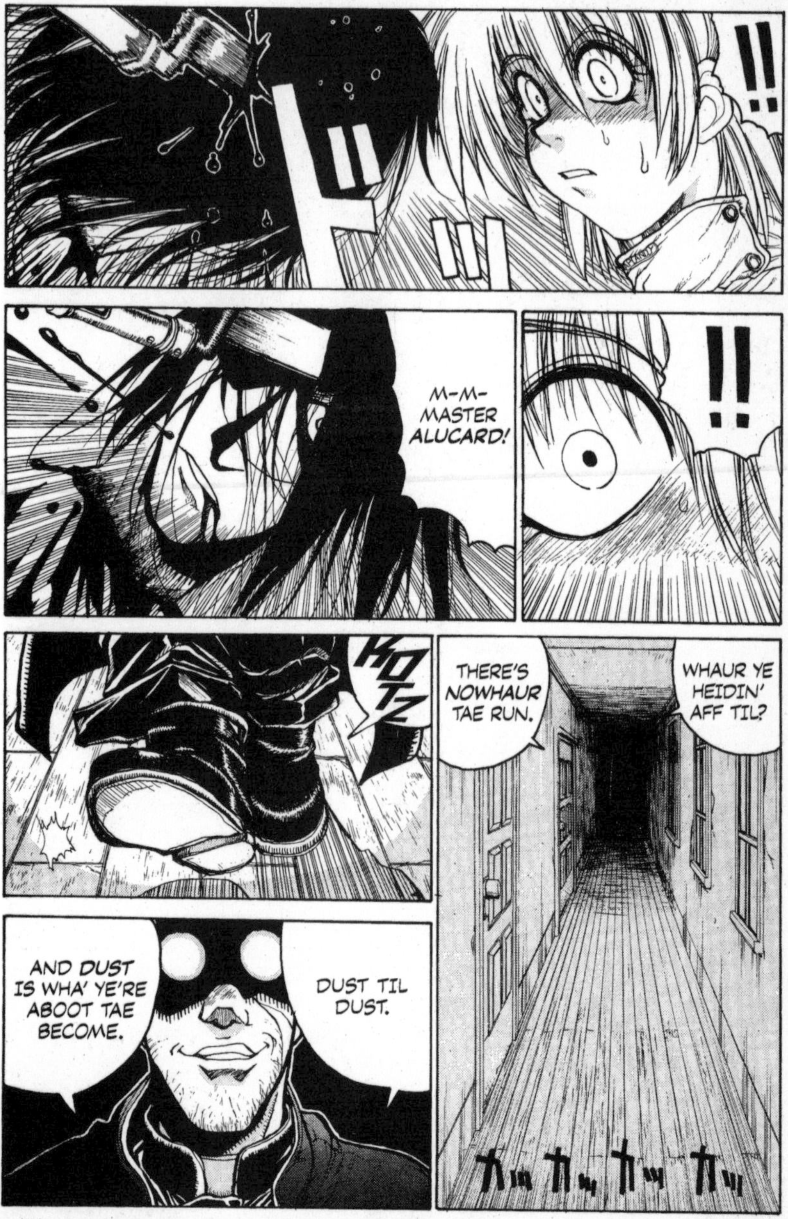
!!
!!
M-M-MASTER ALUCARD!
WHAUR YE HEIDIN' AFF TIL?
THERE'S NOWHAUR TAE RUN.
カッ カッ カッ カッ
KOTZ
DUST TIL DUST.
AND DUST IS WHA' YE'RE ABOOT TAE BECOME.

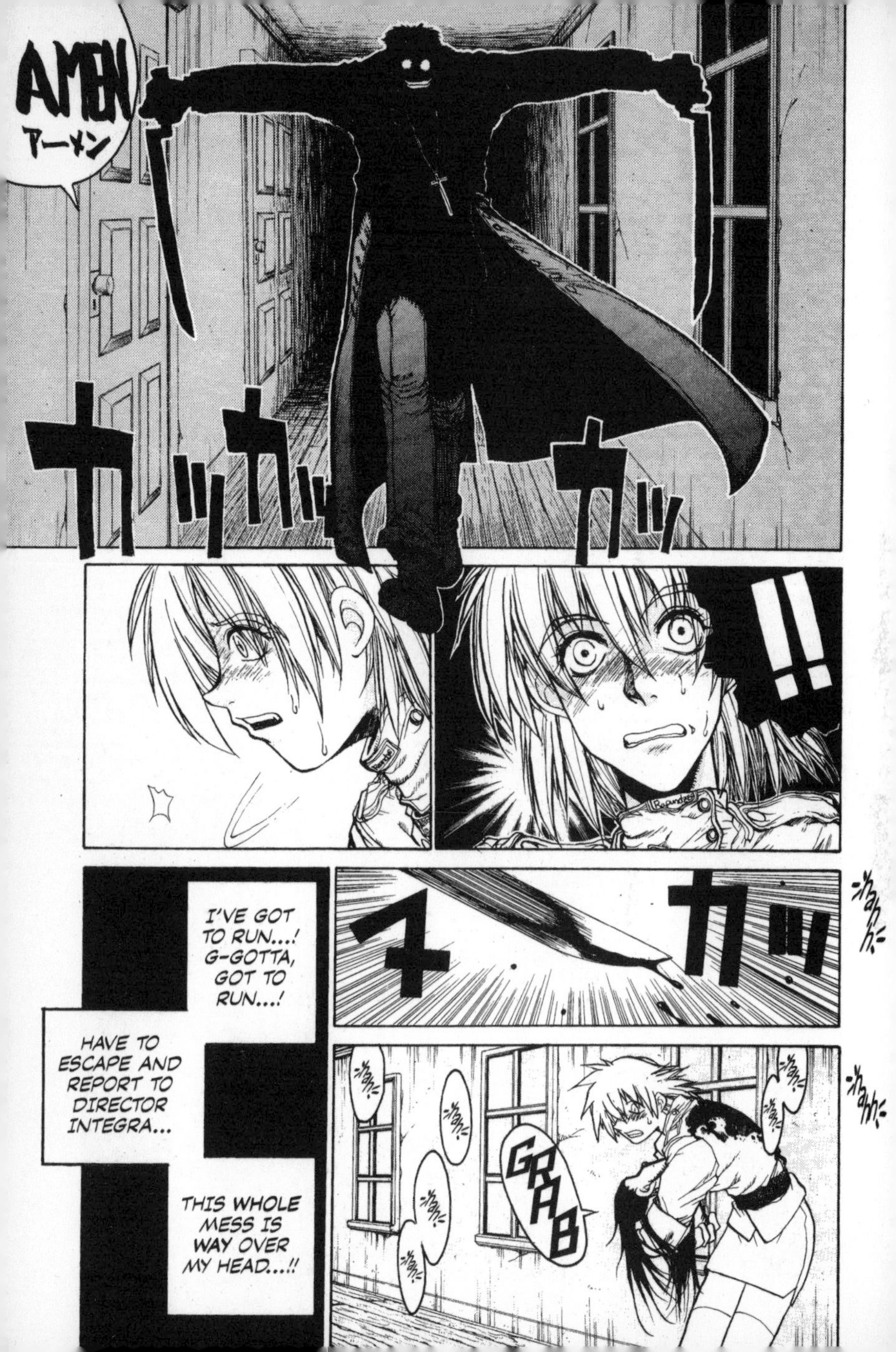
AMEN
アーメン
カッカッ
カッ
!!
-hah hah-
イカッ
-hahh-
-hah-
-hah-
-hah-
-hah-
-hah-
-hah-
GRAB
I'VE GOT TO RUN...! G-GOTTA, GOT TO RUN...!
HAVE TO ESCAPE AND REPORT TO DIRECTOR INTEGRA...
THIS WHOLE MESS IS WAY OVER MY HEAD...!!

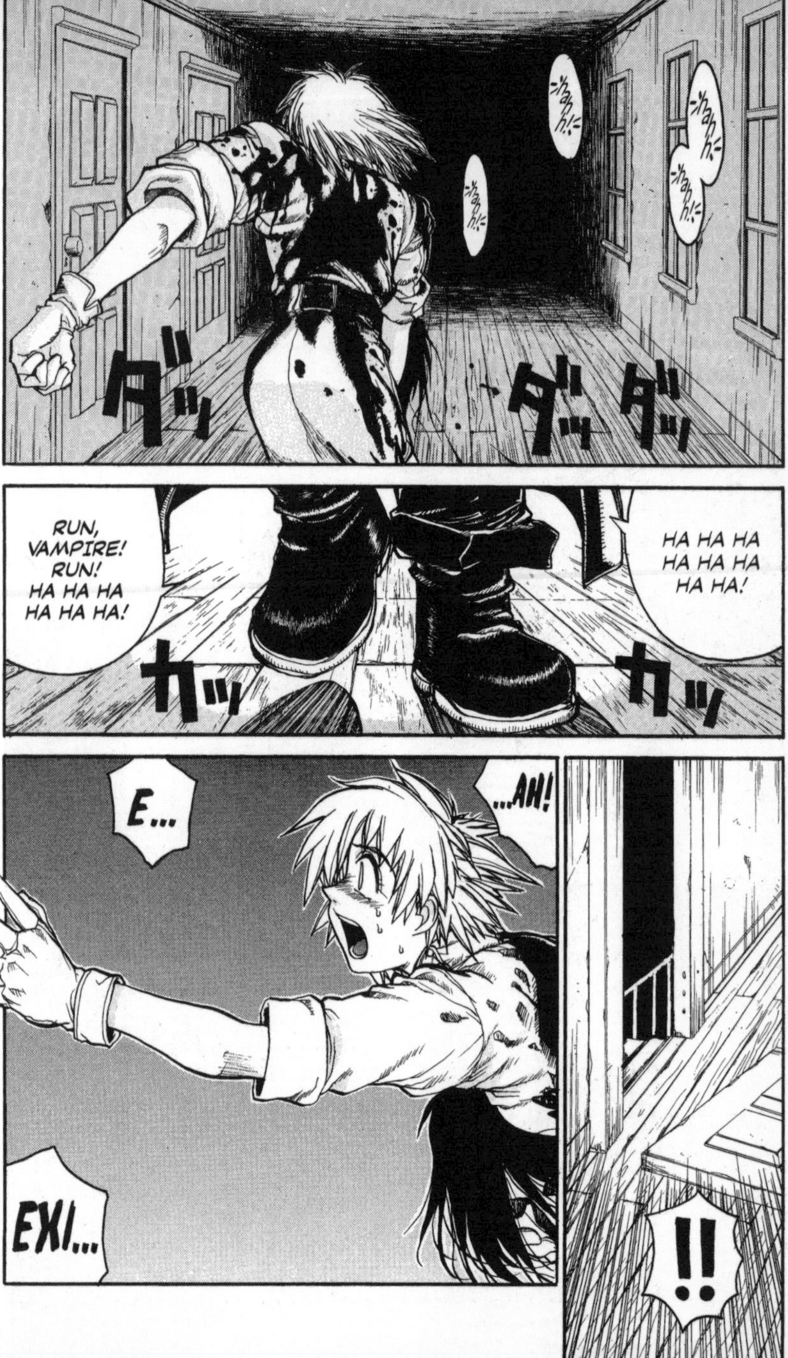

-hahh!-
-hahh!-
-hahh!-
-hahh!-
ダッ
ダッ
ダッ
HA HA HA HA HA HA HA HA!
RUN, VAMPIRE! RUN! HA HA HA HA HA HA!
カッ
カッ
!!
...AH!
E...
EXI...

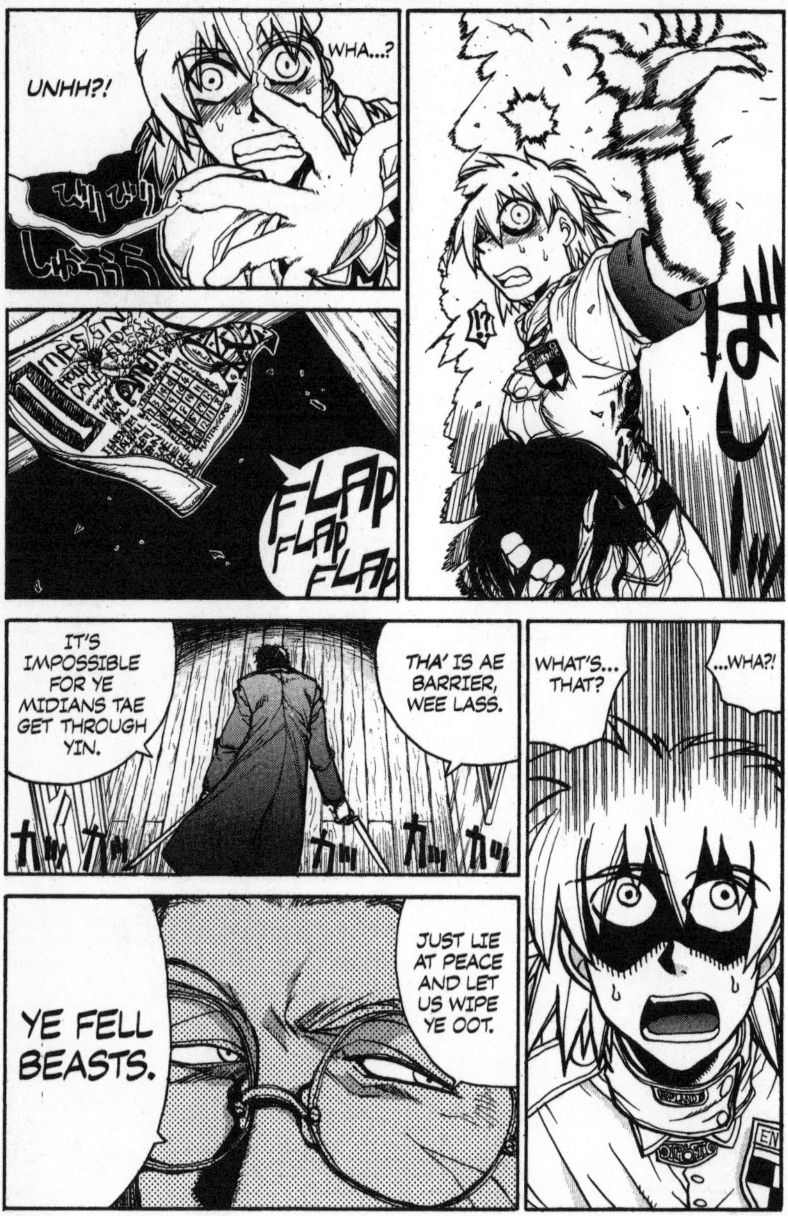
!?
WHA...?
UNHH?!
FLAP FLAP FLAP
...WHA?!
WHAT'S... THAT?
THA' IS AE BARRIER, WEE LASS.
IT'S IMPOSSIBLE FOR YE MIDIANS TAE GET THROUGH YIN.
JUST LIE AT PEACE AND LET US WIPE YE OOT.
YE FELL BEASTS.

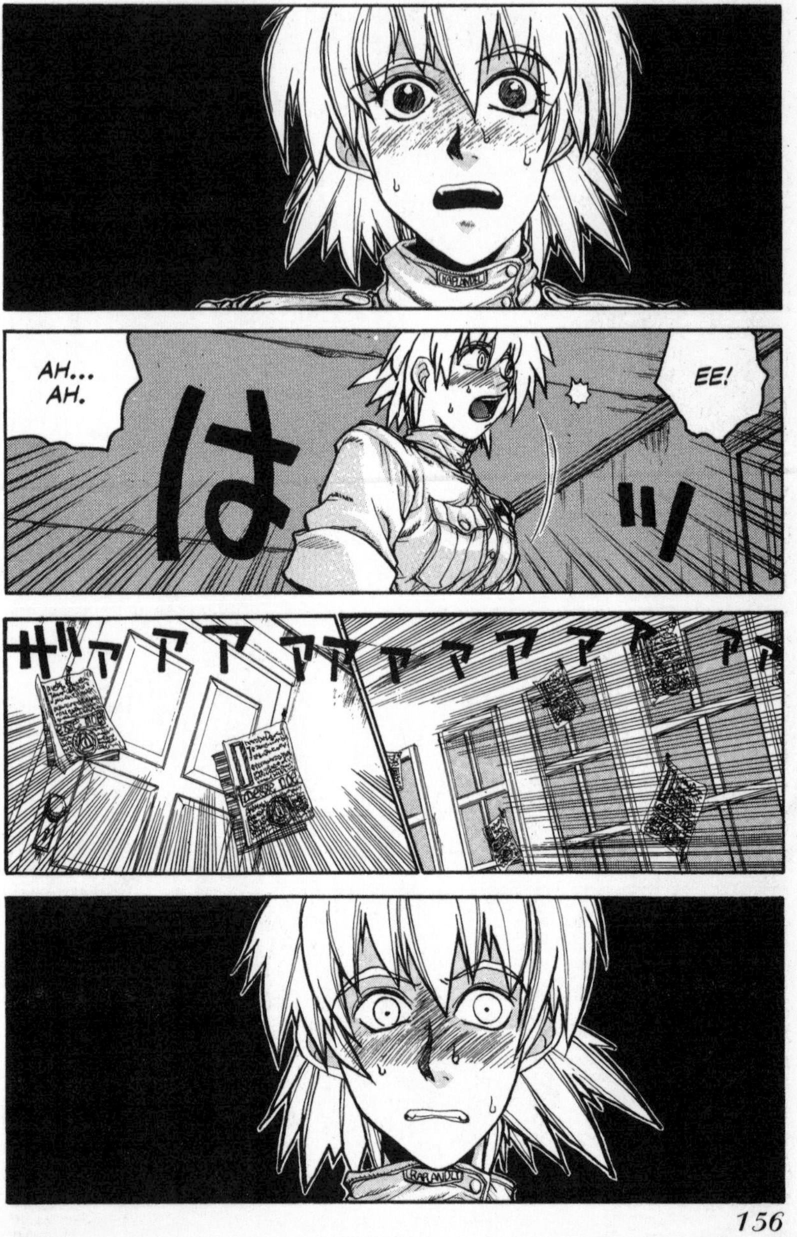
EE!
AH... AH.
はッ

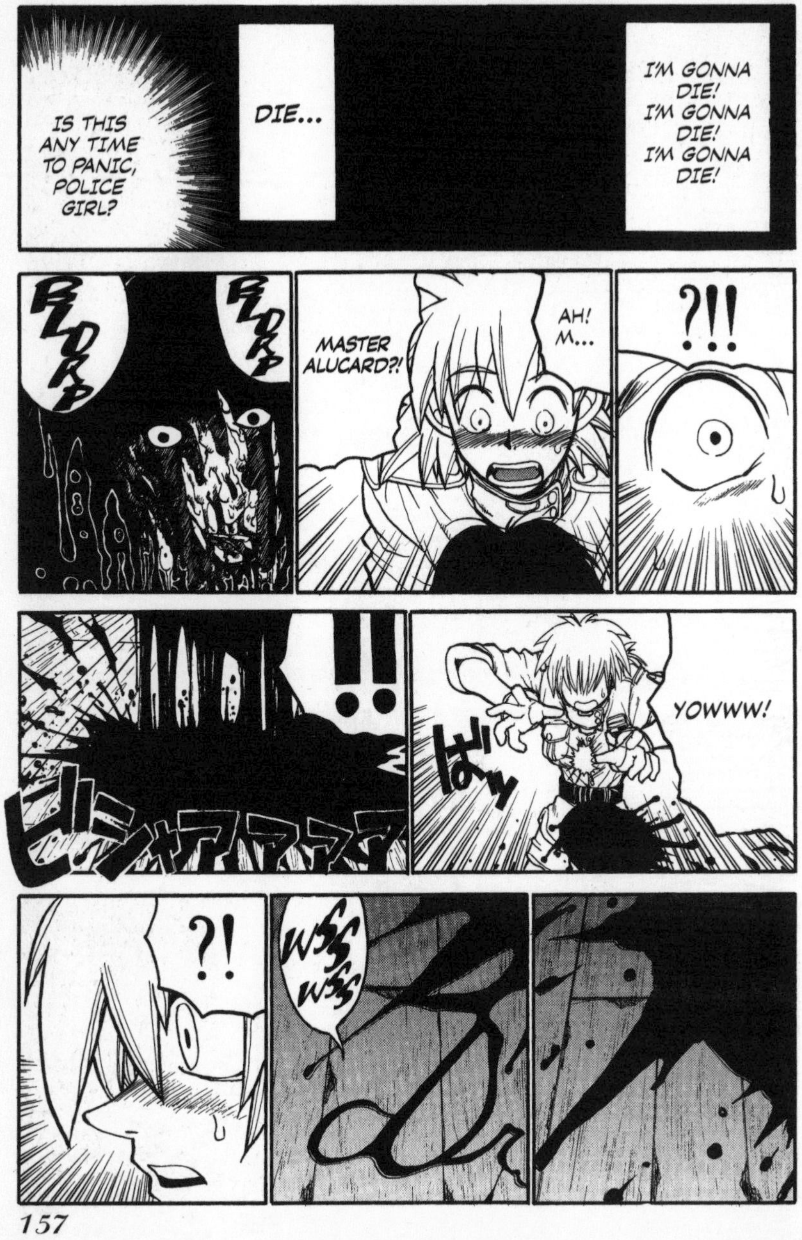
I'M GONNA DIE! I'M GONNA DIE! I'M GONNA DIE!
DIE...
IS THIS ANY TIME TO PANIC, POLICE GIRL?
?!!
AH! M...
MASTER ALUCARD?!
BLORP
BLORP
YOWWW!
!!
WSSS WSSS
?!

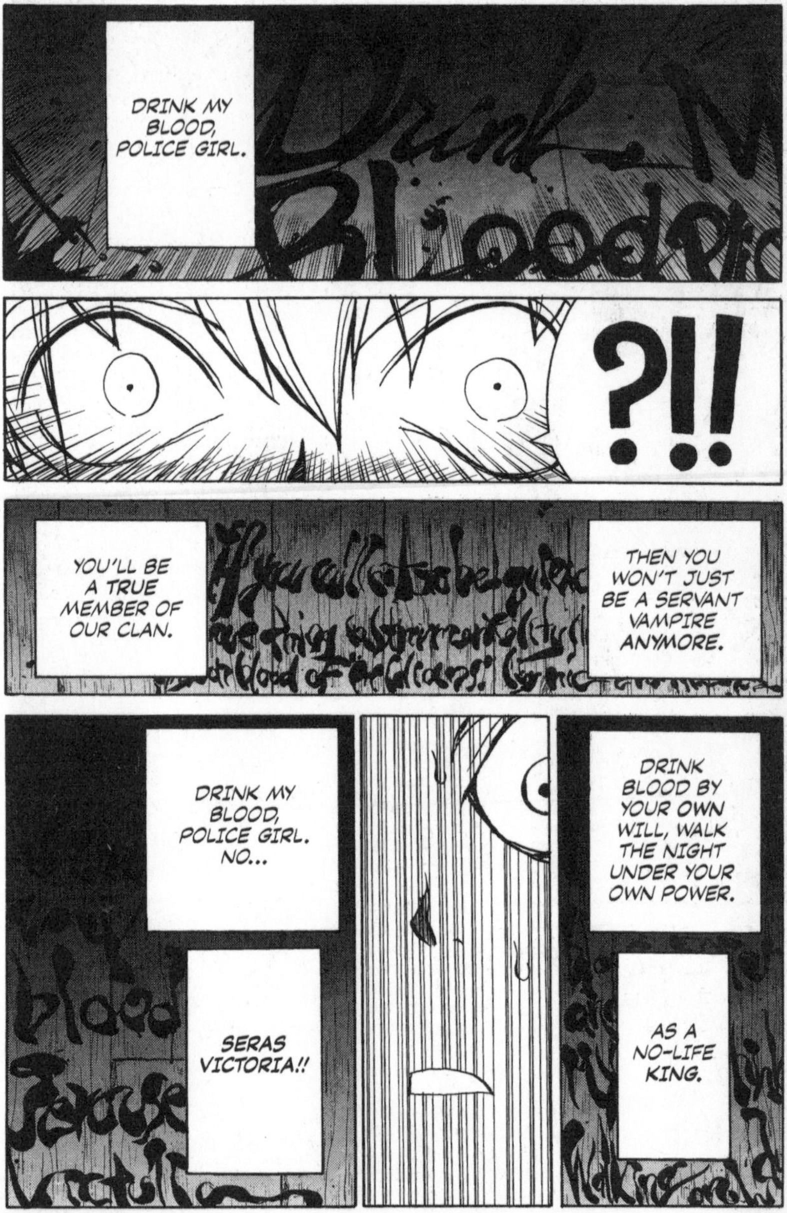
DRINK MY BLOOD, POLICE GIRL.
?!!
THEN YOU WON'T JUST BE A SERVANT VAMPIRE ANYMORE.
YOU'LL BE A TRUE MEMBER OF OUR CLAN.
DRINK BLOOD BY YOUR OWN WILL, WALK THE NIGHT UNDER YOUR OWN POWER.
AS A NO-LIFE KING.
DRINK MY BLOOD, POLICE GIRL. NO...
SERAS VICTORIA!!

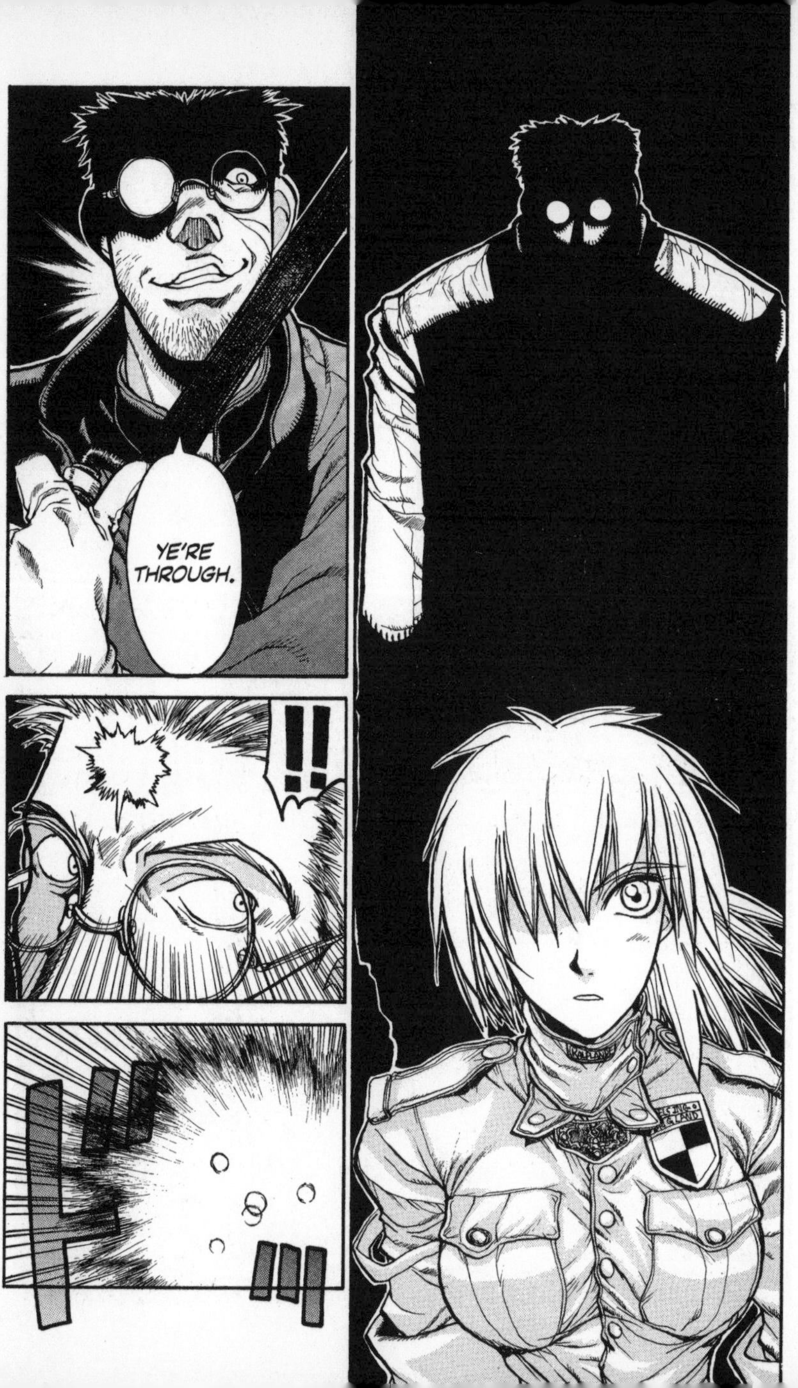
YE'RE THROUGH.
!!

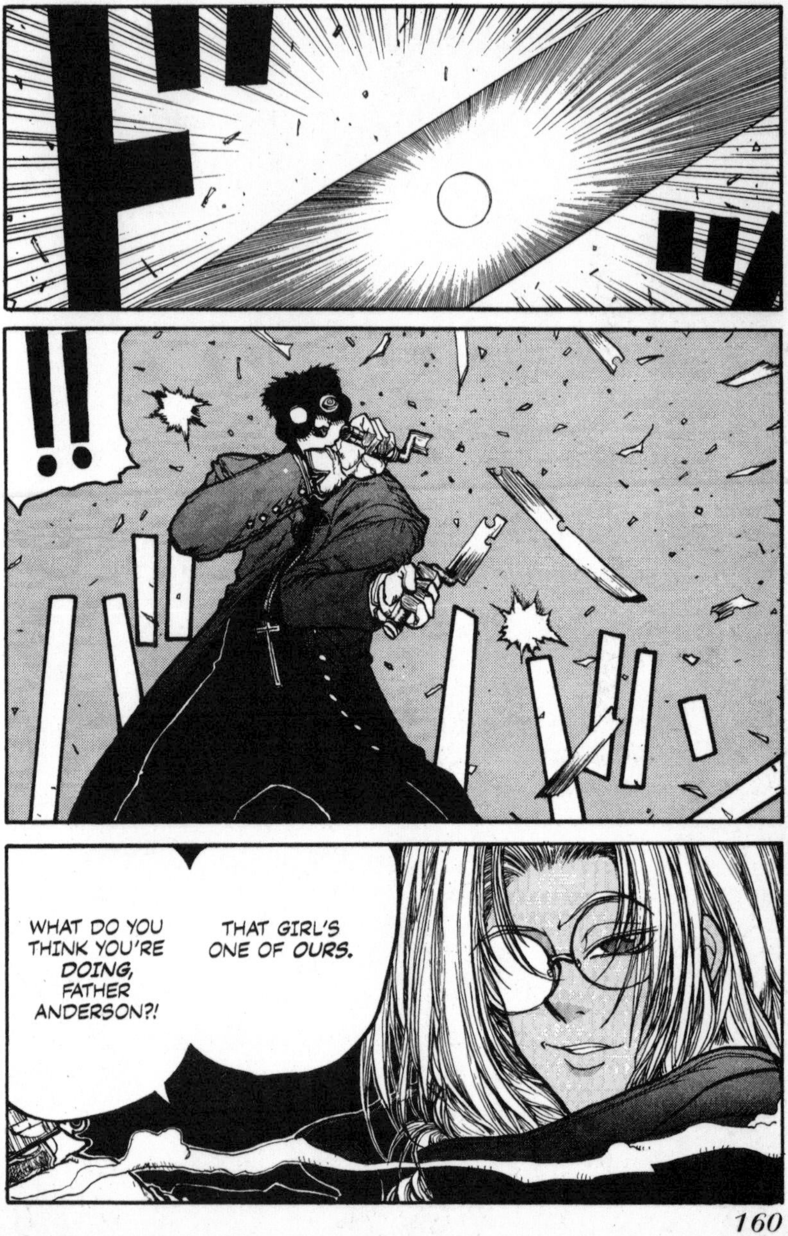
!!
THAT GIRL'S ONE OF *OURS.*
WHAT DO YOU THINK YOU'RE *DOING,* FATHER ANDERSON?!

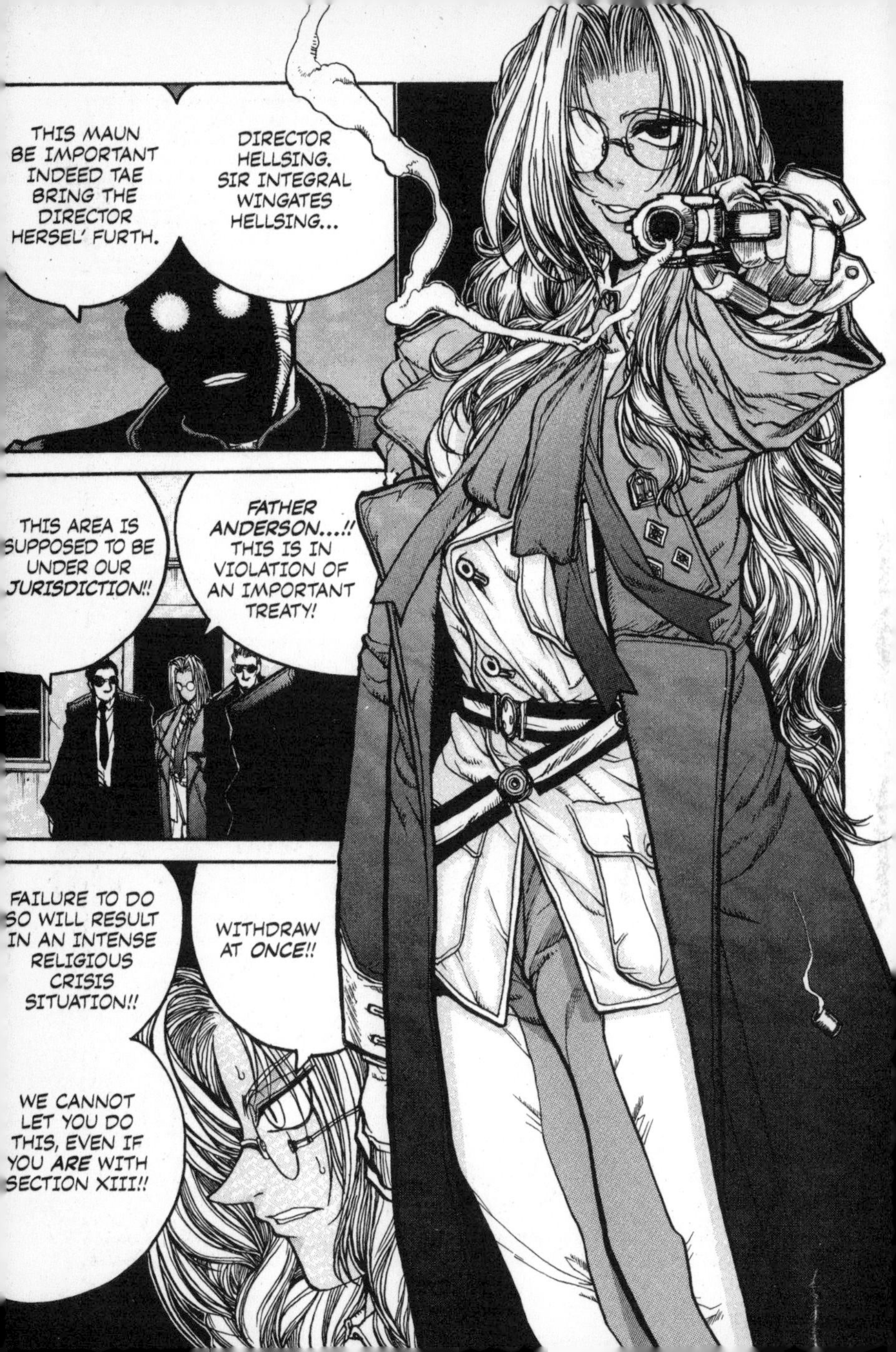
DIRECTOR HELLSING. SIR INTEGRAL WINGATES HELLSING...
THIS MAUN BE IMPORTANT INDEED TAE BRING THE DIRECTOR HERSEL' FURTH.
FATHER ANDERSON...!! THIS IS IN VIOLATION OF AN IMPORTANT TREATY!
THIS AREA IS SUPPOSED TO BE UNDER OUR JURISDICTION!!
WITHDRAW AT ONCE!!
FAILURE TO DO SO WILL RESULT IN AN INTENSE RELIGIOUS CRISIS SITUATION!!
WE CANNOT LET YOU DO THIS, EVEN IF YOU ARE WITH SECTION XIII!!

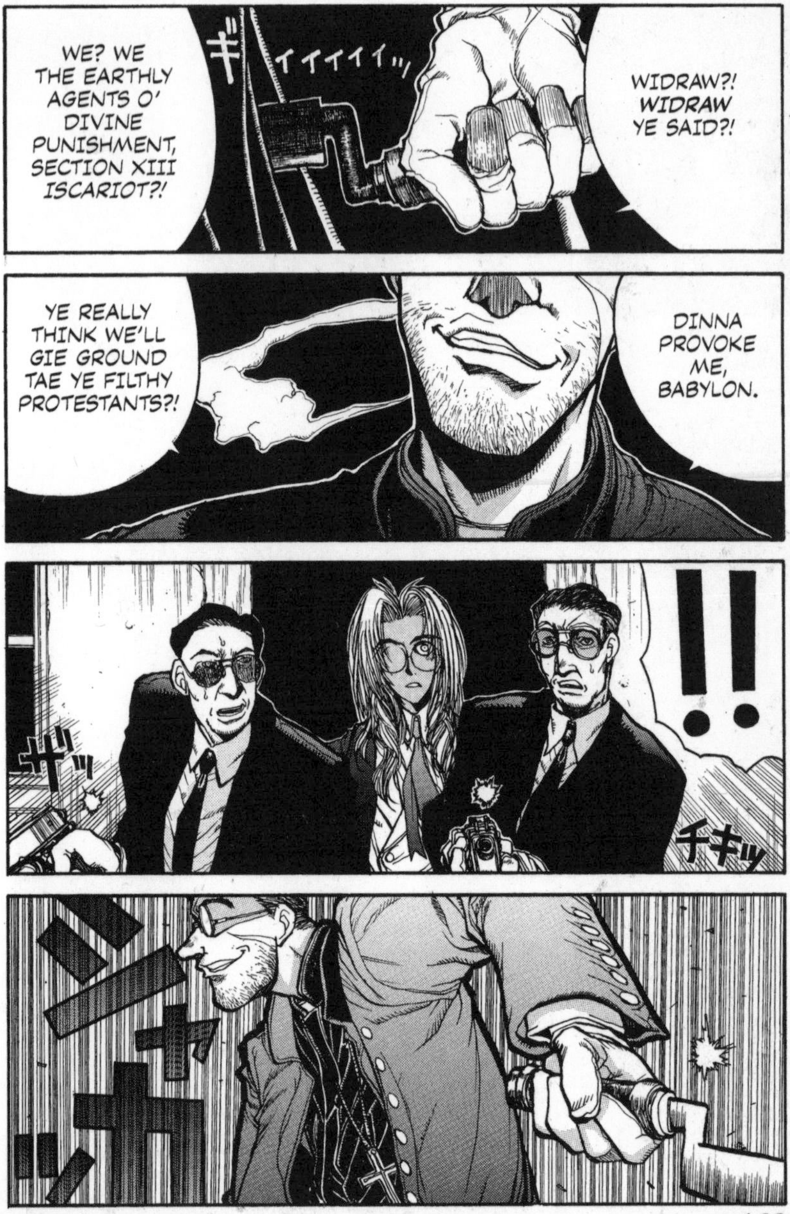
WIDRAW?! WIDRAW YE SAID?!
WE? WE THE EARTHLY AGENTS O' DIVINE PUNISHMENT, SECTION XIII ISCARIOT?!
ギイイイイイッ
DINNA PROVOKE ME, BABYLON.
YE REALLY THINK WE'LL GIE GROUND TAE YE FILTHY PROTESTANTS?!
!!
チキッ
ザッ
ジャキッ

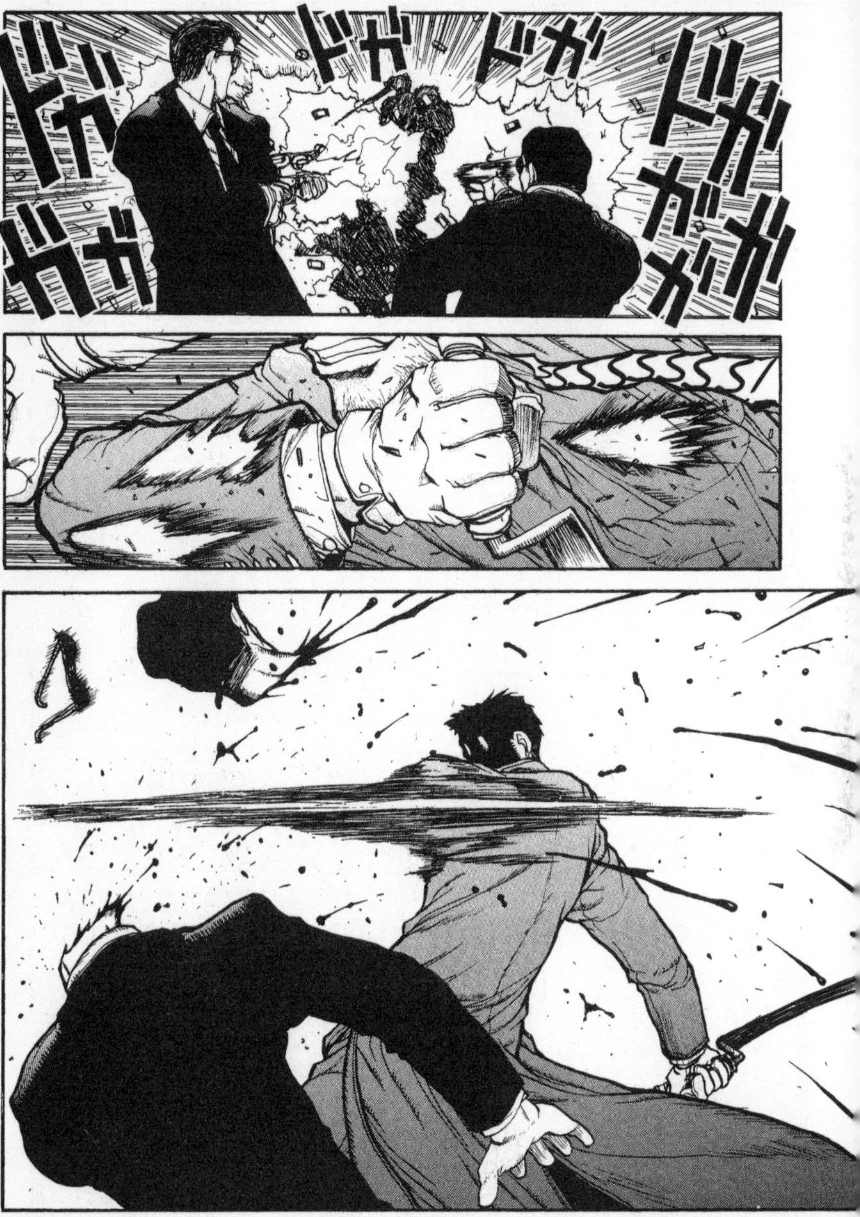
ドガガガ
ドガ
ドガ
ドガガ

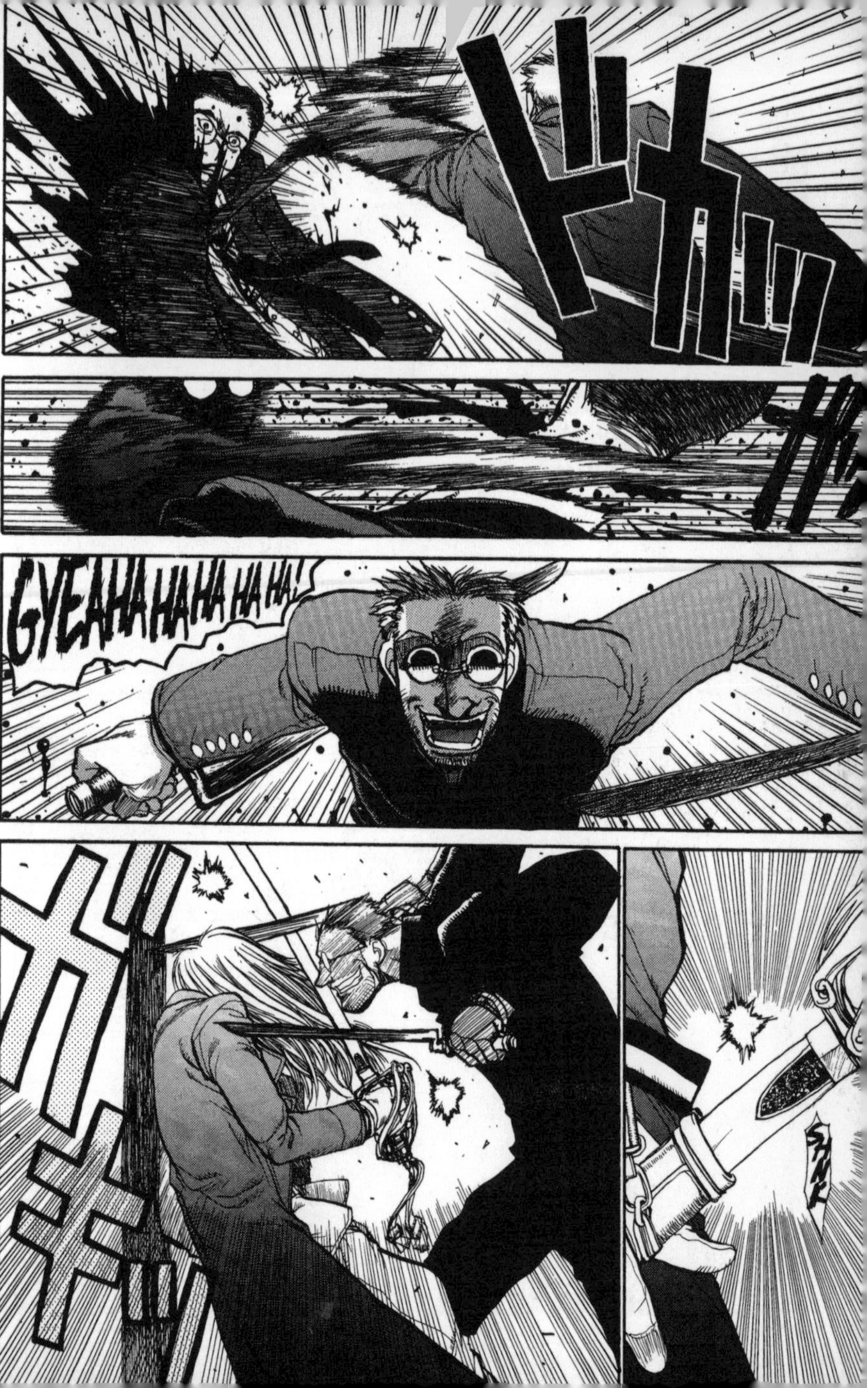
ドカッ
GYEAHA HAHA HA HA!
SHNK

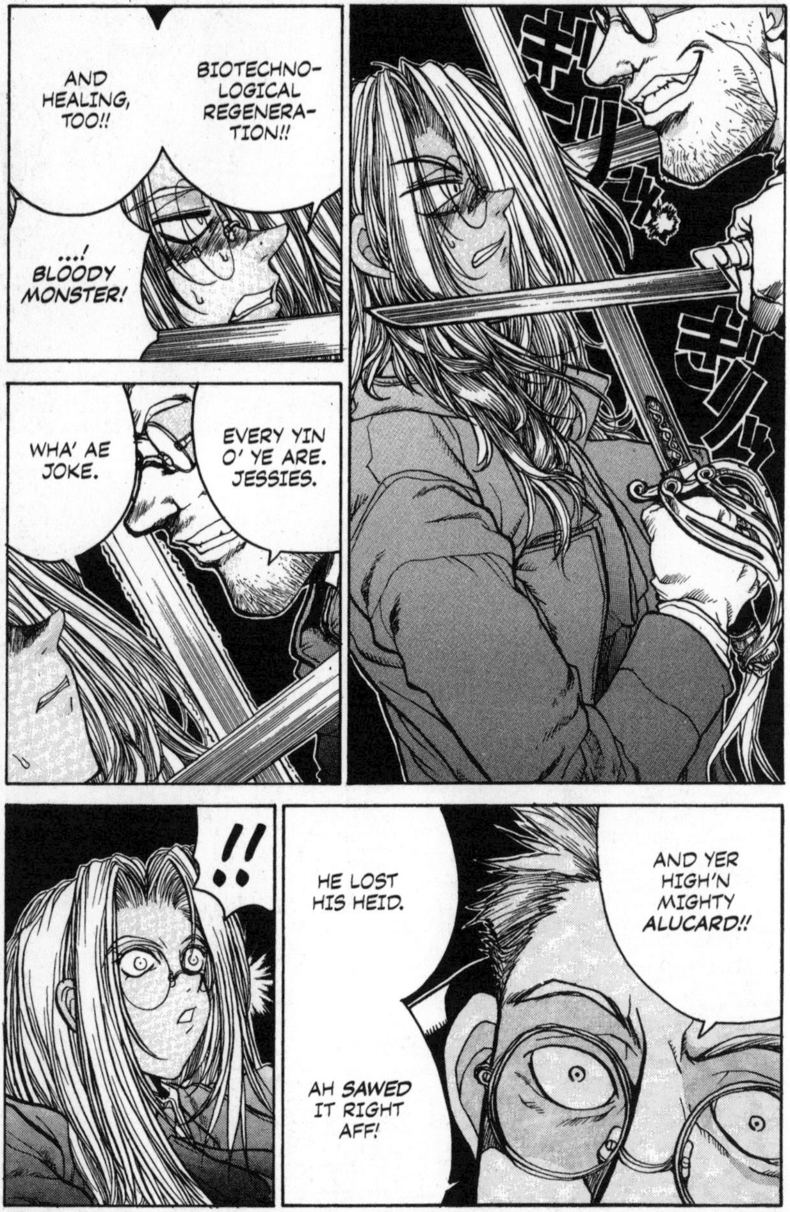

BIOTECHNO-LOGICAL REGENERA-TION!!
AND HEALING, TOO!!
...! BLOODY MONSTER!
EVERY YIN O' YE ARE. JESSIES.
WHA' AE JOKE.
AND YER HIGH'N MIGHTY ALUCARD!!
HE LOST HIS HEID.
AH SAWED IT RIGHT AFF!
!!

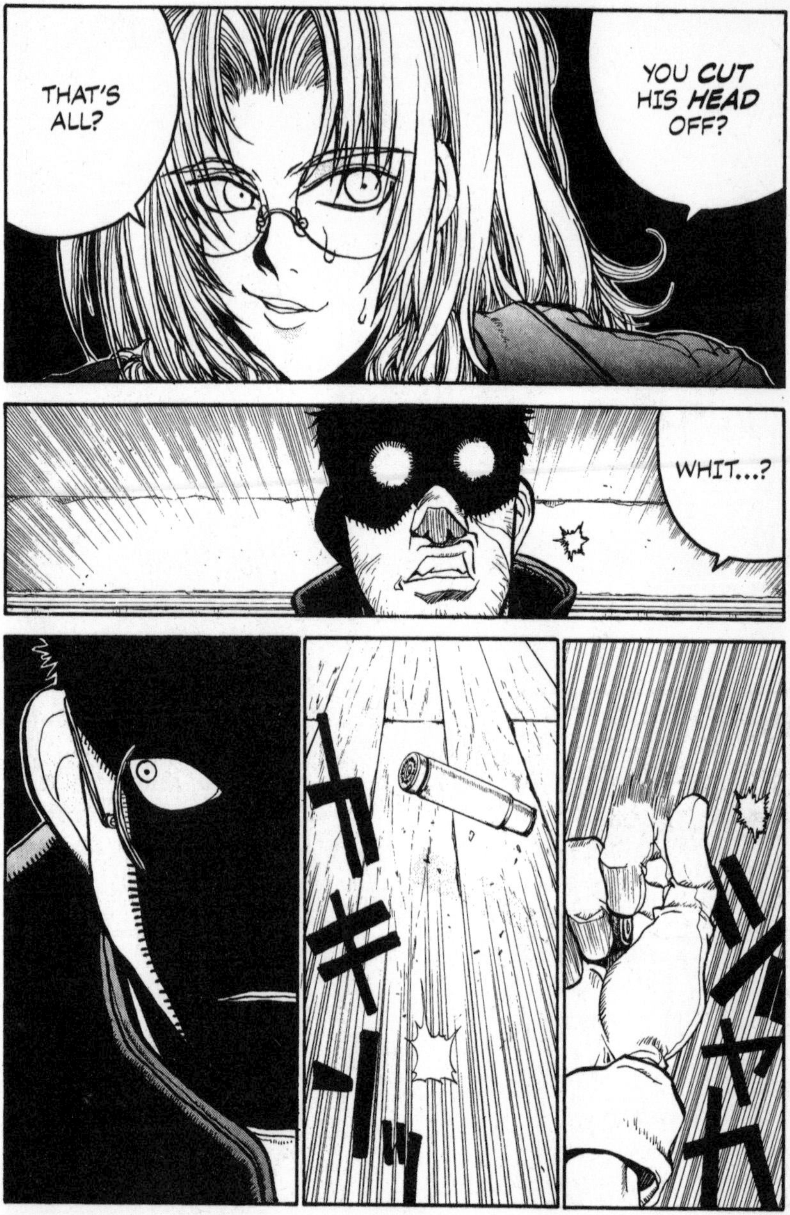
YOU **CUT** HIS **HEAD** OFF?
THAT'S ALL?
WHIT...?

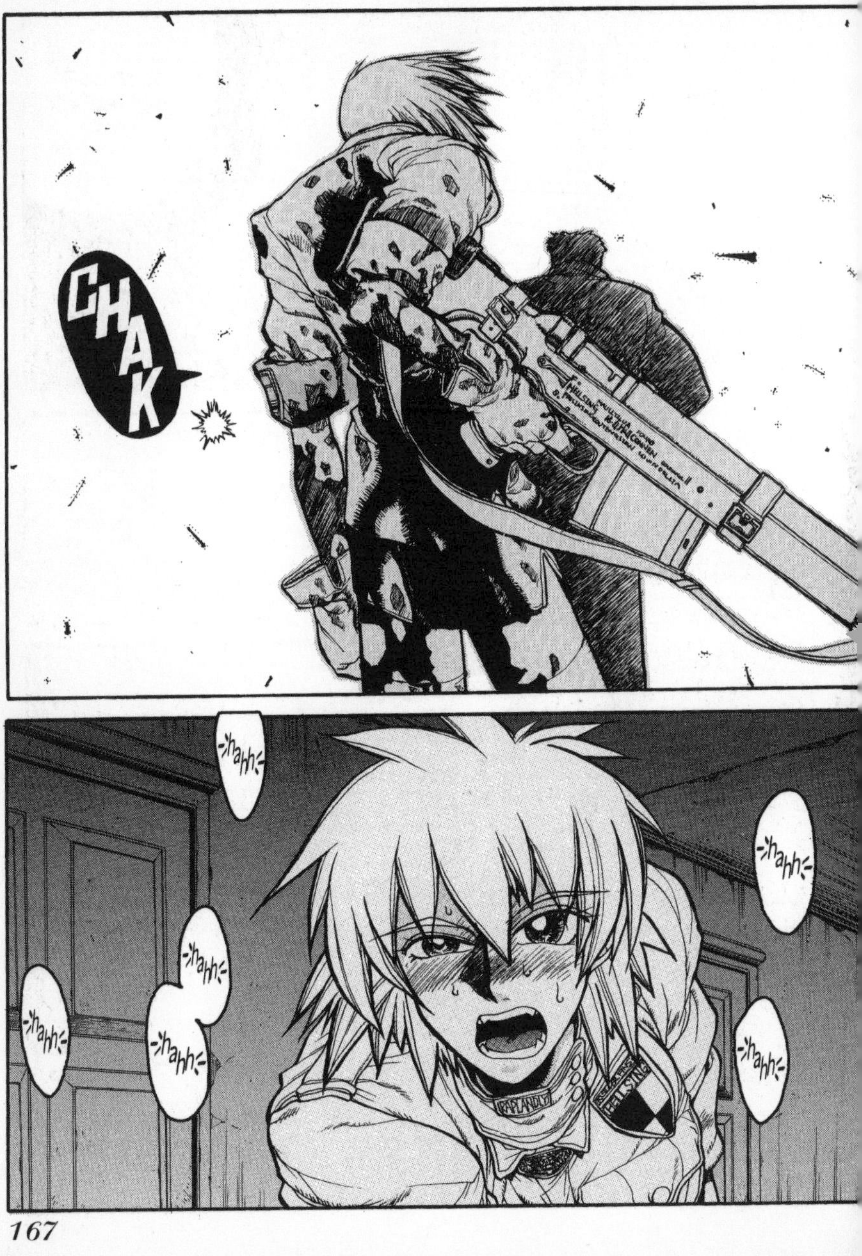
CHAK
hahh
hahh
hahh
hahh
hahh
hahh

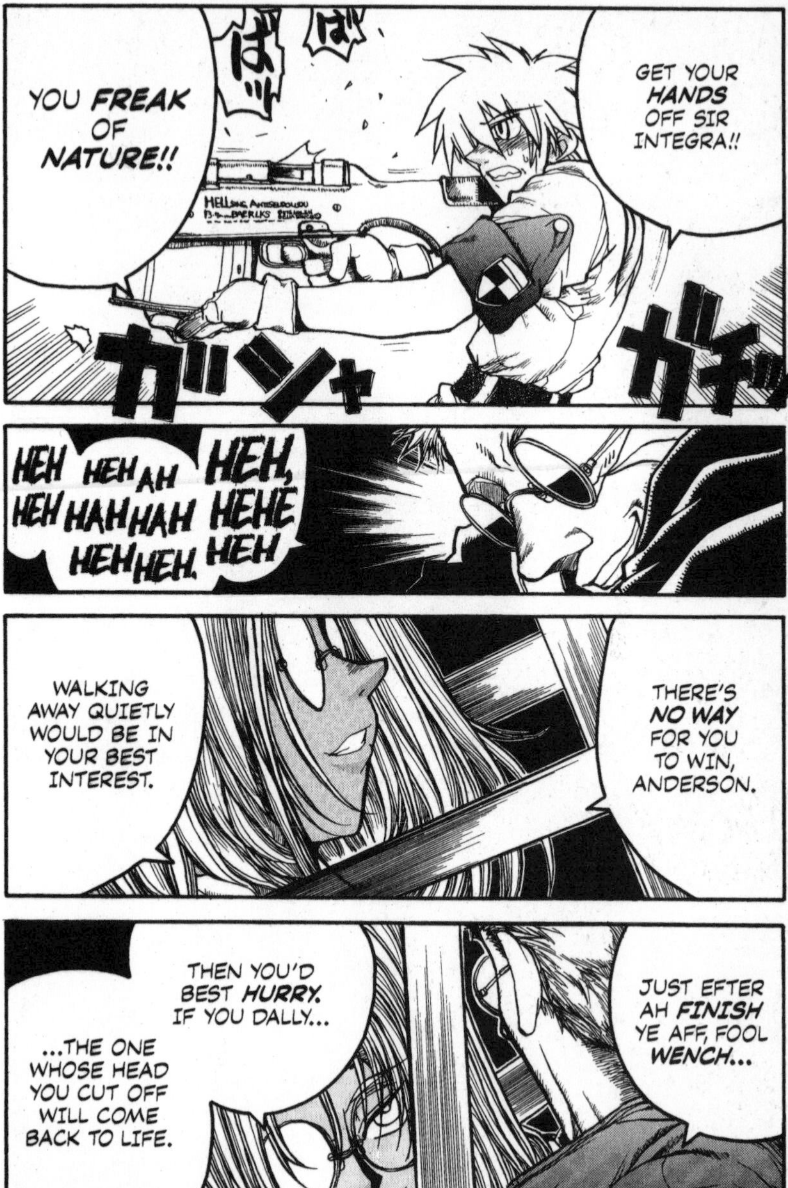
GET YOUR HANDS OFF SIR INTEGRA!!
YOU FREAK OF NATURE!!
ガチッ
ガッシャ
HEH HEH AH HEH,
HEH HAH HAH HEHE
HEH HEH. HEH
THERE'S NO WAY FOR YOU TO WIN, ANDERSON.
WALKING AWAY QUIETLY WOULD BE IN YOUR BEST INTEREST.
JUST EFTER AH FINISH YE AFF, FOOL WENCH...
THEN YOU'D BEST HURRY. IF YOU DALLY...
...THE ONE WHOSE HEAD YOU CUT OFF WILL COME BACK TO LIFE.

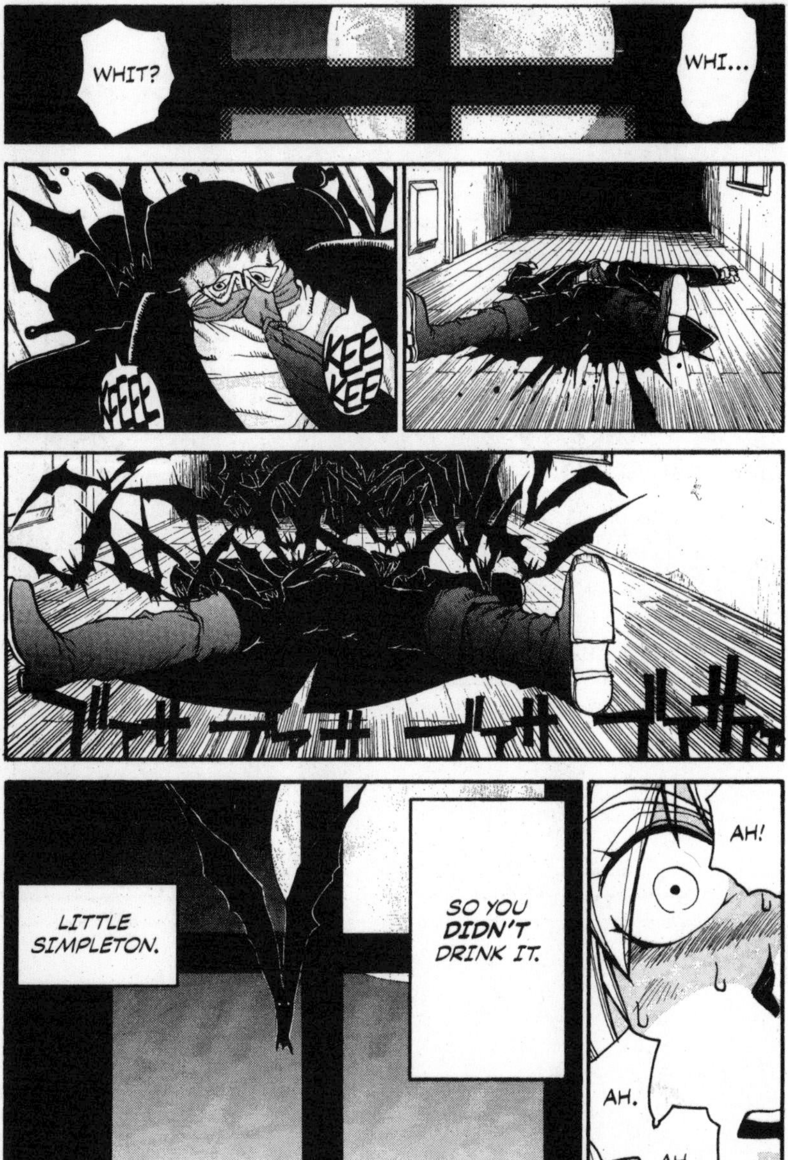
WHI...
WHIT?
KEE KEE
KEEEE
AH!
AH.
AH...
SO YOU DIDN'T DRINK IT.
LITTLE SIMPLETON.

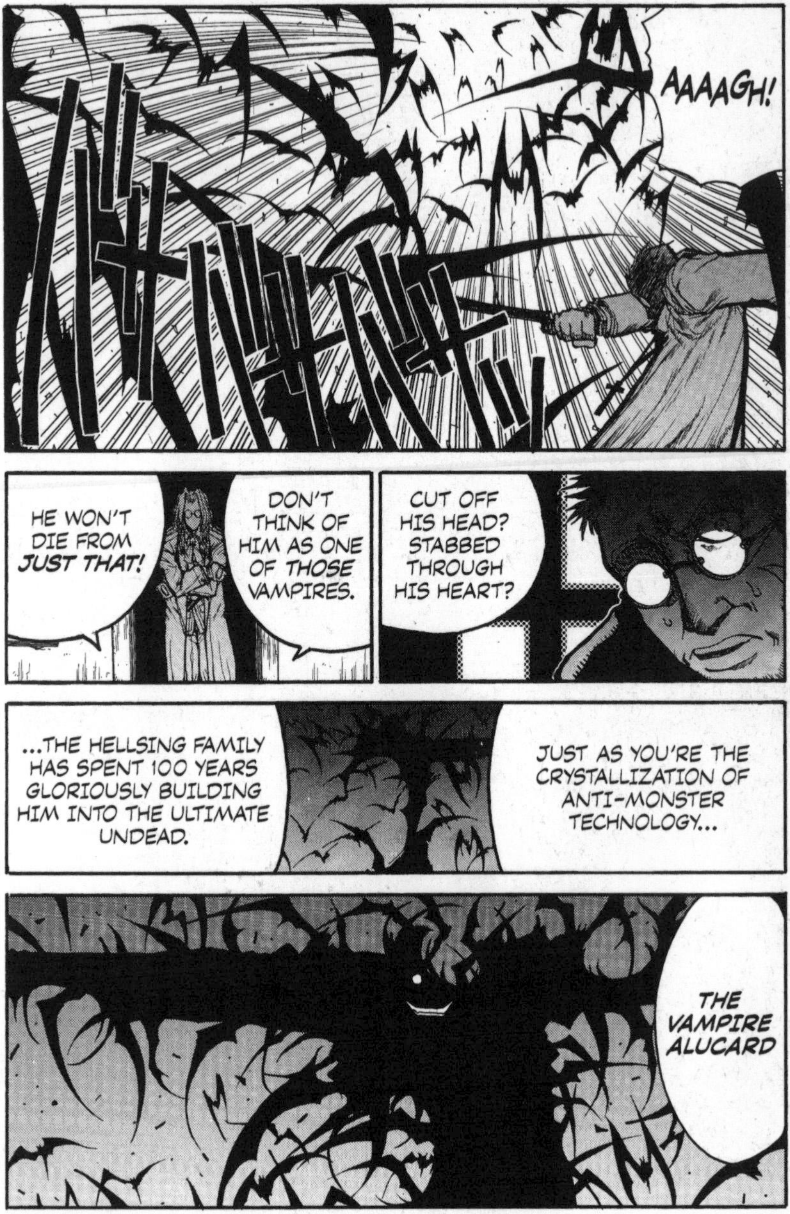
AAAAGH!
CUT OFF HIS HEAD? STABBED THROUGH HIS HEART?
DON'T THINK OF HIM AS ONE OF THOSE VAMPIRES.
HE WON'T DIE FROM JUST THAT!
JUST AS YOU'RE THE CRYSTALLIZATION OF ANTI-MONSTER TECHNOLOGY...
...THE HELLSING FAMILY HAS SPENT 100 YEARS GLORIOUSLY BUILDING HIM INTO THE ULTIMATE UNDEAD.
THE VAMPIRE ALUCARD

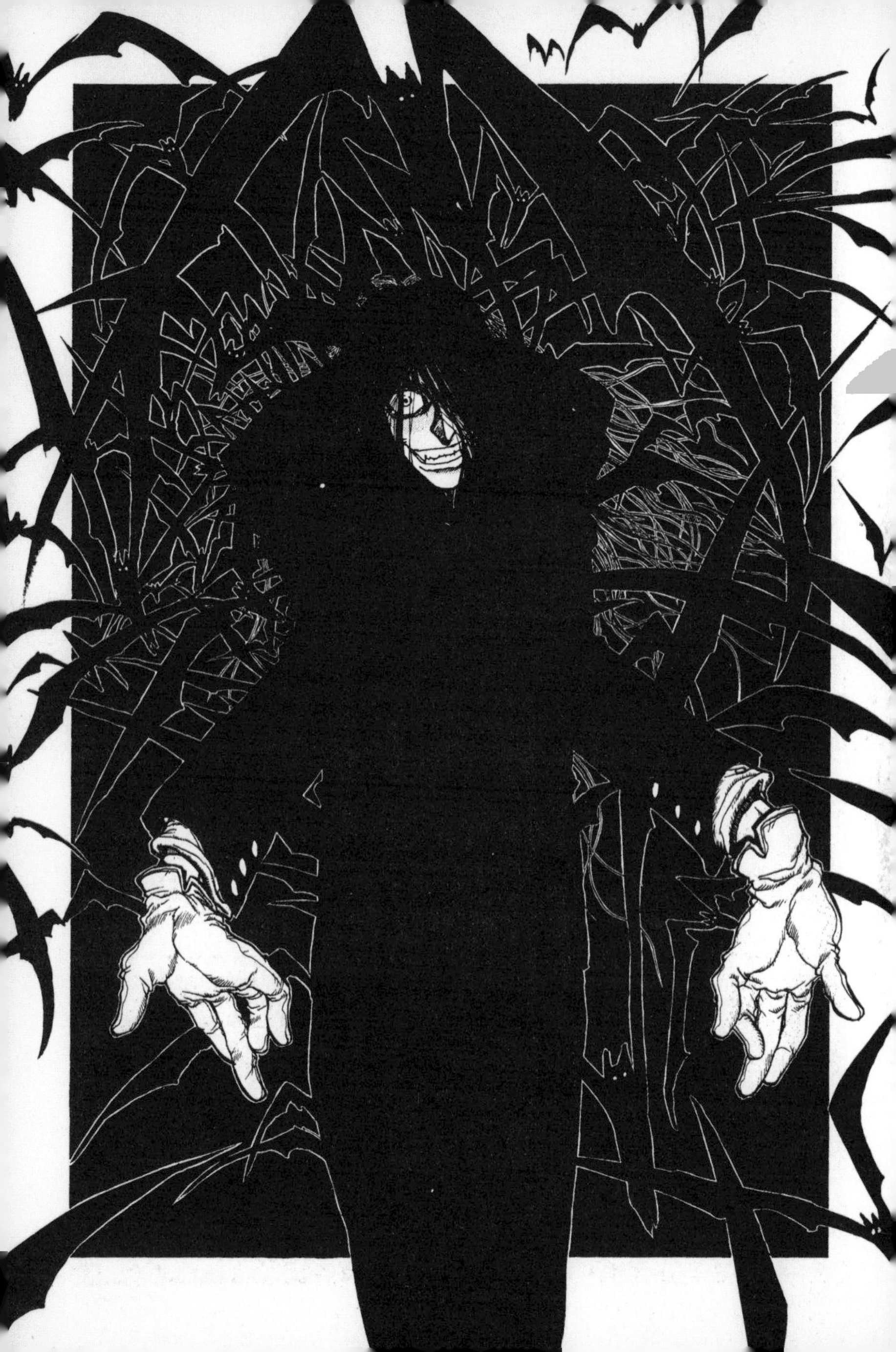

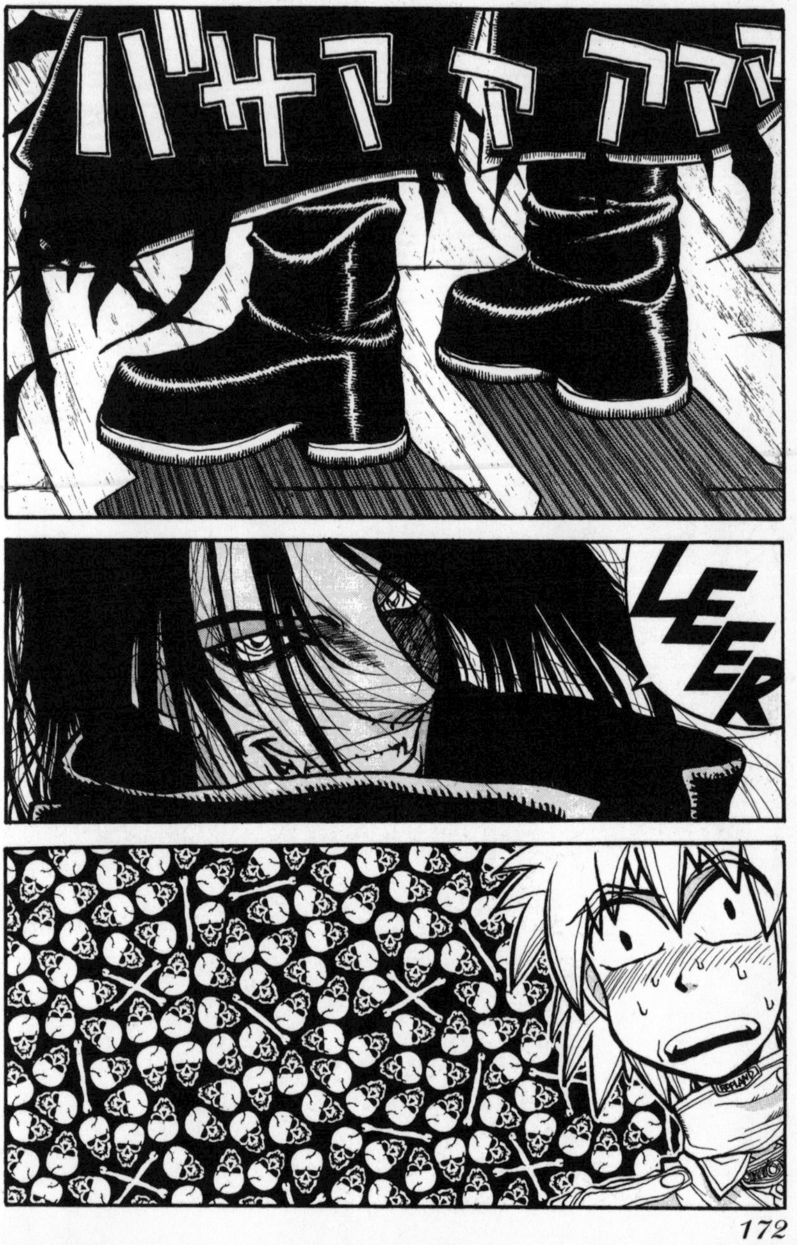
バサア アアア
LEER

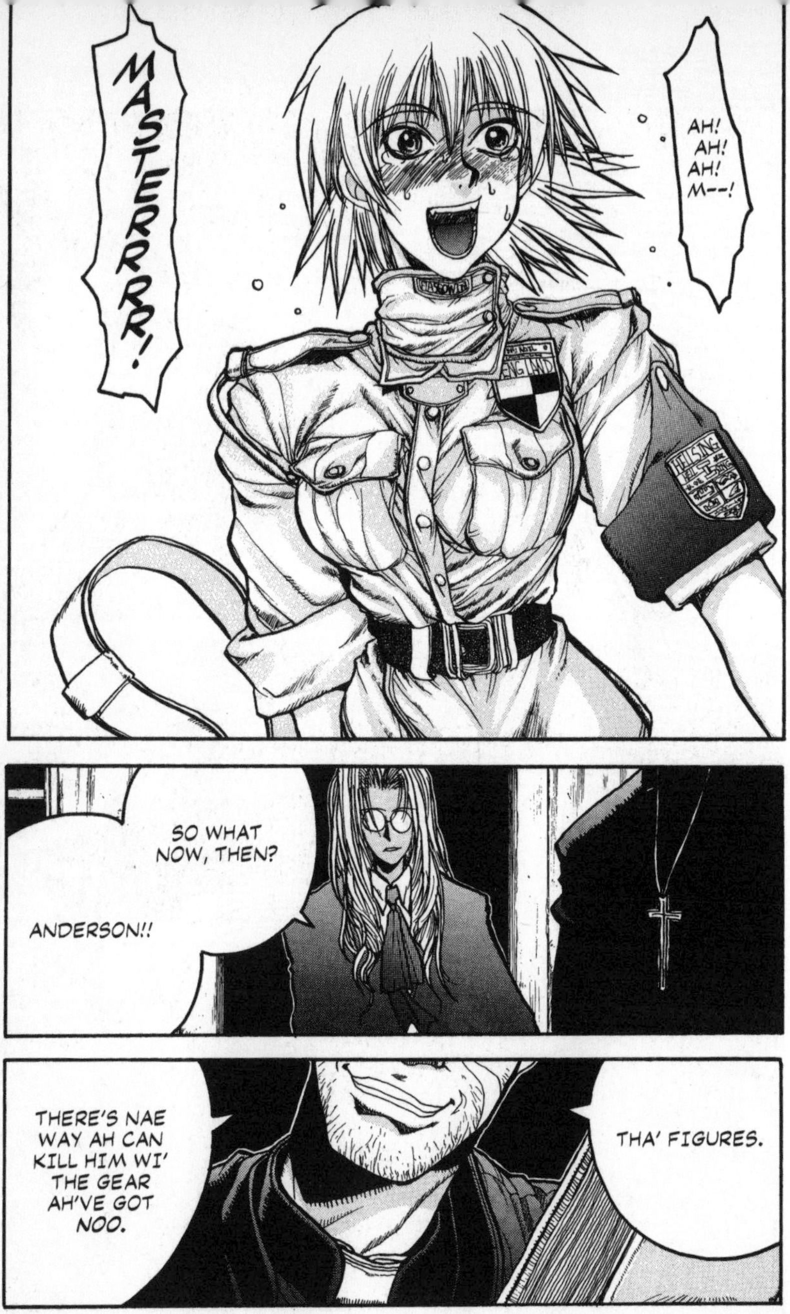
AH! AH! AH! M--!
MASTERRRR!
SO WHAT NOW, THEN?
ANDERSON!!
THA' FIGURES.
THERE'S NAE WAY AH CAN KILL HIM WI' THE GEAR AH'VE GOT NOO.

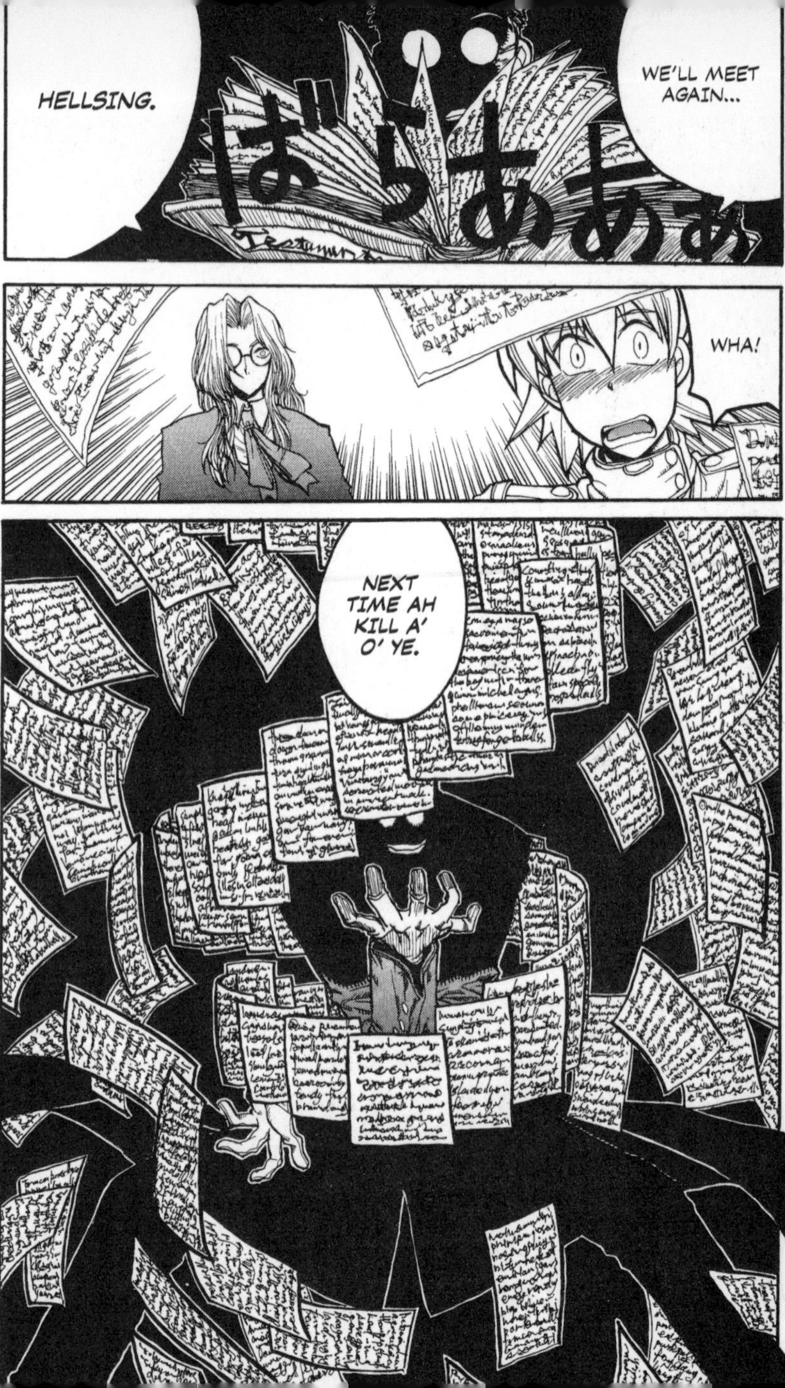
WE'LL MEET AGAIN...
HELLSING.
ばらあああ
WHA!
NEXT TIME AH KILL A' O' YE.

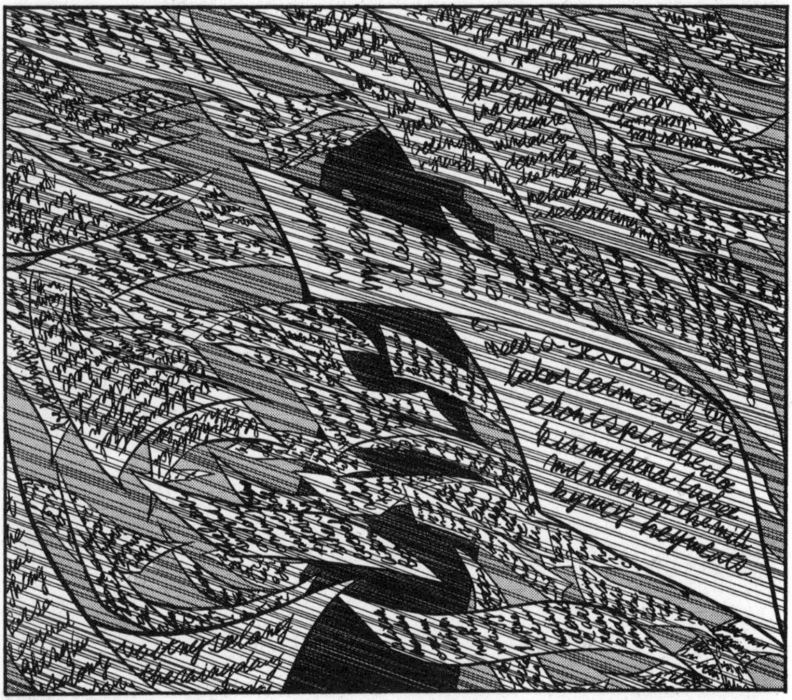

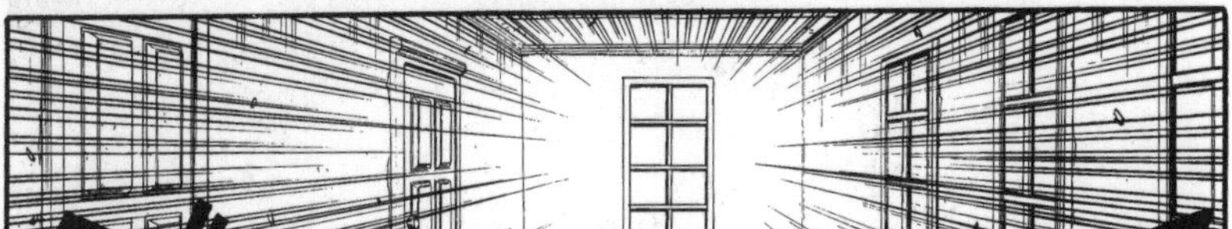

ブァサアアアアアアア

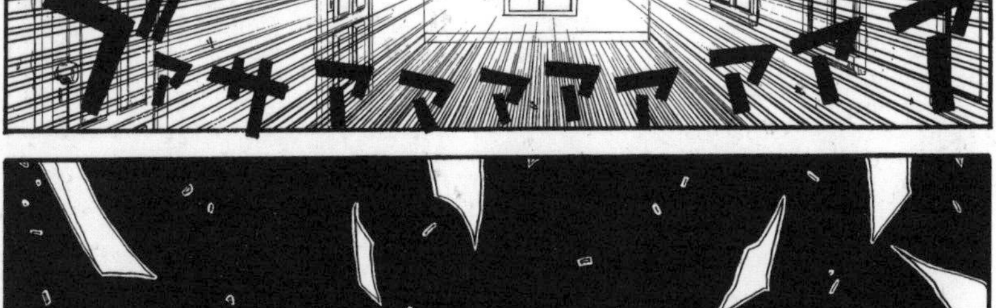

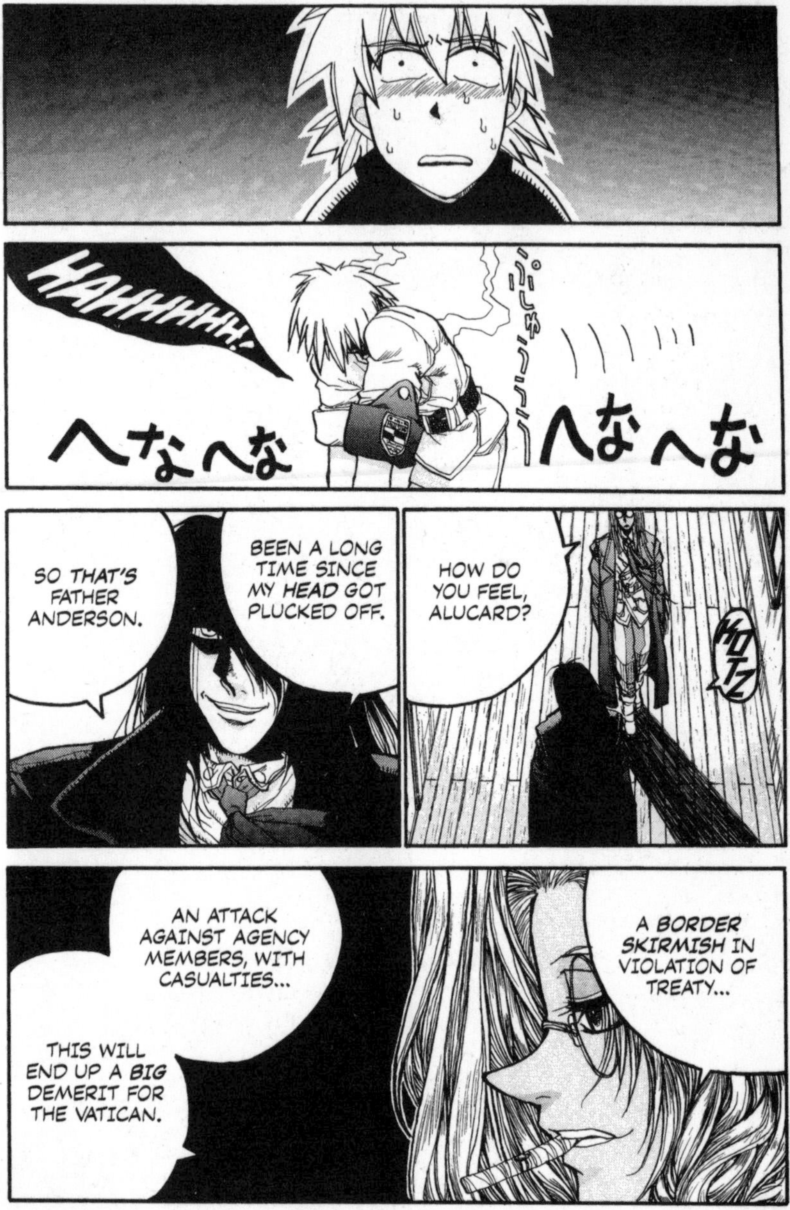

ぷしゅンンンン
HAHHHHHH!
へなへな
へなへな
HOW DO YOU FEEL, ALUCARD?
KOTZ
BEEN A LONG TIME SINCE MY *HEAD* GOT PLUCKED OFF.
SO *THAT'S* FATHER ANDERSON.
A *BORDER SKIRMISH* IN VIOLATION OF TREATY...
AN ATTACK AGAINST AGENCY MEMBERS, WITH CASUALTIES...
THIS WILL END UP A *BIG* DEMERIT FOR THE VATICAN.

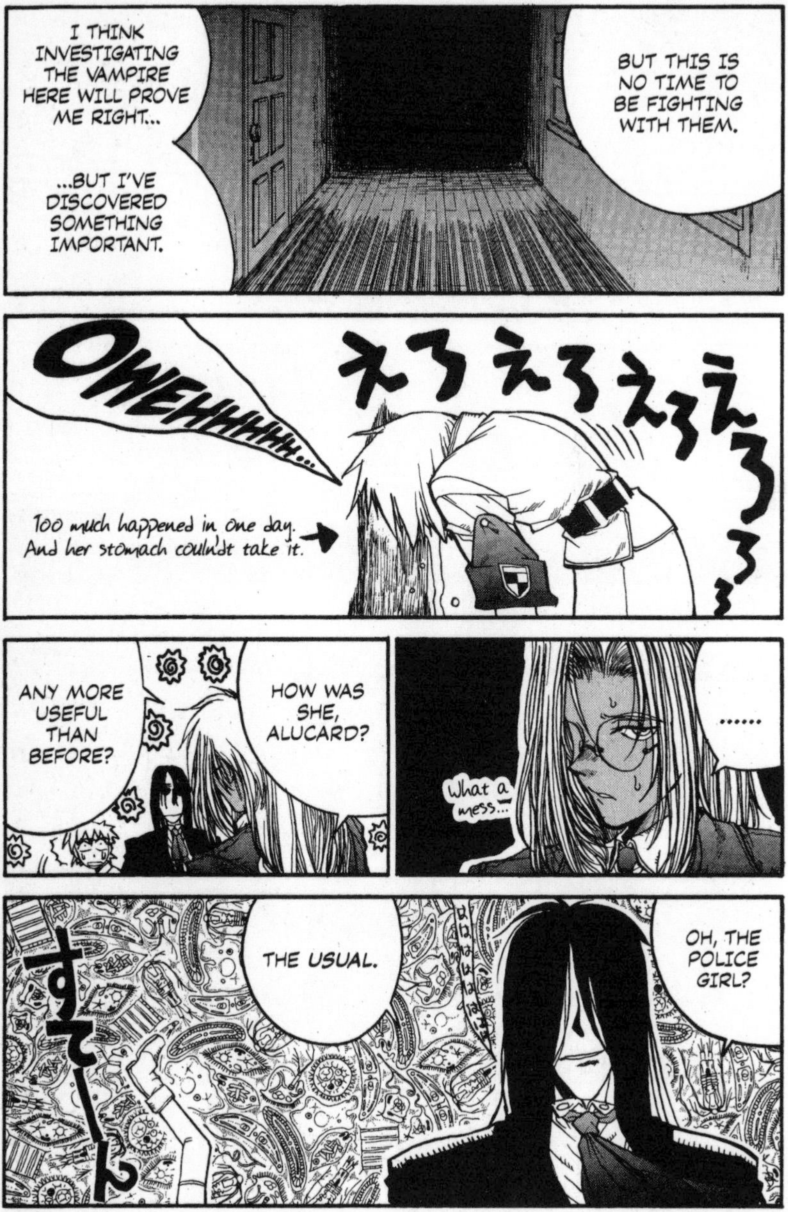

I THINK INVESTIGATING THE VAMPIRE HERE WILL PROVE ME RIGHT...
...BUT I'VE DISCOVERED SOMETHING IMPORTANT.
BUT THIS IS NO TIME TO BE FIGHTING WITH THEM.
えろえろえろえろろろろ
OWEHHHHHH...
Too much happened in one day. And her stomach couldn't take it.
......
What a mess...
HOW WAS SHE, ALUCARD?
ANY MORE USEFUL THAN BEFORE?
OH, THE POLICE GIRL?
THE USUAL.
すてーん

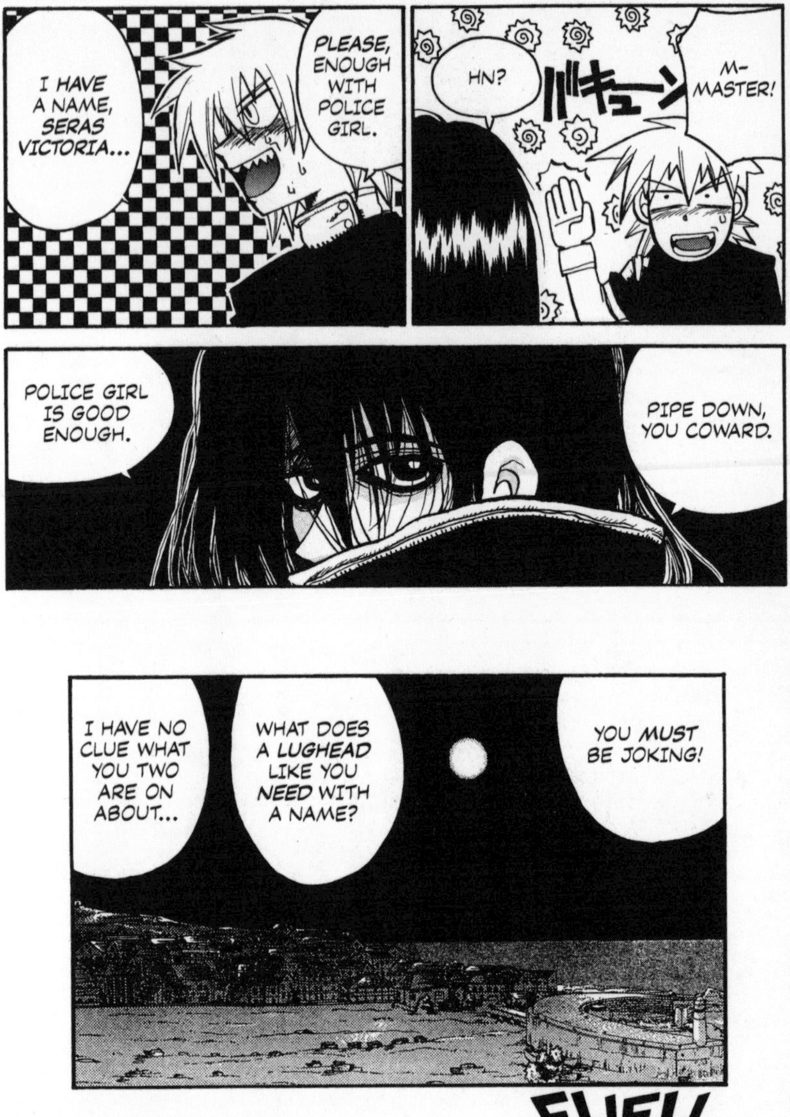
M-MASTER!
ドキューン
HN?
PLEASE, ENOUGH WITH POLICE GIRL.
I HAVE A NAME, SERAS VICTORIA...
PIPE DOWN, YOU COWARD.
POLICE GIRL IS GOOD ENOUGH.
YOU MUST BE JOKING!
WHAT DOES A LUGHEAD LIKE YOU NEED WITH A NAME?
I HAVE NO CLUE WHAT YOU TWO ARE ON ABOUT...
EHEH
END

ORDER 06 / END

後記

■ RIGHT! WELL, UM, AND SO, (SPOKEN LIKE KAKUEI) I AM KOHTA HIRANO. TO THOSE I DON'T KNOW, NICE TO MEET YOU. TO EVERYONE ELSE, WASSAP? HERE YOU HAVE IT, HELLSING VOLUME 1. IT'S NOT AN ADULT BOOK, AND TO BE ABLE TO FINALLY DRAW SOMETHING I WANTED TO ON MY OWN HAS BEEN ONE OF THE BEST THINGS I'VE EVER DONE IN MY LIFE. SO...WHAT DO YOU THINK? I DON'T HAVE TO LISTEN TO ANYONE'S DIREC- TIONS NOW SO IT'S LIKE THE ULTIMATE IN INDEPENDENCE! YEAH! IT'S SORT OF LIKE A STUDENT RIDING HIS MOTORCYCLE INTO THE STAFF ROOM DURING CLASS BECAUSE NO TEACHERS ARE PAYING ATTENTION! THAT'S ABOUT HOW FREE I AM TO DO WHATEVER I WANT! IN "FIST OF THE NORTH STAR" TERMS IT'S LIKE BEING JAGI...OR OTHERWISE SOUTHER. IN THAT CASE THIS BOOK IS THE HOLY EMPEROR CROSS MAUSOLEUM! POLE STAR CROSS FIST! RASHAA! AND OF COURSE SHUU OF THE SOUTH STAR WHITE HERON FIST SITS UP ON THE PEAK AND SAYS NOTHING. GINYAA! THAT'S WHY EVERY DAY I LIVE IN SHIVERING FEAR THAT ONE-DAY KENSHIROU WILL COME ALONG AND BEAT THE CRAP OUT OF ME. OR I'LL DIE.

(*NOTE: KAKUEI TANAKA WAS A FORMER JAPANESE PRIME MINISTER. HE WAS SOME- WHAT AKIN TO RICHARD NIXON, CHARISMATIC BUT ALSO INVOLVED IN A CAREER- DAMAGING SCANDAL. HE TENDED TO HAVE A VERY GUTTERAL VOICE AND SPOKE HIS MIND QUITE FREELY.)

■ ANYHOW, ABOUT THIS MANGA. IT FIRST RAN IN "YOUNG KING OURS", JUST AS YOU'VE READ IT. IT RAN ALONGSIDE SUCH OTHER TITLES AS "GEOBREEDERS" AND "TRIGUN." YOU KNOW, IT WAS ROUGH FEELING HAPPY, EMBARRASSED, AND LIKE THE AYATOLLAH AT THE SAME TIME. I WAS WORRIED TO DEATH THAT MY WORK WOULDN'T BE HIGH ENOUGH QUALITY TO HANG IN THERE. <MUSIC IN> IF THE COSMOS FLOWERS WITHER AWAY AND DIE... <MUSIC OUT> I EVEN CUT MY HAIR SHORT. JUST KIDDING.

■ OH, ALL THE REST OF THE GUNS THAT APPEAR IN THIS MANGA ARE UNREAL, SO DON'T GO SAYING "THIS GUN DOESN'T EXIST." OR "HIS SENSE OF WEAPONS SUCKS." THEY'RE ALL COSMOGUNS THAT CAN HOLD A MILLION ROUNDS.

■ FINALLY, I THINK THERE ARE SOME PEOPLE WONDERING WHERE FATHER ANDERSON HIDES ALL THOSE BAYONETS. ANDERSON IS ACTUALLY FOURTH DIMENSIONAL, SO THERE.

■ CHARACTER EXPLANATIONS (WHICH DON'T EXPLAIN ANYTHING)

■ ALUCARD: HE WAS A LOT OF TROUBLE. VAMPIRE CHARACTERS HAVE BEEN DRAWN LIKE THIS FOR AGES! LIKE MASTER MOSQUITON OR NIGHTWALKER! GEEZ! I MEAN, VAMPIRES LIKE HIM HAVE BEEN ALIVE FOR HOW MANY YEARS? BUT YES! THIS HAPPENS TO BE A SPECIALTY OF MINE TOO! SO YEAH! I GOT A LOT OF FEEDBACK AFTERWARD. ONE THING I HEARD A LOT WAS "HE'S TOO SIMILAR TO VASH SO GIVE UP AND GET LOST, YA PIG." WHO WAS THAT FROM?! RYOUTAROU. WHO?! BUT DO THEY REALLY OVERLAP THAT MUCH...? MAYBE I SHOULDN'T HAVE GIVEN HIM THE SUNGLASSES...

■ POLICE GIRL: SHE LOOKS LIKE SHE'S ON THE VERGE OF DEATH. YEAH. THAT'S ABOUT IT.

■ INTEGRA: IT'S HARSH TO HEAR "IS THAT A MAN?" OR "IS THAT MONTINA MAX?" OR "IS IT MUSKA?" RYOUKO SAKAKIBARA IS WONDERFUL AS HER VOICE (MMMM).

■ ANDERSON: A WHILE BACK, I WAS DRAWING A MANGA CALLED "ANGEL DUST" FOR THE MAGAZINE PAPIPO. THE MANUSCRIPT? OF COURSE THEY DIDN'T SEND IT BACK... SO FOR REVENGE I WROTE IN ANDERSON. HOW MEAN OF ME, HUH? WELL IN THAT CASE, HOW ABOUT WE GET FRANCE SHOIN TO PUBLISH IT? HOW ABOUT THAT? RIGHT, DAIYA? (WITH A TAKARA RUBY HAIRSTYLE). SO, OF COURSE HIS VOICE ACTOR IS NACHI NOZAWA. AS FAR AS I'M CONCERNED ANYWAY.

FULL NAME: CROSS FIRE; KUFU FOR SHORT; COMMONLY KNOWN AS RO.

◀ THE PAGE COUNT ENDED UP TOO LOW, SO THE REST OF THIS BOOK IS TAKEN UP BY A ONE-SHOT I DID FOR THE NOW DEFUNCT COMIC MASTER. IT'S A MANGA WHERE MEMBERS OF THE VATICAN'S SPECIALIZED SECRET AGENCY SECTION XIII ISCARIOT, WHICH APPEARS IN HELLSING, ARE THE MAIN CHARACTERS. IF YOU LOOK AT IT A CERTAIN WAY, YOU SEE THAT IT'S WHAT BECAME THE SPRINGBOARD FOR HELLSING. IT HAS SIMILAR CHARACTERS, TOO. IN ALL THERE ARE THREE STORIES, AND PERHAPS THEY'LL RUN IN VOLUMES 2 AND 3. THAT IS, IF 2 AND 3 COME OUT...

SPECIAL THANKS

RYOUTAROU TANAKA (YAB), SANKICHI MEGURO (GROGGY), THE GREAT IMAMURA TAKEDA TSUNU, ETC... OF COURSE, YOUNG KING OURS EDITOR-IN-CHIEF FUKUHARA! AND MY EDITOR, VICE-CHIEF FUDETANI!

AHHHHHHH, I'M REALLY REALLY SORRYYYYYYY! SORRY! SORRY!

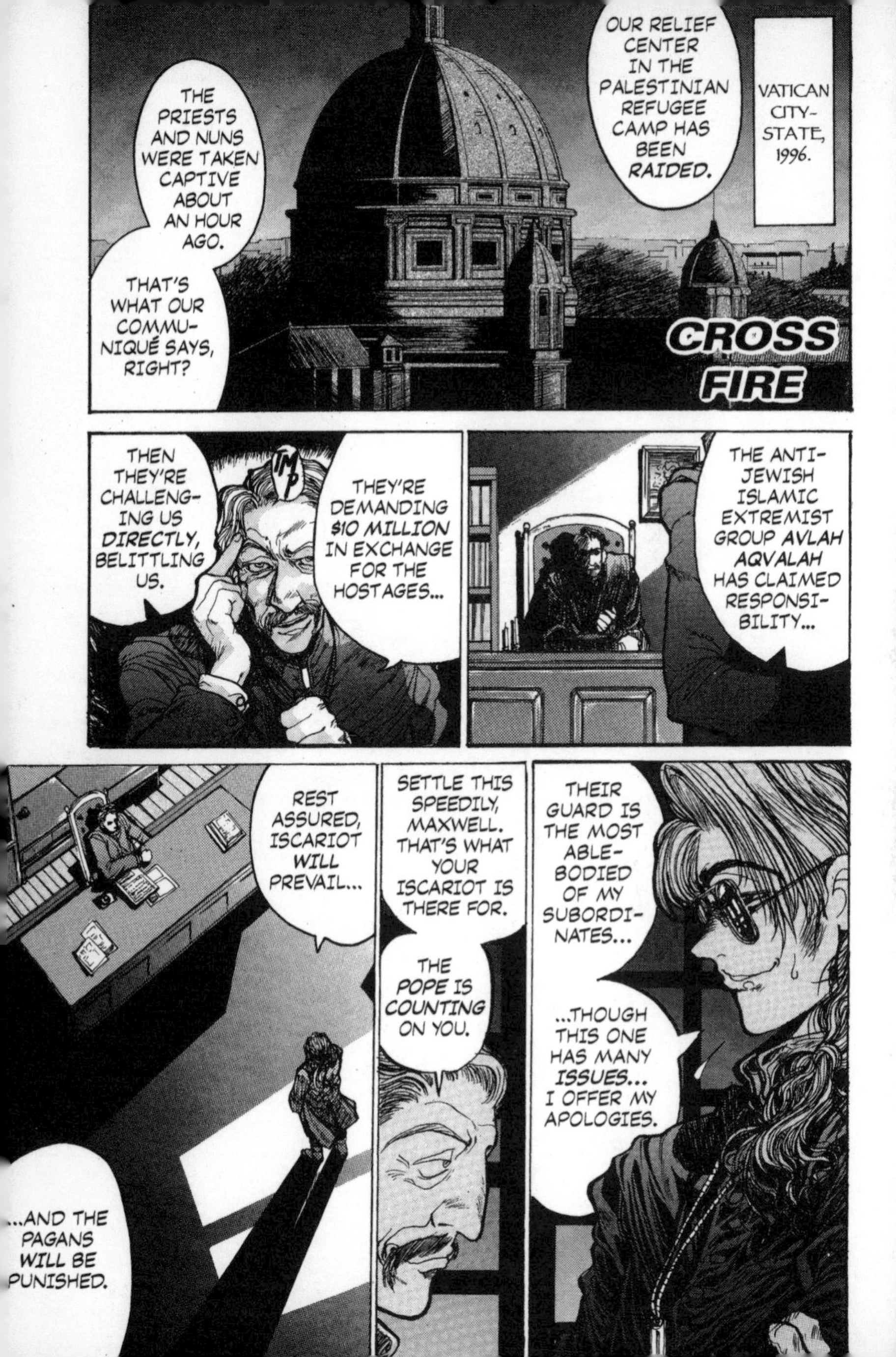
VATICAN CITY-STATE, 1996.
OUR RELIEF CENTER IN THE PALESTINIAN REFUGEE CAMP HAS BEEN RAIDED.
THE PRIESTS AND NUNS WERE TAKEN CAPTIVE ABOUT AN HOUR AGO.
THAT'S WHAT OUR COMMUNIQUÉ SAYS, RIGHT?
CROSS FIRE
THE ANTI-JEWISH ISLAMIC EXTREMIST GROUP AVLAH AQVALAH HAS CLAIMED RESPONSIBILITY...
THEY'RE DEMANDING $10 MILLION IN EXCHANGE FOR THE HOSTAGES...
TMP
THEN THEY'RE CHALLENGING US DIRECTLY, BELITTLING US.
THEIR GUARD IS THE MOST ABLE-BODIED OF MY SUBORDINATES...
...THOUGH THIS ONE HAS MANY ISSUES... I OFFER MY APOLOGIES.
SETTLE THIS SPEEDILY, MAXWELL. THAT'S WHAT YOUR ISCARIOT IS THERE FOR.
THE POPE IS COUNTING ON YOU.
REST ASSURED, ISCARIOT WILL PREVAIL...
...AND THE PAGANS WILL BE PUNISHED.

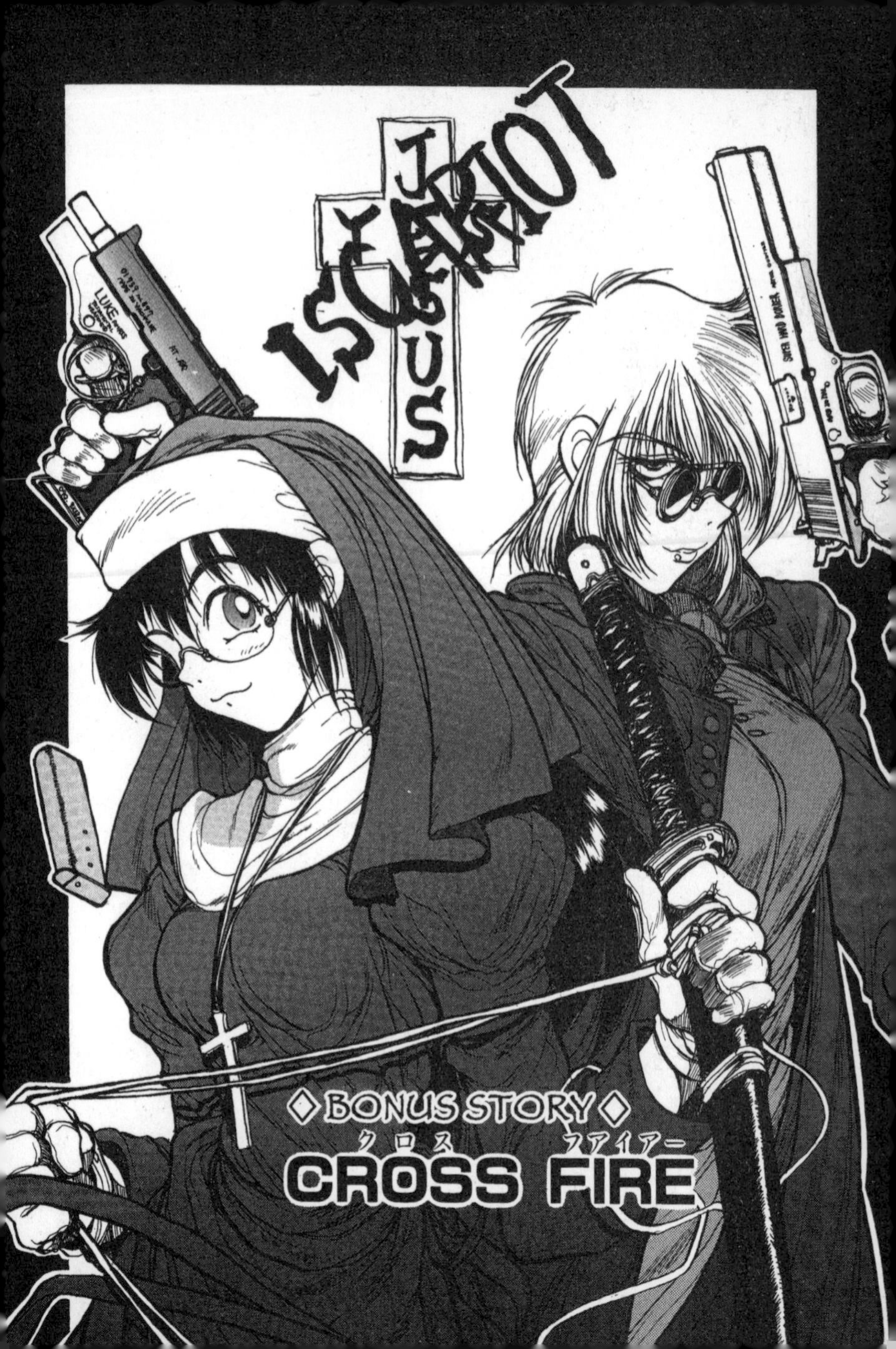
ISCARIOT
◆BONUS STORY◆
クロス ファイアー
CROSS FIRE

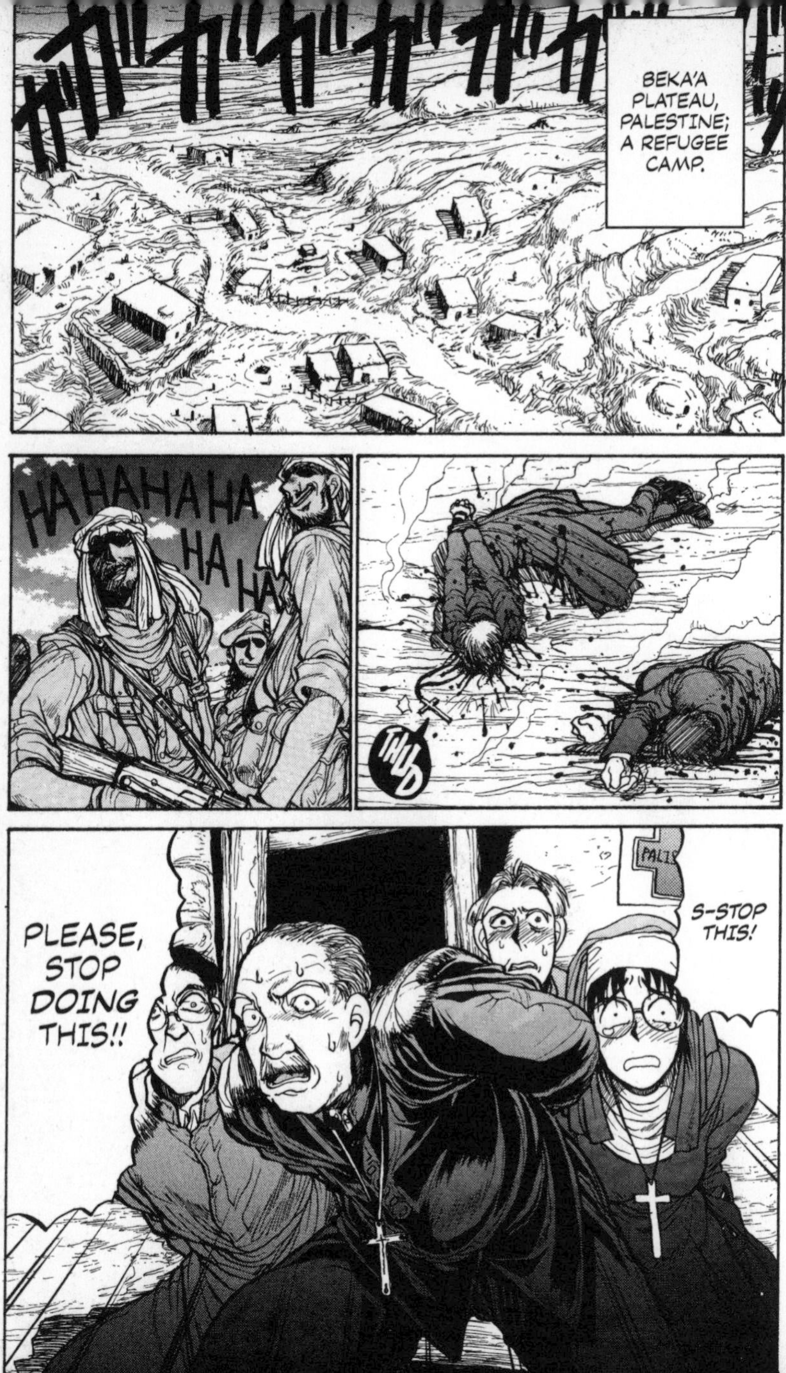
BEKA'A PLATEAU, PALESTINE; A REFUGEE CAMP.
THUD
HAHAHAHA HA HA HA
S-STOP THIS!
PLEASE, STOP DOING THIS!!

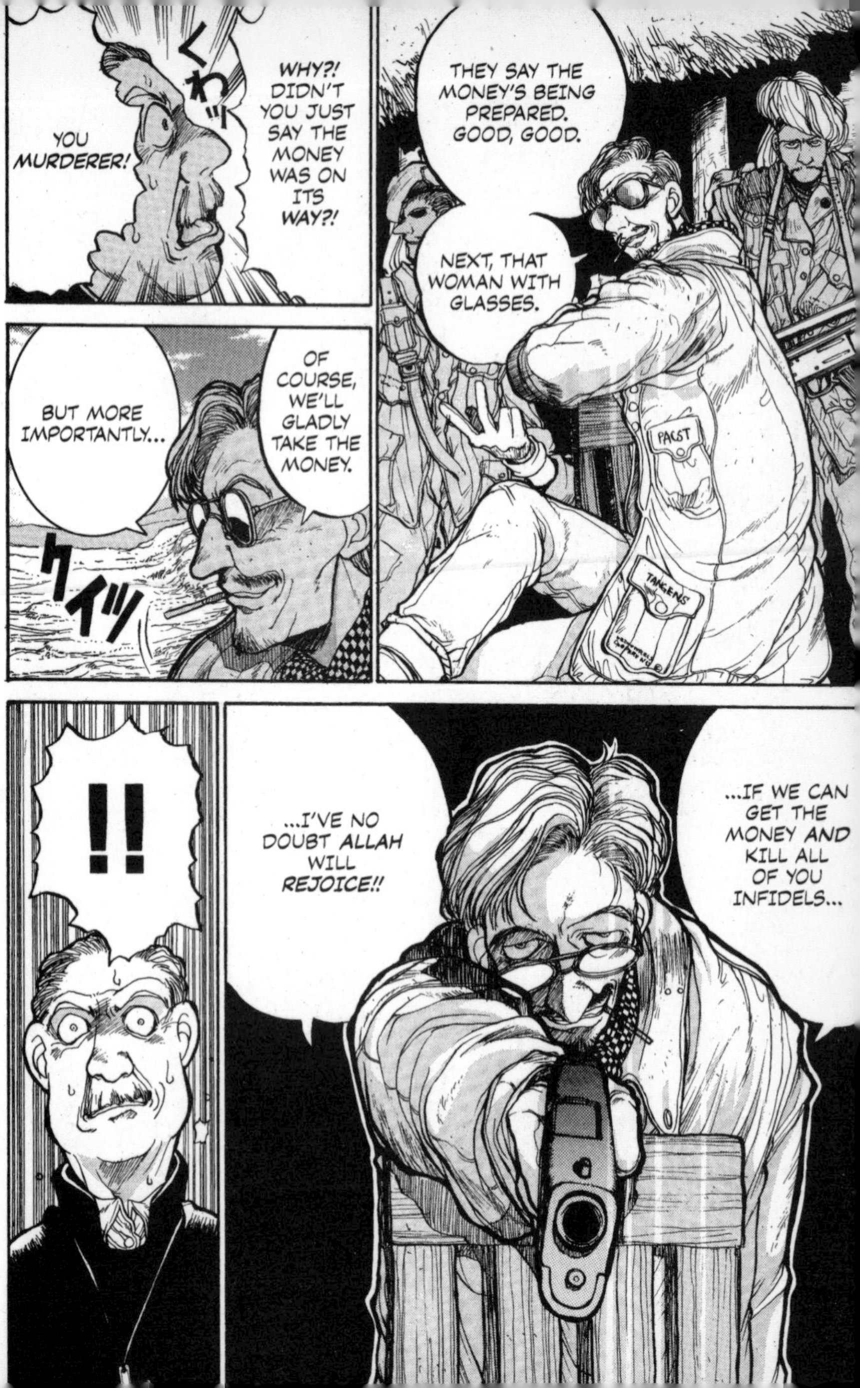
THEY SAY THE MONEY'S BEING PREPARED. GOOD, GOOD.
NEXT, THAT WOMAN WITH GLASSES.
WHY?! DIDN'T YOU JUST SAY THE MONEY WAS ON ITS WAY?!
くわッ
YOU MURDERER!
OF COURSE, WE'LL GLADLY TAKE THE MONEY.
BUT MORE IMPORTANTLY...
クイッ
...IF WE CAN GET THE MONEY AND KILL ALL OF YOU INFIDELS...
...I'VE NO DOUBT ALLAH WILL REJOICE!!
!!

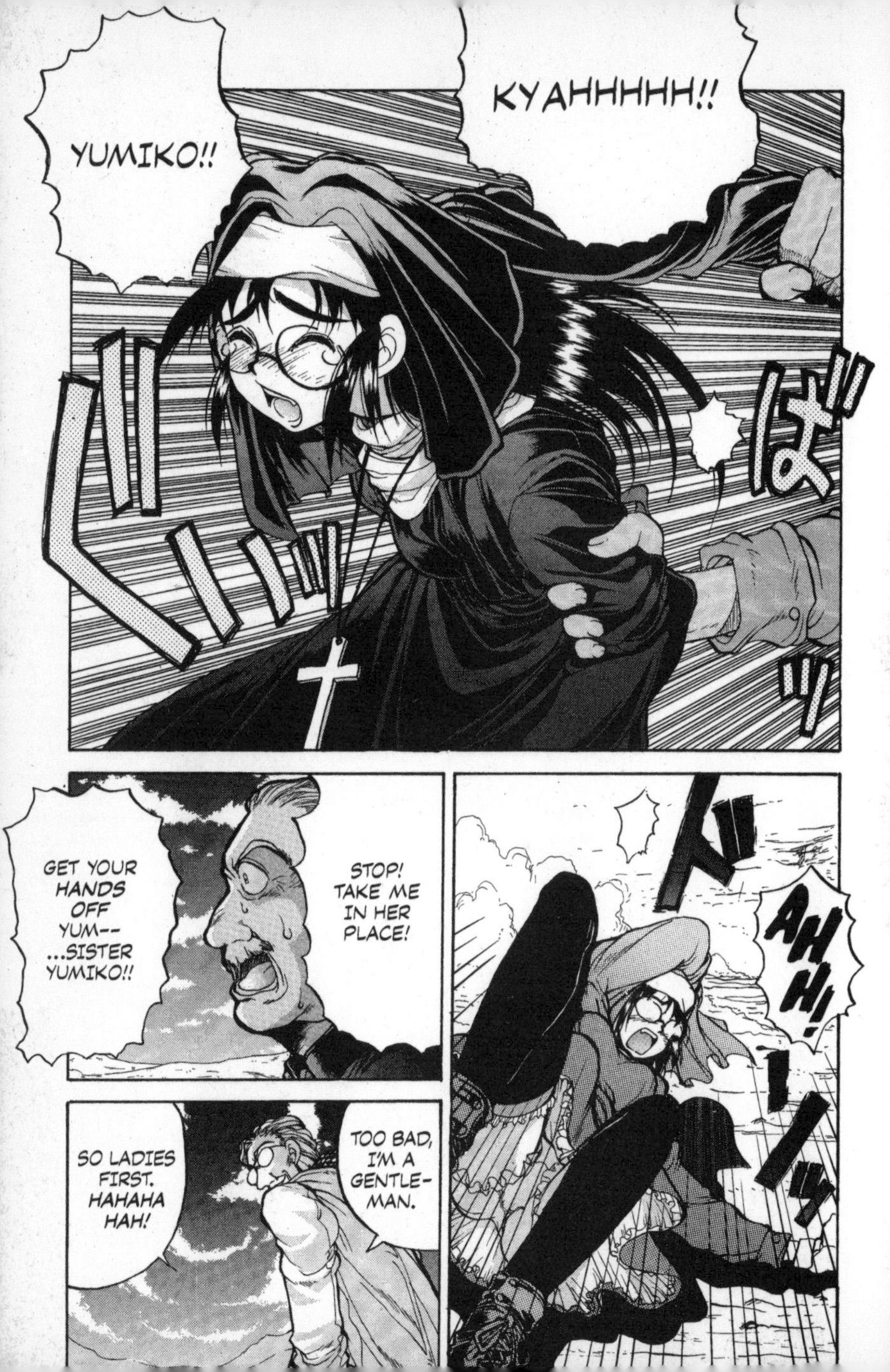
KYAHHHHH!!
YUMIKO!!
AHH!
STOP! TAKE ME IN HER PLACE!
GET YOUR HANDS OFF YUM-- ...SISTER YUMIKO!!
TOO BAD, I'M A GENTLE-MAN.
SO LADIES FIRST. HAHAHA HAH!

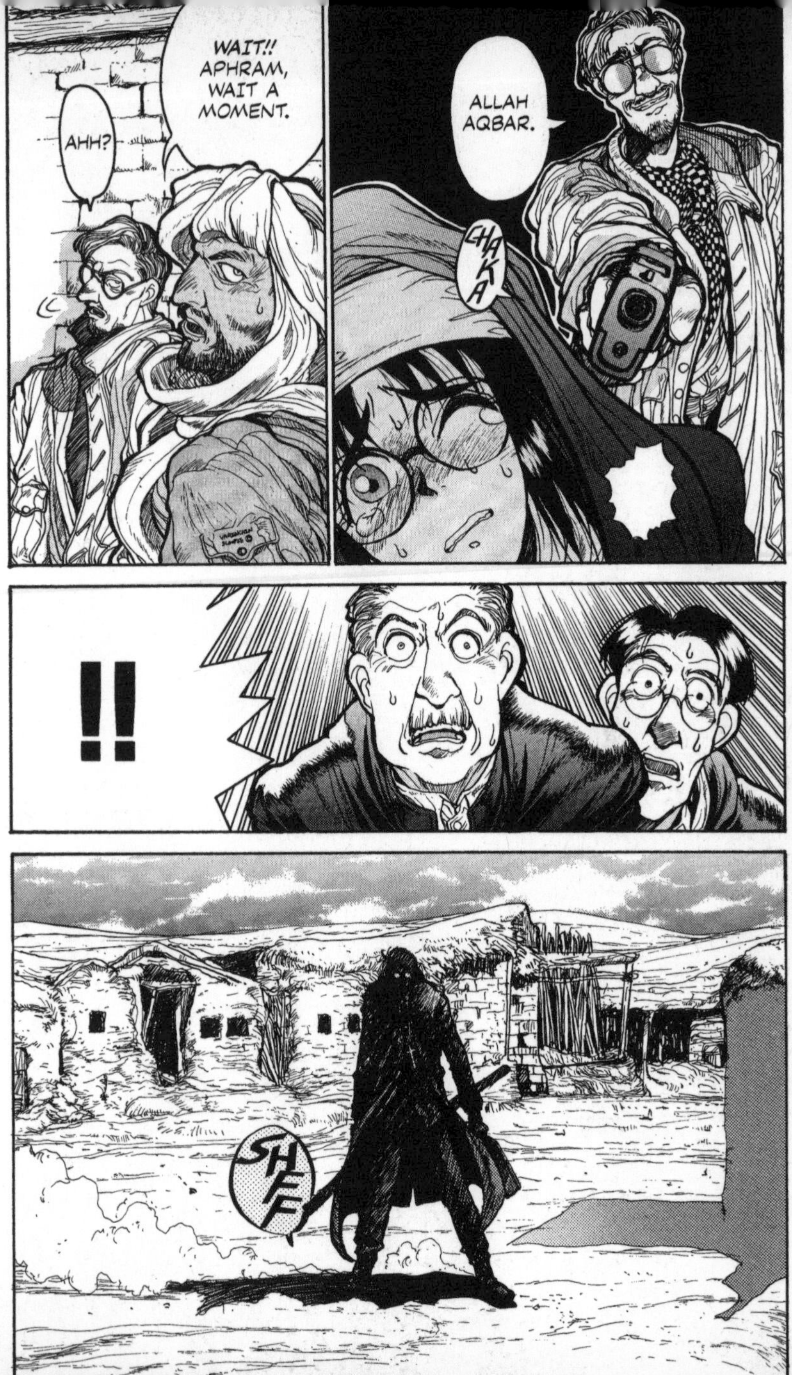
ALLAH AQBAR.
CHAKA
WAIT!! APHRAM, WAIT A MOMENT.
AHH?
!!
SHFF

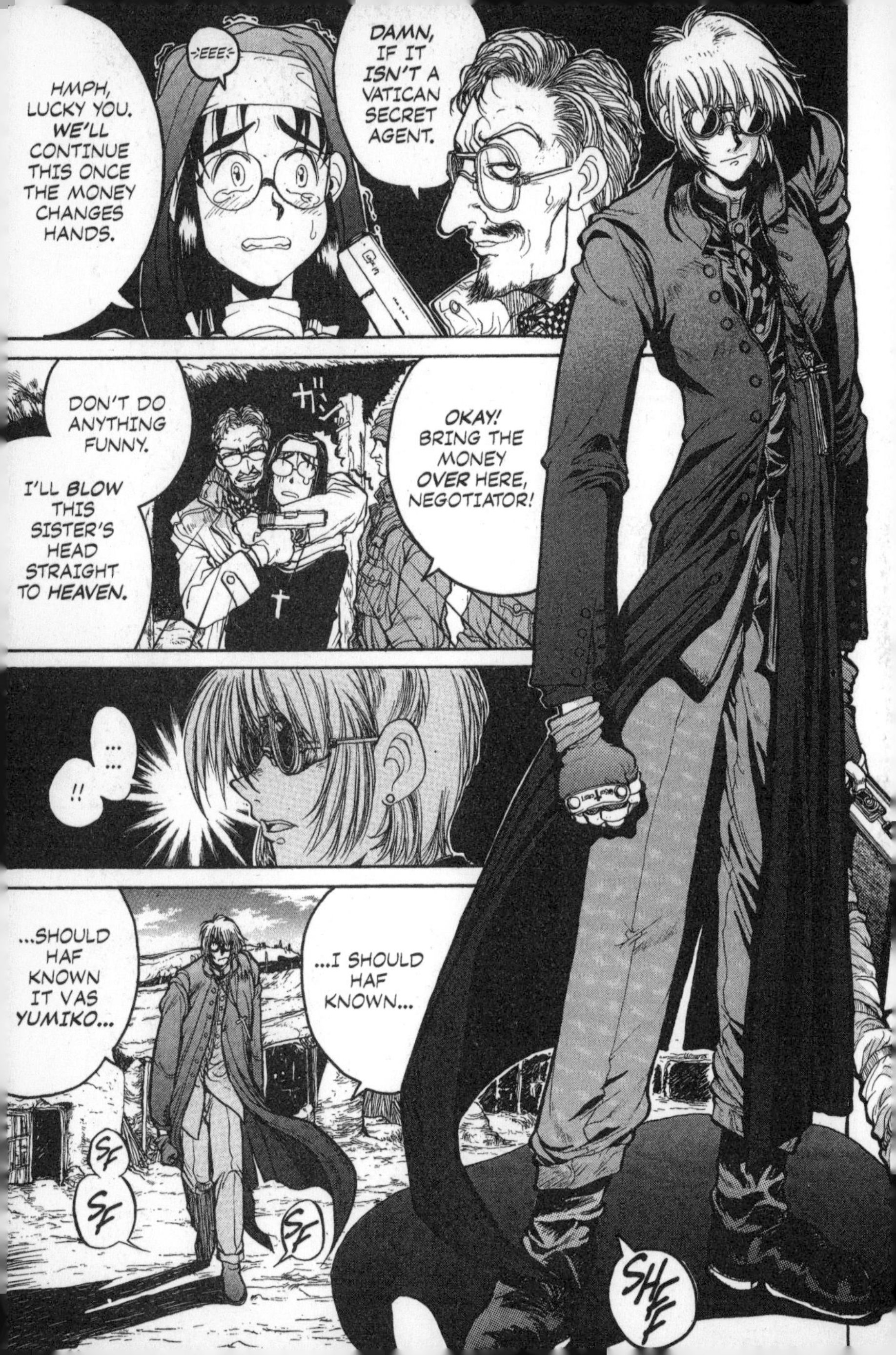
SHFF
DAMN, IF IT ISN'T A VATICAN SECRET AGENT.
EEE
HMPH, LUCKY YOU. WE'LL CONTINUE THIS ONCE THE MONEY CHANGES HANDS.
OKAY! BRING THE MONEY OVER HERE, NEGOTIATOR!
DON'T DO ANYTHING FUNNY.
I'LL BLOW THIS SISTER'S HEAD STRAIGHT TO HEAVEN.
......!!
...I SHOULD HAF KNOWN...
...SHOULD HAF KNOWN IT VAS YUMIKO...
SF
SF
SF

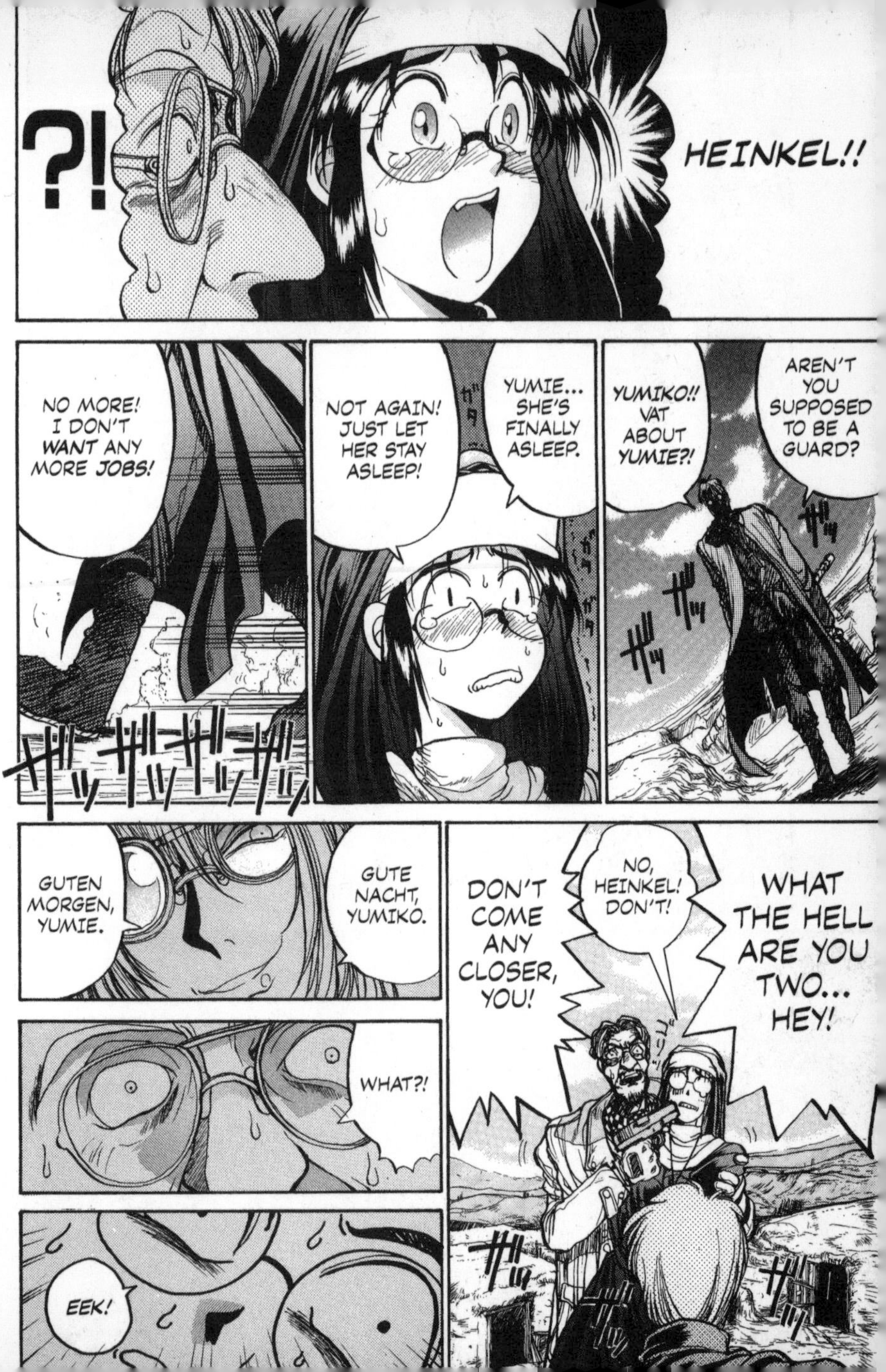
HEINKEL!!
?!
AREN'T YOU SUPPOSED TO BE A GUARD?
YUMIKO!! VAT ABOUT YUMIE?!
YUMIE... SHE'S FINALLY ASLEEP.
NOT AGAIN! JUST LET HER STAY ASLEEP!
NO MORE! I DON'T WANT ANY MORE JOBS!
WHAT THE HELL ARE YOU TWO... HEY!
NO, HEINKEL! DON'T!
DON'T COME ANY CLOSER, YOU!
GUTE NACHT, YUMIKO.
GUTEN MORGEN, YUMIE.
WHAT?!
EEK!

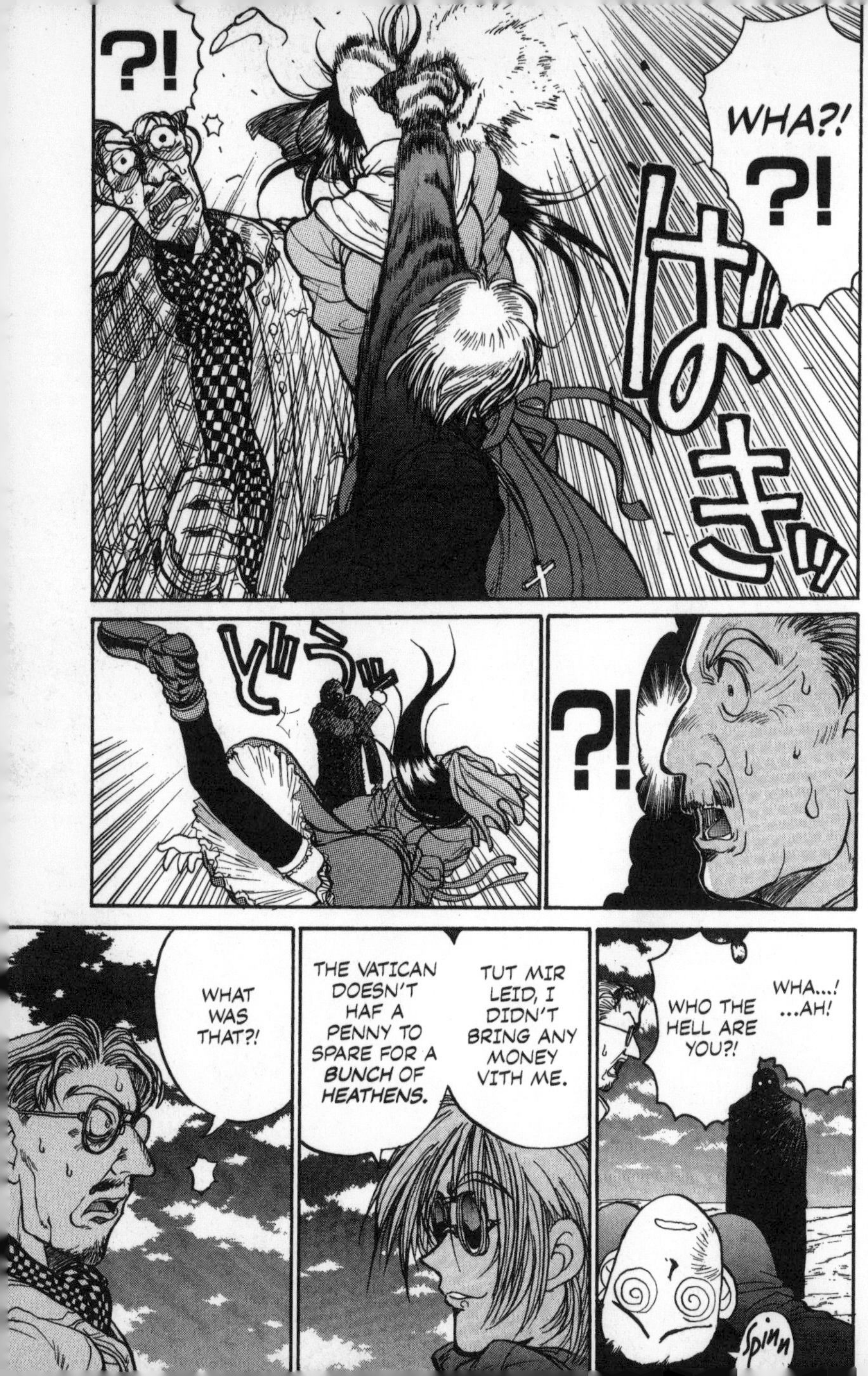
WHA?!
?!
?!
?!
WHA...! ...AH!
WHO THE HELL ARE YOU?!
SPINN
TUT MIR LEID, I DIDN'T BRING ANY MONEY VITH ME.
THE VATICAN DOESN'T HAF A PENNY TO SPARE FOR A BUNCH OF HEATHENS.
WHAT WAS THAT?!

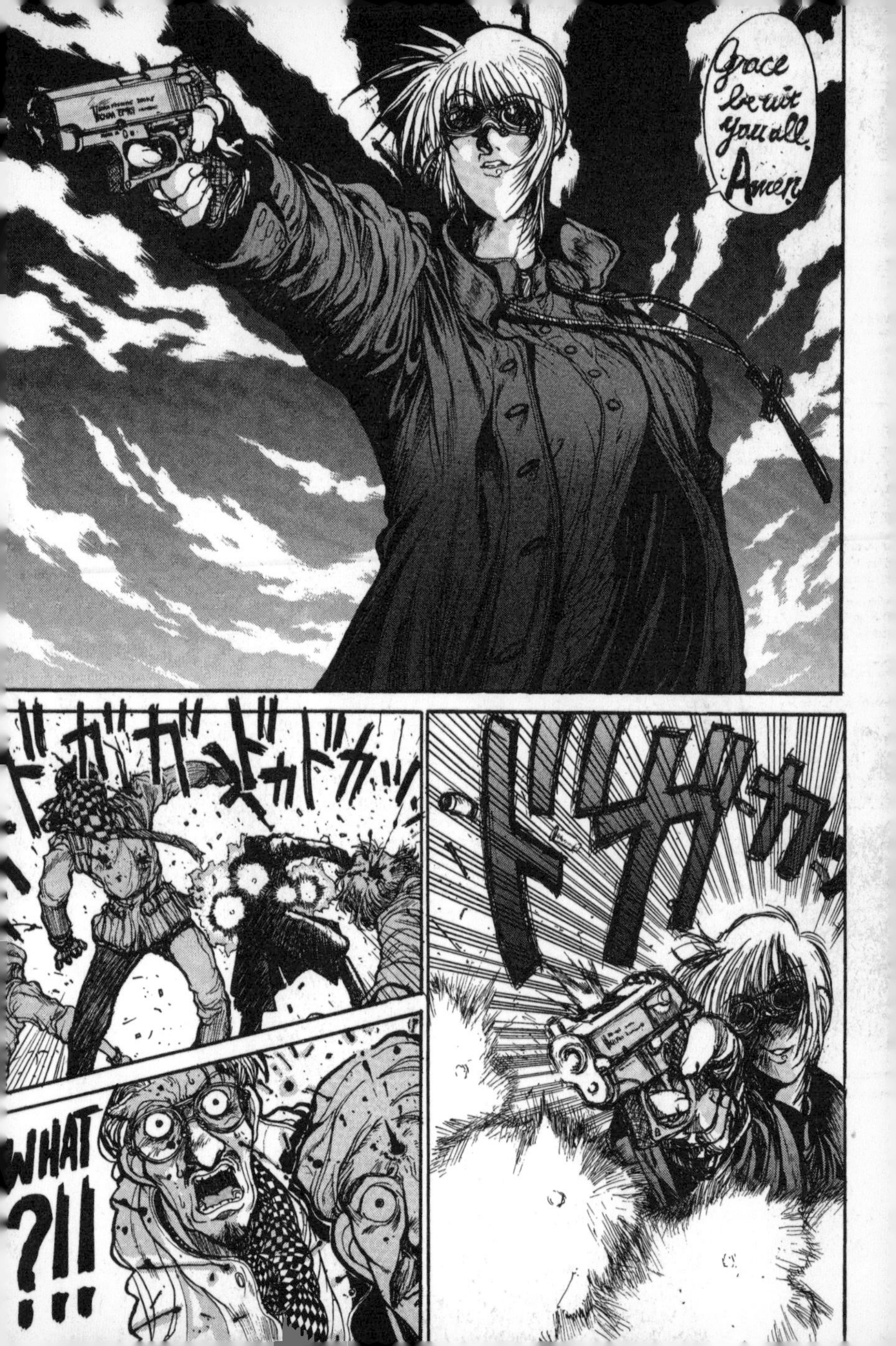
Grace be wit you all. Amen.
WHAT ?!!

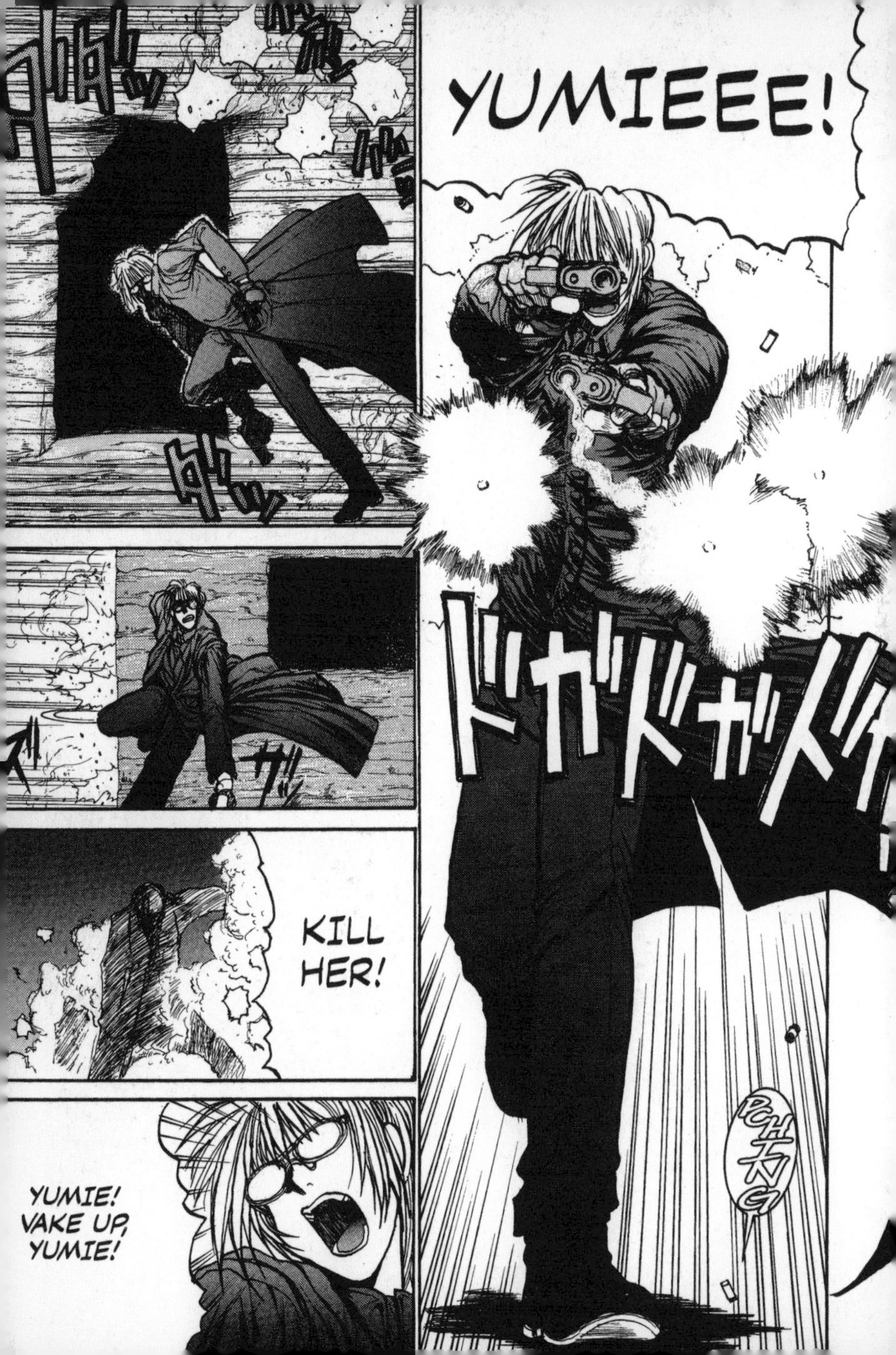
YUMIEEE!
PCHING
KILL HER!
YUMIE! VAKE UP, YUMIE!

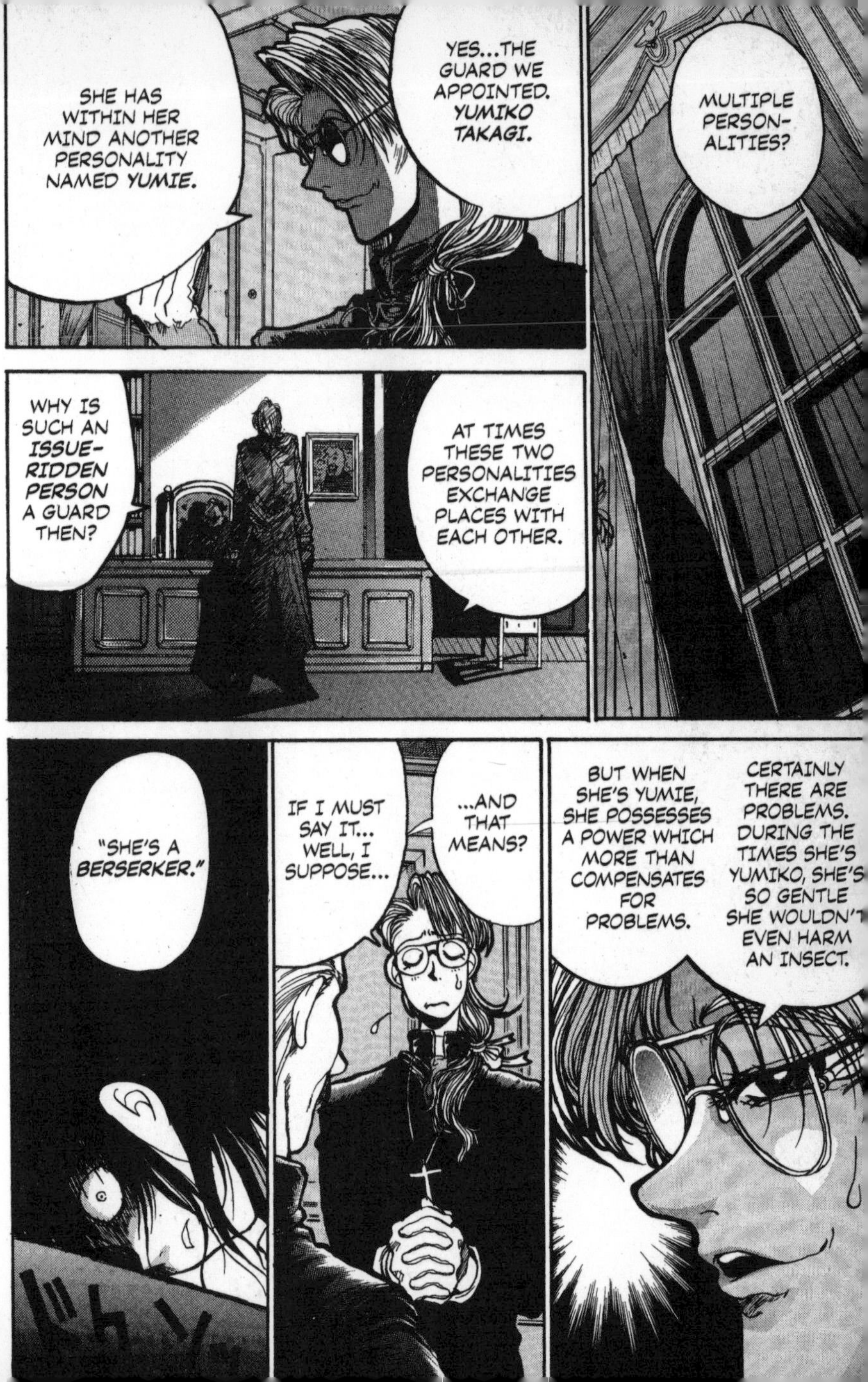
MULTIPLE PERSONALITIES?
YES...THE GUARD WE APPOINTED. YUMIKO TAKAGI.
SHE HAS WITHIN HER MIND ANOTHER PERSONALITY NAMED YUMIE.
AT TIMES THESE TWO PERSONALITIES EXCHANGE PLACES WITH EACH OTHER.
WHY IS SUCH AN ISSUE-RIDDEN PERSON A GUARD THEN?
CERTAINLY THERE ARE PROBLEMS. DURING THE TIMES SHE'S YUMIKO, SHE'S SO GENTLE SHE WOULDN'T EVEN HARM AN INSECT.
BUT WHEN SHE'S YUMIE, SHE POSSESSES A POWER WHICH MORE THAN COMPENSATES FOR PROBLEMS.
...AND THAT MEANS?
IF I MUST SAY IT... WELL, I SUPPOSE...
"SHE'S A BERSERKER."

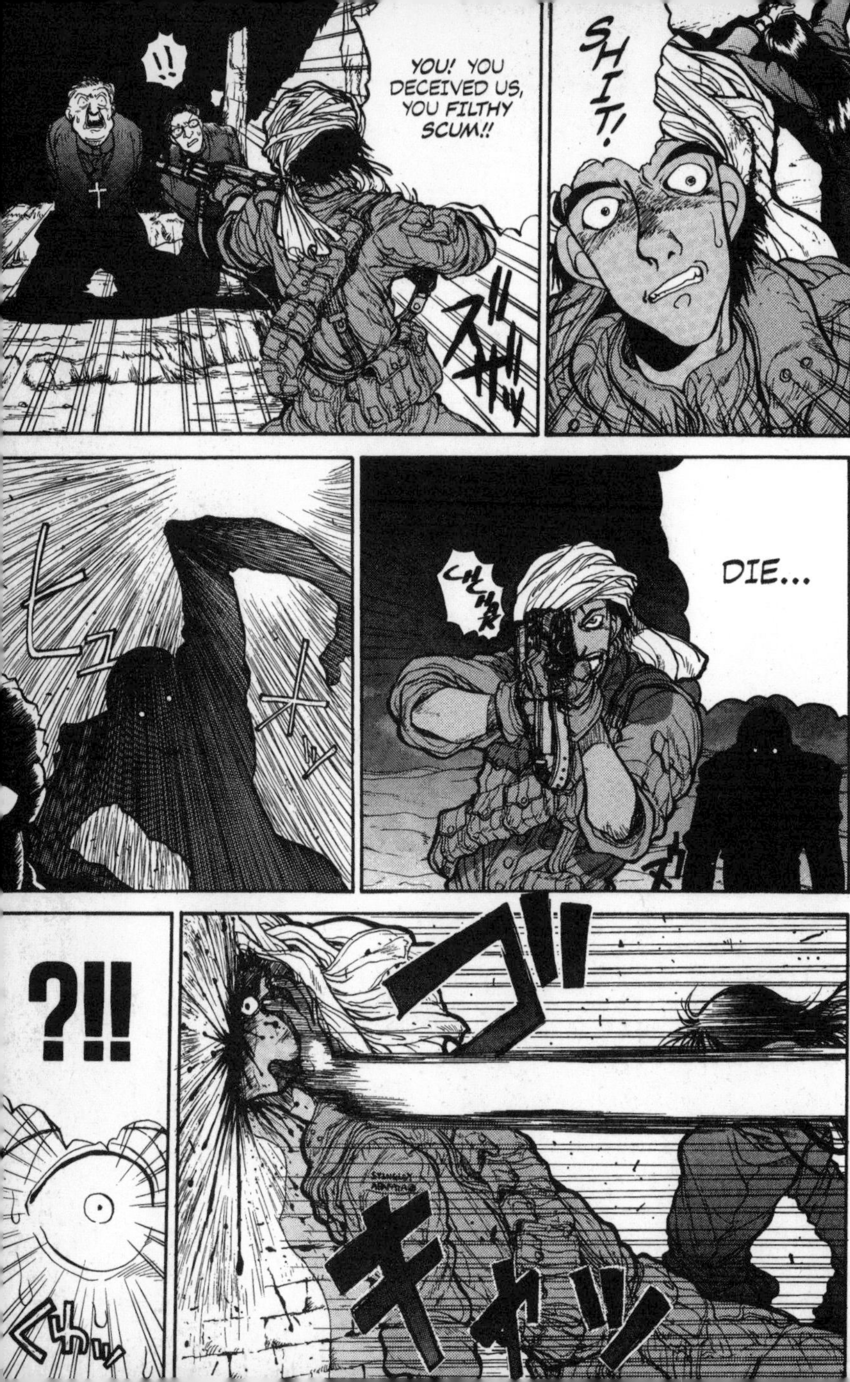
SHIT!
YOU! YOU DECEIVED US, YOU FILTHY SCUM!!
!!
DIE...
CHCHAK
?!!

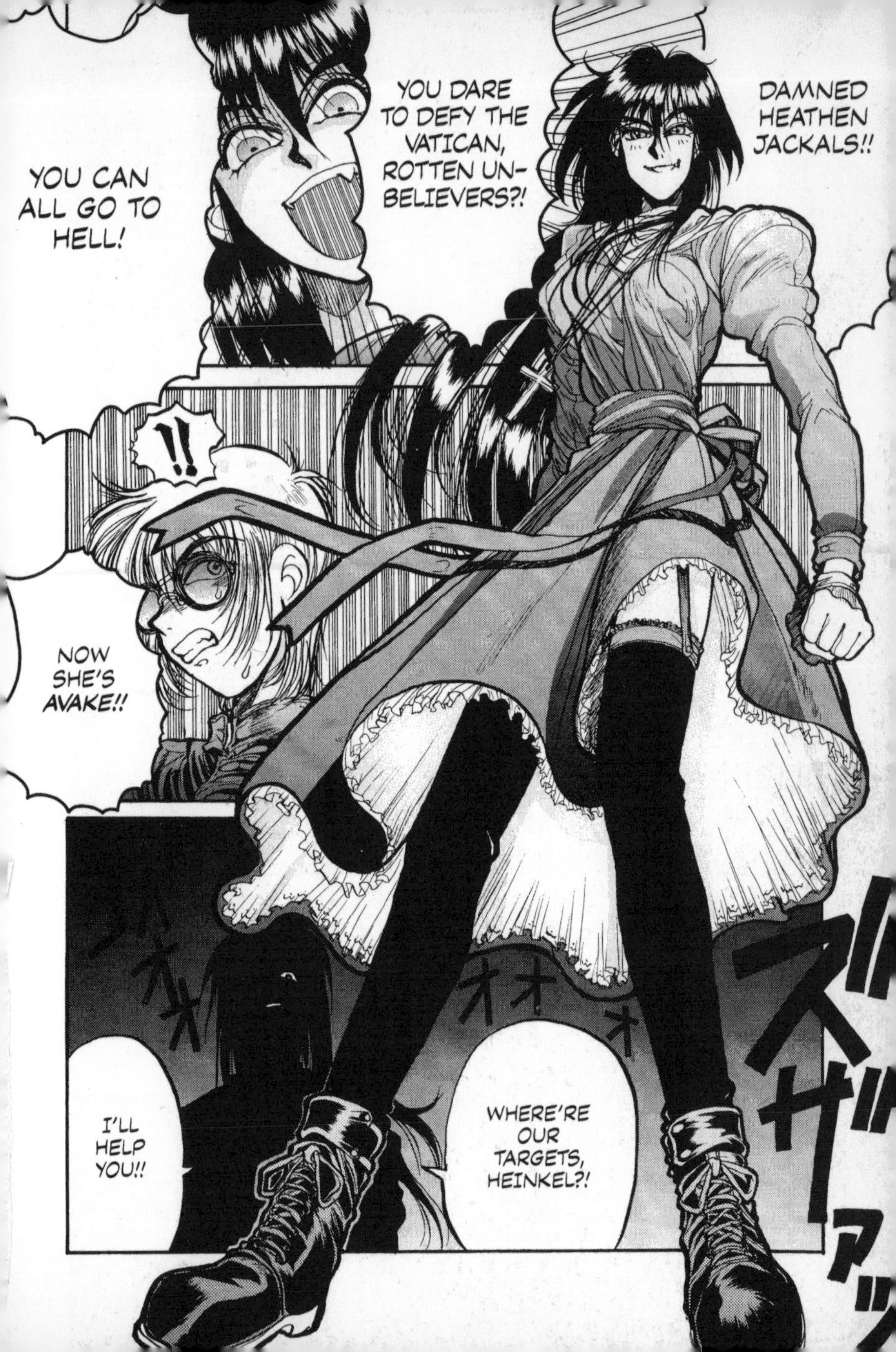
DAMNED HEATHEN JACKALS!!
YOU DARE TO DEFY THE VATICAN, ROTTEN UN-BELIEVERS?!
YOU CAN ALL GO TO HELL!
!!
NOW SHE'S AVAKE!!
WHERE'RE OUR TARGETS, HEINKEL?!
I'LL HELP YOU!!

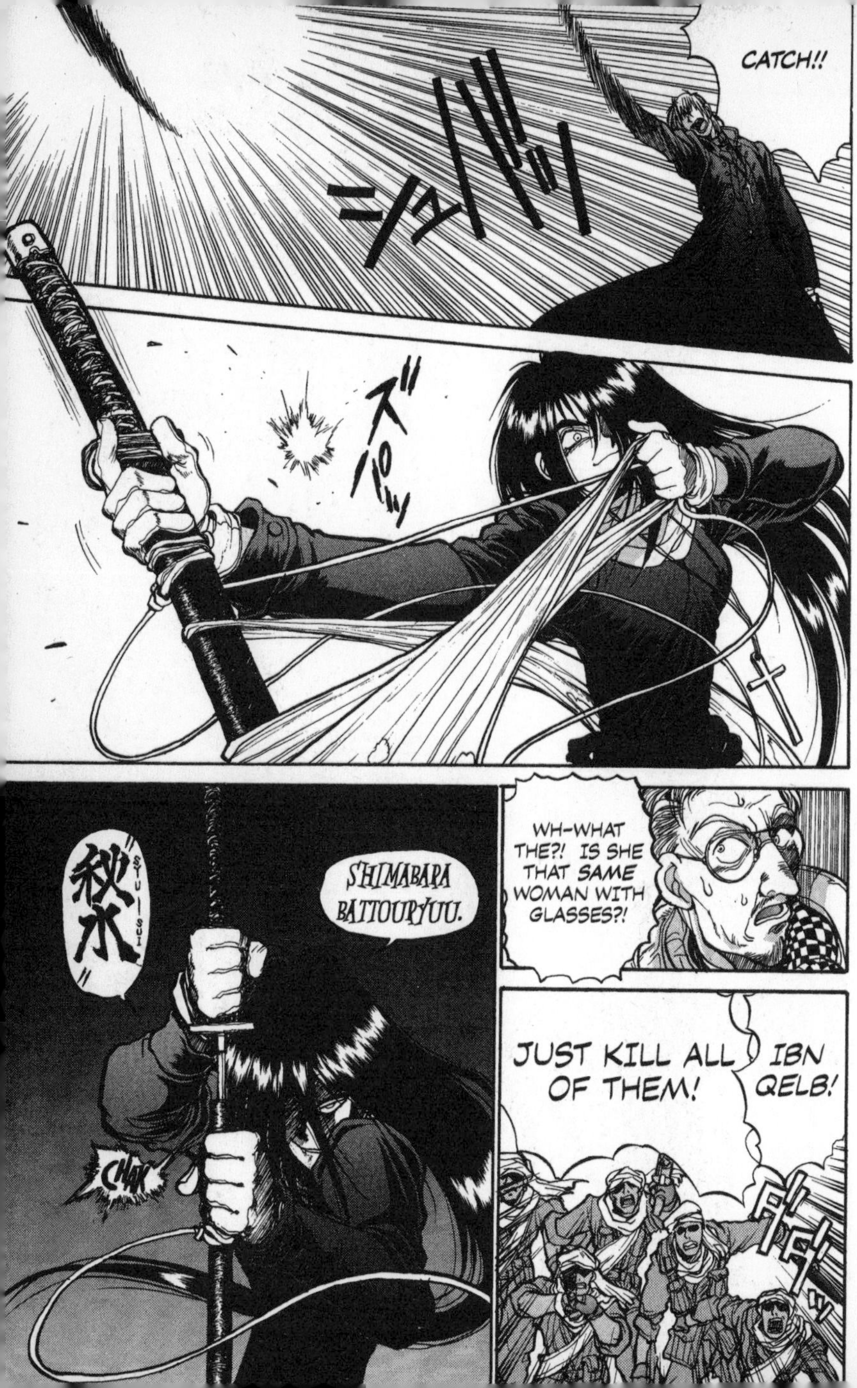
CATCH!!
WH-WHAT THE?! IS SHE THAT SAME WOMAN WITH GLASSES?!
IBN QELB!
JUST KILL ALL OF THEM!
SHIMABARA BATTOURYUU.
秋水 SYU-SUI
CHAK

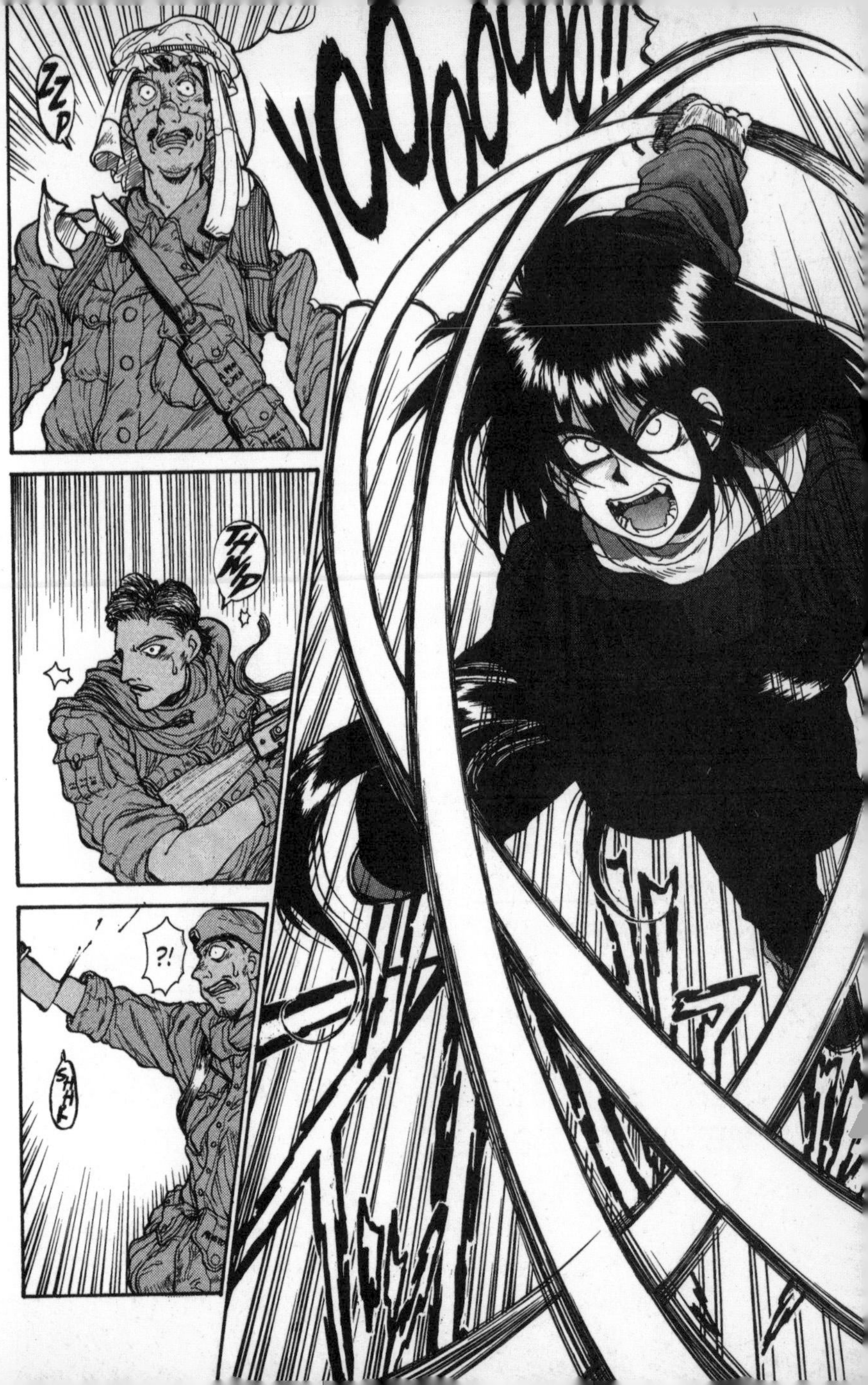
YOOOUUU!!!
ZZP
THMP
?!
SHHK

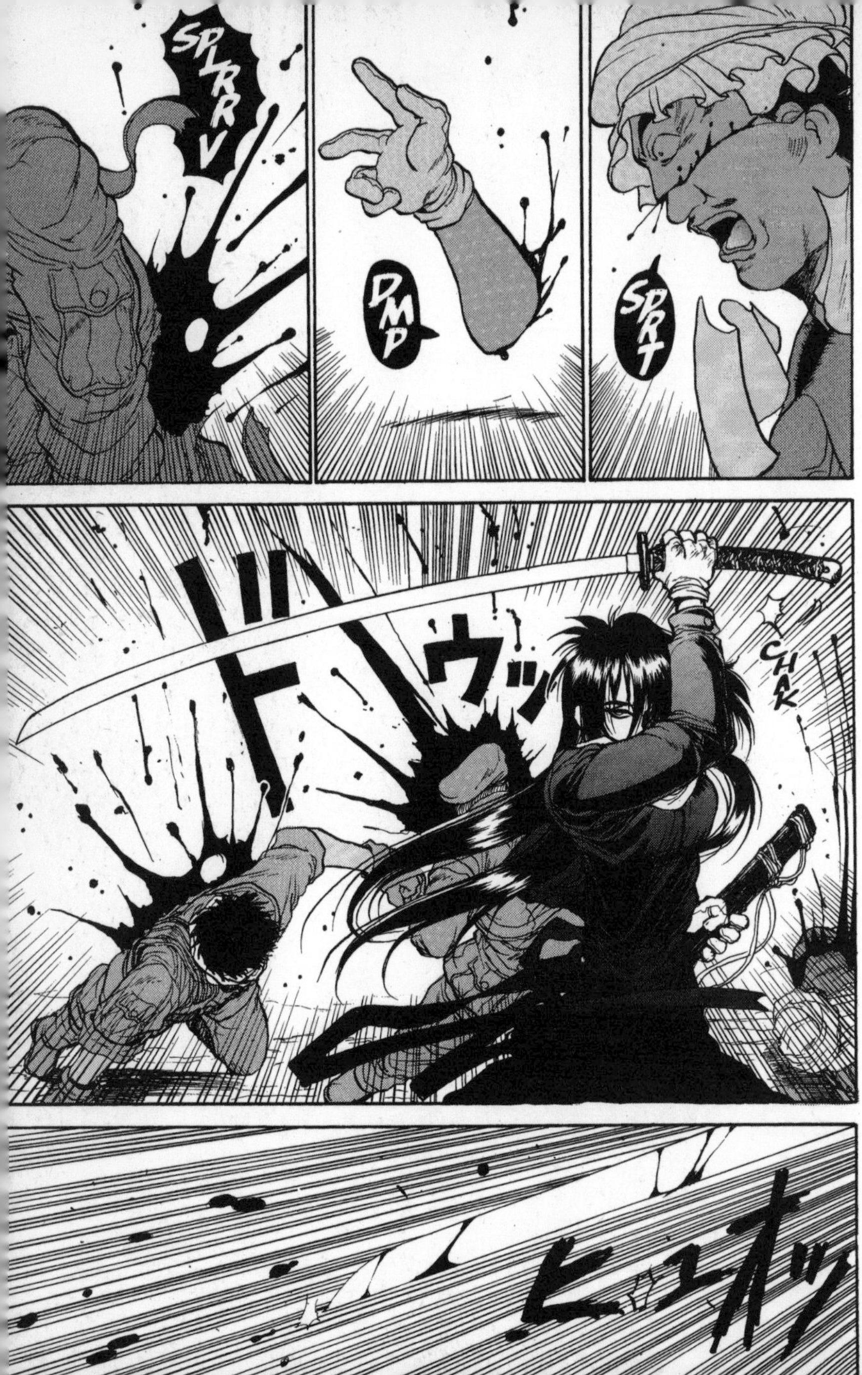
SPRT
DMP
SPLRRV
CHAK
ドウッ
ヒュオッ

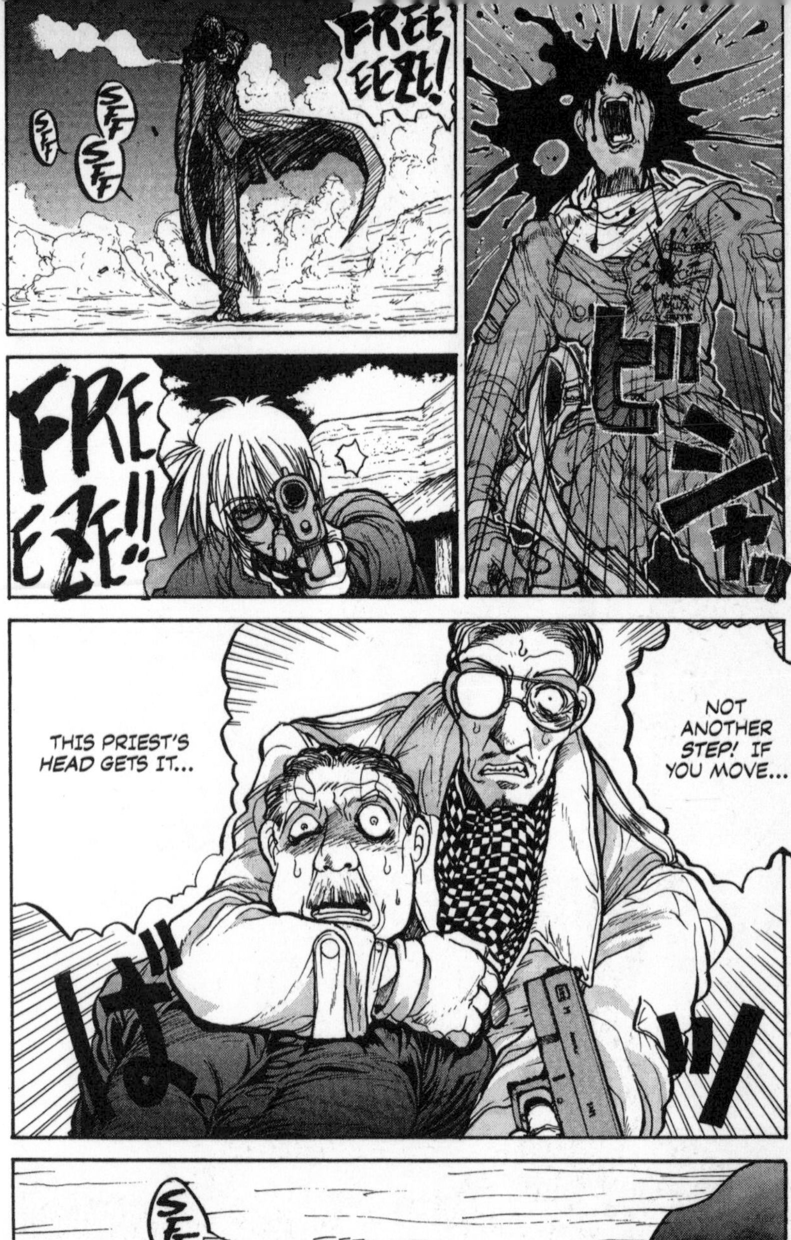
FREE EEZE!
SFF
SFF
SFF
FRE EEZE!!
NOT ANOTHER STEP! IF YOU MOVE...
THIS PRIEST'S HEAD GETS IT...
SFF

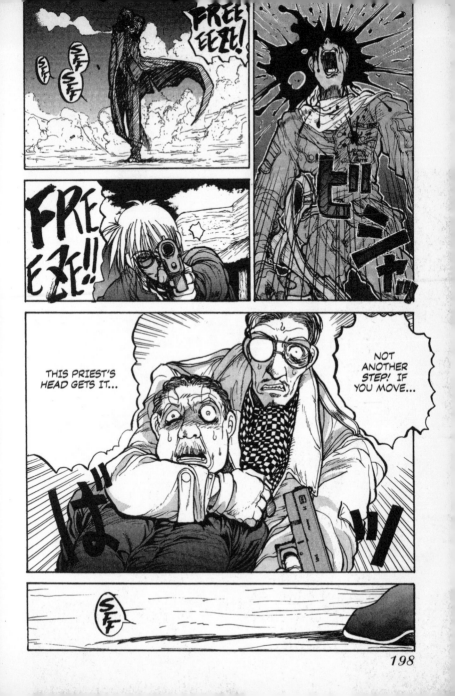

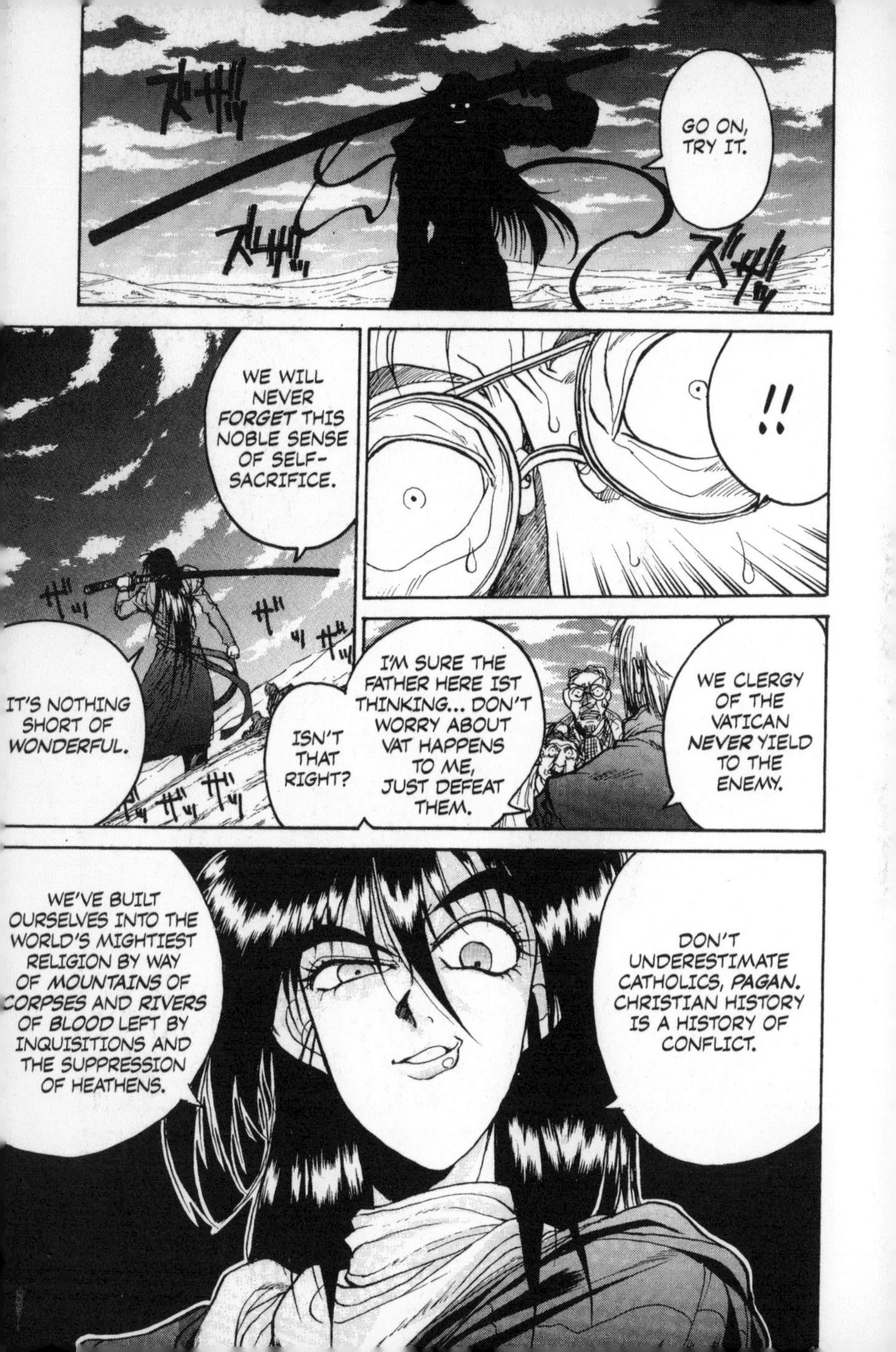
GO ON, TRY IT.
!!
WE WILL NEVER FORGET THIS NOBLE SENSE OF SELF-SACRIFICE.
WE CLERGY OF THE VATICAN NEVER YIELD TO THE ENEMY.
I'M SURE THE FATHER HERE IST THINKING... DON'T WORRY ABOUT VAT HAPPENS TO ME, JUST DEFEAT THEM.
ISN'T THAT RIGHT?
IT'S NOTHING SHORT OF WONDERFUL.
DON'T UNDERESTIMATE CATHOLICS, PAGAN. CHRISTIAN HISTORY IS A HISTORY OF CONFLICT.
WE'VE BUILT OURSELVES INTO THE WORLD'S MIGHTIEST RELIGION BY WAY OF MOUNTAINS OF CORPSES AND RIVERS OF BLOOD LEFT BY INQUISITIONS AND THE SUPPRESSION OF HEATHENS.

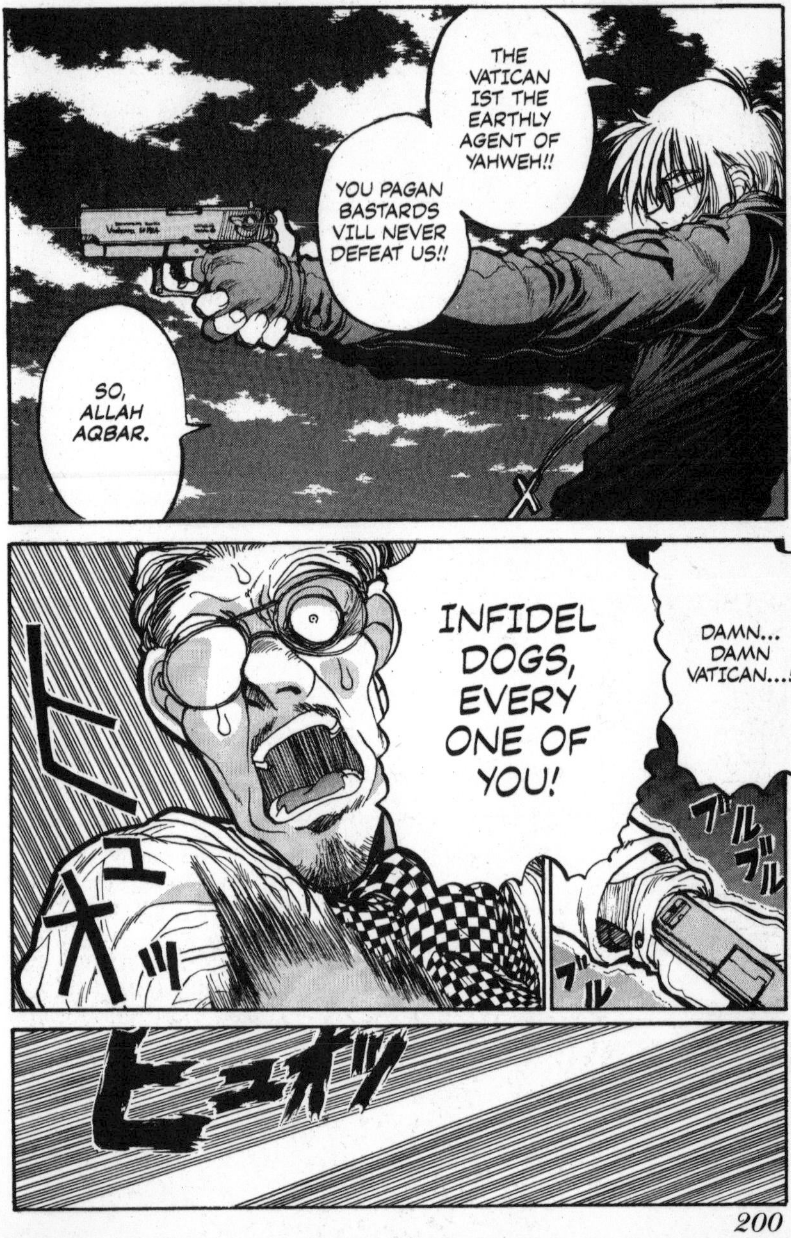
THE VATICAN IST THE EARTHLY AGENT OF YAHWEH!!
YOU PAGAN BASTARDS VILL NEVER DEFEAT US!!
SO, ALLAH AQBAR.
DAMN... DAMN VATICAN...!
ブルブル
ブル
INFIDEL DOGS, EVERY ONE OF YOU!
ヒュオッ

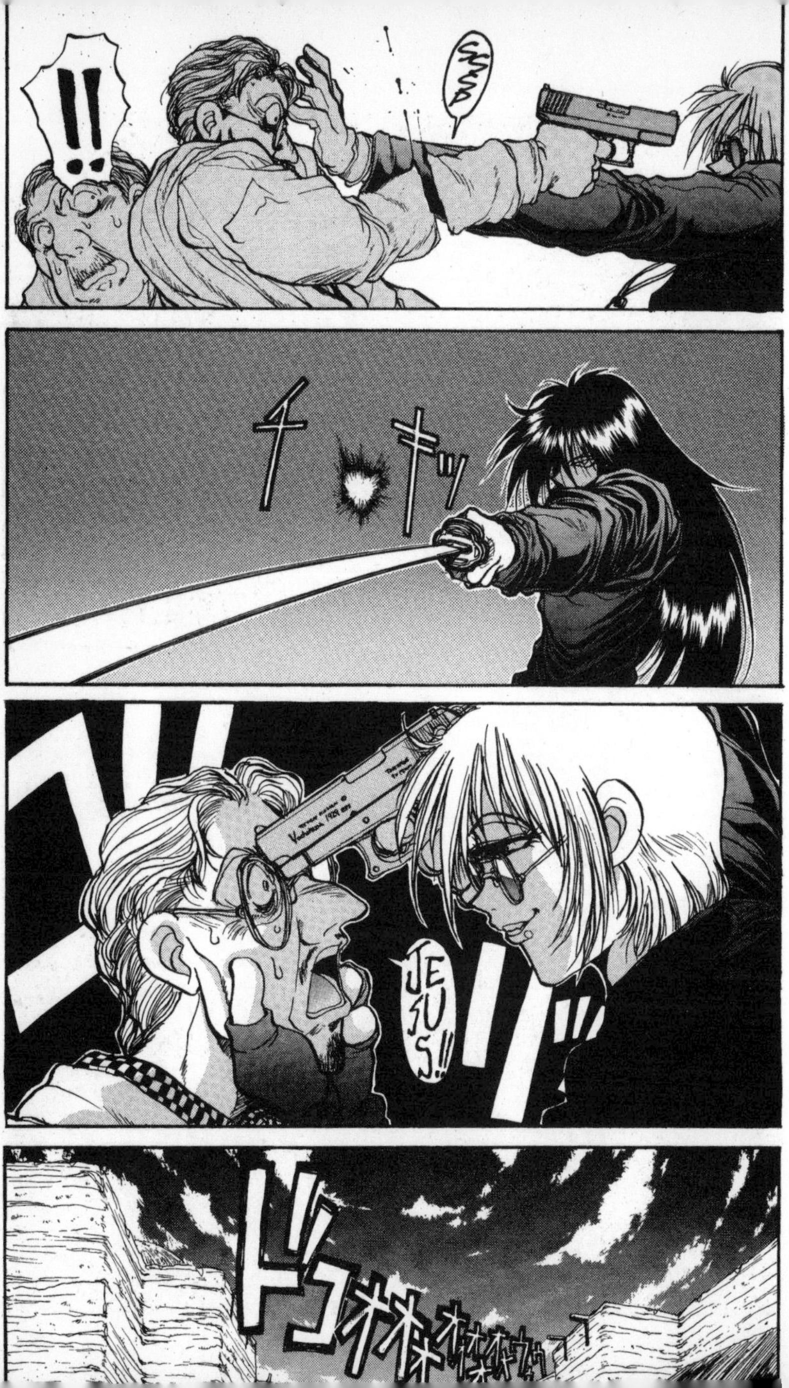
GASP
!!
チキッ
JESUS!!
ドゴオオオ

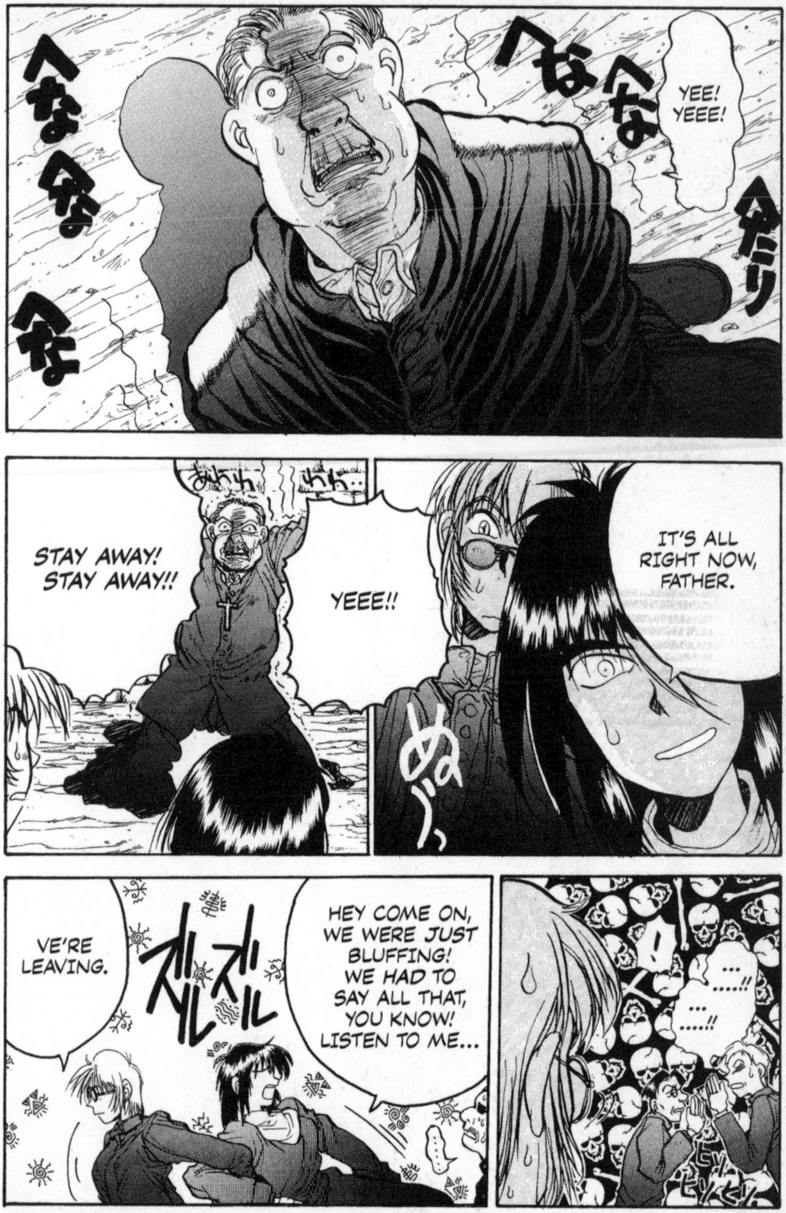
YEE! YEEE!
IT'S ALL RIGHT NOW, FATHER.
YEEE!!
STAY AWAY! STAY AWAY!!
... .!!
... .!!
HEY COME ON, WE WERE JUST BLUFFING! WE HAD TO SAY ALL THAT, YOU KNOW! LISTEN TO ME...
VE'RE LEAVING.

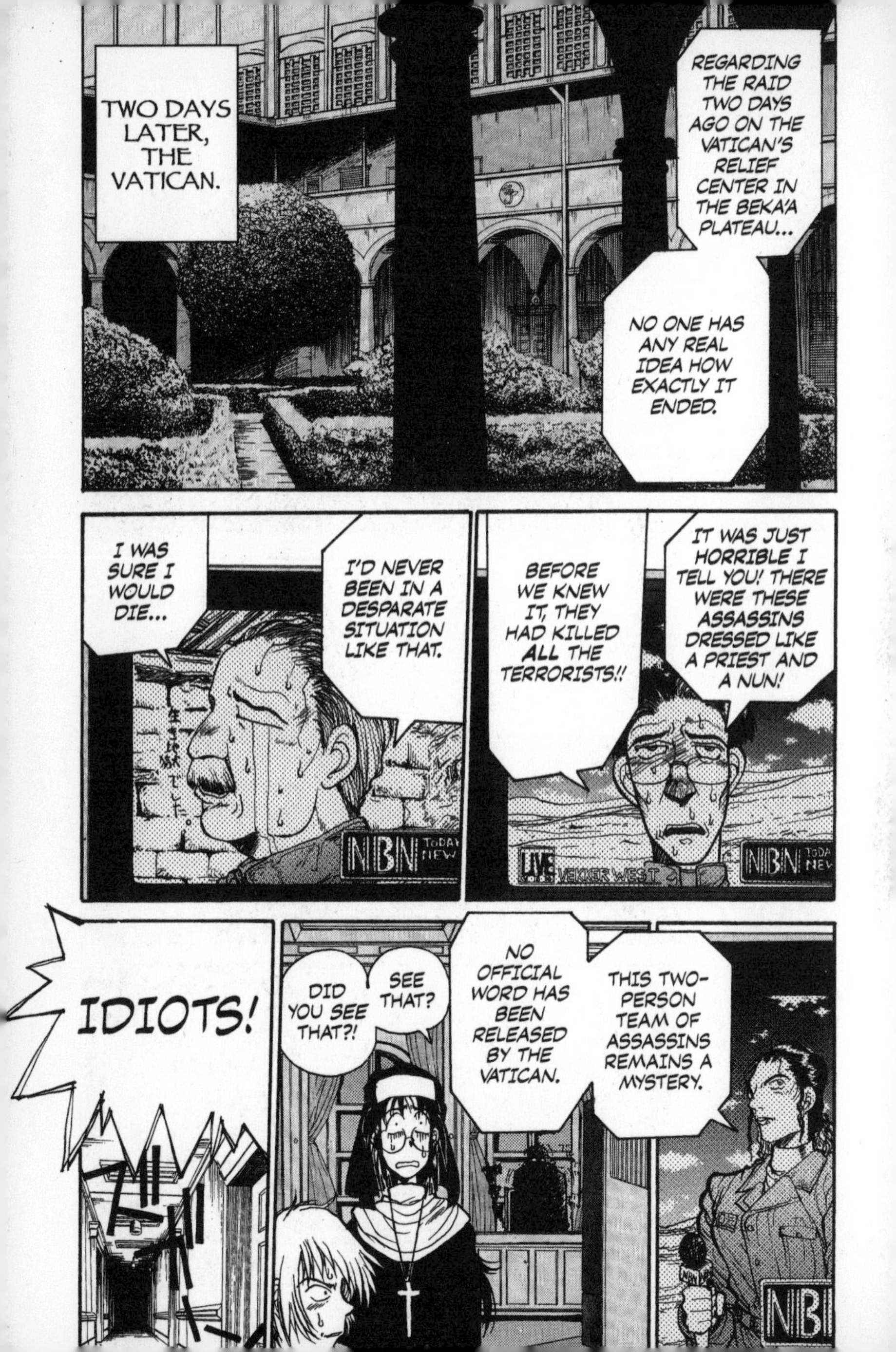
REGARDING THE RAID TWO DAYS AGO ON THE VATICAN'S RELIEF CENTER IN THE BEKA'A PLATEAU...
NO ONE HAS ANY REAL IDEA HOW EXACTLY IT ENDED.
TWO DAYS LATER, THE VATICAN.
IT WAS JUST HORRIBLE I TELL YOU! THERE WERE THESE ASSASSINS DRESSED LIKE A PRIEST AND A NUN!
BEFORE WE KNEW IT, THEY HAD KILLED ALL THE TERRORISTS!!
NBN TODAY NEW
LIVE VEKKER WEST
I'D NEVER BEEN IN A DESPARATE SITUATION LIKE THAT.
I WAS SURE I WOULD DIE...
NBN TODAY NEW
THIS TWO-PERSON TEAM OF ASSASSINS REMAINS A MYSTERY.
NO OFFICIAL WORD HAS BEEN RELEASED BY THE VATICAN.
SEE THAT?
DID YOU SEE THAT?!
IDIOTS!

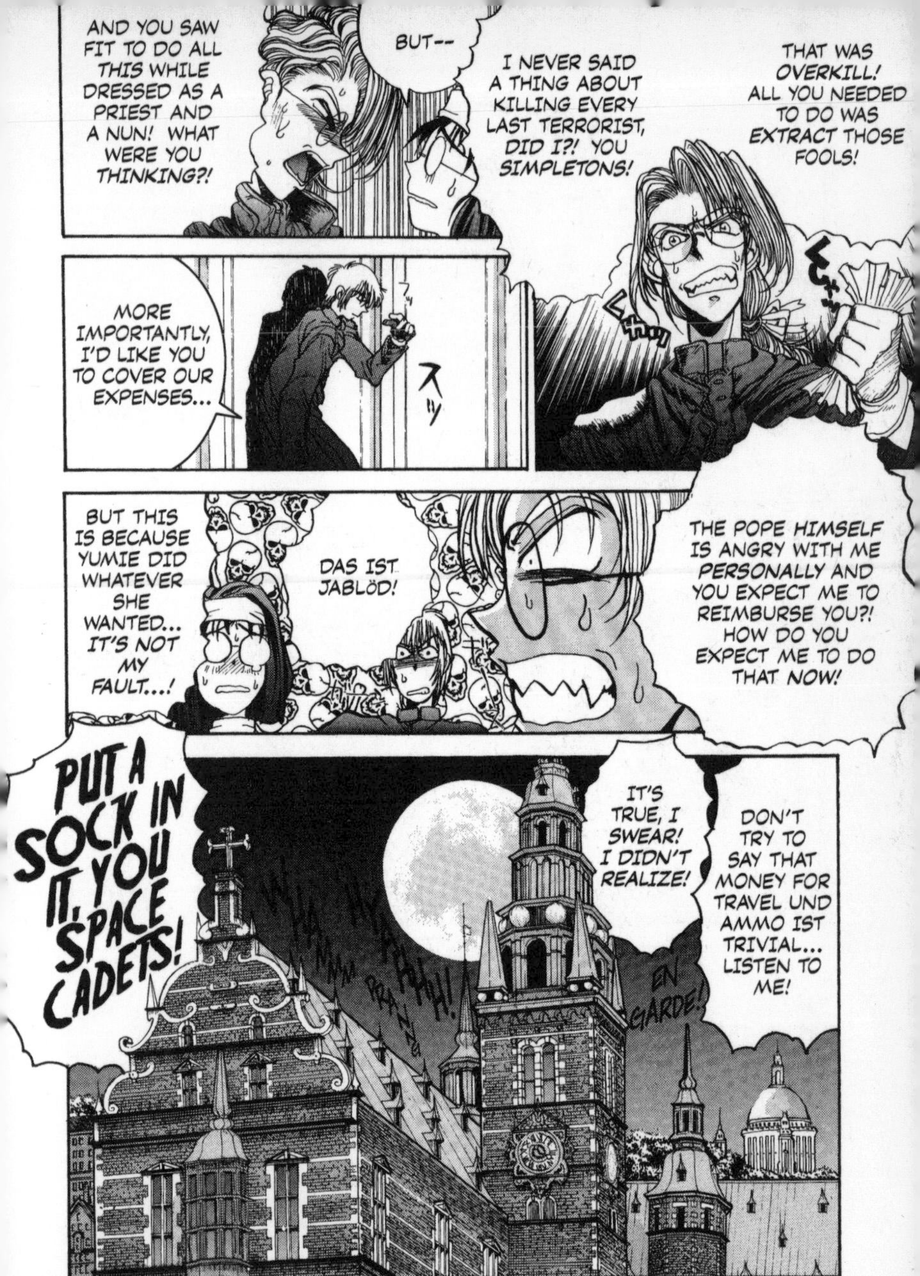
THAT WAS OVERKILL! ALL YOU NEEDED TO DO WAS EXTRACT THOSE FOOLS!
I NEVER SAID A THING ABOUT KILLING EVERY LAST TERRORIST, DID I?! YOU SIMPLETONS!
BUT--
AND YOU SAW FIT TO DO ALL THIS WHILE DRESSED AS A PRIEST AND A NUN! WHAT WERE YOU THINKING?!
MORE IMPORTANTLY, I'D LIKE YOU TO COVER OUR EXPENSES...
THE POPE HIMSELF IS ANGRY WITH ME PERSONALLY AND YOU EXPECT ME TO REIMBURSE YOU?! HOW DO YOU EXPECT ME TO DO THAT NOW!
DAS IST JABLÖD!
BUT THIS IS BECAUSE YUMIE DID WHATEVER SHE WANTED... IT'S NOT MY FAULT...!
DON'T TRY TO SAY THAT MONEY FOR TRAVEL UND AMMO IST TRIVIAL... LISTEN TO ME!
IT'S TRUE, I SWEAR! I DIDN'T REALIZE!
EN GARDE!
PUT A SOCK IN IT, YOU SPACE CADETS!

CROSS FIRE / END

END
EHEH

publishers
MIKE RICHARDSON and HIKARU SASAHARA

editors
TIM ERVIN and FRED LUI

collection designer
DAVID NESTELLE

English-language version produced by
DARK HORSE COMICS and DIGITAL MANGA PUBLISHING

HELLSING VOL. 1

Dark Horse Manga
A division of Dark Horse Comics, Inc.
10956 S.E. Main Street
Milwaukie OR 97222

darkhorse.com

Digital Manga Publishing
1487 West 178th Street, Suite 300
Gardena CA 90248

dmpbooks.com

To find a comics shop in your area, call the
Comic Shop Locator Service toll-free at 1-888-266-4226

First edition: December 2003
ISBN-10: 1-59307-056-X
ISBN-13: 978-1-59307-056-4

7 9 10 8 6

Printed in Canada

T 251385

HELLSING 1

平野耕太
KOHTA HIRANO

translation
DUANE JOHNSON

lettering
WILBERT LACUNA

DARK HORSE MANGA
DMP Digital Manga Publishing